THE
PGA WORLD
GOLF HALL
OF FAME
BOOK

THE PGA WORLD GOLF HALL OF FAME BOOK

GERALD ASTOR

with the Professional Golfers' Association of America

PRENTICE
HALL
PRESS

NEW YORK · LONDON · TORONTO · SYDNEY · TOKYO · SINGAPORE

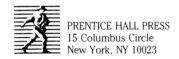 PRENTICE HALL PRESS
15 Columbus Circle
New York, NY 10023

PRENTICE HALL PRESS and colophons are registered trademarks
of Simon & Schuster, Inc.

Library of Congress Cataloging-in-Publication Data

Astor, Gerald, 1926–
     The PGA World Golf Hall of Fame book/by Gerald Astor.
        p.   cm.
     Includes bibliographical references and index.
     ISBN 0-13-661166-4 : $40.00
        1. Golf—United States—History.   I. PGA World Golf Hall of Fame.
     II. Title.   III. Title: Professional Golfers' Association World Golf
     Hall of Fame book.
     GV981.A88   1991
     796.352'0973—dc20   90-36757
                                                      CIP

Designed by Barbara Cohen Aronica

Manufactured in the United States of America

10   9   8   7   6   5   4   3   2   1

First Edition

ACKNOWLEDGMENTS

Charles "Bud" Duffner, editor of *Golfiana* magazine, graciously supplied photographs and advice on where to obtain items. Janet Seale, curator of the United States Golf Association Museum, performed similar services. Joe Steranka, senior director of marketing and communications of the Professional Golfers' Association of America, and Peter Stilwell, director of the PGA World Golf Hall of Fame, lent their valued support. Although this book is a joint venture with the PGA of America, I had a free hand to express my version of history and events.

In the trenches, on picture research and handling of paperwork, was PGA's manager of public relations Kathy Jorden, whose cheerful effectiveness never flagged. Ray Davis, curator at the World Golf Hall of Fame, played an indispensable role. He had the lore of golf at the tip of his tongue, dug into his considerable personal library of photographs, and was always available with the right stuff at the right time.

I am also indebted to Prentice Hall Press editor Paul Aron, his deputy Dave Dunton, and my agent Gerard McCauley for their efforts.

C O N T E N T S

1
Roots and Sources

Winston Churchill described golf as "a curious sport whose object is to put a very small ball in a very small hole with implements ill designed for the purpose." Unlike historians of sports such as baseball and basketball, no one can identify the evil genius who invented the fiendishly fascinating form of competition and recreation we know as golf. Its origins are at least as ancient as the Roman Hills and, in fact, there is some vague evidence of Roman legionnaires amusing themselves playing *paganica*, whacking away at a feather-stuffed piece of hide with a bent stick. But paganica probably did more to sire the Gaelic sport of hurling or shinny, whose modern manifestation is field hockey.

Nevertheless, Roman troops, having exhausted the possibilities of looting and pillaging, introduced the natives of Western Europe to their pastime. Citizens of northern France and Belgium dabbled at their own versions of the game. One authority, Peter Dobereiner, dates the first match as 1296, in the village of Loenen on the Vecht. Documents from the same period speak of a Belgian entertainment, *chole*, in which the contestants employed clubs with iron heads and egg-shaped balls carved from beechwood. The sport featured gambling, and the object was to use the fewest strokes to hit the target. The French also flogged wooden balls and feather-stuffed ones at stumps and posts, and counted strokes.

On a calendar for September in an early sixteenth century Flemish *Book of Hours* there appears a miniature of what looks like a golf match. The implements closely resemble those of golf but the research of Charles Price, for one, suggests this is the Dutch game of *het kolven*, a sport enjoyed on a miniature field rather than over the substantial distances of golf. The alleged French antecedent of golf, *jeu de mail*, with its characteristics of croquet and billiards, also required only limited and enclosed space.

The most enthusiastic adherents of club and ball sports were the Dutch. The Hollanders developed *spel metten colve*, which translates into "game played with a club." The word for club may have transmuted through *colf* and then *kolf*. The "courses," if one could describe them as such, were courtyards, the flat open countryside, or even sections of frozen canals. Some who denigrate the Dutch version claim their targets were such easy marks as church doors, but it's more likely they aimed at elaborately carved poles implanted in the ground. These were items of such beauty that they were frequently stolen and, as a consequence, devotees supposedly sought to aim the ball to the hole left by the purloined stick.

Evidence for the Dutch claim to having originated the sport has been supported by a well-known 1650 painting by Albert Cuyp of a young Dutch boy with a club and ball. But the gear would also suit *het kolven*.

A journal of Dutch navigator Willem Barents, who explored the Arctic regions toward the end of the sixteenth century, notes: "The 3rd of April it was fair and clear with a northeast wind and very calm, we made a baffie to play at golf thereby to stretch our joints . . ." Presumably, a baffie was a club. A few years later another Barents expedition headed for Spitzbergen reported: "On the 5th the wind was north east with a clear sky; this day we still enjoyed four or five hours of twilight, we made wooden cleeks with which we golfed

An illustration of an early Scottish game employs implements that resemble those of golf, but more likely belong to the sport of shinny. (COURTESY THE BETTMANN ARCHIVE.)

upon the bay before our tent for exercise." (The words "baffie" and "cleek" are not Dutch but come from translations of the journal into English.)

Some credit the Dutch for the technique of teeing up on a mound of sand. Their clubs were probably 4 feet or so in length and the balls were about 2 inches in diameter. Some were solid but those of leather stuffed with feathers proved popular enough to become an export.

Even the parentage of the language of the game remains shrouded. "Golf" may indeed be a corruption of *kolf* but then there is *gowf,* Dutch or Teutonic derived, which in the English of Lowland Scotland signified a blow or hit. For example the Hollanders' word for hole is *put* from which some insist came the name for the putter. But then there is the Gaelic word *putadh,* meaning to shove or push, very much like the stroke employed with a putter. Participants began at the sand mound, from the Dutch *tuitje,* pronounced toitee. Yet a Celtic term *dion* through a series of corruptions might also be the source for "tee." An obstacle or an opponent's ball between a player and the *put* was a *stuit mij,* pronounced sty me. Yet those who consider

the Dutch contribution to what we know as golf as about on a level of the cricket genes in baseball argue stymie stems from an ancient Scottish word *styme,* meaning a minimum. Poet Robert Burns speaks of being so dazed he "scarce could wink or see a styme." And there is also a Gaelic root *stigh mi,* meaning "inside me."

Whatever the antecedents upon the Continent,* it was in Scotland that the seeds of golf sprouted most virulently, then blossomed into its present form. According to Sir Guy Campbell, a golf course architect and antiquarian when not a soldier, some rough approximation of golf captured the fancy of residents of St. Andrews, a town thirty miles from Edinburgh, as early as 1100. The University of St. Andrews did not open shop until 1411, by which time St. Andrean Campbell says a crude version of the Old Course was already in play.

A stained glass window at the Gloucester Cathedral dates from the mid-fourteenth century and depicts a golfer, providing pictorial evidence of the spread of the sport in the British Isles from Scotland to other areas.

The pastime of gouff, gowf, then goff, and, finally, golf thoroughly seized the at-

---

* Chinese picture scrolls from the Yuan Era (1271–1368) and the Ming Era, which followed, carry illustrations of *suigan,* described as "a sport in which you hit a ball with a stick while walking." The sticks bear a marked resemblance to modern golf clubs. The Japanese also lay claim to a similar sport, *dakyu,* from an even earlier period. At the time of World War II, official Japan proscribed golf as an activity invented by the enemy but a Japan Golf Association official boldly argued golf came from dakyu.

tention of the Scots during the fifteenth century. So much so that, on March 6, 1457, "The XIIII Parliament of King James II," sitting appropriately enough at Edinburgh, "decreed and ordained . . . that fute ball and golfe must be utterly cryit dune." Fute ball actually had been banned in 1424. The new statute not only reiterated the royal displeasure with that passion but now also added golf. Historians have suggested that James and his legislators feared the pursuit of golfe eroded the skills of archers who, instead of practicing with bow and arrow, spent their hours at a sport that added nothing to national defense.*

The royal decree was largely ignored. The game had already become something of a mania for the recreationally inclined and a cottage industry to the canny as well. Five years before the official ban, a sale of a ball for ten shillings was recorded and local artisans had begun to make and sell equipment for the better-heeled burghers. The government sought to quell the menace with stiffer penalties. A 1491 edict not only called for fines and imprisonment of players but also fixed severe penalties on those who permitted their land to be used for golf.

Courtiers and noblemen devoted to the sport invited King James IV, who took the throne in 1488, to strike a few balls and see for himself that it was not, as he had purportedly sneered, an absurd endeavor that demanded neither skill nor strength. On the castle lawn, the royal duffer swung mightily and squibbed balls for embarrassingly short yardage. Unable to accept failure, he returned the following day for further efforts and quickly succumbed to the fascination of the game. The accounts of the Lord High Treasurer in 1502 note: "The xxi day of September to the bowar of Sact Johnestown for clubbs." And two years later, court documents record: "The third day of Februar, to the King to play at the Golf with the Erle of Bothuile" and lists expenses for clubs and balls for the King.

Scotland lost its monarch and most notable golfer in 1513 when he fell at the battle of Flodden while invading England.

The only enforced restriction upon the freedom to golf turned on the battle for souls. In 1592, John Henrie and Pat Royic, citizens of Edinburgh, were haled before justices for "playing the Gowff on the links of Leith every Sabbath at the time of the sermonses." A few years later, Robert Robertson of Perth, guilty of violating the Lord's day on the links, was sentenced to the stool of repentance. In 1631, a foursome confessed to "prophaning of the Lord's Day" and made public amends. A Stirling kirk session fined a fellow a hefty six shillings and eight pence for a similar offense.

In spite of all of these contretemps and, although Parliament had not rescinded its statutes proscribing golf altogether, the participation of James IV and his successors encouraged not only the upper classes but also tradesmen to take up the game. A theology professor at St. Andrews recalled that when he was a student in 1574 his father, while denying funds for tennis or the tavern, allowed money for bows and arrows, club and balls.

Among the golfing Scottish regents was the notorious Mary Queen of Scots. She had been introduced to the sport as a girl and when she continued her studies in France other students toted her clubs. Mary referred to them as *cadets*, a French word for son. The French pronounced the word cad-day, which some scholars insist is the origin of the term for the now vanishing club bearer. Back home, Mary continued golfing, to the consternation of her numerous critics. Among the places she engaged in the sport was the site known as St. Andrews. Legend holds that shortly after her husband Lord Darnley was murdered, the widow assuaged her grief by practicing her swing.

Scotland prevailed in its wars long enough for Mary's son to ascend to the English throne in 1603 as James I. Whatever else

A mid–fourteenth century stained glass window of the Gloucester Cathedral in Scotland affirms the kinship of the land with golf. The figure appears in the Battle of Cracy window. (COURTESY RAY DAVIS.)

Dutch antecedents of the game seem to combine features of golf and ice hockey. (COURTESY THE BETTMANN ARCHIVE.)

---

* Ironically, James II, in his quest for better weapons, soon turned away from golf's enemy, archery, to become an ardent champion of the new-fangled military science of gunnery. He was killed when a cannon exploded from an overload of powder.

The frozen canals provided a smooth course for Hollanders, who also innovated the sport of skating. (COURTESY THE BETTMANN ARCHIVE.)

he did for his new subjects, James I gave them golf. To satisfy his somewhat bored Scottish associates, the King agreed to a seven-hole course over Blackheath Common, a sandy expanse a few miles from London. He had already indulged his royal prerogative to establish a monopoly. An April 4, 1603, letter from him designates "William Mayne, bower, burgess of Edinburgh during all the days of his lyftime, master fledger, bower, club-maker amd speir maker, to his Hieness, alsweill for game as weir." Some years later, James I awarded James Melvill at St. Andrews a twenty-one-year exclusive franchise to manufacture golf balls, proscribing any balls lacking the bench marks of Melvill and friends as contraband. Imports from the Netherlands were embargoed. The fixed price of a single ball was a whopping four shillings. The monarch endeared himself further to the golfing fraternity by lifting the bans on Sunday golf, albeit with the proviso, "devine services must be attended."

The toleration, and even encouragement,

of golf perhaps owes something to the capacity of humans to improve their efficiency at slaughtering one another. When gunpowder dispatched bow-and-arrow warfare to the dustbins of obsolescence, the conflict between national defense and the passion for golf ceased.* As muskets, cannons, and other firearms replaced the old-style weapons, warring parties killed without the need for the long, tedious practice required by archery. Between international slaughters, there was time for golf. The artisans who crafted bows and arrows were now free to produce the implements of golf, although these remained in short supply—a teenage boy was hanged in 1637 for stealing balls. Both golfers *and* magistrates took the game seriously! One account reports a player became so enraged by the errant behavior of his caddie that he struck the offender on the head with a club, killing him. After hearing the evidence, the court released the murderer with only a reprimand.

One associated British rulers with golf

* In a turnabout, an 1877 issue of *Chambers's Journal* argued, "What hunting does for the cavalry soldier as a training for more important bursts in the battle-field, the like does golf for the infantry soldier in bracing him to encounter forced marching with ease. The Links have formed the training-ground of many a brilliant officer." Logically, one might conclude the modern golf cart instructs prospective soldiers in motorized attack.

for hundreds of years. Charles I was supposedly on the links* at Leith when he first heard of the Irish insurrection. The sincerity of his devotion to golf is questionable, however, since he apparently quit his game forthwith, not even bothering to hole out.

Leith was also the site where the Honorable Company of Edinburgh Golfers held its first annual tournament in 1744. The group temporarily disbanded in 1831, then re-formed in 1836 with play at the Musselburgh links. The oldest continuous operation began in 1754 with the formation of the St. Andrews Society of Golfers, which in 1834, thanks to the membership of King William IV, became the Royal and Ancient Golf Club, the name by which it is now known. The courses themselves were public during the eighteenth and nineteenth centuries, but much of the fun of belonging to a club lay in the colorful uniforms worn during play. One might easily have mistaken golfers in their long scarlet-red coats, knee breeches, and white stockings for the "Redcoats" who came to the Colonies to squelch rebellion. Records of the first aggregations contain long debates on the merits of red versus green outerwear, the cut of the jackets, the color of the buttons. Dandies at the Royal and Ancient squabbled over whether the club coat should be red with yellow buttons or a buff color and later they accepted a resplendent "red coat with dark blue velvet cape, with plain white buttons, with an embroidered club and ball on each side of the cape. . . ." The precedent of the nineteenth hole was established early with meetings at pubs like the Black Bull Tavern or Bailie Glass's favored by the folk of St. Andrews.

Pomp and ceremony were dear to the Royal and Ancient. Consider an 1836 description of the annual ball and banquet:

After dinner the mysteries were entered upon. The silver baton, staff or club which is used to propel the ball onwards, was placed on the table before the President; having silver balls . . . fastened to the body of the baton. Then came a shorter silver club, called a putter, also encircled by silver balls. The candidate on his admission to the Golfing Club by ballot, comes forward to the side of the President, who raising the putter aloft, the former courteously receives it, and kisses one or more of the balls.

The English gentry adopted golf with an enthusiasm that won the plaudits of Scots who had for so long warred against them. When actor David Garrick invited a friend to play on a golf course near Hampton Court during the eighteenth century the Coldstream Guards Regiment on maneuvers nearby broke into cheers at the sight of the golfers, who reminded them of their homes in Scotland.

The eighteenth-century novelist Tobias Smollett, born in Scotland, observed:

Hard by, in the fields called the Links, the citizens of Edinburgh divert themselves at a game called Golf, in which they use a curious kind of bats tipped with horn, and small elastic balls of leather, stuffed with feathers, rather less than tennis balls, but of a much harder consistence. These they strike with such force and dexterity from one hole to another, that they will fly to an incredible distance. Of this diversion the Scots are so fond that, when the weather will permit, you may see a multitude of ranks, mingled together in their shirts, and following the balls with the utmost eagerness.

The French lagged a full century behind the British, with the first club on continental Europe created in 1856 at Pau. A pair of officers from Scotland who, in 1814, were billeted at Pau actually laid out the course. Missionaries of golf carried the gospel from Scotland not only to England and the Continent but also through the British Empire with clubs formed in Calcutta, Bombay, Montreal, and eventually Australia.

Mary, Queen of Scots, learned golf while a student in France. (COURTESY THE BETTMANN ARCHIVE.)

Golf was played at St. Andrews in 1754, nearly fifty years before the creation of this scene. (COURTESY THE BETTMANN ARCHIVE.)

---

* Scotsmen employed the word to describe land that led from the sea inland and the earliest courses of Scotland were along the sea. In the south of England "links" was a synonym for "downs," sloping ground often characterized by sandy dunes.

"The Cock o' the Green" was the title bestowed upon golfing enthusiast Alexander McKellar, who could be found on the Bruntsfield Links every day but the Sabbath from the late eighteenth century to his death in 1813. As darkness would fall he could sometimes be seen playing the "short holes" by lamplight. (COURTESY THE BETTMANN ARCHIVE.)

The early courses in Scotland were hardly more than raw stretches of land leading to the greens and holes. In 1856, the St. Andrews layout consisted of nine holes; one played the course in reverse to complete a round of eighteen. In fact, the rules of the day specified that one should tee off for the next hole a short distance from the previous one, a single club length at first and then two club lengths from the cup. The greens were simply stretches of natural turf, with holes marked by a small iron pin flying a red rag. No architect constructed the hazards: Already existing pits of sand became bunkers, and players frequently contended with balls deeply imbedded in the tracks left by a heavily laden cart, or they might find themselves smack up against an old stone wall that happened to cut across what we today would call a fairway.

The basic rules of St. Andrews, set down in 1754, specified that the ball farthest from the hole be played first. Balls could not be changed after teeing off. Stones, bones, or broken clubs could not be removed when playing a ball except on the green and, then, only if within a club length. "If your ball come among water or any watery filth, you are at liberty to take out your ball and throw it behind the hazard 6 yards at least; you may play it with any club, and allow your adversary a stroke for so-getting out your ball." A lost ball meant returning to the previous lie and loss of a stroke. A later version dictated: "If the Ball lie in a Rabbit-scrape, the Player shall not be at liberty to take it out, but must play it as from any common hazard. If however it lie in one of the burrows, he may lift it, drop it behind the hazard and play with an iron without losing a stroke. If the Ball is half covered or more with water, the Player may take it out, tee it, and play from behind the hazard, losing a stroke. Whatever happens to a Ball by accident must be reckoned a Rub of the green, if however, the Player's Ball strike his adversary or his Caddie, the adversary loses the

hole. . . . All loose impediments of whatever kind, may be removed upon the putting green. . . ."

When St. Andrews first expanded to twelve holes during the eighteenth century, a round added up to a total of twenty-two holes. Golfers, upon finishing the first eleven, then reversed course to play ten backward plus one more. Subsequently, in 1764, the initial four holes were combined to form two longer ones. That eliminated a pair, both going out and returning, again making a round eighteen holes, which, through the status of St. Andrews, became the accepted regimen.

The stymie rule, incidentally, dates from a 1789 ruling at St. Andrews, which stated that if "any ball shall lye in the way of his opponent at the distance of 6 inches upon the hole . . . it shall be in the power of the party playing to cause his opponent to remove said ball." The stymie was briefly eliminated in 1833–1834 and then survived until 1951 when both the Royal and Ancient and the U.S. Golf Association abolished it.

Along with the organization of the sport came some standardization. By 1800, the ball, sometimes overstuffed to a 2-inch diameter, now was supposed to be limited to one and a half in diameter, tipping the scales at twenty-six to thirty pennyweights or roughly one and a half ounces. An artisan stitched three pieces of bull or horsehide together in the size of a duck's egg, turning it inside out and leaving a tiny opening. The ball maker then crammed in a tall hatful of goosefeathers (rather than the hair or wool used by the Dutch). The cover was sewn tight and the ball then soaked in water, causing the leather to shrink. When the interior feathers dried, they expanded to produce a hard, tight sphere. The balls were known as featheries, and a skilled hand could produce four or five a day. Featheries sold for about the equivalent of one dollar apiece and the most dexterous manufacturers like "Old" Tom Morris★ and Allan Robertson sewed,

---

* Whenever a member of the Hall of Fame is first introduced, a star will follow the name.

stuffed, and soaked from 1,500 to 2,500 featheries a year. Featheries seldom formed perfect spheres and contact with damp or wet grounds softened them.

The early clubs were ponderous weapons, as much as four-and-a-half feet in length. A verse from 1721 lyricizes:

> And armed with lead their jointed clubs
>   prepare.
> Intent his ball, the eager gamster eyes,
> His muscles strains and various postures
>   tries
> If with due strength the weighty engine
>   falls,
> Discharged obliquely and impinge the ball
> Its winding mounts aloft and sings in air.

Apart from the idiosyncrasies of spelling and grammar, this account not only reports a stroke preceded by waggles but also implies the blunderbuss quality of the club as a "mighty engine."

A poem in 1743 adds further details about the equipment:

> Long toiled the hero, on the verdant field,
> Strain'd his stout arm the mighty club to
>   wield;
> Of finest ash Castalio's shaft was made;
> Pond'rous with lead, and fac'd with horn the
>   head.

Another early hotbed of the game was Blackheath, established outside London by James I and his courtiers in 1606. (COURTESY THE BETTMANN ARCHIVE.)

The artisans of the early golf era employed a variety of woods for the club heads—ash, apple, pear, blackthorn, or beech—and all inserted lead, hammered into the back of the large wooden heads, to add mass. Hickory gradually became the preferred wood for shafts and remained in favor until steel shafts appeared during the 1920s.

In the beginning the neck formed only a modest angle, requiring players to stand almost directly over the ball. As the angle increased, the golfer could assume a less awkward position and hit farther and more accurately. The very first clubs, their faces set at a 90-degree angle to the ground, performed adequately with balls teed up on a clump of sand. But the configuration severely hampered fairway shots where the ball sat down in the turf. Golfers added to their arsenal a second club that came with an angled wooden face. The players could "baffy" or bounce the clubhead into the ground just behind the ball, causing a modest lift off.

Craftsmen improved the woods in the seventeenth century as clubmakers hollowed out the face to produce a concave shape. The design gave a scooping or spoonlike action, endowing the club with its name. By the nineteenth century, golfers had armed themselves with long spoons, middle spoons, short spoons, and even the baffing spoon to pitch the ball onto the green.

The environment of Scottish links forced other adaptations. Courses frequently stretched over hard-surfaced roads or well-packed ground, with clubs suffering severe damage from contact. To protect the wood, clubmakers nailed a strip of brass on the sole of some clubs, creating the "brassie." And, because of ruts, water-soaked lies, and heavy undergrowth, the wooden niblick,* a club with a smaller head that could dig into narrow areas or slice through rough more readily, became part of the golfers' bags.

During the mid-nineteenth century, Henry Lamb, a pro with a reputation for creative thinking, introduced a driver with a round bump on its face. Lamb argued the protruberance added distance. Many scorned his "bulgur" because, unless struck squarely, the ball veered sharply to the left or right. But modern drivers have a slightly convex face, testifying to the basic wisdom of Lamb.

Although the woods had been refined considerably since the aforementioned "weighty engine," British Amateur champion Horace Hutchinson, a golf historian during the late nineteenth and early twentieth centuries, could still describe the weapons of the 1880s as "stout, stubborn, and bull-headed." Because woods had their limitations, some basic irons evolved. First of the lot came the driving iron, some varieties of the *cleek* (the word has Gaelic origins), a club thicker toward the top of the blade and a putter that was distinguished from a cleek by its shorter shaft and flat face. The traditional wooden putters often caused balls to bounce over the green rather than roll as smoothly with the metal. The niblick included a host of middle irons useful for longer distances from more unpleasant lies. The mashie† had the distinct purpose of pitching a ball dead on the pin.

There was also something known as a lofting iron, which Horace Hutchinson de-

---

* The educated guess on the origins of niblick is a corruption of a Scottish term, *neb leigh,* meaning broken nose, a colloquial description of the niblick's shortened face. During the nineteenth century, the club was also known as a "track iron," useful for lies in cart ruts, horsehoe imprints, and any of the deep impressions due to tracks over the turf. As golf establishments began to prevent wagons and horses from lacerating the courses, the contours of the niblick shifted towards an emphasis upon loft.

† There are a number of explanations for the term. One credits it with a Celtic derivation. "Maise," pronounced mash'-a, is among the synonyms for beauty but it also connotes neatness, elegance, and refined form. It seemed appropriate to the delicacy one theoretically applies to a mashie shot. Another theory says it is from the French "massue" meaning club. Then there is the romantic connection. J. H. Taylor, the outstanding British player around the turn of the century and an expert with the club wrote in his biography, *Golf: My Life's Work*:

scribed as "fascinating, most coquettish, feminine without doubt, delightful on occasion, exasperating and untrustworthy. So full of moods and tenses." Hutchinson's stereotyping of women not withstanding, the lofting iron obviously allowed little margin for error and eventually was abandoned in favor of a more extreme mashie and eventually the wedge. Primitive golfers armed themselves with a sand iron for bunkers, but it bore no resemblance to the sand wedge of today. It was more like a heavy driving iron with a laid back face to add loft. Subsequently, club manufacturers replaced the sand iron with the mashie-niblick.

A set of clubs numbered 8 to 10, and not only was there a caddie to tote them but, frequently, a "fore-caddie" ran ahead to spot the location of balls and clear the way for the featheries. Courses, including St. Andrews, were unfenced areas, created on sites of daily hurly-burly. Sheep and cattle roamed the fairways, soldiers drilled on the grounds, children gamboled across the greens, citizens raced horses over the turf, and cricketers set their wickets there for matches. The caddies chased people or at least opened up space for play, marking the locations of balls with feathers.

Over time, well established clubs like St. Andrews came to depend on professional caddies while some lesser courses continued to hire kids to tote equipment and spot balls. The caddies began to impart to golfers the knowledge they gained from experience and observation. Along with these contributions, caddies also performed valetlike services to club members and did the honors as waiters for postplay bacchanals. Novelist Tobias Smollett in his eighteenth century masterpiece *Humphry Clinker*, reported that caddies "were famous for their dexterity in executing one of the functions of Mercury," his delicate description of procurers.

The golf pro was hardly in evidence, at least not in the form visible today. To survive, club and ball makers of the early nineteenth century also plied the trades of weaver and cobbler. However, some of the earliest of the artisans and caddies exhibited traits not unknown to modern times. There was David Robertson, descendent of a 1743 St. Andrean, "who with matchless art shapes the firm hide . . ." and of whom poet George Fullerton Carnegie rhymed in 1833:

David, oldest of the cads,
Who gives half-one to unsuspicious lads,
When he might give them two, or even
   more,
Is just as politic in his affairs
As Talleyrand or Metternich in theirs.
He has the statesman's elements, 'tis plain,
Cheat, flatter, humbug—anything for gain;
And, had he trod the world's wide field,
   methinks,
As long as he has trod St. Andrews' Links,
He might have been prime minister or
   priest,
My Lord, or plain Sir David, at the least!

Davie Robertson, 'tis plain, was an early hustler, giving half a stroke to innocents who, with handicaps of two or three, would still come up short. And he knew how to cozen the members for his advantage. But Davie Robertson's greatest contribution to golf was the son he sired in 1811. Allan Robertson was the first great pro.

(continued)

I am old enough to remember that in the year of its appearance, 1888, the term "masher" was applied to those ultra-smart young fellows who, with monocle in eye, and arrayed in clothes of the latest fashionable style and cut, we were told, the idol of every lady . . . the new-fashioned club was considered to be a violent departure from the orthodox, a dude among clubs, so what better name could be given it than the mashie, a parody on the popular conception of smartness.

Finally, there is the notion the Scots created the name from a familiar household tool. Golf historian Robert Browning said: "The mashie does not specially resemble the utensil employed to mash potatoes; it took the name from its effect upon the ball when entrusted to unskillful hands."

2

The First Professionals

Allan Robertson, born (1815) in St. Andrews and the first great professional, earned his living from matches and by selling balls. He was known to coddle the amateurs, barely besting them 2 up and 1 to play, in order to restrain the odds for their next meeting. (COURTESY CHARLES "BUD" DUFFNER.)

Allan Robertson spent his boyhood on and about the St. Andrews links, where he was known to rise early enough to practice on a deserted course still wet with dew. In 1842, a local journal reported his brethren prohibited him from competing in a local tournament "on account of his superior play, it being their impression that they would have no chance in any contest in which Allan took part."

Robertson easily defeated the best of the high-born members of the Royal and Ancient. But in his sly-boots style, no doubt inherited from his sire, Davie, he rarely humiliated them, thus retaining their favor and avoiding requests for better odds next time out. A sporty lot, the members soon took to backing him in big money matches. One of the more momentous pitted him against twenty-two-year-old Willie Dunn of Musselburgh. The contest called for twenty rounds (360 holes) stretched over ten days. Robertson triumphed, two rounds up, one remaining on the final day.

His skill included the novel techniques of producing a slice or hook to overcome an obstacle to the green. He was also, a chip off old Davie, adept at gamesmanship. He would disguise the effort he put into a shot to fool an opponent into swinging too hard or soft. If a foe lay a few yards farther off and was scheduled to hit first, Robertson deliberately announced the wrong club for himself, gulling the adversary into a bad choice. He had a cheerful wit: "It appeals to the higher feelings of humanity to see your rival in a bunker."

Allan Robertson has been credited with developing iron-headed clubs employed in approach shots. He also designed one of the more effective iron putting cleeks. Undoubtedly, Robertson also profited from his association with St. Andrews. Edinburgh might boast the oldest Scotch club

but, even in the nineteenth century, St. Andrews was supreme. *Chambers's Journal* firmly asserted:

> . . . the "Royal and Ancient" takes precedence over all, and is indisputably *the* club of the kingdom. What Newmarket is to racing, or Melton to hunting, St. Andrews is to golf. In St. Andrews, it is not a mere pastime, but a business and a passion . . . in St. Andrews no living thing that does not play golf, or talk golf, or think golf, or at least thoroughly knock under to golf can live.

At the peak of Robertson's career, in the mid–nineteenth century, a divinity truly shaped the golfer's ends. A missionary by the name of Patterson, stationed in Singapore, shipped a statue of the Hindu deity Vishnu to his family in Scotland. To protect the icon from damage it had been packed in gutta percha, a resin or gum that resembles rubber. Thrifty Scots who received goods shielded from injury with gutta percha had learned to heat the packing material shavings in hot water and to fashion sheets that, with proper trimming, glue, and nails, sufficed to replace soles and heels on shoes.

The most ingenious use of gutta percha came from Rob Patterson, a younger brother of the missionary. As a ministerial student in St. Andrews, Rob Patterson, in common with succeeding generations of members of the clergy, found golf a healthy outlet. Like so many players he was also not happy with the defects of featheries and he experimented with the gutta percha, kneading it into the shape of a ball and painting it.

On a historic April morning in 1845, he took a few strokes with his new creation. It broke after several hits. Undiscouraged, Patterson returned to the vat. He rolled his

own more carefully and consulted with another brother who boiled the stuff in water to remove all air bubbles. That did the trick and onto the market came balls stamped "The Patterson Composite—Patented Ball."

Gutties, as they became known, rolled much truer than the more bouncy featheries, played well even in damp or wet weather, and held their shape and tightness longer. For golfers, the first experience with them excited the awe primitive man must have felt when he discovered fire. James Balfour authored *Reminiscences of Golf on St. Andrews Links* in 1887. He recalled an 1848 dinner and the comments of a fellow linksman, Sir Ralph Anstruther:

> A most curious thing—here is a golf ball of gutta-percha. Maitland and I have played with it all day in the rain, and it flies better at the end of the day than it did at the beginning.

Balfour remembered that he and a companion obtained some of the new balls and took them to Musselburgh for a tryout:

Gourlay the ball-maker had heard of them, and followed us around. He was astonished to see how they flew, and, being round, how they rolled straight to the hole on the putting green. He was alarmed for his craft.

At first, the makers of featheries like the aforesaid Gourlay sought to hold back the dawn. The threat turned Robertson cantankerous and he growled that gutties were "nae gowf." He and fellow reactionaries tried to buy up and then burn the rival product, but the demand for gutties overwhelmed the opposition. Among the converted was Old Tom Morris, born in 1821 and destined to become "the G.O.M. of Golf."

Golf historian Henry Leach interviewed Morris for a series on great golfers and their beginnings, with an eye to uncovering from each "the most important morals of his experience." Morris recalled his falling out over the guttie with Robertson (Leach bowdlerized the speech of his subjects so they all sounded like Oxford dons when, in fact, most Englishmen found it

An artist memorialized Medal Day at Blackheath. (COURTESY THE BETTMANN ARCHIVE.)

Old Tom Morris began as an apprentice for Allan Robertson, but the pair fell out after the younger man spoke approvingly of the new guttie ball. (COURTESY RAY DAVIS.)

1. Placing the Ball   2. The Drive-Off   3. Putting the Ball   4. A "Bunker"   5. An Uphill Shot

A TOURNAMENT OF THE TROON GOLF CLUB, SCOTLAND

difficult to comprehend the Scotch burr of a Tom Morris):

I had been out playing golf . . . and I had the misfortune to lose all my supply of balls . . . very much easier lost in those days, as the fairway of the course was ever so much narrower then than it is now, and had thick bushy whins close in at the side. Mr. Campbell [the member with whom Morris was playing] kindly gave me a gutta one to try. I took to it at once, and, as we were playing in, it so happened that we met Allan Robertson coming out, and someone told him that I was playing a very good game with one of the new gutta balls, and I could see fine, from the expression of his face that he did not like it at all, and when we met afterwards in his shop, we had some high words about the matter, and there and then we parted company, I leaving his employment.

Tom Morris's earliest memories of golf focused on the scarcity of balls. As a boy he almost always had to be content with an old ball, telling Leach that "very often . . . we then had to be satisfied with only a *piece* of one." And a featherie in those days cost as much a new guttie, half-a-crown, a sum well beyond the ken of Morris's youth.

Although he quickly recognized the value of the guttie, Morris, in his post at Prestwick, accepted the old order. He continued to manufacture featheries for two years before he switched to gutties.

In spite of the opposition of conservative ballmakers, the Patterson Composite quickly drew competition under labels like Eureka, Agrippa, O.K., A.1., White Brand, Henley, and, just as today, balls with the names of the renowned golf figures.

Even Robertson eventually surrendered, and the guttie improved his game. He substituted the niblick for the baffing spoon when he discovered he could now clip the ball cleanly off the turf, pitching it over bunkers and other hazards.

The earliest gutties came with a smooth cover, but golfers soon discovered that

(Opposite) *Troon has survived to serve as a venue for the British Open and British Amateur championships.* (COURTESY THE BETTMANN ARCHIVE.)

The Honorable Company of Edinburgh Golfers commenced play at the Leith Links in 1744, predating the official date for the establishment of St. Andrews. In 1867, the stellar professionals gathered. Some of the more notable include Willie Dunn (fifth from right), Tom Morris (third from right), and pipe-smoking Young Tom Morris (second from right). (COURTESY RAY DAVIS.)

The first trophy for professionals was the Championship Belt, awarded to the British Open victor, starting in 1860. The officials specified that any player who won three years in succession would gain permanent possession of the Moroccan leather belt with its valuable buckle. Old Tom Morris narrowly missed after triumphs in 1862 and 1863 but his son, Young Tom Morris, carried off "The Belt" with wins 1868–1870. Rather than invest further in a new belt, the golfing societies chose a more modest emblem of supremacy, a medal. (COURTESY JEFF MCBRIDE, PGA OF AMERICA.)

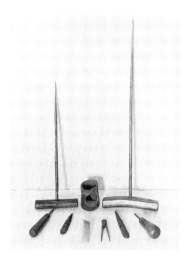

Tools for manufacturing featheries are exhibited by St. Andrews University. (COURTESY ST. ANDREWS UNIVERSITY.)

those with nicks or dents often played straighter. Balfour noted that new gutties did not "fly well, but ducked in the air." Some sought to remedy the problem by banging them with a heavy hammer, but the balls continued their erratic behavior until nicked and cut by clubs.

In their ignorance, the players smoothed out the damage to the balls with a hot bath at night. But, said Balfour:

> . . . this same hot bath, while it cured the wound, spoiled the ball. . . . I and a friend on the day before the medal played with two guttas, and they worked beautifully, so that we resolved to play with them next day for the medal. But as they had been a good deal hacked, we dipped them in hot water overnight, and removed these defects. When, however, we played off the tee next day before an assembled crowd, among whom were the ball and clubmakers, both the balls whirred and ducked amid the chuckling and jeering and loud laughter of the onlookers; we had to put down feather balls next hole. The fact was, they required these indentations to make them fly.

Soon, innovators intentionally scarred balls for more accurate flight. At least one manufacturer laboriously gouged, by hand, a regular pattern on the surface of balls. This was before someone summoned the wit to groove the hemispherical metal molds into which they poured molten gutta percha. The balls were white, except for red ones sold to accommodate those who played in the snows of winter.

The newest balls averaged around 1.70 inches, slightly larger than their modern counterparts, which go from the British 1.62-inch to the American 1.68-inch diameters. They were lighter also, ranging from 1.35 to 1.55 ounces compared to today's standard of 1.62 ounces. With the aid of gutties, golfers hit balls farther and more accurately and play was less subject to weather conditions. Until the advent of the gutties, players opted to use clubs with wooden heads because iron cut the fragile featheries. The new balls brought a pronounced shift to metal heads with more variety to accommodate the demands of fairway play, and wooden putters gave way to iron-faced putters. And the ease of manufacture—simply pouring the softened materials into molds—led to mass production and the price of balls fell to a single shilling.

Innovation breeds imitation and competition. Within a few decades, balls from other substances showed up on courses. Horace Hutchinson remembered a "Commander Stewart" who produced balls under his name that consisted of a "composition" cover filled with steel filings. They were dreadfully heavy and quickly discarded. A more substantial bid for favor came from the "putty," which had the highly desired capacity to restore its shape "even after the most desperate hammering on the head with an iron," noted Hutchinson. Hutchin-

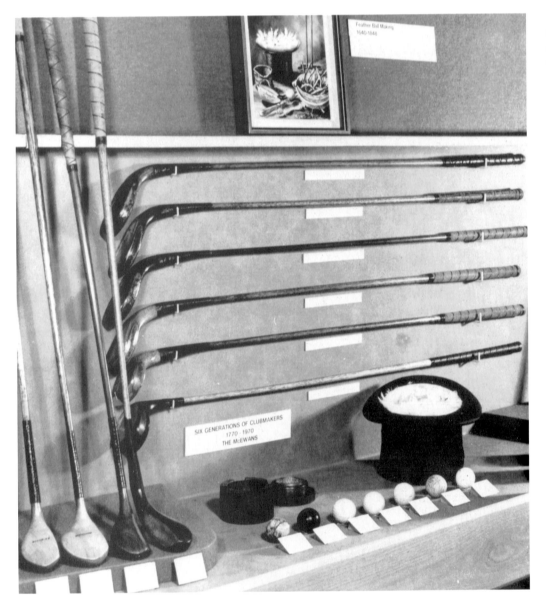

The ball makers packed a "lum," or high hat, full of soaked feathers to fill the inside of a leather covering. (COURTESY PGA WORLD GOLF HALL OF FAME.)

A featherie ball (left) lost its shape quickly. Knives marked gutties before the creation of moulds (center), and the grooves helped cure a tendency to duck. Moulds produced bramble-configured gutties. (COURTESY RAY DAVIS.)

One of the great devotees of golf in the nineteenth century, Leslie Balfour Melville starred in cricket, rugby, billiards, and tennis in the late nineteenth century. He also amassed a pile of medals from the Royal and Ancient. Here the doughty amateur confronts the links of Hayling Island in 1890. (COURTESY THE BETTMANN ARCHIVE.)

In place of crude efforts by hand, a primitive machine cut grooves into gutties to cure a tendency to sudden dives. (COURTESY ST. ANDREWS UNIVERSITY.)

son frequently used a putty when playing with Old Tom Morris, as firm a believer in the guttie as Robertson had been in the featherie. Morris cordially hated what he called "the potty" and when Hutchinson hooked or sliced he chortled, "Eh, they potties—I thocht they potties never gaed aft the line." Potties doomed themselves because they tended to travel shorter distances through the air and over-compensated by running too hard on the green when pitched.

The pros of the era, backed by the club members, began to play matches with significant money at stake. Scheduled to meet Willie Park of Musselburgh in such a contest, Morris trained for six weeks, getting in two rounds every day. In the match, the pair met on four different sets of links before Morris defeated Park.

Before the advent of the gutties, the biggest money event in golf pitted Allan Robertson and Tom Morris against the Dunn brothers who represented Musselburgh. The 1849 match bore a purse of 400 pounds (Morris remembered it as 200 pounds a side), a huge sum in those days; fifty years later professionals played British

Opens for a mere fifty pounds. The St. Andrews pair eventually won out, coming from thirteen holes down, over the home courses of both sets of pros, plus a third neutral territory at North Berwick.

Although they fell out over the guttie, the friendship of Robertson and his pupil Old Tom Morris was soon restored. They were also shrewd enough to realize they stood to gain by pairing up against challengers. While Robertson avoided matches against Morris or Willie Park, Morris met all comers. His one weakness lay on the greens where he was notorious for flubbing close ones. According to Hutchinson, a postman delivered a letter addressed, "The Misser of Short Putts, Prestwick," straight to Morris. As an old man his failing so aggravated him that he often snatched back the ball before it even reached the cup, sometimes stopping one true to the mark. And this gentle, calmest of men once broke a putter, banging it on the ground after a miss.

The new balls became standard during the 1850s, just in time for the seminal event of 1860, the first British Open. In spite of the designation of "Open," only profes-

sionals entered. The trophy was a Morocco belt, which, in subsequent Opens, earned the honorific "the Belt." It was agreed that anyone able to win the Open three years in succession would have permanent ownership of the Belt. At the 1860 debut of the British Open, a total of eight men played three rounds over the twelve-hole Prestwick Course where Old Tom Morris was the pro and Willie Park carried off temporary possession of the Belt with a 174 total.

The following year the tournament was a true Open with both pros and amateurs.

Old Tom Morris took the Belt away from Willie Park and, after a victory in 1862, Morris was only one win away from retiring the trophy. But after the addition of a monetary prize in 1863, Willie Park recaptured the Belt and also pocketed the money. During these first years of organized competition, Park and Old Tom Morris dominated the British Open with Park on top three times and Morris, who had now signed on as the St. Andrews major domo, four. But neither man could manage to string together the requisite three in a row.

In those days scoring was always de-

In this 1892 contest, pro Willie Fernie (in long trousers) is at the top of his backswing. Observing are such knickered gents as "Mr. Horace Hutchinson" (fourth from left), the "Right Hon. A. Balfour, M.P." (immediate right of Hutchinson). A caddie, meanwhile, grabs a handful of grains from the sandbox to form a tee for the next to tee off. Only a few yards away, pro Willie Park, Jr., lines up a putt under the eyes of the bearded Old Tom Morris (second left to Park, Jr.) and the celebrated amateur champion, John Ball (immediate left to Morris). (COURTESY RAY DAVIS.)

A Grand Match over St. Andrews Links pits Sir David Baird and Sir Ralph Anstruther against Major Playfair and John Campbell in 1847 at the fifteenth hole. At this time, the gentlemen players wear the same long trousers as the professionals, and sport jackets better designed for flash than performance. Allan Robertson is to the right of the fellow holding his topper behind his back. (COURTESY GOLFIANA.)

The luminaries gathered at Dudd-ingston in 1898 for a match be-tween two highly regarded pros and a pair of ranking amateurs. The pros are Willie Auchterlonie from St. Andrews (taller, long-trousered player with club in hand, left foreground) and B. Sayers from Berwick (short player right of Auch-terlonie). Their opponents are the redoubtable Lt. Freddie Tait (prepar-ing to putt) and Balfour (extreme right with club under arm). In the center stands a well known cad-die known as "Fiery." (COURTESY RAY DAVIS.)

Willie Auchterlonie won the Brit-ish Open in 1893 and eventually succeeded Old Tom Morris as the paid factotum of the St. Andrews golf operations. (COURTESY RAY DAVIS.)

scribed only in strokes; the concept of what we know as par actually is barely 100 years old. Henry Leach, in *The Spirit of the Links,* published in 1907, reported that the Coventry Club, in December 1890, was the first to assign a scratch number for each hole and that sometime in 1891 a prize was offered in a competition played against the total, which was known as the "ground score."

Around the time the ground score idea spread, a music hall verse of the day warned "Hush! Hush! Hush! Here comes the Bogey man! So hide your head be-neath the clothes, He'll catch you if he can!" When a prominent player of the day kept getting beaten by the ground score, a companion referred to the figure as "a regular bogey man." The now anthropo-morphized ground score for a scratch player subsequently received the rank of Colonel from a club composed of military officers, and that stuck in the language of the game. But the Royal and Ancient never admitted Colonel Bogey to its rules. He was super-seded by "par" with its meaning of equal. Bogey meant par in the U.S., according to a review of competition in 1899. But, Ameri-cans are believed responsible for ultimately stripping Colonel Bogey of his rank and awarding him the inglorious meaning of 1 over par.

The source for birdie, according to Charles Price, is American. In 1899, George Crump, part of a threesome at The Coun-try Club in Atlantic City, hit a drive that struck a bird on the wing. Crump then knocked his second shot to within inches of the pin, enabling him to hole out, 1 under par. His companions kidded him, attributing his feat to the bird shot. The trio then began referring to any score be-low par as a birdie and the term caught on with other club members and finally the entire golfing fraternity, although it did not become part of the British lexicon until after World War I. Ornithologically minded golfers added "eagle" for 2 under par. "Al-batross" is the correct label for the rare 3 below par, although more commonly that rare bird is a "double eagle."

In spite of his putting affliction, Old Tom Morris was an entry in British Opens until age seventy-five. However, he rated one golfer superior to himself and remarked, "I could cope wi' Allan mysel' but never wi' Tommy."

He was referring to his son, not surpris-ingly known as Young Tom Morris.★ By age thirteen he had attracted the notice of the golf cognoscenti of the day. Young Tom has been described as the Arnold Palmer★ of his day, a slasher who eschewed caution and as a consequence frequently hit himself into trouble from which he somehow marvelously recovered. The ferocity of his stroke made Morris the first of the breed to gain the legendary reputation for cracking shafts during his preparatory waggles. In fact, the junior Morris brought an emphasis to the follow through, which was to become a major component of the modern golf swing. He was noted for his skill with irons and he had a noticeable style to his putting, hitting the ball off the toes of his right foot while his left foot pointed at the hole.

Young Tom was a mere eighteen-year-old in 1868 when he captured the Open. He went on to win the next two years to gain permanent possession of the Belt and to show it was no fluke added a fourth in a row with the 1871 tournament. For the day, his scores were phenomenal. His 1868 triumph with a 157 (for eighteen holes) knocked 13 shots off the score by which his father had won in 1867 over the same course. He improved by 3 strokes the following year and followed up with a record 149. In that era courses were considerably shorter than their modern counterparts, but the balls and clubs also played much shorter and the greens sometimes resembled light rough rather than the billiard table smoothness of today.

At age twenty-four, Young Tom succumbed to a ruptured blood vessel. Such was his fame and popularity that a subscription for a monument to him was quickly filled. His grave is marked by a stony image of him, dressed in jacket and tam, about to demonstrate his putting style. The inscription reads:

In memory of "Tommy," Son of Thomas Morris . . . Deeply regretted by numerous friends and all golfers. He thrice in succession won the Champions Belt and held it without rivalry and yet without envy, his many amiable qualities being no less acknowledged than his golfing achievements.

His father carried on for another twenty-nine years at St. Andrews, first as pro and then greenskeeper until his retirement in 1904 and death in 1908 at eighty-seven. He maintained the Old Course at St. Andrews with two undeviating rules. "Mair saund, Honeyman," he would command his assistant. Sand liberally applied to the greens and fairways kept the grass properly. His second dictum: "Nae Sunday play. The course needs a rest if the gowfers don't."

The stymie, captured in this 1896 engraving, dated from the original St. Andrews rules. (COURTESY GOLFIANA.)

Old Tom Morris held the flag as a golfer putted out on eighteen at St. Andrews in 1891. (COURTESY ST. ANDREWS UNIVERSITY.)

The nineteenth hole for Old Tom Morris meant a lemon squash. The purveyor also served home-brewed "ginger pop" from his barrow. (COURTESY ST. ANDREWS UNIVERSITY.)

From 1900 to 1910, Robert Forgan ran a small golf club manufacturing shop opposite the eighteenth green at St. Andrews. (COURTESY ST. ANDREWS UNIVERSITY.)

3

Golf Comes to the United States

Golf was not among the priorities of the first settlers. However, municipal records from 1659, when the Hollanders ruled the region around Albany, New York, state:

> The Honorable Commissary and Magistrates of Fort Orange and the Village of Beverwyck, having heard divers complaints from the burghers of this place against the practice of playing golf along the streets, which causes great damage to the windows of the houses and also exposes people to the danger of being injured and is contrary to the freedom of the public streets. Therefore, their honors, wishing to prevent same, hereby forbid all persons to play golf in the streets, under penalty of forfeiture of 25 florins for each person who shall be found doing so.

Benjamin Rush, the physician-statesman who was among the signers of the Declaration of Independence, became aware of golf during his travels and in his *Sermon on Exercise* he remarked:

> Golf is an exercise which is much used by the Gentlemen of Scotland. A large common in which there are several little holes is chosen for the purpose. It is played with a little leather ball stuffed with feathers and sticks made somewhat in the form of a bandy-wicket. He who puts a ball into a given number of holes with the fewest strokes, gets the game.

Rush added, "The late Dr. McKenzie, author of the essay on Health and Long Life used to say that a man would live ten years longer for using the exercise once or twice a week."

Well before the American Revolution, several ships' lading bills listed "8 dozen Golf Clubs and 3 Groce Golf Balls," and inventories of estates spoke of "gouff" or "goff sticks." The Charleston *City Gazette* in 1788 carried notes concerning the South Carolina Golf Club and a few years later there appeared an item on a "Golf Club Ball." A New York City man printed an advertisement for "veritable Caledonian balls" in 1799 and invitations were sent out for an 1811 Savannah Golf Club affair. But the clubs were more an excuse for a social ramble than homes for golf. No evidence of any golf matches exists, and the game did not really become part of the American scene until almost the end of the nineteenth century.

One claimant for the first site of golf in the States is the area around White Sulphur Springs, West Virginia. No documents attest to the "Oakhurst" course but aged citizens from nearby told a correspondent for the PGA magazine, *The Professional Golfer*, that in the early 1880s half a dozen men, including a quintet of Scottish émigrés, as well as Russell Montague, a Harvard man who had spent time in Edinburgh, were·well acquainted with the sport. The group supposedly enlisted farm hands to carve out several primitive holes on the Montague estate and organized small round robins during the Christmas season.

J. Hamilton Gillespie, a lumberman and real estate developer, is alleged to have driven balls down the main drag of the sleepy village of Sarasota, Florida, in 1883. T. A. Bell insisted he laid out four holes on his father's farm in Burlington, Iowa. Some accounts claim members of the Meadow Brook Hunt Club on Long Island, New York, witnessed a golf exhibition by the British amateur champion, Horace Hutchinson, in 1887 but he says he did not swing a club in the U.S. until a second visit here the following year. In any event, the witnesses yawned and allowed "it might be a good game for Sundays."

Whatever the locale of golf's first U.S. incarnation, it is universally conceded that the sire of American golf, the man from whose efforts the game took root, was one John Reid. He grew up in the Scottish town of Dunfermline, and in his later years recalled childhood scenes of the sport along his native land's seaside. He had left his birthplace to make his fortune in America and he achieved the dream, working himself up to manager of the J. L. Mott Iron Works in the Mott Haven section of the Bronx.

Reid was a close friend of another former Dunfermline boy, Robert Lockhart, a New York linen merchant. Lockhart's business required visits abroad and he occasionally returned with gifts for aquaintances like "Jock" Reid. Once he had returned with tennis racquets and balls. Reid and Lockhart set up a court on Reid's lawn in Yonkers, then a largely rural suburb on the Hudson just north of New York City. Tennis, however, failed to win sustained affection.

In the summer of 1887, Lockhart traveled to St. Andrews. Some accounts say Reid had specifically requested his pal to bring back the equipment used in the sport the foundry executive remembered from his youth. Other reports claim Lockhart bought the balls and clubs on his own as a present for Reid. In any event, Lockhart called upon Old Tom Morris at his St. Andrews shop and ordered six clubs and two dozen gutties. Old Tom made the clubs with his own hand and they included a driver, a brassie or 2-wood, a spoon or 3-wood, and three irons—a cleek or long iron, a sand iron, and a putter. The half dozen clubs cost Lockhart perhaps fifteen dollars.

Lockhart sailed back to New York City before Morris could finish the gear. The Scot finally shipped the goods in the autumn of 1887. When the stuff arrived, the excited Lockhart decided to try out the equipment. Sydney Lockhart, his son, accompanied him on that memorable day and recalled:

One bright Sunday morning, father, my brother Leslie and myself went up to a place on the river which is now Riverside Drive. It was not a wilderness by any means, as I recall there was a mounted policeman near the spot father selected as a teeing ground.

Father teed up the first little white ball and, selecting one of the long wooden clubs, dispatched it far down the meadow. [Lockhart in his youth had learned the game at the Musselburgh course.] He tried all the clubs and then we boys were permitted to drive some balls too. One of father's shots came dangerously close to taking the ear off an iceman, but the policeman did not arrest my father and merely smiled. Later the cop asked if he could hit one of those balls and naturally my father was more than pleased that he was so friendly. The officer got down off his horse and went through the motions of teeing up, aping father in waggling and squaring off to the ball and other preliminaries. Then he let go and hit a beauty straight down the field which went fully as far as any father had hit. Being greatly encouraged and proud of his natural ability at the game that involved a ball and stick, he tried again. This time he missed the ball completely and then in rapid succession he missed the little globe three more times; so with a look of disgust on his face he mounted his horse and rode away.

These first blows struck for golf in New York thus encapsulate the classic experience of the newcomer to the sport.

Having satisfied himself of the quality of the new toys, Lockhart handed them over to Jock Reid who made plans to hold a formal test for friends and associates over a weekend in mid-March. But when a winter thaw set in during the February 22, 1888, holiday of George Washington's birthday, Jock Reid seized the opportunity for the introduction of golf.

Aided by five pals, Reid created three holes in a cow pasture across the street from his home. With only six clubs available, the men agreed Reid and John B. Upham would play the "course," passing the clubs back and forth as needed. The demonstration captured the enthusiasm of the entire band although pursuit of the passion went temporarily on hold after the fearsome Blizzard of '88 arrived on March

In November of 1888, some nine months after the inauguration of golf at St. Andrew's in America, a foursome at the rough-hewn course includes adults, from left to right, Harry Holbrook, A. P. W. Kinnan, J. B. Upham, and the accepted father of the game in the U.S., John Reid. The caddies are Holbrook's sons, Warren and Frederick. (COURTESY THE BETTMANN ARCHIVE.)

12, Reid's originally chosen date for the debut.

With improvements in the weather, and with enough clubs and balls to accommodate the growing number of would-be golfers, the cow pasture course—in what would also become part of the U.S. golf tradition—couldn't handle the demand. Reid and his buddies moved the game to a nearby thirty-acre meadow owned by a butcher who benignly tolerated their usurpation of his property rights.

In November of this same year, after a day of play, Reid and four others from that Washington's Birthday experiment sat down to dinner at his home. Reid proposed they guarantee the future of the pastime by organizing a club that would maintain the course and enhance the camaraderie attending such a joint enterprise. Those present heartily agreed, electing Jock Reid president. He in turn suggested the club be named St. Andrew's, to honor the site of their passion's home.

The Royal and Ancient location bears no apostrophe in its spelling and there were several other distinctions. The Americans, instead of colorful garb, dressed themselves like working stiffs with hobnail shoes, rumpled old jackets and pants, and well-worn derbies or slouch hats. After a round, instead of repairing to a tavern or clubhouse, they sat down at a table constructed of two boards resting on a pair of barrels set up in a neighbor's yard. They drank water from tubs of ice stored beneath the crude table. There were no regular caddies; one of the players' young sons toted the loose clubs for twenty-five cents a round.

The six-hole course itself was basically a batch of unkempt fairways approximating modern light rough. The greens would have been the same texture except the heavy traffic in hobnail shoes soon reduced them to a hard-packed bare ground. Players created the "cups" by scooping out a hole with the blade of a cleek. Course maintenance—mowing of the long grass—was done by an employee of Reid's assisted by the gardener of one of the players.

Reid and his pals had hardly dug their first divots before a correspondent for the Philadelphia *Times* on February 24, 1889, offered readers a breathless description of the new craze:

> As soon as the ball is started in the air, the player runs forward in the direction which the ball has taken, and his servant, who is called a "caddy" runs after him with all the other nine tools in his arms. . . .
>
> Spectators sometimes view games of golf, but as a rule they stand far off for the nature of the implements employed is such

Upon this great apple tree, the early St. Andrew's players suspended baskets of food or hung their jackets in warm weather. The comfort seekers installed a bench around the trunk and a chest for ice and beverages. When the tree finally died, one branch was mounted on a wall in the clubhouse and another hung at the namesake in Scotland. (COURTESY ST. ANDREW'S.)

John "Jock" Reid sparked the U.S. passion. (COURTESY ST. ANDREW'S.)

that a ball may be driven in a very contrary direction to that which the player wishes, and therefore may fall among the spectators and cause some temporary discomfort. Moreover, it would require considerable activity upon the part of the spectator to watch the play of golf, for they would have to run around and see how every hole was gained, from one end of the game to the other.

This was a reasonably accurate if superficial description of the game. But a contemporary account in St. Louis depicted an activity with only a vague resemblance to the game.

No dude can play it because brawn and vigor are essential qualities. The players have servants and sometimes run many miles. . . . In addition to the fact that it appeals to men of athletic development, it is also by the nature of the game itself, a most aristocratic exercise; for no man can play at golf who has not a servant at command to assist him. The truth is the servant is as essential to the success of the game as the player himself.

The writer, who should be the patron saint of caddies, quoted his authority, Alexander MacFarlane:

. . . Having selected a field, the first thing necessary is to dig a small hole perhaps one foot or two feet deep and about four inches in diameter. Beginning with this hole, a circle is devised that includes substantially the whole of the links. About once in 500 yards of this circle a hole is dug corresponding to the one I have just described. The design is to make as large a circle as possible, with holes at about the same distance apart . . .

The "expert" went on to outline a game in which the speed with which one covered the course, using the spoon club to extract balls from the holes, determined a winner, regardless of strokes. Such ignorance was quickly dissipated as the popularity of the game grew, and pros from Scotland, seduced by the economic opportunities, arrived on American shores to instruct the novitiates.

One giant precedent for golfdom occurred on March 30, 1889, when St. Andrew's became the site for a mixed foursome match, breaking the male exclusivity of the American sport for the first time.

When the Yonkers city fathers decided to extend a street through the meadow housing the St. Andrew's course, the club relocated to a thirty-four-acre apple orchard.

The clubhouse of St. Andrew's, designed by its then vice-president, featured a large dining room and vistas of a course that extends from a hillside down to a long valley. (COURTESY USGA.)

In a single day, Jock Reid and his chums designed another six-holer. They did not pare a single apple tree as they twisted the 1,500-yard course through the orchard, giving themselves plenty of obstructions for shots. The *piece de resistance* of the layout was a gnarly, thick-trunked specimen standing near the first tee and final green. It served as a locker room, on the branches of which the players could hang their jackets and picnic baskets along with demijohns of potables familiar to the clubhouses of Scotland. Because of St. Andrew's site and the *al fresco* clubhouse, Jock Reid and his cronies became known as "the Apple Tree Gang." By the end of the year the club numbered twenty members. Instead of their once-tatty clothes, they began to tee off in starchy shirts, bow ties, well-pressed suits, as well as hats ranging from the traditional derby through the straw boater, the pith helmet, and the tweed cap.

The zest for golf had now spread well beyond the confines of the apple orchard. Courses and clubs quickly sprang up in other New York suburbs, New Jersey, Pennsylvania, Connecticut, Rhode Island, and as far off as Kentucky and Illinois.

While St. Andrew's dawdled through the development of its rough-hewn abbreviated courses and rudimentary facilities,

other adherents of golf advanced the state of the sport with stunning swiftness. Theodore A. Havemeyer, who amassed a fortune through sugar, first witnessed golf while at the French resort of Pau. After being rebuffed when he broached the sport to others, Havemeyer, on his own, built a nine-hole course at Brenton's Point in Newport, Rhode Island, a summer colony for the swelling ranks of U.S. millionaires, including the likes of Cornelius Vanderbilt, Oliver Belmont, and John Jacob Astor. With the inauguration of the Brenton's Point course in 1890, these worthies launched the Newport Golf Club with Havemeyer at the helm.

On the eastern reaches of New York's Long Island, industrial potentates W. K. Vanderbilt and Edward Mead, spurred on by another crusading Scottish transplant Duncan Cryder, agreed to create a course in Southampton. For many years, historians credited Willie Dunn, a highly respected architect and pro from Scotland, as designer of the twelve-hole course. However, latter-day scholar David Goddard attributes Shinnecock to Willie Davis, an English professional recruited from Montreal. The group chose land in a 4,000-acre section along Great Peconic Bay in Southampton. About 150 Indians recruited from the Shinnecock Reservation were hired as labor-

Before moving to its current home in the Mount Hope section, the links of St. Andrew's were in an area known as Gray Oaks. Jock Reid stands to the left of the driver, Dr. Moffat. (COURTESY USGA.)

The strokes of women golfers in 1903 were severely limited by the dictates of fashion. (COURTESY THE BETTMANN ARCHIVE.)

Famed illustrator Howard Chandler Christy infused style into the garb of his female player. (COURTESY THE BETTMANN ARCHIVE.)

ers. Horse-drawn road scrapers carved fairways while workers cut away blueberry bushes from the rough. Unlike at Scottish seaside links, with their natural sand bunkers, men had to dig traps at Shinnecock. From the remnants of Indian burial mounds, they fashioned other obstacles. In the growing American style of combining business with pleasure, the organizers opened the course in 1891, selling forty-four shares in the Shinnecock Hills club for 100 dollars apiece, raising enough money to construct a clubhouse designed by the most renowned architect of the day, Stanford White.

Another discoverer of golf during a stay at Pau was Florence Boit. On her return to America, she visited an uncle in Wellesley, Mass., where she fascinated neighbors by practicing the sport on the front lawn. A few demanded to join, the fun spread and, together, they stretched a crude pitch-and-putt layout across neighboring lawns. The fascination with the new game brought a suggestion that The Country Club at Brookline add golf to its program. From Florence Boit's innocent hacking about the yard sprouted a modest six holes and then a full-scale operation that would grow into one of the totems of American golf.

Equally significant in the advancement of American golf were events in Chicago. American-born Charles Blair Macdonald, with the blood of Scotland in his ancestors, was dispatched at age sixteen by his wealthy father to study at St. Andrews University. A grandfather there introduced the boy to the pleasures of the Royal and Ancient. Among Macdonald's golfing buddies at St. Andrews was Young Tom Morris and the American became an excellent player.

Back in the States, Macdonald first constructed a tiny seven-hole arrangement on a friend's estate. He soon persuaded friends at the downtown Chicago Club in 1892 to sculpt nine holes in suburban Belmont. They added another nine a year later for the country's first eighteen-hole layout, which the Royal and Ancient had decreed was the proper total for a full-fledged operation. But Macdonald and company had their sights on a grander scale. The Chicago Golf Club struck out for Wheaton,

twenty-five miles from the city. There they created a full-scale course that continues to be part of the international golf scene.

Macdonald had an ego roughly the size of Lake Michigan and a mouth large enough to back it up. Furthermore, he knew how to display his talents to their best advantage. He put down the holes at Wheaton in a clockwise fashion around the perimeter of the property. The design endangered all hookers who frequently found themselves chasing balls into an adjacent cornfield. The club tried to mollify hookers with an out-of-bounds rule. If a player pulled a drive into the farmer's field he could tee up a second ball rather than desperately thrash about the alien corn before returning to the fairway. But C. B. Macdonald never worried about being out of bounds; he was at worst a slicer and the layout was, in the words of Herbert Warren Wind, as tailor-made "as the short rightfield fence was made for Babe Ruth." The worst that Macdonald could do was slice onto an adjoining fairway.

St. Andrew's also improved as it continued to move. The orchard site was too confining and at the insistence of younger members a new, nine-hole enterprise was erected at another site. Three years later, in 1897, St. Andrew's finally found a permanent and eighteen-hole home in the Mount Hope section of what is now Hastings-on-Hudson. Jock Reid gushed his delight over the layout:

I do not think there is any golfer in the land, certainly there is no golfer who has once seen the present links of the St. Andrew's Club . . . who will not be prepared to apply the reasoning that Dr. Johnson applied to the strawberry when he said that, of course, the Almighty *might* have designed a better fruit than the strawberry, but that He never had! With equal truth it might be said that nature might have prepared a better site for an eighteen-hole golf course, but she never had!

The first courses, like their Scottish antecedents, incorporated not just nature in the raw but a scattering of man-made al-

(Above) *At the exlusive Jekyll Island Club, Brunswick, Georgia, Mrs. William Fellowes Morgan lashed a drive with a unique follow-through.* (COURTESY RAY DAVIS.)

(Left, top) *On the first day of the U.S. Amateur in 1903, a tiny crowd witnessed the play at the Nassau Country Club, Glen Cove, New York.* (COURTESY RAY DAVIS.)

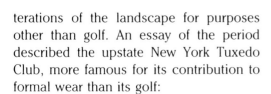

(Left, bottom) *The Westchester Country Club eventually competed with St. Andrew's for regional prestige, but in 1903 facilities were minimal.* (COURTESY RAY DAVIS.)

terations of the landscape for purposes other than golf. An essay of the period described the upstate New York Tuxedo Club, more famous for its contribution to formal wear than its golf:

[It] furnishes great variety in its hazards of hills, stone walls, railroad embankments lined with blast furnace slag, apple-trees, and a combination of terrors in front of what is known as Devil's Hole, consisting of brook, boulders, and road . . . where straight long drives are the only hope for preserving the temper, and the hazards are such that they make glad the heart of man when surmounted, but to the beginner are outer darkness where is weeping and gnashing of teeth.

Apart from the full-length courses, golf's becoming established was indicated by the appearance of even fancier uniforms for play. In the tradition of the Old Country, red coats, brass buttons, blue checked caps, winged collars, gray knickers, plaid

stockings, and gray gaiters were among the prescribed items. And St. Andrew's even regressed to a ban on women. To combat the men-only syndrome, a Morris County, New Jersey, course was founded in 1893 exclusively for women.

Within less than ten years, golf in America had stepped out from a single, three-hole, dung-strewn cow pasture to dozens of elaborately designed layouts replete with luxurious clubhouses that could compete with the best of the British facilities. The *New York Times*, in 1894, took note of the phenomenon on its society page:

Society is as prone to fads as are the sparks to fly upward. And the latest in outdoor fads is golf. Tennis, archery and polo have each had their turn, and golf is now coming in to replace them in the fickle minds of the Four Hundred.

Without being as violent as tennis or polo, the ancient Scottish game furnishes more exercise than either archery or croquet and seems to find favor with those

lovers of outdoor sports who are too stout, too old or too lazy to enjoy any of the severer games.

The index of the paper for that year shows eleven stories on fencing compared to a mere four for golf. But only a year later the *Times* marvelled:

In the history of American field sports there can be found no outdoor pastime that developed and attained such popularity in such a relatively short period of time as the game of golf.

Horace Rawlins captured the first U.S. Open in 1895 at the Newport Country Club with a 173 for 18 holes. (COURTESY RAY DAVIS.)

At the Point Judith Country Club in Rhode Island, sheep "mowed" fairways. (COURTESY RAY DAVIS.)

4

Madness and Order

Some might wonder why it took as long as it did for golf to capture the nation. Modern professional major league baseball had been established in 1876, more than ten years before the gathering of the Apple Tree Gang. By 1895, while thousands of amateur and professional teams met on American diamonds, golfers still numbered in the hundreds and eighteen-hole courses remained a rarity.

American intercollegiate football, hewn from rugby and soccer with some native innovation dates to the 1869 meeting of Princeton and Rutgers. In 1889, the year St. Andrew's was born, Walter Camp chose his first All-American football team and the sport was well on its way to becoming a major feature of every college campus (although the president of Harvard expressed himself as ill disposed toward the student mania for "moving a bag of wind").

Modern tennis, which surfaced in England in 1873, crossed the Atlantic within a year. Horse racing came to America with the early arrivals from England and they broke from the gate in the first Kentucky Derby in 1875.

Obviously, almost from the moment the first colonists stepped ashore in the New World, sporting blood coursed through the States. For that matter, the Indians, too, played games. Why, then, with such a heavy influx of people from the font of golf—a high proportion of the settlers during the late eighteenth and early nineteenth centuries came from the British Isles and particularly Scotland—did the sport make such a late appearance?

One explanation lies in golf's affinity with the landed gentry, folks with leisure time and the wherewithal to support a hobby. Except for the pre–Civil War plantation South that segment did not exist in the United States. Baseball could flourish even in the growing American cities where one could play on a relatively small lot. Golf, on the other hand, required spaces outside of urban areas, and so the clubs sprouted in places like Yonkers, Southampton, Newport, or Wheaton, where land was available and the population sparse. While there were municipal courses almost from the start, the number was limited and, just as today, they quickly became overcrowded.

Besides the formidable costs of building a course with clubhouse, at fifteen dollars for a set of clubs, the basic implements of golf could be afforded only by the well heeled. So it was the new wealth, the industrialists, who first took to the game. In spite of the first municipal course opening for play in Boston in 1890, golf was a clubman's game. Working stiffs and small businessmen labored long hours for six days a week. And even if money and time were not considerations, a dour work ethic frowned upon frivolous pursuits. The battle over Sunday golf was long over for British sportsmen, but in the States the clergy continued to thunder against the intrusion of golf upon the Sabbath and the obligations of worship.

While the infectious attraction of golf grew slowly, it was a grand passion for those who had succumbed. W. K. Vanderbilt, one of the founding fathers of Shinnecock Hills, spoke for his class in 1889 when he announced: "Gentlemen, this beats rifle shooting for distance and accuracy. It is a game I think would go in our country."

Fellow entrepreneurs (revisionist historians have labeled them "robber barons") like Andrew Carnegie and John D. Rockefeller took to the game with the same zest with which they built the trusts to corner markets in steel and petroleum. Carnegie, another Dunfermline boy—a member of

Charles McDonald, the magnificent blusterer, bellowed "foul" after losing the invitation Open sponsored by the Newport CC in 1894. After soaring to a disastrous 100 on the final nine at Newport, he claimed tournaments should be decided by match rather than medal play. St. Andrew's gave him his opportunity a month later, but he blew a playoff with a cornfield slice. The squabbles led directly to formation of the United States Golf Assocation, which henceforth organized the U.S. Amateur championship, the U.S. Open, and wrote the rules governing play and equipment. (COURTESY RAY DAVIS.)

St. Andrew's who personally signed for the 50,000-dollar mortgage that covered the clubhouse—and a benefactor of libraries and universities, seemed to equate golf with these causes when he solemnly declared golf "the indispensable adjunct of high civilization." So enamored of golf was Carnegie that he built a weekend retreat on the St. Andrew's land. Because of the bloody violence attendant upon the strike at his steel plant in Homestead, Pennsylvania, in 1892, the Carnegie cottage had a stone foundation and steel shutters as protection. Despite his fondness for St. Andrew's, Carnegie hurried home before dark to thwart would-be kidnappers.

It was oil tycoon Rockefeller who indulged his zeal for the sport most lavishly. He had discovered golf in 1899 while vacationing at Lakewood, New Jersey. His first round over the nine-hole, 2,800-yard course was 64 and the following day he managed to shoot 61.

Within days Rockefeller installed four holes on his estate at Pocantico, New York. He then hired Willie Dunn, the noted pro and sometime designer, to plot a twelve-hole operation at Pocantico. Simultaneously, he engaged professionals from nearby clubs to come to his estate and hone his technique. And at another of his homes, Forest Hills, New Jersey, he built a nine-hole course.

Rockefeller and his guests rode bicycles between strokes because, he explained, "I like to play golf as much as possible, so I save up energy." (In his dotage some years later, an employee would push him on a bicycle between holes.) Just as he doled out shiny dimes to street urchins, Rockefeller rewarded golfing companions with ten-cent pieces.

Frederick Taylor, the no-nonsense father of scientific management, had become a devotee of golf a few years before Rockefeller, but it was the oil tycoon who brought a rough science to his endeavors. A photographer from Cleveland came to Pocantico for the express purpose of taking snapshots of the Rockefeller stroke. Through study of the pictures, John D. eliminated a troublesome slice. To break a bad habit,

he stationed a boy at tee side who, during his swing, shouted: "Hold your head down! Hold your head down!"

Rockefeller decided he lost distance because his feet tended to shift during the stroke. To correct the problem he practiced with a stone slab across his toes. When that method proved ineffective he hammered a croquet wicket over his foot and into the ground to anchor the offending member. Witnesses from the period say Rockefeller frequently drove balls a more than respectable 200 yards. He refused to allow the weather to prevent play. During the dead of winter, workmen, using horses and snowplows, cleared fairways and putting greens.

Not so curiously, Rockefeller was among the first to learn of the affinity of golf to business. When a friend felt the oil magnate was lonely he suggested Rockefeller make an opening gesture toward those who felt timorous in his presence. John D. forcefully responded, "If you suppose I have not thought about the matter you are mistaken. I have made some experiments. And nearly always the result is the same— along about the ninth hole out comes some proposition, charitable, or financial."

Indeed, the mighty U.S. Steel Corporation was conceived at the nineteenth hole of St. Andrew's. It was there that financier Charles Schwab persuaded Andrew Carnegie to sell his company to J. P. Morgan.

The society page of the *New York Times* had demeaned golf as a "fad," but the fervor of the pillars of the new Society and the profusion of courses and clubs attested to something of far more permanence. And in 1894, the natural competitive aspect of the game and the tendency of Americans to organize united to provide a firm foundation for the future.

The triggering occasion was a joust between two rival enterprises, St. Andrew's and the Newport Golf Club, both of whom organized tournaments to determine the best amateur player in the land. The first contest, in September 1894 at Newport, saw twenty men tee off with dismal results. Many of the players were rank novices; only eight of the starters actually completed the thirty-six holes, four times over the nine-hole course. The burly creator of the Chicago Golf Club, Charles B. Macdonald, figured as the favorite and his 89 for the first 18 led the field. But he blew up to 100 for the final round, allowing Newporter William G. Lawrence to squeak through, 188 to 189.

Macdonald, a fierce stickler for the letter of the rules, was an irascible type; some would have called him a sore loser. He believed himself to be the best golfer in America and complained the strokes that cost him the match were due to a stone wall on the course, an improper hazard in his view, although such obstacles certainly were common on the old courses of Scotland and frequently bedeviled golfers in the U.S. as well. Furthermore, Macdonald blustered, the medal-play system at Newport penalized him and he was confident he would gain revenge in the match-play tournament at St. Andrew's. To his utter dismay he lost again when, in a sudden-death playoff, he sliced his tee shot into a cornfield. He offered the excuse of illness for the errant drive; the source of the malady was diagnosed as one too many bottles of champagne for lunch.

Almost totally ignored was a professional Open, also held at St. Andrew's. Four men entered it, all imports who served as pros at U.S. clubs, and it was almost exclusively a battle of the Willies—Dunn, Campbell, and Davis—plus Samuel Tucker, just named to instruct at St. Andrew's. In contrast to the amateurs, the tournament was match play and Willie Dunn stroked to a title worth 100 dollars in cash and a gold medal.

The dissatisfaction so noisily offered by Macdonald as well as a general sense of anarchy in competitions stimulated a meeting of representatives from a number of clubs to form a group that could supervise national championships and other activities relevant to golf. Men from the five most prominent clubs, St. Andrew's, Newport, Shinnecock Hills, The Country Club, and the Chicago Golf Club, sat down to a dinner a few days before Christmas in 1894. They created the Amateur Golf Associa-

tion of the United States, which a year later took on its current name, the United States Golf Assocation. Theodore Havemeyer served as the first president over a committee, including an early oddity, a golfing minister, the Reverend William Rainsford, and a clubman, Richard Peters, who used a billiard cue on greens—the sort of thing which the USGA would even-

McDonald designed this layout for the Chicago Golf Club. It promises death and destruction for those who hook. C. B. himself tended to slice. (COURTESY RAY DAVIS.)

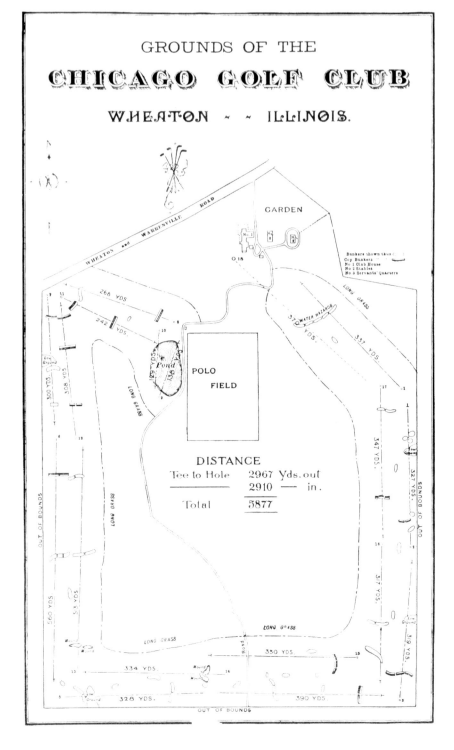

The Chicago Golf Club became the largest establishment of its kind, replete with an appropriately sized clubhouse. (COURTESY USGA.)

(Above, left) *For all of his noisome behavior, McDonald devoted himself to the purity of the game. Horace Hutchinson, the renowned British expert on golf, visited the U.S. in 1910 and described McDonald's National Golf Links on Long Island, New York, as the best of the American courses.* (COURTESY RAY DAVIS.)

(Above, right) *Fred Herd fired a 328, a record high score, in the first seventy-two-hole U.S. Open of 1898 at the Myopia Hunt Club, South Hamilton, Massachusetts. With a layout of only nine holes, Herd went around eight times in two days.* (COURTESY RAY DAVIS.)

tually outlaw. For the time being, the USGA announced its aims as uniform rules, a standard system of handicapping, establishment of itself as the final authority on all golf controversies and to "decide on what links the Amateur and Open Championships shall be played."

The organization sponsored its first three tournaments in 1895, the Men's Amateur (the British did not get around to an amateur championship until 1885, twenty-five years after the inauguration of the nation's Open), the Men's Open and the Women's Amateur (there were no female professionals to necessitate a Woman's Open). Newport served as the site for the Men's Amateur, in match-play as Macdonald had demanded—and he carried off the cham-

pionship, easily winning his five matches, culminating in a 12 up, 11 to play in the final encounter. With such a pleasing result for Macdonald, the USGA could now count on his steamroller support for its efforts. Horace Rawlins captured the Open on the following day at the same course, beating out Willie Dunn for the 150 dollar prize money and the medal.

The first female champion, Mrs. Charles S. Brown from Shinnecock Hills, triumphed over a dozen other women in a tournament at the Meadowbrook club in Hempstead, New York. Her score for the eighteen holes was 132, remarkably low considering the clothing foisted upon women players. Brown, like her sisters on the links, was encumbered with a wide-brimmed bonnet, a starched, leg-of-mutton sleeve blouse, a tight corset, and a flowing skirt that hung over her ankles. The men, in spite of regrets offered by the likes of C. B. Macdonald, had begun to shuck their extravagant finery in favor of clothes that did not interfere with their strokes.

Macdonald is often depicted as an overbearing boor. However, the USGA—of which he was a principal founder—brought some order to the chaos threatening golf in the States. And he backed the development of the out-of-bounds rules, subsequently adopted by the Royal and Ancient across the sea. Until this revision golfers were required to recover from lies along the railroad line bounding several holes. Macdonald would later take up the cause of a new type of ball and the National Golf Links at Southampton, which he designed, set a standard of excellence. Two of the holes replicated ones at the Scotland St. Andrews Old Course.

In the role of a golf course architect, C. B. came on as an Old Testament prophet, heaping fire and brimstone upon those who strayed: "The object of a bunker or trap is not only to punish a physical mistake, to punish lack of control, but also to punish pride and egotism." On another occasion he thundered: "If I had my way, I'd never let the sand be raked. Instead, I'd run a herd of elephants through them every morning."

The USGA had written the rules and fellows like Macdonald enforced them. But competition against the courses and other golfers from the start tried the integrity of men's souls. Henry Howland wrote in an 1895 issue of *Scribner's Magazine*:

Golfers as a rule are an exceptionally honest race of men, but uncertain arithmetic is occasionally encountered on the green. "I aim to tell the truth," said one; "Well you are a very bad shot" was the reply,

At Ardsley, New York, in 1898, Beatrice Hoyt lines up a putt that made her 5 and 3 for her third consecutive victory in the USGA's Women's Amateur. (COURTESY RAY DAVIS.)

Mrs. Charles S. Brown required 132 strokes to gain the women's amateur title in 1895 at the Meadow Brook Club, Hempstead, New York. (COURTESY RAY DAVIS.)

The Shinnecock Hills Golf Club in eastern Long Island boosted a clubhouse designed by Stanford White. (COURTESY SUFFOLK COUNTY HISTORICAL SOCIETY.)

and there is often an area of low veracity about a bunker.

Even earlier, in 1890, the redoubtable Horace Hutchinson advised:

> It is an un-Christian counsel, but the mood for success in golf matches is silent hatred —temporary only, be it observed of your opponent. . . . Do not, of course, be aggressively rude to an opponent, but do not bother your "dour" mood to make yourself agreeable. All your powers of charming will be needed for the ball.

Interest in the sport was sufficient to import Willie Park, Jr., twice winner of the British Open, to play exhibitions in 1895, and people actually paid to watch him. Had he not inexplicably sailed for home just before the 1895 U.S. Open, the results might well have been different. He was not only an excellent player but also a shrewd sort who on hot days toted a bucket of ice with him to keep his gutties round and hard. The Country Club in Boston engaged Park to meet its own pro Willie Campbell, and Park won 6 and 5 for a 100 dollar prize. There was no second money. Park drew a crowd of 400 at the Morristown Golf Club, where he destroyed Willie Norton 17 and 16 in a thirty-six-hole match. One phenomenon to surface during Park's tour was widespread betting.

Shinnecock included a pair of eighteen-hole layouts. (COURTESY SUFFOLK COUNTRY HISTORICAL SOCIETY.)

Enthusiasm for golf led to two separate courses in the bucolic resort of Lakewood, New Jersey. On a wintery January 1, 1898, one of them, the Ocean County Hunt and Country Club, invited the public to witness a contest among professionals. Ten hardy professionals bundled up in heavy coats, mufflers, and hats and shivered through thirty-six holes over the frozen turf. A reporter of the time wrote:

> The meeting was one of golfing giants, to each of whom was granted an unknown degree of skill and each of whom had their particular partisans. The purse [150 dollars] offered an incentive which invited their best effort.

The winner, Val Fitzjohn, who beat his brother Ed in a playoff, was hardly a household name, yet the correspondent noted the ". . . large attendence [actually about 100 chilled souls] proving it a sporting event of greater interest than any that has ever been held here."

Other resorts, like Hot Springs, Virginia; Asheville, North Carolina; Augusta, Georgia; Ormond and Jacksonville, Florida, all created courses, charging a princely fifty cents for nine holes.

The eagerness of Americans to learn the game seemed to guarantee employment to any applicant for the job of pro, provided his first name was Willie and he had a Scotch accent—a dialect many pupils could barely understand.

The esteemed *Harpers Weekly* of June 29, 1901, carried a piece "A Country Gone to Golf." Wrote Gustav Kobbe:

> . . . we have all gone golf mad.
> "Fore!"—the click of wood or iron against gutta percha, and the white globe sails through the air, strikes the ground, continues with little leaps and bounds, and rolls along, bobbing up and down with the unevenness of the surface until at last it comes to a stop.
> Or perhaps there has been a dull thud and you have ploughed up the ground before hitting the ball, or have "drawn" off into "whins" and it is a case of a lost ball. But be you golfer or "duffer" you are equally

ready to acknowledge that golf is a great game.

Kobbe compared the interest with baseball and rhetorically asked where was the baseball club with 300 members. He described the sport as one where "thousands play," while in baseball two nines compete and thousands only watch.

I have seen "kids" whose clubs although children's size, were larger than the players toddling over the links and then, too, grayhaired men and women who ten years ago would have been laid on the shelf. Golf has robbed old age of its regrets, for it can be played from the cradle to the grave.

After noting at least a thousand listed clubs in the U.S., Kobbe detailed what he considered the heavy investment by the players, as much, he swore, as 100 dollars apiece. Club dues were twenty-five dollars. Clubs and bags cost fifteen dollars, and caddies for the year five dollars. Golf balls took another seven dollars, and special clothes and boots fifty dollars. The total was 102 dollars, but, Kobbe warned, one should allow another thirty-three dollars for travel to and from the clubs plus the refreshments, "especially those of a liquid character."

Three years later the magazine offered an insight into the popularity of the sport:

To a certain extent, golf is an old man's game, the older players hold their own in it, as they cannot pretend to do in any other purely athletic sport. Doubtless it is the judicious mixture of force and art in golf . . . in the winning of a hole, the 200-yard drive and the 14-inch putt count the same.

The first periodical in the United States entirely devoted to the sport, *Golf Magazine*, appeared in 1898. Newspapers had begun to cover tournaments and exhibitions, and carried items about local clubs. Two famous humorists of the day, George Ade and Finley Peter Dunne, made golf a subject for columns.

An article in the June 1902 *Atlantic Monthly* noted:

Empire, trusts and golf were three new topics of conversation in the land . . . the future historian if he should ever come to know our life . . . should [he] have a right sense of values in civilization and a keen eye to the sources of national character, will not rate golf as the least of three new things which came with the end of the century.

Shades of Jacques Barzun, the French-born philosopher who some fifty years later said, "Whoever wants to know the heart and mind of America had better learn baseball." The American brand of the sport had teed off.

(Top) *With its flat, wind-swept terrain, Shinnecock recalled the seaside links of Scotland.* (COURTESY USGA.)

(Bottom) *A mixed foursome on the U.S. links bespeaks the growing informality of male garb.* (COURTESY RAY DAVIS.)

5

Clubs, Balls, and Hands Across the Sea

The sport held a growing beachhead of players as well as golf clubs in the United States toward the turn of the century, but the game still depended upon supplies from abroad. A. G. Spalding —the one-time star pitcher for the Boston Red Stockings and Chicago White Stockings, owner of the latter club and a pivotal figure in the formation and establishment of major league baseball since he was only twenty-six—had exploited his baseball connections to establish a sporting goods company. Spalding continually sought to expand the market for his goods, going so far as to spend 20,000 dollars of his own dearly held money for a round-the-world tour of the American game in hopes of introducing the sport to other countries, who would then buy equipment from A. G. Spalding & Brothers. That 1888–1889 venture was an abysmal flop. The most notable incident in the British Isles was a flap over Spalding's behavior as he explained the action in an exhibition game to the Prince of Wales, destined to become Edward VII. The American committed a grand gaffe when he sat himself down beside the Prince and touched the royal shoulder after Edward had slapped him on the knee following a long hit by White Stocking star Cap Anson.

Later Spalding went to extraordinary lengths to prove his beloved baseball bore no British ancestry. However, he was also an astute businessman and, when he observed golf courses mushrooming over the landscape with fairways populated by deep-pocketed folks, he seized an opportunity. As early as 1892, a buyer for Spalding brought back 500 dollars worth of clubs and balls from Scottish manufacturers.

Other officials of the company were aghast at the investment in so much inventory for what many believed a fad, but the company chief approved it.

Within a few years, the Spalding concern began to import golf club heads from Scotland and attach shafts in the U.S. Actually, the industry in Scotland had operated in the reverse, using for its shafts hickory wood imported from the U.S. The Spalding firm later claimed it was the first to market a wholly made-in-America club. This is in some doubt, but the baseball magnate's company was the first to develop an American guttie and replace hand-hammered irons with a pioneering drop-forge process.

By 1900, several other U.S. firms were turning out clubs. Most notable was a shoe-last outfit named Crawford, McGregor and Canby, which was manufacturing wooden clubheads on the same lathes employed to shape shoe lasts. Eventually, the first and final names of the firm disappeared, leaving the familiar McGregor label.

Among those prospering through golf was the B. F. Goodrich Company, beginning to flex its muscles as an industrial giant. Goodrich turned out gutties at its Akron, Ohio, plant. The appropriately named Bertram Work supervised the factory for Goodrich. One day, Coburn Haskell, a Cleveland sportsman and a man with the right connections—Haskell was married to a daughter of the president-maker Mark Hanna and was an occasional golfing companion of Rockefeller—arrived to pick up Work. The foreman was busy and suggested Haskell stroll through the plant. Haskell meandered by a pile of thin rubber stripping and mused about golf balls.

His chain of thought led to the idea of wrapping a rubber core in a gutta percha cover.

Bertram Work, also a golfer, agreed to experiment with a design by Haskell. Goodrich employees first hand-wound the yarn about the core and then built a crude mechanical contraption to wrap the rubber strands about the center. When a local pro tested what was to become known as a "Haskell," the ball soared over a bunker where previously the best drives barely rolled into the sand. Work and Haskell patented the ball in 1898. Later, balata would replace gutta percha as the cover substance.

Haskells were not an instant success. Some referred to them as "Bounding Billies," since accuracy seemed sacrificed for distance. In mid flight the balls frequently ducked abruptly. The lively Haskells seemed particularly difficult to control around the green. In Britain, where the opposition was particularly fierce, guttie adherents referred to Americans and those who used Haskells as "bounders." Difficulties with putting brought comments such as "a guttie on the green is worth two billies in the bushes." Henry Leach, while conceding the American creature's capacity for flight, denigrated the newcomer as "more wayward, fickle." He spoke of the guttie as:

> . . . a dull unimaginative thing, that only knew its duty was in the hole, and went there and down with no coy antics round about the rim, and no changing of mind and out again when once it had touched the metal lining.

In contrast he called the Haskell:

> . . . often as unreliable as any human genius is in the most matter-of-fact duties of human life. It is almost as if it, made for fine unsurpassable flight, resents such stodgy work, and in its resentment is aided by the increasing nervousness and inefficiency of its would-be master . . . the short putt becomes less and less dead than it used to be.

The distance achieved led to the sneer, "A good ball for a tired man." To secure control, manufacturers pocked covers with slight indentations but the white paint tended to fill these in. Horace Hutchinson remarked:

> The general, the natural objection to the ball at first, was . . . that it was too dear. The ball cost twice as much as a first class "gutty." Naturally it looked expensive. The fact that it never was knocked out of shape and would last out three or four gutty balls only became obvious on fuller trial . . . what did not take any time to prove, but was obvious at once, was that if you lost a ball that cost half a crown it was a far more expensive matter than the loss of a ball that cost a shilling, and also that if you were one of the class of players that hits the ball hard and often on top of the head with the iron, the American ball was a very doubtful item of economy, because a hit of this kind cleft a very serious wound in it. [Maimed and lacerated gutties could simply be heated and reinserted in the mold to restore them. Injured Haskells could not be repaired.]

Hutchinson also noted marked advantages to the play of what he called "the American ball." Compared with a guttie, the ball could easily be picked up from a "hard, unfriendly cuppy lie" and it traveled greater distances, not only with woods but also with irons. While he conceded that the tendency to run and bounce increased difficulty upon the greens, he also foresaw that the existing courses would become too short.

Apart from its aerodynamics, the Haskell offered an advantage that eventually transformed how one held a club. Golfers had always been pained by the shock of impact when the clubhead struck the rock-like gutties. To cushion the trauma to hands the grips consisted of thick woolen cloth covered with sheepskin. The resilient rubber-cored balls all but eliminated the stinging sensation. As a consequence, grips shrank in thickness enabling players to tighten their hands and have much better feel of the clubhead.

Golf folklore says the Haskells gained respectability after one pro accidentally put one into a press for gutties, giving it a bramblelike pattern. The marking substantially tamed the wilder spirits of Haskells.

According to Henry Cotton★—the scholarly British pro who dominated golf in his country and who could compete with the best of the Americans during the 1930s and 1940s—the new balls added 20 yards to a shot, even though the ball often wound up somewhere other than intended. A par 4 with a guttie measured from 310 to 380 yards, but the advent of the rubberized ball eventually stretched comparable par 4s to distances of 390 to 450 yards.

Cotton has contended that the new ball "managed to turn the ordinary clumsy golfer overnight into a moderate performer, for even misshits achieved a 75 percent result." But that did not elevate the duffer to equality with the pro; Cotton figured a skilled player who could out-hit an 18 handicapper by 25 yards with a guttie now opened a gap of 75 yards. To take full advantage of the distance, you couldn't simply flail away. Instead, the new ball forced discipline on the backswing and encouraged more lofted clubs whose backspin imparted greater control when the ball sat down on a green.

Among those initially antagonistic to the rubber-cored ball was the Spalding company, which had a vested interest in the guttie. In spite of A. G. Spalding's Anglophobia, his brother James had arranged for the most prominent British golfer, Harry Vardon,★ to put his name on the newest Spalding gutties. The company engaged Vardon to tour the United States in 1900, shilling for the Vardon Flyer and whipping up interest in golf and the equipment sold by Spalding.

Vardon was the best known of the "Great Triumvirate," a trio that dominated tournaments around the turn of the century. The others were James Braid★ and John H. Taylor.★ The only Scot in the crew was Braid, who at six feet one-and-a-half inches was a taller fellow than most of his rivals and who, in his youth at least, weighed a wiry 174 pounds.

Born on the Fifeshire coast in 1870, Braid said: "At Earlsferry and Elie, and all about there it is all golf, and everybody must play unless he wishes to be taken for a crank, or as somebody with whom there is something constitutionally or mentally wrong."

While his parents "did not view golf with any great amount of favour," they did not object to his carrying clubs for visiting gentry or practicing shots when no caddie jobs were to be done: "When a golfer begins his life in this way he needs no tuition in the game, and I never had any

Standing for their group portrait, the "leading professionals of the year" (1902) hew to their uniform of long trousers, with the exception of Harry Vardon. In the twenty-one years from 1891 and 1911, only two outsiders, the amateur Harold Hilton and the Frenchman Arnaud Massy, won British Opens. (COURTESY RAY DAVIS.)

lessons. I simply watched the grown-ups at the game and imitated them like a monkey."

At thirteen he quit school and, to his disappointment, his mother and father would not countenance a career in the sport. Braid practiced the trade of a joiner or carpenter while indulging in amateur golf. A friend who produced clubs for the Army and Navy Stores in London offered him a job as his assistant. He had never made a club in his life but Braid applied his craftsmanship to making them. Meanwhile, he had graduated from the amateur ranks to those of the local professionals. Bernard Darwin,* a grandson of the author of *On the Origin of Species*, and considered by many the patron saint of golf writers, remembered "hearing rumors that there was a wonderful golfer (name to me unknown) at the Stores, who would do terrific things if he could only get the chance."

Braid's opportunity arrived in 1895 when, in an impromptu exhibition match against the then-reigning champion, J. H. Taylor, Braid halved the contest. However, Braid labored several years before reaching the zenith. Once in command of his game, he would win five British Opens between 1901 and 1910.

Observers celebrated his aplomb under the most dire golf situations. During the 1908 Open, Braid plunged into an abyss of a bunker. Trying to extricate himself, he cuffed a ball that glanced off the boarded wall twice before it caromed out of bounds. When he finally arrived at the green, nothing in his demeanor or stride indicated anything untoward, even as he eventually got down in 8. His 291 for that tournament, good enough for an 8-stroke victory, stands as a testament to his resolution.

He drove well and smacked fine irons but usually putted badly. He experimented with clubs and techniques in a desperate

(Above) *"As regards golfers ... nobody could look so wise as James Braid is. There is nobody whose every word and action is so redolent of sagacity. He has a great twinkle of humor, too, humor such as the Scots call 'pawky,' ... Certainly no man ever played golf with a cooler head, though I have heard him say that he liked to feel just a wee bit nervous before starting. Oddly enough, he combined with this quality a power of hitting at the ball with an almost reckless abandon, as if he meant to kill it. ..."—Bernard Darwin,* American Golfer, *January 1934.* (COURTESY ST. ANDREWS UNIVERSITY.)

(Left) *Braid was the first man to win the British Open five times, a mark he shares with Tom Watson. Both are runner-up to Harry Vardon's six titles.* (COURTESY ST. ANDREWS UNVERSITY.)

---

* An excellent golfer in his own right, good enough indeed to have filled in a British team during an international amateur tournament, Bernard Darwin was celebrated for legendary tantrums on the course. He occasionally fell to his knees, tore clumps of turf from the ground with his teeth and then howled, "Oh God, now are you satisfied!"

effort to correct his weakness but green disasters haunted him throughout his career. His Achilles' heel was probably his diminished eyesight, a much more telling factor on the green than from down the fairway.

Like most of the well established pros, he dabbled in golf course design. Darwin appraised his approach:

> . . . though the kindliest of men, [he] is rather ruthless in the matter of bunkers. His old friend, J. H. Taylor, once got into one of Braid's creations at Prestwick and remarked that the man who made that bunker ought to be buried in it with a niblick through his heart.

John H. Taylor starred on the golf scene even earlier than Braid, winning the first of his five Open titles in 1894 and 1895, then losing to Vardon in the 1896 playoff. Born in Devon near the sea, Taylor was reared in a rented cottage. So impover-

"In 1894 the Open was at Sandwich. From the first to last there was one, and one only, most likely winner—J. H. Taylor. His driving was so marvellous a correctness that it was said the guide flags were his only hazards, and his pitching was perfect."—Horace Hutchinson, Fifty Years of Golf. (COURTESY RAY DAVIS.)

ished was the family that his father, a laborer, could not afford a clock. Fearful of being late for work, Taylor's father occasionally hiked to the square in the village of Northam where he could learn the hour from the town clock.

Taylor earned his keep tending boots for the local gentry and as a caddie at the Westward Ho! course. He vividly remembered the first day he caddied and expressed pity "for the unfortunate gentleman upon whom my services were inflicted, for I managed to lose three balls for him in one round."

The going wages for a round amounted to six pence. A lost ball cost Taylor a three-penny fine. Like Braid, Taylor taught himself the rudiments. He observed the best golfers from around the country who came to try out Westward Ho! and analyzed their efforts, "to skim the cream from each style." In addition, he and a few companions created a few holes on the sandhills near the course: "They were short holes, merely calling for pitches from the tee, but they conduced to the learning of the most accurate short play, for the holes were placed in almost un-get-at-able places." Taylor attributed his excellence with the mashie to this early cultivation of the stroke.

Devonshire, however, offered no opportunities for a career in golf and at fifteen Taylor became a gardener's boy attached to a gentleman's house. He continued to play as part of his job at Westward Ho!. As the best of his ilk, Taylor competed against some of the finer amateurs including Hutchinson. Because of his superior performances on the links, the members at Westward Ho! offered him a menial post as a groundskeeper. Within a year he was pro and greenskeeper at a new course.

Taylor developed his own unique style, a flat-footed, abreviated swing. Accuracy marked his play, enabling him to attack boldly. This suited a personality marked by a quick wit and a low flashpoint of temper. Considerably shorter than Braid at five foot eight but stocky at 161 pounds, his movements, said Peter Dobereiner, were "bird-like." He was only twenty-three when he captured his first Open. He was forty-three when, for his fifth championship, he outplayed the likes of Vardon, Braid, and Ted Ray, a new behemoth in British golf, to take the 1914 Open in a howling gale at Hoylake.

Vardon was an inch or so taller than Taylor at five foot nine and a half, weighing 154 pounds, but he possessed an outsize pair of hands that undoubtedly helped him control the club in that era of thick grips. He outshone all other golfers for close to twenty years, copping six British Opens. It was his overlapping grip and his straight up-and-down style that golfers most often sought to emulate. Born on the Isle of Jersey in 1870, he was a lad of seven when he first began to caddie over the new course at Grouville—built only a year earlier at the behest of English tourists on holiday. Like Taylor he collected six pence per round, but his parents regarded the pay insufficient and demeaning, and they forced him to quit.

Undaunted, Vardon and playmates fashioned some homemade clubs from tree limbs, using rough-hewn chunks of wood for club heads. When he grew older, Vardon worked as a gardener, but continued to play golf, joining, like Taylor, the Workingmen's Club. Vardon never took a lesson in his life; his style, which seemed unique, was actually a series of adaptations from observations.

After younger brother Tom became a pro, Harry followed suit, taking jobs at Yorkshire courses. Taylor had already demonstrated his brilliance with his second Open when Vardon played an exhibition match against him and won. Taylor was heard to worry that he had met the fellow who would challenge him most in the coming defense of his title. And indeed, Vardon tied the champion at the Muirfield over seventy-two holes, then conquered him in the playoff.

Vardon rapidly demonstrated the skills that would enable him to stand as the foremost player of his day. One rival, Andra Kirkaldy, frequently second to him, said:

He smiles as he plays, but it is not a broad smile, just a faint flicker over his features. It is what you might call the Vardonic Smile. He was never a worrier or recounter of lost strokes. Nothing ruffled him. He sank into the game, but there was nothing grim about him. No teeth grinding or setting of jaw; just a twiddling of the left toe to make the nails [spikes of that time] grip the ground.

Hutchinson rated Vardon 2 strokes a round superior to Braid and Taylor. He was also the first professional to take the field in knickerbockers. Until Vardon donned them, one could easily distinguish the club members from the hired hands in a painting or photograph merely by observing whether the player wore trousers or knee britches.

Later in his career, beset by illness and the deterioration of his skills, Vardon seemed grim. But in his early days, Hutchinson insisted:

. . . with the flower at his button-hole he set a mode of gaiety and smartness to the rest which younger men were not slow to follow. There was a gay *insouciance* about his whole manner of addressing himself to the game which was very attractive. It was as different as their styles were different from the imperturbability of Braid or again from the tense and highly strung temperament of Taylor.

By the time of Vardon's 1900 arrival in the United States, he had already won the British Open three times and U.S. golfers were eager to see how he would fare in the U.S. Open at the Chicago Golf Club. Impressively large galleries turned out for what had been a sport that drew sparse numbers of spectators. The Vardon tour did not lack venues. There was at least one course in every state; New York boasted 165 while Massachussetts registered 157. To increase the market further, the A. G. Spalding company had employed one Tom Bendelow, beginning in 1895, to serve as an architect for those who wanted to build a course. Bendelow's credentials were minimal. He did speak with a Scotsman's burr but his experience was actually as a compositor on a New York newspaper. He had one great virtue: He charged only twenty-five dollars to design a course. The results were predictable, and Charles Price said of his efforts:

> ... he would mark the first tee with a stake. Then he would pace off a hundred yards and stake off that spot with a simple cross-bunker. Then he would march another hundred yards and mark this location for a mound that was to be built in the shape of a chocolate drop. Then he would walk another hundred yards, more or less, and mark the location for a green. All of Bendelow's greens assumed one of two shapes, perfectly round or perfectly square. None of the greens was protected by hazards, most of them were indistinguishably flat, and all of them had to be plowed under within a few years after they had been planted because, as anyone with a smattering of agronomy would see, they were nothing more than weed nurseries.

Bendelow is credited with creating as many as 600 of these monstrosities.

A course became one more bauble for the wealthy to possess. John D. Rockefeller was no longer the only man to have his own private course. Havemeyer, John Jacob Astor, and even A. G. Spalding had installed layouts on their estates.

With all of this interest in the sport, the Vardon tour was a great success. Vardon barnstormed 20,000 miles across North America, playing more than sixty matches in the U.S. and Canada, before crowds of as many as 1,500. Vardon destroyed the redoubtable Willie Dunn in match play twice, 16 and 15, then 15 and 14. In the midst of his travels, Vardon sailed home for the British Open. He finished second to J. H. Taylor, who won with a 309.

Vardon played subpar golf where such achievement had never been seen. He wrote of his reception:

> At that period, the Americans were not sufficiently advanced to appreciate some of the finer points of the game. They did, however, appear to thoroughly enjoy the type of ball I drove. I hit it high for carry, which resembled a home run.

Vardon's rival countryman, Taylor, was also showing his wares in America. He and a boyhood pal had started a clubmaking company with a branch in Pittsburgh. Taylor and his partner, who now lived in the States, agreed they might cash in by duplicating Vardon's promotional efforts. To bankroll the venture, Taylor accepted the handsome sum of 2,000 dollars from *Golf* magazine.

Their homeland found little to praise in the twosome's conquest of America. Britain's *Golf Illustrated* harrumphed:

> It cannot be said that the visit of either Vardon or Taylor to the States has been productive of much apparent good to the best interests of Golf. It is true that our American friends have had the opportunity of seeing and studying the playing methods of the two best living exponents of the game. But, unfortunately, the presence of the Champions in the States has been the occasion of attempts to exploit their abilities for business purposes and has been the cause of an unpleasantness which all true sportsmen, both in the States and in this country, must deeply regret.

It was still an age in which snobbery prevailed toward those who earned a living off sport and toward entrepreneurs seeking to cash in on what was perceived as an endeavor that ought not be sullied by commerce.

Vardon's successes in America came in spite of the obvious advantages that accrued to opponents who used a rubber-cored ball. During an exhibition at the Chicago Golf Club, inventor Coburn Haskell approached J. H. Taylor and invited him to try his creation. Taylor teed up at a 220-yard hole while the group ahead still occupied the green. To his astonishment the drive bounded among them, forcing him to apologize. But not even such a spectacular long hit by the ordinarily moderate-driving Taylor converted him. And Vardon, of course, was contractually obliged to use the Spalding product bearing his name.

The climax of the expedition came at the same Chicago Golf Club where the two Britons entered the U.S. Open. While the two most prominent visitors were odds on, a handful of other fine British players comprised an excellent field. Neither Taylor nor Vardon could hole putts the first round but when the morning ended, the former at 76 led Vardon by 3 strokes. Their positions reversed in the afternoon as Taylor blew to an 82 while Vardon struggled home in 78, giving him a 1-shot margin. On the following day, Harry Vardon extended his lead with a third round 76 to J. H. Taylor's 79.

On the final afternoon, Vardon cranked up an amazing, though wind-aided, drive of 270 yards with his guttie on the seventh hole. However, the feat must have roused mixed emotions for the ball ended in a bunker. To the despair of Taylor, Vardon then lofted a niblick shot so close to the pin he could hole out for a birdie three. Taylor, however, whittled away at what was then a 6-stroke lead until he trimmed it to a bare 2 by the next-to-last hole. But on seventeen, Vardon blasted a brassie to the back of the green to take down his par 5 and close the door. His victory was so sure that on the final hole with a 2-inch putt left, Vardon flicked his club at the ball in the manner of one brushing away a fly and missed the cup. He then addressed the ball more formally to end the round. The winner scored 313 for the seventy-two holes while Taylor finished at 315. The next two were at 322 and 327.

Vardon's triumph notwithstanding, the guttie was an endangered species, soon to follow the feathery and the baffing spoon into extinction. Technology was the first aspect of golf in which the States would compete with the game's birthplace.

Proponents of the guttie reeled from a staggering blow when Charles Hutchings won the 1902 British Amateur with a rubber-cored ball. The ball died in Great Britain as the result of a fatal wound suffered in the Open in 1902, at the demanding Hoylake course. All of the members of the Triumvirate had entered the tournament with Braid as the defending champion. Among those in a field expected to be an also-ran was Alex "Sandy" Herd, a slender, young, and mustachioed pro representing Huddersfield. Like so many of his "low-born" peers, Herd learned the game with makeshift equipment, supposedly hewing stumps from the woods around St. Andrews for his club-

heads and practicing with balls whittled from discarded champagne corks weighted with nails. Many years later, Herd related a tale of the 1902 Open:

Mr. John Ball,★ the finest amateur golfer who ever lived [He won the Open in 1890 and the Amateur Championship of the British Isles eight times with his last victory coming at age 51], asked me to have a practice round with him. During the round he produced a funny ball and asked me to

(Top) *At St. Andrews in 1905, the Triumvirate temporarily became a quartet with the addition of Alexander "Sandy" Herd (standing left). In 1902, Herd became the first man to win the British Open while playing a rubber-cored ball. He was the brother of Fred Herd, the victor in the American Open of 1898.* (COURTESY RAY DAVIS.)

(Bottom) *While James Braid and Sandy Herd stand at the left, Harry Vardon ponders his putt at Prestwick in 1903. To the right of Vardon, J. H. Taylor his rival.* (COURTESY RAY DAVIS.)

Crawford-MacGregor & Canby were among the new American manufacturers of clubs. (COURTESY RAY DAVIS.)

Dapper H. Chandler Egan reigned as U.S. amateur champion in 1904–1905. (COURTESY RAY DAVIS.)

Alex Smith shot a record 295 for the U.S. Open crown in 1906. He repeated his win in 1910. (COURTESY RAY DAVIS.)

Johnny McDermott, the first U.S.–born pro to win his homeland's Open (1911, 1912), burned out quickly. (COURTESY RAY DAVIS.)

have a go at it. The ball was a Haskell from America.

At the end of the round Mr. Ball told me that Jack Morris [nephew of Old Tom Morris], the Hoylake professional, had four in hiding, and I got hold of them. They were a bit cracked, but I played with them in the championship, and won. [His 307 tied the record previously set by Vardon in 1898.]

When I putted out a winner on the last green the ball was in such a bad state that its "stomach" was hanging out.

I never saw the balls again. Everybody was shouting for Haskells and the four Jack Morris graciously gave me vanished.

Actually, Herd's was a very narrow victory as he edged out Vardon only on the final green. Some accounts give a less charitable view of Herd. Supposedly, after he had obtained Morris's entire stock of rubber-cored balls, he went about complaining that the balls were no good.

Regardless of gamesmanship from Herd, the new balls converted even the most hidebound. The editor of *Golf Illustrated* grudgingly wrote, ". . . interesting, just as a spirited horse is more fun to drive than a quiet one." A last-ditch defense by the hidebound proposed that the Royal and Ancient create a "standard ball," which in reality would have outlawed the American creation. No less a golfing enthusiast than the newly designated Prime Minister Ar-

thur Balfour decried the movement, issuing a statement that the proposed "standard" "would destroy the unlimited freedom of selection which, among all games, belongs, so far as I know, alone to golf." England's top politician declared: the guttie is dead, long live the Haskell.

Before 1901, the United States imported most of its golf balls from Great Britain. By the middle of 1903, American manufacturers had shipped across the Atlantic 40,000 dozen balls in five months.

Only two years after his company had spent a large sum promoting its Vardon Flyer through the appearances of its namesake, A. G. Spalding abandoned the guttie. His 1903 catalog heralded the "Spalding Wizard Golf Ball." The copy claimed when "Well drove, 'twill fly from tee to green. It is not an experiment but a pronounced success." It was still a bramble-marked ball but the company was innovative in using balata, a tree gum from South America, in place of the Malaysian gutta percha that cracked more readily. In 1906, Spalding introduced its "Dot" label, marking the varieties with color.

A British engineer, William Taylor, provided the next significant improvement. He received a 1908 Crown patent, stating:

. . . its principal object to obtain better results in the flight of the ball, in the direction of a sustained, hanging flight giving a flat trajectory with slight rising tendency, particularly toward the end of the flight. . . . It has been proposed to invert this [bramble] marking so that the spherical surface . . . consists of numerous ridges enclosing isolated polygonal cavities.

In short, Taylor had devised the modern, dimpled configuration for the cover. Spalding adopted the Taylor dimples in 1909. Other refinements included liquid cores in a shell and the introduction of the vulcanizing process to harden the balata exterior.

Peter Dobereiner on
HARRY VARDON

Harry Vardon is often described in such terms as the inventor of the modern golf swing, the father of technique, or the great innovator. The shy and painfully modest Vardon would have been thoroughly embarrassed by those expressions and would have rejected them as being entirely inappropriate. Although he accepted progress and predicted with remarkable accuracy the way the game of golf would develop, he saw himself not as a pioneer of a new way of golf but as one of the last exponents of a superior and more demanding game that was supplanted by the invention of the rubber-core ball.

The essayist Bernard Darwin, no mean player himself, wrote of Vardon: "I do not think anyone who saw him play in his prime will disagree as to this, that a greater genius is inconceivable." That genius enabled Vardon to succeed with the new Haskell ball when it was introduced shortly after the turn of the century. He and his contemporaries who had been brought up on the stonelike gutty ball referred to the newcomer as the Bounding Billy (incidentally giving the English language a new noun, "bounder," to describe one who flouts the conventions of good taste and honesty).

Vardon appreciated well enough that the rubber-core ball would be of enormous benefit to golf since it made the game easier and would therefore attract many new recruits, but he deeply regretted the changes it brought in the style of play. The unresponsive gutty required a stroke of absolute precision and, since it stopped pretty much where it landed, golf was a game of carry through the air. The Bounding Billy pitched and then ran and, to Vardon's dismay, indifferent golfers could match him for distance by the technique of a slinging, pull shot that hit the ball low and produced an inordinate amount of roll. This style made the game too easy for Vardon's taste and he reckoned that with the introduction of the Haskell ball his own game suffered by four strokes a round, not in terms of scoring but in his advantage over other players.

This paradox of a traditionalist who is revered as a great innovator is a theme that runs through the Vardon story from the time he was a seven-year-old boy, one of eight children of a gardener on the island of Jersey in the English Channel off the coast of France. At that time a group of holidaymakers began laying out a golf course on the links near the village of Grouville, and Vardon and his schoolfriends were caught up in this new craze.

They built themselves a course of their own, four holes of about 50 yards apiece. They had to make their own equipment and here they showed them-

selves to be astonishingly proficient and prescient. They learned quickly from their errors and settled on oak for the heads and on blackthorn for the shafts of their rudimentary clubs. But how could they attach one to the other? Clearly, the method of shaping splices, glueing, and whipping in the manner of the professionally made clubs used by the lordly visitors was beyond their powers. The solution was to pierce one end of the roughly whittled head with a red-hot poker and drive the shaft into this hole, securing the joint with wedges. Those small boys thus anticipated by several years the invention of the socketed joint for wooden clubs. Although Vardon was thus a pioneer in a major club-making advance, he remained all his life a devotee of the spliced shaft. He felt that the socket clubs had a dead feel about them and that the spliced, or scared, clubs brought an extra whip into the shot at impact.

For balls the boys used taws, large earthenware marbles about half the size of a golf ball. These unyielding missiles soon necessitated a measure of reinforcement of those wooden heads and the boys devised a method of sheathing the club heads with tin. With such improbable implements, and often playing by moonlight, the greatest golfing talent the world has known was nourished. As the new Grouville golf club (later Royal Jersey) became established, the Vardon boys and their friends earned pocket money by carrying the clubs of the players, acquiring now and then the priceless treasure of broken clubs and even complete clubs that had lost favor with their owners. They found golf balls on the course and no doubt, like children from the earliest days of golf, were occasionally less than diligent in searching for a client's ball in order to make the finding easier afterward.

Vardon left school at thirteen and followed his father's example by becoming an apprentice gardener. Although he had increasing opportunities to play golf, his sporting interests at this time lay more with cricket and football. He estimated that by the time he was appointed to his first job at age twenty as professional and greenskeeper at a new nine-hole course in Yorkshire, he had played no more than twenty full rounds. He had, however, won his first competition, an artisans' event, playing off a handicap of plus 3, which he later judged to be about 8 or 10. No trophy he won later gave him greater pleasure than the modest vase that adorned his mantelpiece for the rest of his life.

His first club appointment was undemanding, with so few calls on his services that he played more cricket than golf as captain of the local team. Vardon moved to Bury (Great Britain), and it was here that his game really developed and he gained competitive experience. He played a few tournaments but at this period, toward the end of the nineteenth century, the commoner form of spectator golf was at the individual challenge match. Established players such as Willie Park had standing advertisements proclaiming that they would meet any man for 100 pounds a side (in U.S. currency about 500 dollars then), winner to take all after head-to-head matches at their two clubs. Vardon was no great enthusiast of the individual challenge because he felt that playing a man for his own money

"He [Vardon] was the first of the long line of so-called 'mechanical golfers' who bring off bullet-like shots with the consistency of a press printing tomorrow's headlines. While the consistency of many of these has often reached monotony, Vardon added a fillip to his shots. He 'typed' them, cutting the cloth, so to speak, to fit the pattern of the hole. Depending upon the architectural characteristics of a hole, he would draw the ball or fade it and if the wind so dictated, loft it high or punch it low in the process."—Charles Price, The World of Golf.
(COURTESY U.S. GOLF ASSOCIATION.)

threatened the camaraderie of the profession, even though wealthy backers put up the purse in many cases. His preference was for the exhibition match, another popular form of spectator golf during an era when new golf clubs were opening with increasing frequency. To those who suggested that such exhibitions were insipid, since the players had no incentive to give of their best, he had a ready answer. A true professional, he proclaimed, played to the utmost of his ability on every occasion in order to protect his hard-won reputation, and this single-minded pursuit of excellence was the major factor separating the professional from the amateur golfer.

That dedication brought its rewards when he won the (British) Open championship in 1896 at Muirfield, the new course of the Honourable Company of Edinburgh Golfers. That victory by an unknown Englishman shocked the locals, who had confidently expected the winner to come from among the strong contingent of Scottish professionals. One of those defeated favorites, Andra Kirkaldy, blamed his failure on the course, which he described as "nothing but an auld watter meddie."

Vardon's victory brought him an invitation to become the pro at Ganton, the famous old Yorkshire club near Scarborough, and he was much in demand as the champion golfer for lessons and his views on golf technique. This was a subject to which Vardon had never really given much thought. Having played golf for as long as he could remember, without ever receiving a formal lesson, he had acquired his markedly upright swing by trial and error and by copying points from players he admired. Professional golfers are notoriously touchy about being described as natural golfers, as if they had inherited their talent at birth. Sam Snead and Christy O'Connor both resented being described as "naturals," pointing out that their swings had been painfully acquired through long months of practice on the pastures of West Virginia and the beaches of Bundoran, respec-

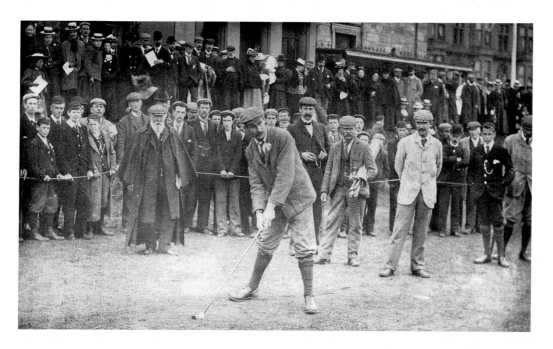

Under the eyes of white bearded Old Tom Morris, Harry Vardon, boutonniere in place, addresses the ball on the first tee at St. Andrews. (COURTESY USGA MUSEUM AND LIBRARY.)

tively. Likewise, Vardon had experimented and practiced exhaustively, but now he had to analyze his technique and to articulate why he had settled on his style of play.

A small gathering turned out to watch the celebrated Briton as his Spalding-sponsored tour reached Pinehurst, North Carolina. (COURTESY RAY DAVIS.)

Up until this time, golf had been played with the St. Andrews swing, with variations on that theme. The St. Andrews swing involved playing from a very closed stance and grasping the club with the palm of the right hand well under the shaft in an extremely light grip. The club was swung back low to the ground in a flat plane with a marked sway to the right and an even more pronounced sway into the shot, with the ball being swept away in a direction somewhat behind the golfer's left shoulder. The rationale for this style was that it was the only effective method of hitting a golf ball with the long and cumbersome clubs of the day. The main objective was to cover the distance of the hole with the wooden clubs that comprised the bulk of the golfer's armory and then switch to the accuracy mode for the delicate task of getting the ball close to, and then into, the hole. Young Tom Morris, outright winner of the championship belt the year Vardon was born, had refined golf technique by exploiting the possibilities of backspin and thus starting a vogue for a greater proportion of iron clubs. Still, the written and personal instruction at the time of Vardon's first Open, and for some years afterwards, was essentially the old St. Andrews swing.

Vardon, as we have seen, had never been exposed to the received wisdom of golf technique or equipment. In this he resembled Severiano Ballesteros nearly a century later on the beach at Santander, a young and innocent mind finding out for himself the most effective way of striking a golf ball. Vardon had a further advantage. Ballesteros began his golf with a proper club; Vardon had to make his own clubs right from the start, having had no preconceptions of what a club should be like beyond the broad outlines of what he had seen the real golfers using. But in the personal details of length and weight he had literally suited himself, whittling his clubs down to the size and feel that felt right to his juvenile physique. As a professional, his duties naturally included making up and repairing golf clubs and his own clubs were considerably lighter and shorter than those of his contemporaries. On those occasions when he was engaged for an exhibition match, and for some reason his own clubs were not available, he invariably borrowed women's clubs. This preference for light, responsive clubs was undoubtedly a major influence on the development of his technique, particularly the unusually upright swing.

The other vital factor was what has come to be universally known as the Vardon grip, acknowledged today to be the classic method of gripping a golf club and preferred by 99 percent of accomplished players. Yet Vardon did not invent the overlapping grip and never claimed credit for it. The Scottish amateur champion Johnnie Laidlay was probably the first prominent golfer to employ the overlapping grip although Vardon's great friend and rival, J. H. Taylor, had also experimented with it before Vardon came to prominence. It was probably named the Vardon grip in 1900 when Vardon made a promotional tour of the United States and popularized golf by his virtuosity, of which more later.

The combination of an effective grip and manageable clubs released Vardon from the constrictions of the St. Andrews swing and enabled him to develop his exceptional talent. Playing from an open stance with the left foot turned well towards the target, he made a full pivot, allowing his left arm to bend naturally to accommodate a full backswing. In this matter of the bent left arm Vardon was at variance with modern ideas, and he relished the prospect of meeting opponents

Artist Michael Brown chose the occasion of the 1905 British Open for a painting that includes the then-surviving winners. They are: (standing from left to right) J. H. Taylor (1894–1895, 1900); Jack White (1904); Harold Hilton (1892, 1897); John Ball (1890); James Braid (1901, 1905); Old Tom Morris (1861–1862, 1864, 1867); Bob Ferguson (1880–1883); Willie Auchterlonie (1893); Jamie Anderson (1877–1879); David Brown (1886); Bob Martin (1876, 1885); Willie Fernie (1883). Seated from left to right are: Alec Herd (1902); Harry Vardon (1896, 1898–1899, 1903); Willie Park (1887, 1889); Jack Burns (1888). The cigarette-smoking Hilton and Ball, as "gentlemen," wear knickerbockers while all of the others, as professionals, dress in long trousers. Vardon's choice of breeches made his own quiet statement about class distinctions. Vardon copped the British Open twice more after 1905, winning in 1911 and 1914. (COURTESY RAY DAVIS.)

who kept the left arm ramrod stiff on the backswing. Technically, the point is not a major one. Rigidity of the left arm is a method of stabilizing the club at the top of the modern fast upswing and thus retaining control of the swing arc. In the case of Vardon's leisured take-away, when the club head lagged noticeably behind his hands as he started his backswing, almost as if dragging a weight on the end of a string, there was no danger of his "losing the club" at the top. The whole swing was a movement of measured grace, clearly conveying that he was exerting much less than his full reserve of physical power. That quiet tempo, not to be seen again until Julius Boros came on the scene, exemplified the golfing truth that distance comes from hitting the ball well, not hitting it hard. Vardon was long enough in all conscience with his regular swing but when the situation demanded he could find an extra 30 yards to the astonishment and dismay of his rivals.

Vardon's technique not only profoundly influenced golfing style but also revolutionized golf thinking. Instead of playing purely for distance with the long clubs, he was able to combine distance with accuracy with every club in the bag. Contemporaries said that he was as accurate with his brassy (No. 2 wood) as they were with their mashies (5-irons), and so everyone had to switch to the Vardon way of golfing.

Vardon was singularly fortunate in his contemporaries since they included two other extraordinarily gifted golfers, J. H. Taylor and James Braid. Between 1894 and 1914 these three golfers, dubbed with ponderous Victorian wit as the Great Triumvirate, won no fewer than fifteen Open championships among them. The third major factor, then, in the development of Vardon was the strength of the competition he had to compete against.

Vardon consolidated his supremacy by winning the Opens of 1898 and 1899, giving him three championships in the space of four years. That third victory—at Royal St. George's, Sandwich, which he regarded as the best golf course in the world because it was unforgiving of anything less than a well-planned and perfectly struck shot—probably represented the peak of Vardon's genius. His exploits had been lauded around the world, prompting the Spalding company to engage him for a tour of the United States to popularize the growing game of golf and, in particular, to promote sales of the Vardon Flyer golf ball. In this last respect the tour was a flop because Mr. Coburn Haskell's invention of a method for winding elastic thread under tension around a central core was already under patent and the gutty ball was therefore under sentence of banishment from the game. But as an evangelical exercise, the tour was an unconditional success. Vardon made an exhaustive tour, the routine being that he would play the better ball of the two best golfers at every club he visited. His standard of skill was a revelation and gave rise to a constellation of Vardon mythology. The story went around, for instance, that he had problems playing in the afternoon because such was his accuracy he was driving his ball into the divot scrapes he had made on his morning circuit. No wonder the crowds flocked so avidly to watch

"He was very long, so that he could reach in two wooden club shots holes at which most other people needed two and a chip. He was so accurate with those high-floating, quick-stopping brassie shots that he would put the ball as near the hole in two as his toiling, sweating adversaries would put theirs with their third, the chip. What hope was there against such a man? In truth, in his great years, nobody had any real hope."—Bernard Darwin, The American Golfer, *February 1943.* (COURTESY USGA.)

the golfing superman. He did not disappoint them. Throughout the tour he was beaten only twice, by a single opponent—on a Florida course that had not a single blade of grass on it, by Bernard Nicholls, a man armed with much local knowledge and cunning. In matches against two opponents playing their best ball, he won more than fifty times, losing on eleven occasions. He also thrashed the best U.S. pro, Willie Dunn, 16 up, 15 to play.

He won the U.S. Open at Wheaton, Chicago, and further added to his reputation when he was engaged to hit balls into a net in the Boston department store of Jordan Marsh. The sheer boredom involved in this exercise prompted Vardon to challenge himself to hit a fixture the size of a quarter set in the ceiling. An apprehensive floor manager begged him to desist, explaining that the target he had selected and which he was threatening to hit with his stream of near-misses was a fire extinguishing device which, if struck by a Vardon Flyer, would flood the store with water.

That tour, broken only by a trip back to Britain for an unsuccessful attempt to defend his championship title, was a huge promotional success but exhausting and Vardon felt later that he left something of his game back in America. He also lost some of his competitive edge with the introduction of the rubber-core ball but even so he adjusted well enough to win his fourth Open in 1903 at Prestwick. He felt terrible that week and was close to fainting several times during play. The problem soon became apparent; he had contracted tuberculosis, the debilitating lung disease that today is cured by antibiotics but that at the turn of the century necessitated complete rest in a sanatorium. Vardon was thus robbed of five years of his golfing career. He made a good recovery but, like most TB victims, never regained his full vigor.

He won his fifth Open when the championship returned to his beloved Sandwich in 1911 and, three years later, capped his career with a sixth Open at

Prestwick. Between those two victories, he returned to the United States to play the 1913 U.S. Open at The Country Club, Brookline, the most momentous championship in the history of American golf. Vardon was accompanied on this visit by his friend and fellow Jersey islander, and from the same tiny village, Ted Ray, a giant of a man noted for his enormous hitting rather than for golfing finesse. The two visiting champions were established as the hottest of favorites, not one Goliath but two of them. In a scenario which would have been rejected by any boys' adventure magazine as being too fanciful, there arose a David in the unlikely form of a twenty-year-old shop assistant who held a junior membership at an unfashionable Boston club. Francis Ouimet had been persuaded to file an entry for the Open only by the pressing request of an official of the United States Golf Association, which was anxious to increase the number of entries for its championship. In fact, Francis tried to withdraw his entry so that he could go and watch Vardon and Ray, but the list had already been published and his boss insisted that he should play. The certainty that he did not stand a chance was probably Ouimet's most valuable asset, for it enabled him to play with an abandon unaffected by nerves or a sense of occasion. The inconceivable story unfolded over successive rounds, with Ouimet matching Ray and Vardon and then beating them handsomely in the playoff to create the greatest sensation in the history of golf. America exploded with delight and golf caught the public imagination as never before. American golf was on the march, on a journey that was to dominate the world during the game's rapid expansion after World War I.

The gigantic achievements of Vardon have created in the public mind the impression that his physical stature must have matched his mighty deeds but in

Vardon embarked on a third tour of the States in 1920, accompanied on this occasion by Ted Ray (far left). He shucked his usual customary jacket as he punched an iron at Morris County, New Jersey. (COURTESY USGA.)

fact he was of medium height, five foot nine, and of slight build (150 lbs) but in common with such champions as Arnold Palmer and James Braid he had inordinately large hands. Those hands, fashioned in the grip to which his name is universally associated, are preserved in the form of a bronze cast, which is displayed at South Herts golf club where he spent his last years as professional. He is remembered by older members as a reserved and gentle man with a deep love of nature. Every morning he left his assistant in charge of the shop and walked out onto the course to feed the birds.

Although the most consummate professional of the day in his dedicated and analytical approach to the playing of golf, his attitude resembled more that of an amateur such as Bob Jones. He put everything into the playing of each shot but when the match or tournament was over he shook hands and with that symbolic gesture he shook off any feelings of elation or disappointment. As a

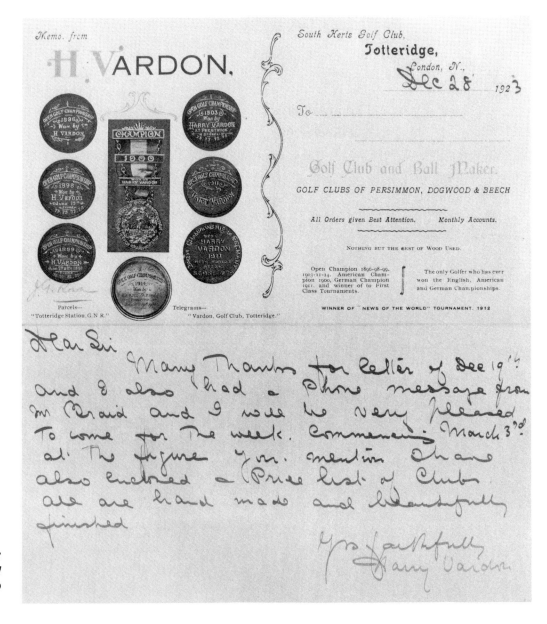

The Vardon letterhead in 1923 spells out his golf history and his business. (COURTESY PGA WORLD GOLF HALL OF FAME.)

consequence he earned a reputation among those who did not know him well of being a rather dull personality, a cold fish. His taciturnity on the course is well illustrated by an incident during the 1920 U.S. Open championship at Toledo when he was drawn to play with the youthful Bob Jones. On the seventh hole Jones committed the ultimate sin of the weekend golfer. Faced with a short pitch shot over a bunker, he feebly topped his ball into the sand. "Did you ever see a worse shot in your life?" he asked. "No," replied Vardon.

It is inconceivable today that the winner of the Open championship should quietly disappear after the presentation of the trophy and travel back to his club by train in order to fulfill the terms of his engagement by playing the regular Sunday morning round with the club captain. But to his intimates this apparent lack of emotion did not mean he felt no pain or joy, merely that he suppressed them according to the dictates of the poet Rudyard Kipling:

> If you can meet with Triumph and Disaster
> And treat those two imposters just the same,
> You'll be a Man, my son.

And, so, on to the impossible task, which cannot be shirked, of trying to evaluate Vardon, comparing him with the golfing giants of other ages and seeking to place him in the order of precedence on the golfing pantheon. It goes without saying that direct comparisons of scores is quite irrelevant because of the huge disparity in equipment and courses between the nineteenth century and the modern era. One line of perspective is quite clear: It can never be said of Vardon that he achieved his victories in weak fields, that he did not have to overcome the full might of American, Australian, and Japanese professional golf. At that time there were no overseas players worthy of championship honors. So Vardon faced the world's best golfers every time he played and he beat them more often, and more soundly, than anyone else. No complete record of Vardon's career has ever been compiled. We know that by the time of his third championship victory he had also won forty-eight other tournaments. The historian Charles Price discovered in his researches that at one period Vardon won fourteen tournaments in succession. And the records clearly show that he won a higher proportion of the championships he entered than any other golfer.

More pertinently, perhaps, he must be given full credit in the acid test of greatness: By how much did he influence golf and leave it a better game than before? Here we are on rather more solid ground because Vardon made a huge contribution in popularizing golf and elevating the standards of the professional game to a new plane. He gave golf a new horizon, exposing a vision of its exciting potential, to be so brilliantly exploited by those who followed such as Ben Hogan and Jack Nicklaus.

"It will be seen at once that I do not grasp the club across the palm of either hand. The club being taken in the left hand first, the shaft passes from the knuckle joint of the first finger across the ball of the second. The left thumb lies straight down the shaft just to the right of centre. The right hand is brought up so high that the palm covers the left thumb leaving very little to be seen. The first and second fingers of the right hand just reach around to the thumb of the left. The little finger of the right hand rides on the first finger of the left."—Harry Vardon, The Complete Golfer, *1905.*

The Vardon Trophy, awarded by the PGA of America to the tour player who posts the best scoring average with adjustments for tournament play levels, bears a cast of the British pro's grip. (COURTESY PGA OF AMERICA.)

Rivals and Jingoes

"The 'Old Man,' Walter Travis, studied the game of golf as if it were an ancient papyrus script to decode. 'From the very first I became an infatuated devotee. Every available opportunity found me endeavouring to put into practice the various strokes described in the works of Badminton, Park, and all the other authorities I could seize upon. Otherwise unaided I worked away, encouraged by gradual improvement. I was too much concerned with what I then conceived to be the more essential elements—driving and approaching—to devote any close study to such a trivial and unimportant thing as putting. And it was not until three or four years later that I managed to acquire any real grasp of this vitally important art.'" —*Walter J. Travis*, Great Golfers in the Making. (COURTESY THE BETT-MANN ARCHIVE.)

Amerian players were still—as the Britons had so clearly demonstrated in their U.S. expeditions—not prepared in 1900 to challenge British skill. In fact, the best of those listed as Americans were almost inevitably Scots who had been attracted by the economic possibilities of golf in the U.S. Only one professional of any stature, Johnnie McDermott, was a native-born American. In its account of the 1900 U.S. Open, the British publication *Golf Illustrated*, with pardonable jingoistic pride, declared:

> The outstanding feature of the meeting was the pronounced superiority of the two English professionals over native and naturalised talent. . . . The English and Scots professionals fought out on American soil and no American, either amateur or professional was worth taking into account.

The first fellow to make his mark as an American golfer was not a transplant from Scotland but an émigré from Australia, Walter J. Travis.★ He had come to the States as a boy, and although a cyclist and tennis player, until age thirty-five Travis never even held a club. However, during trips to England he had occasionally hiked alongside golf courses and watched players. Neighbors on Long Island persuaded him to support a local golf course, and in the autumn of 1896, at the new Oakland course, Travis took up the game at an age when many modern stars begin to slip.

Having sampled golf and silently savored the taste, Travis went at it in the fashion of a cloistered monk seeking to unveil the mysteries of an arcane biblical papyrus. Travis devoted his winter to reading the best literature on the game. He pored over the dynamics of the swing as expounded by the prolific Horace Hutchin-

son (whose observations were part of a series from the Badminton Library). Travis absorbed the instruction of Willie Park, Jr.'s, manual. He dissected the sport and then analyzed himself. He recognized that his slight physique meant he could not overpower courses but would have to concentrate on accuracy. And he was among the first to perceive that all of the derring-do on the fairway could be tossed away in the short span of the greens.

His appearance has been compared to one of the cough-drop box Smith Brothers and General Stonewall Jackson of the Confederacy. Sporting a beard in the style of Civil War hero and President Ulysses S. Grant, wearing a slouch hat, Travis, during the spring of '97, tramped the courses, puffing away at his one concession to pleasure, a perennial cigar, presenting an image somwhere between an old-style prophet and a silent steam engine. He is said to have actually played only three or four rounds but experimented and practiced hour upon hour, just as his spiritual descendant Ben Hogan★ was to do when he revealed to moderns almost forty years later how to hone one's game to precision.

Practice made him near enough to perfect for a try at the U.S. Amateur title a scant two years after his first stroke. He performed well enough to reach the semifinals and in 1900, the same year that Vardon put the Americans to the rout in the Open, Travis clubbed his way to the Amateur championship. His relatively advanced age led to the nickname, "the Old Man."

In style, Travis pioneered with the putting stroke. He was among the first to use a reverse overlapping grip, hooking the index finger on his left hand over the little finger of his right. He grasped the club first with his right hand, thumb pointed straight down the shaft. Then he placed his left thumb on the shaft, in the palm of his right hand. His putting stroke began with the left wrist guiding the backswing, but on the return of the pendulum the right hand dominated. He insisted the right forefinger should act as captain of the operation. And he counseled that under no circumstances should the body move; the entire stroke was to be conducted by the wrists.

Travis choked up on the putting shaft by as much as 6 inches with the ball played off the line near his right foot. He tucked his right elbow against his side while lining up his left elbow to point parallel to the hole. And he was a vigorous proponent of the theory, "Never up, never in." His near obsession with putting arose from his study of the game:

> The first thing that strikes you when you come to analyse the game is that of the total number of strokes played in a perfect round of golf nearly half the number are absorbed in these little putts on the green. . . . very few golfers seem to put it to themselves . . . that they have twice as many putts—and, alas! sometimes more —as drives . . . therefore bad putting at a hole is twice as costly as bad driving, and excellent putting infinitely more remunerative than the finest play from the tee.

Using the rubber-cored ball now—when it first appeared he was among those who scorned it—his short-but-straight game off the tee combined with his dead-eye Dick putting won him a repeat title as the best U.S. amateur in 1901 and third place in the U.S. Open. After a hiatus of a year he again topped the amateurs. His all-business approach, with hardly a word to exchange on the links (another flash forward to Hogan), may not have unnerved opponents but the way he dropped putts from 20 feet out unraveled many.

During his sojourns abroad, Travis had played a number of matches against the best of the Scottish and English golfers. Convinced that he was in their league, the Old Man invaded Great Britain with his sights set on that land's amateur championship. Though now a middle-aged forty-

three, he was undaunted by the prospect of the site's 6,135 yards across the wind-swept dunes of Sandwich.

In his inimitable way, Travis mapped out a campaign to conquer the field. He arrived in the British Isles three weeks before the tournament, figuring on ten days of practice in Scotland, with the remainder of the time tuning up his game at the tournament venue, the Royal St. George's course.

But to paraphrase the best-known Scottish poet, Travis's best laid scheme fell aft-agley on the St. Andrews course. He lapsed into the kind of despair that particularly afflicts those who believe that through reason and science they can reduce problems to manageable proportions. Nothing seemed to work; not even a new set of clubs or more time at St. Andrews experimenting and practicing.

When he arrived at the Sandwich course, Travis experienced further discomfort. The locals in charge of the Royal St. George's club treated him as if he were personally responsible for the loss of the Colonies. Instead of staying at the club's digs, Travis was forced, with other Americans, to live at a hotel. He had asked to play a few practice rounds with some of the best Britons but that was denied. In fact, he grumbled, some of the very fellows whom he and other Americans entertained when they

At the Oakland Golf Club, Bayside, New York, in 1900, spectators milled about during a pause in the match between the touring Briton, Harry Vardon, and the U.S. Amateur Champion, Travis. Vardon whipped the home boy. (COURTESY RAY DAVIS.)

Never a long hitter, Travis relied on his accuracy on the fairways and a deadly stroke on the greens. (COURTESY RAY DAVIS.)

came to the States now cut them dead. The finally indignity was a cross-eyed caddie, whom the authorities refused to replace.

In their defense, the British claimed that when they originally offered the hospitality of dinner parties to Travis, he, in his typically cold fashion, had rejected it. From then on, they said, they gave him the same chilly shoulder.

The simmering Travis, his fury no doubt exacerbated by his poor play, stepped out onto the course for a practice round. In his rage he started to bang the ball around using only one of his new clubs, a putting cleek. To his astonishment, his stroke off the greens returned:

The first ball I struck I knew I was on the road to recovery. For the first time in two weeks I could "feel" the ball. The necessary "touch" and the resultant "timing" were there in such sharp contradistinction to the entire absence of these . . . that I was transported into the golfer's seventh heaven of delight.

However, in successive practice sessions the man credited with the ability to putt the eyes out of a squirrel at 60 feet felt he could not find the Grand Canyon from a yard off. Having lost faith in his putter, he accepted the loan of what was known as a "Schenectady," a club with the shaft in the middle of its mallet head and so named because the maker of the putter came from that city in upstate New York.

The putting touch now returned and with the restablishment of his normal, short but highly accurate game from tee to green, Travis was at his sharpest. All of the slights, real or fancied, reinforced his determination and concentration. In fact, he began to take a kind of perverse satisfaction from his experiences. To a friend he quoted the homespun philosopher David Harum: "A reasonable number of fleas is good for a dog. It keeps the dog from forgetting he is a dog."

The Schenectady served beautifully in the opening match as he canned several long distance putts to wipe out an opponent in less than two hours while rain pelted down. He did not endear himself further to the Britons when he publicly scolded his foe for having touched his club to the sand in a bunker.

He paid for this remark when officials denied his request for some extra time to change into dry clothes for his afternoon match. The best he could do was to towel off in a hallway of the clubhouse—as an interloper he was not granted locker facilities. The match against James Robb was a squeaker, and Travis was nearly done in by the cross-eyed caddie. On the eleventh hole, both men hit the green with their second shots. Travis, away, putted to within inches of the cup. Travis's caddie was standing on his post at the flagstick when the opponent, well out of stymie range called, "Take it out!" The confused caddie misinterpreted the order and reached down to pick up Travis's ball. The American shouted to him, but too late—the ball was lifted a couple of inches off the ground. Technically, Robb could have called for a penalty but he proved a sportsman and refused. Nevertheless, the incident unnerved Travis. He blew the twelfth hole. Fortunately, after dropping the next to last hole, Travis recovered to halve the final one and win 1 up.

After the match, Travis politely asked Robb if he could borrow his bag-toter. The loser graciously agreed, but the caddie-master—the ultimate authority—refused. Travis choked down his rage and reverted to his implacable demeanor. He defeated his next opponent with a steady performance. But in his fourth round, Travis fell behind and, as they came to the fifteenth tee, H. E. Reade teed off, 2 up. Still, the steady plumes of cigar smoke indicated no panic, and Travis cut the deficit in half with a par 4 to Reade's bogey over a long hole. On the sixteenth, a 180-yard part three, the American swatted a drive that left him only 12 feet from the pin. He knocked it home for a birdie and tied the match. When Reade blew his putt on seventeen for another bogey, Travis holed his to assume the lead. They halved the finale and Travis moved on to meet one of the outstanding Britons, Harold Hilton.★

Twelve years before, Hilton had captured the British Open and he copped the honors in again in 1897. All told he would be British amateur champion four times, with his final victory coming in 1913 at age forty-four. Although he was a scholar of the game, he seemed, unlike Travis, a free swinger. Bernard Darwin said of Hilton:

The first sight of him hitting a ball did not convey a notion of accuracy but rather of a wholehearted flinging himself at the ball. His address to the ball was, to be sure, very careful and precise; he placed his feet and faced his club to the line with great exactness. These preliminaries over, he seemed to throw care to the winds and one had a wild and whirling vision of a little man jumping on his toes and throwing himself and his club after the ball with almost frantic abandon. Yet this was the most deceptive possible appearance, for though he certainly hit for all he was worth, he had a gift of balance such as is given to few. His cap might fall off the back of his head, he might twist his shoulders round in producing the hook which he used so skillfully, but he was always firmly poised, the master of himself and the ball.

The cigar and campaign hat were trademarks of Travis. "I conceived the idea that my game would be improved if I stopped smoking and drinking ... so a couple of weeks or so prior to one of the Lakewood tournaments, I cut out both. I found that while it made no difference in my long game my work on the green was simply childish— I couldn't putt at all .... I have never since allowed even golf to interfere with my smoking or drinking when I feel like it."—Walter J. Travis, Great Golfers in the Making. (COURTESY RAY DAVIS.)

Hilton became the first fellow ever to win both the British and American amateur titles the same year, 1911. He had one other distinction: He was almost never seen on a course without a cigarette dangling from his lips.

Obviously, Travis faced formidable opposition in his quarter-final. Indeed, the two had met in 1901 and the Briton had trounced the American. Their repeat encounter seemed to stir up memories of past unpleasantries between Great Britain and the U.S. The locals, having formed a personal dislike for the Old Man, now rooted hard for one of their own. The American contingent, which had come with Travis to compete and remained to support the surviving U.S. entry, boosted him as their paladin. They stoked him with stout and diverted him from his grievances with after-golf cribbage games. Shrewdly, they praised Hilton's talents, thus adding to Travis's determination.

Hilton never had much of a chance. The Old Man won the first three holes and for the front nine fired a par-busting 34. A slight rally by Hilton as they turned for home failed and Travis romped to the semifinals, 5 and 4.

The next match pitted him against Horace Hutchinson, the golf correspondent who, at forty-five, was even more ancient than the Old Man. Although Travis botched the final nine for his worst golf in the tournament, he had built such a commanding lead with his opening 34 that Hutchinson fell 4 and 2.

The last obstacle to the first American victory in the British Amateur was Ted Blackwell, one of four prominent golfing brothers. Tall and strong, Blackwell's major asset was his prodigious drive. Using a guttie, he had smacked a ball at St. Andrews an estimated distance of 366 yards. On the same hole in 1964, Jack Nicklaus,★ aided by a blustery wind and of course using modern balls and equipment, reached the green 380 yards off several times.

The pressure seemed to affect the pair as they began the final, a thirty-six-hole affair. On the par 4, 366-yard first hole, Travis scored a bogey 5, but Blackwell went him one worse with a double bogey. Both recovered to reach the second green with two shots but to the dismay of the gallery, Travis holed out from 36 feet for a birdie and went 2 up. Either as a psychological ploy or perhaps because of the euphoria of the early lead, Travis uncharacteristically cracked the silence of the competitors with a compliment for Blackwell's drive off the third tee. The Briton glowered beneath his heavy eyebrows and responded with an undecipherable grunt. From then on, the match continued in dead silence.

The chauvinist spectators trashed courtesy on the sixth hole, applauding a muffed putt by the Old Man. ("Some day I hope I may entirely forget the slight cheering which greeted the failure," brooded Travis years later.) But he clung to a two-hole advantage. Blackwell was well positioned to cut the gap on the thirteenth when his drive and wood off the fairway left him only a pitch to the green. The shorter-hitting Travis lay well over 100 yards off, facing a brisk wind. The Old Man eased the crisis, drilling a low-angle shot onto the green while Blackwell hooked his pitch and, instead of trimming the lead, fell further behind.

On the fourteenth hole—known as the Suez Canal because of a deep ditch that crossed the fairway well over 400 yards out—Blackwell was undone by his own strength. Like Travis, he planned to play the second shot safe, dropping the ball before the Suez Canal. While the American had hit a brassie and sat down nicely behind the obstacle, Blackwell, whose drive had sailed close to 40 yards farther, went to his cleek. But those who live by power can be destroyed by it and, even though Blackwell restrained himself, the ball dropped into the ditch. Travis hammered another nail into the coffin with a good pitch, and one putted from far off. An outrageous air of confidence accompanied such feats. Wrote Herbert Warren Wind:

> After he stroked a putt, he would stand absolutely still and eye the ball like Svengali as it dipped off the rolls and found its way into the cup. He acted as if there were no other possible outcome for the stroke.

They broke for lunch and then began the final eighteen. The pulses of the gallery quickened as Travis foozled the first hole for a ghastly 7. But he steadied quickly and on the fifteenth closed out the match, 4 and 3. There was no ovation as the Old Man's final putt fell into the cup, even though many certainly realized the winner had demonstrated superb skill under adverse conditions.

Some, however, denigrated Travis as an ordinary player who rode his odd Schenectady putter to victory. One well-preserved comment was, "Travis could *write* with his putter if you put a nib on it." The final indignity came with the cup presentation. John Bull, in his most overbearing form, a certain Lord Northbourne, delivered a tedious speech, recounting the early history of the local county under the Romans, reciting the glorious achievements of golf and British players before a brief word of congratulations to the American winner. He concluded with his fervent and tacky hope that such a disaster as this should never again humble his nation's sports.

Norman Hunter, a member of the Oxford & Cambridge Golfing Society, heaped further insult upon the victor. Upon learning Travis intended to carry the emblematic trophy cup to show off for the homefolks, Hunter remarked, according to Travis: "Umph! We'll never see that again." A fellow American player, W. W. Burton rebutted sweetly: "You needn't worry. We've managed to take pretty good care of the America cup for a good many years." (At the time the U.S. had held the yachting honor without a loss since 1851.)

In the United States, of course, Travis's triumph was greeted with chauvinist hosannahs including a tribute from an editorial writer at the *New York Times:*

The mere fact that Travis was born in Australia need not detract from his Americanism for he has spent the better part of his life here and learned to play golf in this country—has met the best golfers that England and Scotland can muster on their own ground and beaten them at their own game.

And a few years later, in 1909, the Royal and Ancient took Pyrrhic revenge by outlawing the Schenectady putter. In so doing, the R&A incurred the ire of local clubmakers who were forced to scrap thousands of models of Travis's weapon. The ban on center-shafted putters was not rescinded until 1952 and, appropriately enough, one was in the hands of Ben Hogan when he won the British Open a year later.

Oddly, Travis himself abandoned that disputed club almost immediately after he returned to the States. He said, "I have never been able to do anything with it since. I have tried it repeatedly, but it seems to have lost all its virtue." And, although he could not repeat as winner of either the U.S. or British Amateur champion, he remained a competitor into his mid fifties, winning the prestigious Metropolitan Amateur at fifty-four with a typical stunt, a 30-foot putt on the final green.

He also designed a number of golf courses and the avocation caused the imperious souls then running the USGA to revoke his amateur status temporarily. The Old Man founded and edited one of the finest early magazines on the sport, *The American Golfer.* It flourished under his

intense editing but after he died, not even so professional and so devoted a golf fan as Grantland Rice could keep the publication alive. To Rice, Travis once offered his theory on why he could beat younger, stronger men. "I never hit a careless shot in my life. I only bet a quarter, but I play each shot as if it were for a championship."

Americans had been winning their own U.S. Amateur since that first official tournament of the USGA in 1895, and had held their own against foreign invaders. Now the country had produced a golfer good enough to beat the founders of the sport on their home turf. Amateur golf still drew much more attention in the U.S. than the

(Top) *During his unsuccessful effort for a fourth national title at the U.S. Amateur of 1904, Travis blasted out of a trap at Baltusrol in New Jersey.* (COURTESY RAY DAVIS.)

(Bottom) *Hunched over his Schenectady putter, Travis scans the line during the great 1904 British Amateur at Royal St. George's Sandwich.* (COURTESY RAY DAVIS.)

Willie Anderson (center, bow tie) sat with other pros and caddies, the lower class of U.S. golf in the early twentieth century. Anderson copped his four U.S. Opens, 1901, 1903–1905 before losing in 1906 to Alex Smith, posing to the right of Anderson. Smith also won in 1910. (COURTESY RAY DAVIS.)

death, Gene Sarazen★ was demonstrating his own talent for recovery from a bunker. An ancient pro and course architect named Bill Robinson was among those watching Sarazen's practice session. Gene, aware of Anderson's legendary skill, yelled to Robinson, "Could Willie Anderson get out of traps like that?"

The oldtimer scornfully replied, "Get out of them? He was never in them!"

Success, however, did not cure Anderson of his melancholy and alcoholism. He faded from the rank of contender before his twenty-sixth birthday and died at only thirty-four.

Meanwhile, on the U.S. amateur front, the Old Man's domination was usurped by a rich kid, Jerome D. Travers. Travers grew up on an estate in Oyster Bay on Long Island, a village celebrated as the home of Theodore Roosevelt, who occupied the White House during the years when Travers first began to achieve fame.

As a nine-year-old boy in 1896, Travers smacked golf balls from a back-lawn windmill towards the family mansion. A year later, teed up at the same site, he clouted one through a window in the house and his father ordered a change of venue to the front lawn. The youngster designed a three-hole, triangular course using a flagpole and two trees as the equivalents of the holes, unwittingly mimicking the ancient Dutch game of *hel met kolven*.

Several years later, his father joined the Nassau Country Club. Alex Smith, the gregarious pro at Nassau, approached Jerry who was hacking at balls and asked if he wanted to be serious about the game or simply duff around. When Travers indicated he'd like to play properly, Smith began to coach him. In the first lesson he counseled the boy to quit overswinging, to relax the stiffness of his arms, and to shift his hand from an extreme top-of-the-shaft position.

Persistent practice and Smith's instruction paid off two years later when seventeen-year-old Jerry Travers not only won the Interscholastic Championship but also defeated Walter Travis, the Old Man himself, in the final of the Nassau Invitation. The Young Man lagged behind, 2 down with 5 to play, but squared the match on 18 and then birdied the third hole of the sudden-death playoff. Ironically, Travers had armed himself with the same sort of center-shafted or Schenectady putter with which Travis had confounded the British.

Considering his steely, stiff-necked approach to the game, one might have expected Travis to resent the upstart kid. But he was most gracious following the Nassau encounter. "There is no aftermath of bitterness in such a defeat. It is a match I shall always recall with pleasure."

Although their styles of play were poles apart, they respected one another and actually enjoyed a rivalry that stretched over a number of years. Both brought a cool detachment to the links, seemingly oblivious to all but the challenge at hand. However, their shots took a far different trajectory. Travis, often almost pitifully short from the tee, hardly ever strayed from the fairway. Travers, on the other hand, had rounds when he seemed never on the fairway. His woods were so wild that he frequently drove with a cleek. But he possessed, as Walter Hagen★ and Arnold Palmer did years later, the ability to follow an apparent disaster with a dazzler that could destroy any but the most stouthearted of foes.

During one match, Travers's opponent drove to the green 220 yards off. Jerry skulled his shot. The ball landed in a mudbank along a ditch, seemingly a spot where his feet could not find a purchase. Travers selected a niblick and coiled himself in the ditch. In midswing, he leaped forward and managed to whack the ball while both feet were off the ground. The ball soared over the green to a wheat field. Displaying no more emotion than if he had dropped the ball hole high, Travers resorted to the niblick again and set the ball down 12 feet from the cup. His rattled companion 3-putted, while Travers banged in his putt to halve the hole. Still expressionless, Travers strolled from the green and went on to win the tournament.

The T men met innumerable times after that first playoff at Nassau. In 1905 the eighteen-year-old Travers beat the Old Man in the Metropolitan Amateur Championship, but a few weeks later in another tournament it was Travis who whipped the whippersnapper. Later the same season came another contest and another outcome as Travers upset the older man.

At age twenty-one, Jerry Travers had begun to play consistently fine golf. Not even the harping of Alex Smith could cure him of a tendency to move through the backswing too quickly nor shorten his stroke, but with Travis now declining, the youngster seemed ready to dominate tournaments.

And indeed he whizzed through the early rounds of the 1907 Amateur championships into the finals where, against Archie Graham, he could close out the match with a simple 4-foot putt on the thirteenth green. But the seemingly cool Travers suddenly lost his nerve. He froze over the ball, walked away after several moments and explained to Graham he had no feel of his hands or putter and couldn't continue. Graham offered no sympathy. "Drop it anyway and end the agony. You couldn't miss it with your eyes shut." A chastened Travers returned to the ball and without further fuss knocked home the winner.

A year later he defended his title at the Garden City Golf Club. In the semi-finals, once again the challenge came from the Old Man. They were dead even as they arrived on the seventeenth tee. From the fairway, the Young Man fired a 240-yard brassie close enough to the pin to allow a birdie. Travis went 1 down and needed the eighteenth.

The course had been designed by Travis and this par 3 called for travel over water to a deeply bunkered green. Club members had often chided the architect for the difficulty of the hole, but Travis stubbornly refused to ameliorate conditions, including the most savage trap of all, a 6-foot-deep pit with perpendicular walls. Travers drove first and plopped the ball nicely on the green. Travis, however, hooked enough to plunge into the unforgiving bunker.

On the green, Travers waited while his elder disappeared from sight into the trap. From the post, Travers heard the heavy thump as the club dug into the sand, which sprayed onto the green but no ball appeared. A second blast of iron into dirt spewed more sand; still no ball appeared. Out of the bunker trudged Travis who conceded the match, hoisted by his own petard or, as a spectator declared, "I guess the Old Man dug his grave that time." The final proved an anticlimax, as Travers destroyed another challenger 8 and 7.

Having supplanted Travis as the best American amateur, Travers sought to duplicate the feat of winning the British title. But he came an ignominious cropper, losing in the first round of the 1909

Harold Hilton, the fine British amateur was the last non-pro to win the British Open (1897) until the American Bobby Jones did it in 1926, '27, and '30. Hilton also triumphed on four occasions in the British Amateur, and in 1911 beat all comers in the U.S. tournament. (COURTESY RAY DAVIS.)

championship. And when he failed to defend his U.S. title that year, did not enter the following two seasons, and then lost in the 1911 third round, he was written off at age twenty-four as a burned-out case.

In 1912, however, during a blaze of torrid heat throughout the Midwest—to add to fiery ambience, the clubhouse of the Chicago Golf Club burned down—Travers returned to form. In the final round he was up against a hometown entry, twenty-two-year-old Charles "Chick" Evans,★ a graduate of the caddie ranks and one of the first without a moneyed background to play in the highly exclusive Amateur championship. As an Easterner, Travers was accorded by locals in the gallery the same warmth the British gave interlopers like Travis when he came to defeat their best. With a sizeable contingent of visitors from the East on hand, the betting reached frenzied heights.

The day began with Travers missing most of the fairways and battling his hook with a cleek off the tee. Only the fabled recoveries from woods and rough, coupled with no less than 3 putts from at least 20 feet out, including one from a distant 35 feet on the eighteenth, kept him in the match as Evans, possessing one of the smoothest swings in the history of golf, played immaculate golf.

As they went out for the afternoon round, Travers was only 1 down and by the fourth hole the match was even. Travers appeared to have hooked himself into deep trouble with his drive on the fourth, but the ball caromed off a mound that detoured it away from deadly rough and back onto the fairway. More than the heat, Travers's luck and pressure wilted Evans. Those wagering on him saw his smile fade; his brisk marches down the fairway were replaced by the reluctant plod of a man on his way to the executioner. Travers captured hole after hole, wiping out Evans on the twelfth hole, 7 and 6.

In the qualifying round of medal play for the 1913 U.S. Amateur at Garden City Golf Club, Travers barely squeaked through. On the eighteenth hole where a few years before he had prospered by the catastrophe that befell Walter Travis he too leaped into bunkered jaws of defeat. He posted a

horrendous 7, tying him with twelve others seeking the remaining eleven openings. Fortunately, he survived the playoff.

In the actual tournament, Travers continued to scramble because of errant woods and shanked irons. When practice between rounds failed to cure the damning hook, he again resorted to the driving iron off the tees during the semi-finals. His opponent on this occasion was another one-time caddie, a twenty-year-old from the Boston suburb of Brooklyn, Francis Ouimet.★ Only a 20-foot putt on the final hole of the morning round gave Travers a 1-up lead. But even though the defending champion doubled the margin on the first hole of the afternoon, Ouimet squared everything over the second and third and sprinted ahead by 1 as they played the eighth hole. A 180-yard iron sat him pretty, less than 10 feet away with an opportunity to increase his advantage. Travers, from slightly closer on the fairway, surveyed the challenge. He swept through one easy practice swing, then sailed the ball in a graceful arc to the green where it came to rest only 10 inches from the cup. Somewhat unnerved, Ouimet missed his birdie shot enabling Travis to even the contest. From then on, the senior man, a ripe old twenty-six, dominated. He disposed of Ouimet and went on to victory in the finale, becoming the first to ever take four U.S. Amateur titles.

Oddly, Travers abruptly stopped being a factor in the Amateur championships but he made one more dramatic appearance, in the 1915 U.S. Open. This was not a tournament ordinarily suited to his game. His erratic play, which could lead to a 7 on one hole and a birdie 3 on the next, made match play more appropriate than medal scoring. However, he was now a resident of New Jersey and familiar with the Open site at Baltusrol, so the gallery would offer support.

He fired a 78 and 72 in the first two rounds, which left him only 2 strokes off the pace. And with a 73 on the morning of the final day he eased out in front by one. All of his potential faults showed, however, as he started the last eighteen. His driver failed him again with a hook that spelled bogey on the first hole; a 3-putted fourth and some more mistakes and he was out in 39, certainly not championship play.

Nothing seemed to work. He overcorrected on the tenth and sliced out of bounds; topped his drive on the eleventh and then hammered one over the green on twelve. But his putter saved him. Deft work on the green trimmed the losses to a single stroke.

Travers calculated he would need to par the final six holes to earn even a tie. He steadied himself enough to reach his goal on thirteen and fourteen. But his midiron on the 465-yard, par-5 fifteenth seemed destined for the bunker as it caught the lip. Luck extended a hand as the ball bounced forward to within 10 short yards of the green. He pitched well enough to can a birdie and now 3 pars meant victory.

Rather than gamble for the extra distance, Travers bagged his woods and for the final holes drove with his iron. He copped the necessary pars and added a U.S. Open trophy to the four cups awarded for his Amateur titles.

Somewhat of a playboy in his first years as a champion, Travers experienced a series of financial reverses. He double-bogeyed in several business ventures and there were no miraculous recoveries. Among the sacrifices made was tournament golf. He tried to succeed as a professional after the Stock Market Crash of '29, but no one cared to pay for exhibitions by an over-the-hill former star. Following one match he offered his jigger* for auction and it brought a paltry six dollars. He attempted to sell golf equipment, peddling the Spalding Red Dots that he had popularized. A former caddie bought some, then handed them back to Travers saying he needed them more. After he died in 1951, his medals from the Open and his Amateur championships were found in the safe-deposit box of a friend, along with a note that said, "in appreciation for your many favors."

Travers, of course, was native born, as were some of the best of the other U.S.

Jerry Travers captured four U.S. Amateur titles and one Open. "[Jerry] Travers was the greatest competitor I have ever known. I could always tell just from looking at a golfer whether he was winning or losing, but I never knew how Travers stood."—Alex Smith. (COURTESY RAY DAVIS.)

amateurs. But the first home-bred, as opposed to naturalized, citizen to qualify as a professional champion was Johnny McDermott. When Alex Smith beat out his brother Macdonald in the playoff for the 1910 Open, the third person who had tied at the end of the regulation seventy-two holes was McDermott, the eighteen-year-old son of a Philadelphia mailman. Unlike the carousing Scots imports, McDermott was known as a nonsmoking teetotaler who regularly attended Sunday mass.

While his personal habits were above reproach, McDermott, a near jockey-size man at 120 pounds, floated an ego of championship proportions. Almost from the start of his career he believed he could beat anyone and he had the skill to make his boast respectable. He paid the dues required. Beginning at the first light of a 5 A.M. dawn, he practiced until it was time to open the pro shop at the Atlantic City Country Club around eight. After he closed the shop for the day, McDermott would play until dark and then work on his putting by the light of a lamp.

His size mitigated against power, but his mashie accuracy was legendary. Supposedly, McDermott developed his accuracy by hitting shots aimed at a large tarpaulin spread out on a fairway. As his technique improved, he substituted a newspaper for the tarp, becoming furious if balls failed to stop on a targeted paragraph.

Following his runner-up status in 1910, he put his money where his mouth was, challenging Philadelphia professionals to 1,000-dollar winner-take-all matches. After he cleaned out the first three to take him on, he ran out of opponents.

He was a nineteen-year-old stripling when he entered the U.S. Open at the Chicago Golf Club in 1911. Again McDermott finished regulation play in a three-way tie but this time his 80 beat out the competition in the playoff, making him not only the first U.S. homebred Open winner but also the youngest. He even gave himself something of a handicap. The

* An iron with a shaft slightly longer than a putter and with the loft of a modern six. It was used around the green for run-up shots.

Bernard Darwin, the first truly professional writer on golf, displays the "President's Putter," a trophy awarded by the Oxford and Cambridge Golfing Society. The club originally belonged to Hugh Kirkaldy, who used it while winning the 1891 Open. (COURTESY SPORT & GENERAL.)

maker of a new ball called "Colonel" offered him a quick 300 dollars if he'd use it during the playoff. McDermott put away his customary Rawlings Black Circle balls and promptly belted two Colonels out of bounds on the first tee. Nevertheless, he overcame the potentially fatal 6 for that hole.

McDermott demonstrated that his supremacy was no fluke as he successfully defended his championship in 1912 at the Country Club of Buffalo. His reign had seemed in peril as Tom McNamara burst into fire with a finale of 69 for a total of 296, even par on a course with a generous par 74 per round. But McDermott was equal to the challenge, demonstrating a popular U.S. putting stroke with heels together, the stance erect and the stroke a pendulum effect. He scored a 71 to preserve a lead.

After the triumph at Buffalo, the cheeky McDermott decided it was time to teach the British a lesson on the quality of U.S. golf. The Europeans were undoubtedly much gratified that, after some very good practice rounds, McDermott humiliated himself with an awesomely awful 96 in the qualifying competition and was on a boat back to the States before the British Open even began.

In 1913, McDermott and two colleagues, Mike Brady and McNamara, sailed again, bound for the Open at Hoylake. McDermott endured a typically miserable downpour with strong winds on the final day for an 83 that ballooned his total to 315. It was good enough for a 5th-place finish, best ever by an American, but 11 strokes off the pace set by J. H. Taylor.

However, McDermott, instead of becoming an incandescent beacon of U.S. golfers, fizzled into a short-lived Roman candle. Financial reversals and the competitive drive within him so consumed McDermott that he lost his aplomb. Subsequently, golf officialdom chastised him for some unseemly remarks to visiting Brits. He missed a ferry and forfeited an opportunity to qualify for the 1914 British Open on the eve of World War I. Returning home, he was forced to flee in a lifeboat as his ship collided with another and foundered. He sank into a steep emotional decline and at only twenty-three years of age entered into a life of rest homes and sanatoriums terminated only by his death at eighty.

7

Snatching the Torch

Moving into the second decade of the twentieth century, British golf hegemony was no longer assured. While the Americans had failed to carry off an Open prize, a visitor from France, Arnaud Massy, "a mountain of a man [who] carried himself like a grenadier," according to Bernard Darwin, had the temerity to enter the lists at Hoylake and defeat the ripest of the British crop, finishing with a 2-stroke lead over Taylor. In celebration of the site of his success, Massy christened a new-born daughter, Hoylake. (There was a precedent; James Braid dubbed his son Muirfield.) Darwin later said of the first foreigner to win the tournament:

> [He] had a fine swashbuckling air and a cheerful, chuckling way with him that was most engaging. His account of his career as a bomb-thrower at Verdun, where he was wounded, was as picturesque as his description of his matches against rich Spanish visitors . . .

The Frenchman's triumph, according to writer Pat Ward-Thomas was warmly received even by his rivals because of Massy's good humor. However, J. G. McPherson, in an issue of *Baily's Magazine* shortly afterwards was moved to inquire, "Is British golf declining?"

But as Ward-Thomas said:

> In those days it was not too difficult to be tolerant of defeat for the great British professionals. The better part of a generation of supremacy remained before the invaders began to plunder in earnest. . . .

No American had come closer than Johnny McDermott's 5th-place finish in 1913. And while Travis had beaten all comers in the Amateur in 1904, after that date the play-for-no-pay championship bounced between John Ball, Harold Hilton, and other Britons.

On the other hand, the U.S. golfers (albeit mostly naturalized citizens) now steadfastly repelled invaders. After Vardon's 1900 victory in the Open, only Hilton's win in 1911 of the Amateur championship interrupted all-American domination of the two major tournaments.

Nevertheless, the rivalry across the seas simmered. The *Country Gentleman* in England argued a distinction between the approaches taken in the two lands.

> As played across the Atlantic, golf is fundamentally different from the British variety of the game. At bottom the game in America is a business. At bottom the game here is a pleasure, a relaxation, and a means of taking pleasant exercise. The American likes to satisfy himself as to who is the best player in the country, and to be eternally comparing the merits of various performers. These comparisons and criticisms are also very harsh.
>
> America is a land of championships—a happy hunting ground for the pot hunter. The continual playing of golf with an object does away with lighthearted and cheery matches and foursomes which form the main part of golf as it is played in the United Kingdom. Hence American golfers are for the most part serious-minded, haunted with the fear of losing the reputation they have gained in past competitions. Golf under this treatment soon loses its title to be called a game at all, and, so far from serving as a relaxation, it tends merely to an increased consumption of physical and mental energy. This being the case, it is not strange that the vast majority of good American players are comparatively idle men, or undergraduates at the various universities, who can give up their whole vacation to the exigencies of the American golfing spirit.

The logic of the 1911 *Country Gentleman* diatribe rested on the rock of Rule Britannia petulance. Tournament play began in the United Kingdom and flourished there before it arrived in the U.S. The best of the British amateurs like John Ball, Horace Hutchinson, and Harold Hilton had all taken the game seriously. The latter two wrote detailed treatises on form and proper strokes. Still, the audience of *Country Gentleman* continued to regard the lesson-giving, greenskeeping, club making professionals as low-born hired hands unworthy of being considered golfers. Certainly they must have been aware of the positions held by those who bore the Union Jack—Vardon, Braid, Taylor, and the like—but *Country Gentleman* would not have these fellows in for lunch, to say nothing of the distance they insisted be kept by the lesser pros. The attitude in the States was no more egalitarian: Travis and Travers wined, dined, and rubbed shoulders with the club members, but the likes of the many transplanted Willies and even the homebred McDermott were not welcome in the locker room, much less to share the grub.

For that matter, the bulk of the U.S. professionals (and not a few of the better amateurs) came from parts of the Empire where they learned the importance of the shilling, and then the buck. As for the comment about the better Americans being either "idle men or undergraduates," who else could afford to engage in competitive golf? The better nonprofessional British players also had to come from the ranks of the moneyed.

The American magazine *Outing* reprinted the *Country Gentleman* farrago and appended a comment:

> Some one once defined a lobster as a red fish that walks backward. To which Huxley responded: "A lobster is not a fish, it is not red, and it does not walk backward. Otherwise the definition is correct."

The snobbery of *Country Gentleman* towards those who earned a living through golf was nothing new. *Golf Illustrated* had already written off the adventures of Vardon and Taylor as beyond the pale.

The best of the British and Americans, as the second decade began, were now like a pair of boxers in the opening rounds, stalking one another, looking for an opportunity to strike a devastating blow. However dismal the logic of *Country Gentleman*, the rivalry packed a full head of steam.

In the summer of 1913, a writer for *Punch* tortured his native tongue and expressed the national pride in verse:

> German and Yank, you may can keep your
>   swank
> With the quivering lath and the diver's
>   tank.
>
> But who shall best o'er the bunkers caper
> And joust in the sand-filled trough?
>
> None, I think but the loved of Heaven
> Whose path is the ancient green
>
> Whose hearts are buoyed with the sea-
>   dog's leaven
> Whose brand is the iron keen.
>
> I will wager a crown to a mere piaster
> That Teuton and Gaul and Greek
>
> And the faraway Japs and sledge-borne
>   Laps
> Shall fall to our plus-four handicaps
>
> And the god shall fashion the oleaster
> To the blade of a British cleek.

That same year the Brits aimed their biggest cannons at the prizes across the Atlantic. Harry Vardon, having recovered from a siege of respiratory ailments that forced him into a sanatorium in 1903 and which would trouble him the remainder of his life, returned for a second tour. Symbolic of the new era in Britain despite *Country Gentleman*'s sneer, the expedition was not financed by an American manufacturer seeking to spread the gospel of golf and increase the market but by Lord Northcliffe, publisher of the London *Times*. There was no need to thump the tubs to lure spectators. The golfing public of the U.S. was now large enough and sufficiently sophisticated to appreciate the artist coming to display his wares. Huge crowds flocked to the courses in hopes of learning from the master.

Accompanying Vardon was Ted Ray, an oversize specimen for the times. He stood over six feet and weighed better than 200 pounds. Ray was often wild but he could play well enough to knock off the entire Triumvirate plus Sandy Herd and win the 1912 Open at Muirfield. His flamboyant mustache, his ever-present pipe in mouth even as he hurled himself into an explosive thrust through the ball, offered a stark contrast to the mild mien and graceful, seemingly effortless strokes of Vardon. The tremendous tee shots of Ray added to the excitement generated by the fine touch of Vardon. Between the two they massacred American opposition.

They suffered only a single setback. At the Shawnee Open in Pennsylvania, Johnny McDermott, a year from his crackup, put together a series of rounds that gave him an 8-stroke victory over Alex Smith, 13 better than Vardon with Ray behind one more. At the presentation ceremonies, McDermott committed the gaffe that contributed to his eventual collapse. He began with some mild remarks of welcome to the two Britons. Then, in a spasm of arrogance, McDermott blurted out, "We hope our foreign visitors had a good time, but we don't think they did, and we are sure they won't win the National Open!"

If he singed the ears of Vardon and Ray, they had the grace not to respond. But the Americans, other players and tournament officials, cringed. Later, McDermott apologized, but surely the broadside must have spurred Vardon and Ray to get revenge.* The opportunity was the U.S. Open held at The Country Club in Brookline, outside of Boston. Not only did the Brits now have personal reasons for wanting to take the Open but also this was the trophy most desired by their employer, Lord Northcliffe.

A record 165 men entered, causing the USGA to initiate thirty-six-hole qualifying rounds to be played over two days. Based

upon their devastation of all comers, the foreigners had to be the favorites. The best hopes for the host country lay on the shaky shoulders of McDermott; two other well-known U.S.–born pros Mike Brady and Tom McNamara, both of whom where familiar with the course; the redoubtable Jerry Travers, who had won his fourth Amateur title; and a couple of recent transplants, Macdonald Smith, a younger brother of Willie, and Jim Barnes.★ There were also some tyros of mild distinction. A twenty-year-old pro from Rochester by the name of Walter Hagen introduced himself to McDermott and enlisted himself in the ranks of the national defense. "I'm here to help you boys take care of Vardon and Ray." Supposedly, even the tight-wound McDermott burst into laughter. Present, too, was another twenty-year-old, Francis Ouimet, the young amateur and sporting goods salesman from Boston who had startled

Young Francis Ouimet learned to play hacking around the street and then in a homemade course laid out in a pasture. (COURTESY FRANCIS OUIMET ASSOCIATION.)

---

* Another account of the incident says McDermott, while holding the cup awarded for his Shawnee win, said, "You are not going to take back our cup!" He meant obviously that emblem of the coming U.S. Open. In this version of the affair, even after he apologized to Vardon and Ray, maintaining he had no intention of hurting their feelings, he reiterated the remark about the cup.

Travers and almost beaten him in the semi-finals of the Amateur.

Born in 1893, Francis Ouimet grew up in Brookline, across the street from the site of the 1913 Open. He recalled his initial acquaintance with golf:

The first golf course that I played over was laid by my brother and Richard Kimball in the street in front of our home which forms the boundary of one side of The Country Club. This golf course, as I call it, was provided by the town of Brookline, without the knowledge of the town officials. In other words, my brother and Kimball simply played between two points in the street. With the heels of their shoes they made holes in the dirt at the bases of two lamp posts about 120 yards apart and that was their "course."

Francis tagged along behind his elders until he was seven, when his brother gave him a birthday present, "a short brassie." He already had seven or eight balls, found while trudging to and from school on a pathway alongside of the sixth hole. He progressed to his own "course," a layout of 130 yards over pasture behind his home. There he contended with natural hazards, a ball-swallowing marsh on the left, a yawn-ing gravel pit in the middle of the "fair-way," and, most forbidding of all, a swift-flowing brook about 100 yards out. He could ill afford to lose one of his precious stock of balls in the stream. Thus, he learned accuracy and also to play within himself; in his early days he always played short of the water. "At last came the memorable morning when I did manage to hit one over the brook." Success brought not only satisfaction but the ambition to carry the hazard consistently.

Those first balls were gutties, so Ouimet knew he had found a genuine treasure when he discovered a rubber-cored ball. Misguided shots sent him on long searches for the treasure and when he had knocked off all the paint he recovered it in white, then set the ball in a hot oven to dry. To his dismay his treasure melted into a soft mess.

Ouimet's brother added a mashie to the brassie and now he became bold enough, with other boys, to sneak onto the grounds of The Country Club until chased. At home, he and his companions lengthened the pasture course to a 230-yard hole with several 90-yard placements for mashie prac-tice. Tomato cans sunk into the ground served as cups.

"There is this boy—for born on May 8, 1893, he is nothing more—beating our Harry Vardon and Edward Ray when they are at the prime of their golfing lives and at something uncommonly like their best."—Henry Leach, The American Golfer, *October, 1913.* (COURTESY RAY DAVIS.)

By his eleventh birthday, Francis had begun to caddie and his brother Wilfred offered some sound advice. Ouimet had been taking a half swing, bringing the club around as if it were a baseball bat. Wilfred counseled that distance demanded a full swing. The pupil attempted the correction and indeed he drove balls much farther, but all of his carefully developed accuracy vanished with it. Facing the question of which stroke to choose, the young Ouimet astutely opted to start with distance. And after much practice, the accuracy returned.

A member for whom Francis had caddied contributed significantly to the boy's meager equipment, passing along four clubs, a driver with a leather face, a lofter, a midiron, and a putter. When not called on to tote clubs and shag balls, Ouimet and a friend would spend a Saturday on a nine-hole public course at Franklin Park.

> To get to Franklin Park, we had to walk a mile and a half with our clubs to the car line. Then we rode to Brookline Village, transferred there to a Roxbury Crossing car, arrived at Roxbury Crossing and changed again to a Franklin Park car. After getting out of the last street car, we walked about three quarters of a mile to the clubhouse, checked our coats—that is all we had to check—and then played six full rounds of the nine holes, a total of fifty-four holes.
>
> Then we went home the way we had come, completely exhausted. All this at the age of thirteen!

At Brookline High where he was only a freshman, Ouimet organized a golf team that played squads from neighboring schools. At fifteen Ouimet obliterated his opponent in the Greater Boston Interscholastic Championship, 10 up, 9 to go. At seventeen, he tried to enter the U.S. Amateur scheduled for The Country Club, borrowing twenty-five dollars from his mother to obtain the necessary junior membership in the Woodland Golf Club. He promised to pay off the loan from his four-dollar-a-week summer job in a local store. However, he failed to qualify by a single stroke and the same unhappy 1-stroke deficiency barred him in 1911 and in 1912 as well. Then came the 1913 Amateur championship in which he not only qualified but also gave the eventual winner, Jerry Travers, his toughest match in the semi-finals.

Ouimet actually was on hand at the Open almost by accident. The USGA, anxious to make a fine showing for the visiting firemen, had gone to great lengths to build up a strong field. It was largely at the behest of the USGA that players like Travers, whose inconsistent game was ill suited for the medal play of the Open, and Ouimet entered. The boyish Ouimet seriously considered withdrawing because he felt he had taken too much time away from his job by playing in the National Amateur and then the Massachusetts State Amateur where he was a surprise winner. A week before the qualifying rounds, a local newspaper carried the names of entries. When Ouimet's boss asked if it were true he was in the Open, the young salesman stammered he'd only entered because he had been importuned by a USGA official. He really did not plan to play because of the time involved but he wondered if he might be granted a few hours off to see Vardon and Ray at work. His superior dismissed Ouimet's qualms and actually ordered him to play.

Rain soaked the ground as the contestants played the qualifying thirty-six holes over a demanding par-71 layout. Form held up as Vardon copped the first day medal at 151. Ouimet occasioned mild surprise coming home only a stroke behind Vardon. On the second day of qualifying, Ted Ray beat Vardon's round by 3, giving the Britishers the honors for qualifying. Also surviving the cut was the bumptious Hagen who posted a creditable 157, as well as Jim Barnes, Mac Smith, McDermott, and Brady (although the last two barely muddled through).

Once the tournament began, the visitors struck out vigorously. After thirty-six holes, Vardon at 147 was tied by another excellent English player, Wilfred Reid. Ted Ray was only 2 off the pace, recovering from a scary 79 with a subpar 70. Then came the naturalized Americans, Smith and Barnes. The best U.S.–born hope, Jerry Travers, had blown in 156, putting him 9 big strokes behind the leaders. McDermott and Brady had been unable to effectively harness their games and now fell back in the ruck. Hanging close, however, were the two American kids, Ouimet and Hagen. Both racked up 151, putting them just 4 behind the top Britons.

The pressure of the qualifying rounds and the intensity of the rivalries boiled over in a noisy scene, surprisingly among the visitors rather than between the locals and them. At dinner in the formal precincts of the Copley Square Hotel, Ted Ray and Wilfred Reid argued over the British system of taxation. When both sought to enhance their views with disparaging remarks aimed at their respective birthplaces, Ray drove his point home—by reaching across the table and punching Reid in the snoot, twice. Reid picked himself up from the floor and, with blood gushing from his nose, rushed at Ray. Waiters halted the debate.

On his third round, Vardon slipped somewhat, shooting a 78 and Ray, unfazed by the brawl and controlling himself on the green, carded a 76 to tie his countryman. Reid, however, fell apart and out of contention as he stumbled to an 85 and then 86. To the astonishment of all, the slender, hollow-cheeked salesman for Wright and Ditson, Ouimet, outscored everyone with a 73 and now it was a three-way tie for first. Still, no one could expect an inexperienced amateur to withstand the pressure of a final round against the two best players in the world. And for those who really liked long shots, Walter Hagen was still in the hunt, only a couple of strokes behind.

Conditions worsened. The rain hardly ever let up and the grounds were so saturated with water that puddles and rivulets pocked the fairways. No one would break 300 in this Open. On the final eighteen, Ted Ray virtually staggered home first with a 79 for a 304-stroke total. Vardon, who had trouble with his putter, could do no better and he too punished himself with a 79 to tie Ray.

Meanwhile, young Hagen seemed a quick loser. He began with three bad holes, then suddenly charged at the leaders. On the fourth hole, after a fine drive, he hit a full mashie that put the ball in the cup for an

eagle 2. He followed that feat with a more orthodox pair of birdie 3s and teed off at the tenth hole, even with Vardon and Ray. He remained their equals through ten and eleven. On the next hole he missed his 12-foot putt for a birdie that would have given him a lead. When Hagen smacked a long drive on the par-5 fourteenth, he determined to go for a birdie kill. The ball lay in one of the many fairway patches of water but Hagen ignored the potential problem. He launched a mighty brassie. Possibly he overswung or perhaps he miscalculated the lie of the ball in the water. Whatever, he topped the target and it skittered through the grass, shedding water like a dog shaking itself after a swim. Angered by the paltry result, Hagen then compounded his troubles with a vicious hook. When he finally got down he had a double bogey 7 instead of his anticipated bird and he was a loser, finishing eventually at 307.

The only person with a shot at Vardon and Ray was now Ouimet, and his chances were somewhere between dim and nil. He had gone out in 43, which meant he would need a 36 for the final nine if he were to win or a 37 to tie. Considering the state of the course it would not be easy. Then on the tenth hole he dug himself a pit from which there seemed no escape. It was only 140 yards from tee to green but Ouimet committed the duffer's cardinal sin, jerking his head up during the swing. The ball rolled a bare 20 feet. He lofted his second shot to the green all right, but then flubbed his putts for double bogey 5. The arithmetic now dictated he shoot the remaining eight holes in one under par just to draw even with the Englishmen.

He managed to par the eleventh but another bogey on the 415-yard twelfth hole meant he must play the final six in 2 under. Ouimet figured there were two holes where he might save strokes. On the thirteenth, one could pitch onto the green from the drive and then sink a birdie putt. The other possibility was the sixteenth, a short hole where a well-placed drive could set up a single putt.

His chances appeared respectable after his drive on thirteen placed him with an opportunity for an easy pitch toward the pin. However, the youngster skewered himself with a mishit that barely avoided a bunker and he left himself a tough chip even to get close enough for a par-saving putt, never mind a birdie. With nothing more to lose, Ouimet executed the abbreviated arc of the chip. The ball hit on the green and rolled over the soggy grass into the cup for the requisite birdie.

Saved for the moment, Francis parred fourteen and then teetered on the brink of extinction on fifteen with another poorly executed approach that stuck him in the rough. Again he chipped for survival, setting the ball down less than 3 feet from the pin and scoring the necessary 4.

Then came the opportunity on sixteen. He blew it. His second shot left him still a grim 9 feet from the pin. Not only was there no bird but bogey loomed. Ouimet hung in, however, and at least had his 3. But now he would have to birdie either the 360-yard seventeenth or the 410-yard eighteenth. The first of these doglegged left around a bevy of bunkers. He drove decently but stayed to the right, avoiding the bravado of saving yardage by flirting with the traps. For his second shot he chose his jigger, which in this case approximated a shallow-faced version of a 4-iron. He lofted the ball, which plonked onto the green at a distance estimated by latter-day historians of between 15 and 20 feet.

Many of the spectators, particularly after Francis muffed his chance for a birdie on sixteen, drenched by the rain and convinced the British had conquered, had fled for home. The weather and the pell-mell evacuation created a monumental traffic jam. Those on the course heard a cacophony of auto horns from the soaking and impatient drivers. But Ouimet, as he measured what was a long, sidehill, downhill putt, heard nothing. He huddled over the ball and struck boldly—almost too boldly, as it rushed across the grass, skipped across the hole to smack the backside of the cup, and, only then, fall. Those present broke into wild cheers, poked one another with their umbrellas. On hand, the phlegmatic Jerry Travers said he jumped three feet into the air.

But, of course, it was far from over. Ouimet still needed a par on eighteen and the sodden course meant the 410 yards would play even longer. Francis began by clouting a fine, straight drive. He took a long iron and walloped a beauty that rose towards an elevated green. Ouimet watched the ball hit the ground and disappear. He was certain he was on the green and turned to his ten-year-old caddie, Eddie Lowery. "I've got a putt to win." When he caught up with his ball, however, he discovered that instead of bouncing onto the green, the ball had stuck in the dirt surrounding the green. He could only chip to 4 feet away and then resolutely smack it home to tie Vardon and Ray at 304.

The gallery of 3,000 went berserk. Men and women, members of The Country Club

Ten-year-old Eddie Lowery, retained by Ouimet as his caddie for the playoff, received 100 dollars after the victory. (COURTESY RAY DAVIS.)

and other institutions that placed a premium on dignity shouted at one another, hugged and even kissed, oblivious to the continuing downpour. They mobbed the new hero. They bore him on their shoulders and put him down only after the cooler heads warned the boy would still need his wits and his body for the playoff the following morning. In the crowd was a pair of reluctant admirers, Vardon and Ray. The latter, not known for his magnanimity, allowed he had never seen such a pressure-laden putt.

The morning dawned or more correctly drizzled. Ouimet awoke from a sound sleep, still young enough for his mind not to be clouded by fear of failure. While others worried the two British golf giants would devour him, he kept his equanimity even as he accepted the occasion as momentous. "I realized I was just an amateur. I played golf for fun. I considered professionals as something like magicians who had an answer for everything. I felt I was in the playoff by mistake."

Once again, ten-year-old Eddie Lowery (who grew up to become a successful West Coast automobile dealer, to sponsor a number of promising professionals like Ken Venturi and Harvie Ward, and to serve as a USGA official some forty years later), expected to caddie. Ouimet spent half an hour loosening up and practicing shots on the polo field that also served as the fairways for the first and last holes.

When summoned to the first tee to begin the match, Ouimet was accompanied by a handful of spectators. Among them was McDermott, who stepped forward to encourage the American hope: "You're hitting the ball well, kid. Go out there and pay no attention to Vardon and Ray. Play your own game." It was the soundest advice one could offer any competitor, and particularly one so inexperienced.

Just before they reached the tent where the golfers would draw straws to determine the honor of starting, an adult friend called out to Ouimet and offered to act as caddie. The man was a good golfer who understood the finer points of play and tactics. His counsel could be most useful. Ouimet suggested he approach Lowery. The boy refused and when Ouimet saw tears begin to form, he firmly announced, "Eddie's going to caddie for me." Lowery's chief contribution throughout the playoff was to iterate and reiterate: "Be sure and keep your eye on the ball."

Once again the heavens declined to shine on the Open and instead doused the grounds with water. Francis drew the short straw, walked to the sandbox to scoop the makings for his tee and then belted a drive down the middle of the fairway. The trio bogeyed the hole. Ouimet putted home a 4-footer and his confidence surged.

Vardon and Ouimet were even after four, with Ray a shot behind after 3-putting on the third green. On the 420-yard fifth hole,

The final putt on the eighteenth green of the playoff was a formality; a birdie 3 on seventeen had given the American an insurmountable lead. (COURTESY RAY DAVIS.)

The locals bore their boyish conquering hero about the course. Herbert Warren Wind believes that the triumph of the modest Ouimet, a youngster of humble origins, helped give golf more mass appeal in the U.S. (COURTESY RAY DAVIS.)

both Vardon and Ray missed the green with their second shots. Ouimet, who had outdriven them, saw an opportunity to seize command. He chose his brassie, swung for the green. But the club slipped in his hands and the ball veered sharply to the right crashing off tree branches and falling in the brush.

Ouimet remembered:*

We finally found the ball deep in a virtually unplayable lie, just out of bounds by a margin of inches. . . . If the ball had stopped a few inches closer to the fairway and been in bounds I'd have had to play it from that position and I'd probably still be trying to get it out.

But because he was out of bounds, Ouimet dropped a ball over his shoulder onto the fairway and then coolly struck a brassie to the edge of the green. From there he chipped close enough for a single putt and scored a 5 including the out-of-bounds penalty. When both of his opponents required a chip and 2 putts it meant that even with the penalty he had not lost a stroke. Recalling the event, Ouimet insisted the slice into the trees was "the greatest shot of my life even though it was out of bounds."

The match continued as tight as could be, with all three recording 38 for the front nine. On the tenth hole, with a green that sloped down towards the tee 140 yards off, Vardon and Ray landed toward the front of the green and when their balls rolled backwards several inches they were forced to putt across the gouges left by the impact of their balls on the mushy green. Ouimet carried over the pin and although his ball also was mud-covered it left its impression on the green behind it. As a consequence, his elders took 3 putts each while he maneuvered his ball down the watery incline in 2, giving him the lead.

To the consternation of Vardon, Ouimet padded his advantage by another stroke with a par on the twelfth, while his adversaries suffered bogeys. Vardon soon reduced the margin to one. The first to fold was Ray. He pushed too hard, found himself hacking his way through trees on the fourteenth, was saved from the rough on fifteen only after his drive bounced off the derby of a fan and onto the fairway and, by the sixteenth, he had fallen an insurmountable 4 behind. As the kid continued to keep the pressure on, even the ordinarily imperturbable Vardon succumbed to stress, lighting a rare cigarette on the course.

The 1900 Open winner desperately tried to close the 1-stroke gap on the seventeenth, gambling he could save ground on the

---

* His recollection was recorded in 1938, and Ouimet said the wild blow on the fifth hole came on a tee shot. But memory played him false as golf historians have noted the mishap occurred with the fairway brassie.

The Boston Traveler *splashed the news of Ouimet's great feat over the front page.* (COURTESY RAY DAVIS.)

dog leg by lying up close to a bunker that guarded the angle. But he hooked enough to throw himself into the pit. The ball rolled up so close to the front wall he had no chance to recover with an iron onto the green. Instead, he could only blast out, then reach the green in 3 and 2 putt for a fatal bogey rather than the hoped for birdie. For Francis, playing safe, had hit straight out, then jiggered himself close enough to fire a birdie putt.

Ouimet now held a 3-stroke lead with only a single hole remaining. It would take a cataclysm of megamagnitude for him to lose. And when he calmly split the fairway with his final drive, no one could doubt the outcome. The enormous crowd, certain their David had slain both of the overseas Goliaths, flowed onto the course. The marshals bawled at them through megaphones to clear room for Ouimet to finish. At last Francis could address his ball, take a practice swing and then hammer an iron right to the flag. He was about 18 feet off, and his first attempt left him another 4 feet to go. "For the first time, I thought about the championship. I couldn't get my breath. The green began heaving beneath me. I couldn't even see the hole." The inner

turmoil hardly showed as he tapped the ball in a swift path into the cup for a 4 and a 1 over par, 72. A disconsolate Vardon double bogeyed to end 5 back at 77, while Ray scored a 78.

Paraded around the grounds on the shoulders of rooters, Ouimet at one point leaned over to speak to a small woman: "Thank you, Mother. I'll be home soon."

At the presentation, John Reid, Jr., secretary of the USGA handed the cup to Ouimet and said: "It is customary to receive security for this trophy, but in this case the only security which the United States Golf Association will demand is that the Woodland Golf Club shall see that Francis keeps up his game."

The twenty-year-old clutched the silver ornament and demurely swatted the British hopes in the teeth:

> Naturally it was always my hope to win out. I simply tried my best to keep this cup from going to our friends across the water. I am very glad to have been the agency for keeping the cup in America.

On the day after the tournament, they celebrated at The Country Club. The hero walked across the street from his home to the clubhouse as the honored guest. He downed a handful of drinks—Horse's Necks they were called, mixtures of lemon juice and ginger ale. The young man became an instant hero in the States. He was perfect material for idolatry, loving and concerned for his mother, a teetotaler, an amateur when professional athletes were still regarded as unfit for the company of respectable people, and above all the stripling who singlehandedly repelled the British.

Grantland Rice honored him in verse:

If I was a Homer, a Milton or Byron,
And felt that an epic was due,
I'd sing of your magic with wood and with iron
And weave further laurel for you;
I'd crown you the King of a Game that's eternal
In rhapsodies shorn of restraint;
I'd wreathe you an olive bough endlessly vernal
If I was a Burns—but I ain't

O Soul of a Stalwart, for history's pages
If I was a Keats or a Gray,
I'd tell how, for those of the far, unborn ages,
You slipped it to Vardon and Ray;
I'd sing every stroke of your conquering battle
Until I was fagged out and faint;
I'd make you the subject of every child's prattle
If I was a Keats—but I ain't.

Rice carried on the doggerel for two more full verses, demonstrating that *Punch* held no monopoly on poetic panegyrics of dubious distinction, but praise showered down upon Ouimet. The American magazine *Outlook* opened its tribute with a triple apostrophe:

Impossible! Nonsense! It cannot be! No other comment seemed reasonable when the dispatches announced that Harry Vardon and Edward Ray, who are generally regarded as the greatest golf players living, both of them British professionals, were beaten for the Open Championship of America. . . .

"Ouimet the enemy and they are ours" was the brief bulletin that was posted in the clubhouse at the Woodland Golf Club at Brookline, Massachussetts, on Saturday afternoon, September 20. That bulletin not only gives the name of the victor but indicates to a host of his new-made admirers how his name is pronounced.

Americans are said to excel in those competitions that require brilliance, but lack steadiness, persistence, patience, unflagging courage. It is gratifying to have this record that Ouimet scored up to the credit of an American, for if ever in any game a player showed just those qualities, Ouimet showed them in playing those 126 holes of the qualifying round and of the tournament.

While the U.S. press seemed intent on hurling back the sneers of *Country Gentleman*, British publications took the defeat with good sportsmanship. Said the London *Evening Star*:

Ouimet, beyond a doubt, played the most dazzling golf in the annals of the royal and ancient game. No precedent can parallel Ouimet . . . an obscure young man who started life as a caddie, was pitted against two of the greatest golfers in the

Ouimet added U.S. Amateur titles in 1914 and 1931. (COURTESY FRANCIS OUIMET ASSOCIATION.)

Throughout his life, Ouimet favored the place across the street from where he grew up. "To me the ground here is hallowed. The grass grows greener, the trees bloom better, there is even a warmth to the rocks ... somehow or other the sun seems to shine brighter on The Country Club than any other place that I have known." —Francis Ouimet, 1932. (COURTESY FRANCIS OUIMET ASSOCIATION.)

world, men of years, ripe in skill. Yet, this boy coolly and calmly outplayed them under circumstances that might have shaken the nerve of a man of iron. This marvelous boy did not crack under the strain and stress. It was the veterans that cracked.

We note that there is a disposition to make excuses for Vardon and Ray because they were upset by the gallery. What rubbish! They are always playing before a gallery. What upset them was the pitiless accuracy and unshakable nerve of a boy who beat them at every stage of the long battle.

The London *Daily Mail* was similarly gracious:

Golfers at this moment are engaged the world over in the single, simultaneous and irrepressible act. They are taking off their hats to Ouimet with a flourish of profound respect. . . . The mere stripling of twenty carried off the American Open Championship by beating in the final round two of the finest and most seasoned warriors Britain could put on the links against him.

J. H. Taylor, who had won the British Open that year, offered a discordant note. He grumped about the stress of a three-player playoff, ignoring that the pressure was no greater on his countrymen than on the American amateur. One English journalist succinctly summed it up:

There will never be another like it. When we are old men, little golfing children will ask us to tell them again the romantic story of the 20th of September in 1913.

Ouimet rarely placed himself in as disagreeable a location as here. (COURTESY RAY DAVIS.)

8

Sir Walter and the Rise of the Pro

At the time Francis Ouimet vanquished the all-powerful British, for all of the enthusiasm shown by those who relished any event in which Yankee Doodle humbled John Bull, fewer than 350,000 Americans played golf. *Outlook* may have celebrated Ouimet's victory, but golf received little attention in most newspapers. Grantland Rice had been unable to convince the sports editor of the *New York Evening Mail* that he should cover the Open at The Country Club; the editor sneered at golfers as "unemployed sheepherders and coupon-clipping stiffs."

It is a measure of the state of the sport that Ouimet did not try to cash in as a professional; he was far better off continuing as an amateur and pursuing a livelihood through endeavors other than golf. He did, of course, continue to compete, venturing abroad in 1914 under the sponsorship of his Woodland Club members. He fared dismally in the British Amateur, losing in the second round. But he recouped his reputation with a win in the French Amateur against a field quite similar to the one in Great Britain. He returned that same year to the U.S. to win his first U.S. Amateur championship, a title he would regain seventeen years later in 1931, after having been runner up in 1920. He was a semi-finalist seven times.

Naturally, Ouimet prepared to defend his U.S. Open title in 1914 at the Midlothian Country Club near Chicago. Also on hand were the old stalwart Tom McNamara and the chipper amateur, librarian's son, and former caddie, Charles "Chick" Evans. As they readied themselves for the opening rounds at Midlothian, Evans already had been to the U.S. Amateur semi-finals on three occasions. The perennial bridesmaid of tournaments, Evans was renowned from tee to green but from there to the cup he proved Walter Travis's point. In fact, he inspired *American Golfer* to a verse entitled "A Chronic Semi-Finalist":

> I'm a semi-final hoodoo, I'm afraid.
> I can never do as you, Jimmy Braid.
> I've a genius not to do it,
> I excel at almost to it,
> But I never can go through it, I'm afraid.

Midlothian and the 1914 Open were destined to be the stage for the grand entrance of the first truly great U.S. professional, Walter Hagen. When last seen, Hagen had in effect slunk off from The Country Club after his ill-advised go-for-broke brassie from a puddle bankrupted him on the fourteenth hole of the final regular round.

After his highly respectable finish, 3

In electing Ouimet to its captaincy in 1951, The Royal and Ancient Club named the first of three Americans who have held the post. Latter-day successors from the U.S. are the USGA and PGA official Joe Dey and the amateur star William Campbell. (COURTESY RAY DAVIS.)

At age fifteen, Charles "Chick" Evans, born in 1890, demonstrated signs of his golf prowess. After several sharp disappointments, notably as runnerup in the 1914 U.S. Open, he crashed through with the first U.S. double, the 1916 Open, and the Amateur. Second to him in the Open was the St. Andrews-born Jock Hutchison who chirped, "Look at that little pissy-assed medal of yours. I got real dough." (COURTESY RAY DAVIS.)

strokes behind the trio of leaders, the young pro from Rochester returned home briefly, then headed south for the Florida season. A blacksmith's son, he had been an excellent baseball player, going so far as to teach his sister how to catch in order that he might practice pitching in the backyard. He became friendly with Pat Moran, manager of the Philadelphia Phillies, who gave him a tryout. Moran seemed impressed enough for Hagen to believe that the following spring he would be offered a genuine opportunity to show the Phillies what he could offer, either on the mound, where he threw right-handed, or as a left-handed hitting outfielder. His ambidexterity benefitted him later as a golfer, when he sometimes used a left-handed club because of the lie.

Back in Rochester, Hagen figured to bide his time at his job with the Country Club of Rochester, supplementing his income with semi-pro baseball. He had no plans to enter the Open again until Ernest Willard, editor of the local *Democrat and Chronicle*, offered to cover Hagen's expenses.

From the beginning, Hagen seemed possessed of the notion that he should exude star quality. When he had first appeared at The Country Club in 1913 he had drawn bemused and amused stares with his duds—a checked cap, a silk dress shirt with bright red and blue stripes, a red bandanna knotted around his neck, long white flannel pants, and white buckskin shoes with flamboyant red rubber soles. When he went to Chicago in 1914, he changed his attire slightly. On social occasions, in place of the checked cap he sported a rakish straw skimmer and on the course he wore hobnailed shoes. The short round-headed nails enabled him to dig into the ground that he believed betrayed him in Brookline.

Typically, he celebrated his unspectacular but nevertheless qualifying round of 152 at Midlothian. He gobbled an extravagant dinner of lobster in a dingy restaurant without tablecloths. He awoke with a belly ache. Partially assuaged by potions and pills administered by a physician, he endured a hot, sooty train ride to the site of

the club and then, still crampy, set out on the initial leg of the tournament.

He started out in the style that was to become his trademark: a drive sliced deep into the rough followed by a fine recovery and 2 putts to meet par. He duplicated the effort on the second hole and shook off the last complaints of his still unhappy stomach. After the first nine he was 1 under par at 35 and then he exploded for 4 birdies on the final five holes, to set a course record of 68. His elation lasted only until he discovered the gentle Ouimet had fired a 69 to be only one behind.

In the afternoon round, Hagen cooled off to a 74 for a 142 total. Tom McNamara pulled close with 143 but Ouimet sprawled to a 76 in the afternoon and now was 3 behind. On the second and final day—in that era tournaments were grueling two-day affairs—Hagen posted a 75 in the morning. His two closest rivals, McNamara and Ouimet folded but now the amateur Chick Evans, as usual relying on only seven clubs: brassie and spoon woods, a mid-iron or modern 2-iron, a jigger for the run-up shots, an equivalent of a modern 7 or 8, a niblick to serve as a 9 or wedge and a putter. With this limited arsenal, however, he constructed a 71 for the third round to bring him within 4 strokes of the lead.

As they played their final eighteens in the afternoon, Evans, as a Chicago boy, gathered a gallery of more than 1,000 while the unknown Hagen, playing ahead of him, was attended by only a corporal's guard. Hagen teetered on the brink of defeat, losing a horrendous 3 strokes to par on the eighth and ninth holes and as Evans finished his first nine he was only one behind. He could have been even had he not, as usual, betrayed himself blowing a 3-foot putt on nine.

As the tournament headed for the climax, the hordes following Evans cheered lustily as he delivered magnificent strokes on and off the green. The roars reached Hagen's ears as he himself endeavored to escape damage from an errant shot or concentrated upon a critical putt.

Now Evans began to stagger, missing a putt of under 10 feet on the eleventh and following up with a 3-putt debacle on the twelfth. Meanwhile Hagen sputtered and groped ahead. On the sixteenth he hooked his brassie, stubbed his chip but buried a long putt to save par. On the next hole when he could have salted away the match with a 7-footer he missed but he canned a slightly longer putt on the final hole.

Evans seemed doomed when he barely missed a 15-footer on the sixteenth but when his 25-footer dropped on the penultimate hole he lay but two behind. Ordinarily, the eagle necessary to tie Hagen would be out of the question. But the last hole at Midlothian was a par 4, 277 yarder. The powerful Evans was fully capable of reaching the green.

Hearing that Evans could equal his score, Hagen joined the mob crowding the green. Chick blasted off the tee and drove to the edge of the green, 50 feet from the pin but still with a longshot possibility. The locals hushed for the benefit of the hometown boy and all heard the click of iron against balata. The ball struck the green smoothly and rolled directly at the cup. A long group "Oooh" turned to "Awwwww" as the ball slowly veered left to halt a foot away. Walter Hagen had won the 1914 Open with a score of 290, tying the record set previously by George Sargeant in 1909.

Gone were thoughts of baseball. The 300 dollar first prize bought Hagen an automobile plus offers to play exhibitions. Still, when the champion returned to Rochester, he was not hailed as the conquering hero. While the newspapers had given modest recognition to his efforts, there was no celebration. In his memoirs of the time, Rochester newspaperman Henry Clune remembered:

Hagen returned to Rochester with little more panache than a factory hand punching a time clock in the morning. His vacation was over; he went back promptly to instructing club members in the niceties of a game in which he had won supreme honors. There was no dancing in the streets and streamers were not festooned between the lampposts with huge stenciled letters

"Welcome Home, Champ." The country club members were conservative souls; they liked their pro, they were pleased with his victory, but golf was a game with them, not a passion. Hagen had grown up around their course and learned the game there, and overnight they couldn't canonize him merely because he had played a winning round. . . .

Indeed, so low was the state of even a pro with Hagen's credentials that he was expected not only to give golf lessons but also had the duties of teaching tennis and skating. Still, as Open Champion, he now added from 200 to 300 dollars for an exhibition, and he was known to hustle millionaires into 500 dollar nassaus.*

To some, Hagen must have seemed a flash in the pan. For he did poorly in 1915 defending his title at Baltusrol, when Jerry Travers wrested the Open championship back for the amateur brigade. Hagen fared no better in 1916, as Chick Evans finally put together all of the strokes at the Minikahda Club outside of Minneapolis. Harry Vardon had once called Evans the best amateur he had seen in America and Jerry Travers remarked that "if Evans could putt like Walter J. Travis, it would be foolish to stage an Amateur tourney in this country." Now his 3- and 4-foot putts fell with consistency, and his total of 286 brought him home 4 ahead of his nearest competitor, Long Jim Barnes, and broke the record set by Sargeant and Hagen.

Evans refused the temptation to cash in on his celebrity. However, he agreed to make a series of phonograph recordings on golf with the proceeds turned over to the Western Golf Association for the benefit of caddies. By 1930, the fund amounted to 12,000 dollars, and Evans shifted the program into scholarships for caddies to attend his alma mater, Northwestern University. By 1990, well over 5,000 caddies had received aid towards higher education through the Chick Evans Fund.

Hagen's failure to follow his first great victory with a string of similar achieve-

A gauche young pro from Rochester, Walter Hagen startled the golf world in 1914 with his victory in the U.S. Open at Midlothian, outside of Chicago. (COURTESY THE BETTMANN ARCHIVE.)

---

* In a nassau, the winner of each nine holes earns a point and the low score for the eighteen holes is worth another point.

At the 1918 North-South Open, Pinehurst, North Carolina, Hagen now slicked his hair and added panache to his attire. "If Hagen were not a great golfer, I fancy he would have been a great actor. He loved to do his stuff for the gallery—and for an opponent when it was match play. His bold, confident, deliberate personality impinged on a single human opponent with such effect that so good and game a player as Leo Diegel said to a friend in the gallery following the match between him and Diegel in 1925 in the Professional Championship, where Hagen picked up a deficit of five holes and won on the fortieth green, 'Bill, I never want to play him again; he's killing me.'"—O. B. Keeler, The Bobby Jones Story. (COURTESY RAY DAVIS.)

"Hagen could relax sitting on a hot stove. His touch was as sensitive as a jeweller's scale. If he estimated a club's weight and the scales didn't check with Walter's guess, the scales were wrong." —Tommy Armour. (COURTESY THE BETTMANN ARCHIVE.)

ments is no mystery. The boy from Rochester never developed a classic stroke and in his early days he was a textbook of don'ts. He gripped the club like it was a baseball bat and shifted his body too much as the club moved toward the ball. A compatriot from the early days said, "Hagen sways like a rocking horse." The stroke was less of a swing and more of a lunge.

Over time, Hagen programmed better control into his attack and some insist that underlying what seemed undisciplined mechanics lay a sense of rhythm that Ben Hogan later described as "the order of procedure." Others would drive longer and straighter but few could equal his skill with irons or his touch on the green. Still, Hagen never developed an automaton approach that guaranteed consistency. As a consequence he incited cries of dismay succeeded by exultant hollers. He thrilled those who followed him on the course, and they soon showed up in droves, with an almost endless spectacle of self-inflicted damage followed by redemptive acts of Herculean proportions. Hagen added excitement to golf; both the cognoscenti and the innocents marveled at his heroics. Ouimet's popularity reflected his 1913 win; Hagen brewed his fame wherever he played.

World War I eliminated British tournament golf after 1914, and when the United States joined the Allies, competition in the States also ceased. None of the major events were held in 1917 through 1918. Like the handful of other well-known golfers, Hagen played in exhibitions for the benefit of the Red Cross or war relief agencies. Another featured performer was a child prodigy out of Georgia, young Robert Tyre Jones,★ destined to become Hagen's chief rival for golf headlines during the Roaring Twenties.

Meanwhile, Hagen moved on to become the pro in residence at Oakland Hills outside of Detroit, where he ingratiated himself with the cream of the automobile executives and also acquired a patina of polish for his manners and dress. Tournament golf reappeared in the U.S. in 1919 with the Open at Brae Burn Country Club, West Newton, Massachusetts. Hagen trailed from the beginning but, true to form,

slashed his way back into contention until he arrived at the final green, needing to sink an 8 footer to eke out a win over Mike Brady. The leader had retired to the locker-room but Hagen insisted he be brought out to witness the shot. And with Brady glumly watching, Hagen tapped the ball towards home. It caught the lip of the cup, then spun out setting up a playoff.

Undaunted, Hagen threw himself a late-night party that included Al Jolson and some of the cast from the musical show "Sinbad." Hagen had been a teetotaler until his mid twenties, but now he enjoyed what he called a "hoot" or a "hyposonica," belts of Scotch whiskey. As the bunch tippled and toasted the day's feat, a guest suggested Hagen should get some sleep before the playoff. After all, it was pointed out, Mike Brady had long since gone to bed. Hagen supposedly responded: "He may be in bed, but he ain't asleep." (The same quote has appeared in an anecdote about a match against Leo Diegel, ten years later.)

Though Hagen caroused until 4 A.M., when his day's work began, he gained an immediate edge. As he and Brady, who had his sleeves pushed up in the heat, stood on the second tee, Hagen not so casually remarked, "Listen, Mike, hadn't you better roll down those sleeves?"

"What for?"

"The gallery can see your muscles twitching." Brady then walloped a murderous hook that cost him 2 strokes on the hole. On the seventeenth tee, Hagen still held a 2-stroke lead. Strategy called for a player to draw the ball but Hagen launched a rocket that missed the fairway and fell like a rock into a patch of soft muck. In the search party hunting for the ball, it was Brady who discovered what appeared to be it, deeply embedded. Because the ball was all but buried, Hagen insisted a spectator must have stepped on it, but his request for a free lift was denied. Walter now filed a new petition. Since the ball was obscured, how could anyone be sure that it was Hagen's? He demanded his right to identify his ball and the request had to be granted. Hagen plucked the ball from the goo, wiped it clean and solemnly pronounced it his own. Then he delicately placed it back on the soggy ground. It did not sink and he had a playable shot. He lost a stroke on the hole but when the playoff ended, Hagen was Open champion by 1 stroke.

Unlike the cool reception in Rochester after his 1914 victory, Oakland Hills hailed Hagen with a banquet. He thanked the members, then astounded them with his resignation. He declared his intention to become the first, unattached, full-time touring pro golfer. He offered a balm to the stunned group as he introduced, ". . . just the fellow to replace me. He's here tonight —Mike Brady." Because of his generous ways, few opponents could stay angry at Hagen when he beat them, even when he resorted to the ploys of gamesmanship.

When the British Open was revived in 1920, the cocky Hagen, funded by one of his Detroit millionaire pals, sailed with four trunks stuffed with clothes, a press agent, and an adviser. When he learned he and other pros would eat in a tent while the amateurs dined in the clubhouse, he arranged for champion-style luncheons, elaborately served by a footman beside Hagen's chartered limousine, in full and painful view of the club swells dining inside. (On another occasion, he hired an airplane to fly him daily, with companions, to a famous inn.)

But to the British he was all flash and no substance. Warned of the dangers of the many bunkers lying in wait, he scoffed: "There are no bunkers in the air." However, his American game with its soaring, high drives and its recoveries from less-punishing rough would not play on the wind-swept, gorse-laden course at the seaside town of Deal in the United Kingdom.

To say Hagen was not a factor in the British Open of 1920 puts a gloss on his performance. He seemed to spend more time in the sand than a Bedouin trekking the Sahara. On the final day he found himself paired with a sixty-two-year-old gent who finished dead last at 56th, 1 behind Hagen, who averaged 82 strokes a round. Without offering an alibi, he tweaked the beaks of the locals: "I tried too hard, just like any duffer might play. Guess I figured

these boys were tougher than they were."

He retained some of his reputation in Europe by winning the French Open, beating British Open champ George Duncan as well as Abe Mitchell, another fine English player. At the La Boulie course near Paris, Hagen served notice he would no longer put up with the indignities piled upon professionals. Shown a stable with

"Hagen spent money like a King Louis with a bottomless treasury. In the credit-card age he might have broken American Express."
—*Al Barkow,* Golf's Golden Grind. (COURTESY RAY DAVIS.)

"... up to the vicinity of the green, a dozen players might be adduced who were his equal, but around the greens, within chipping and putting range, Hagen very likely was the greatest. Hagen was also celebrated for his recovery shots which reputation collaterally implied an inclination to wildness. This implication is accurate. Walter was one of the wildest of all the front-rank golfers, and this disposition to wallop the ball off the visible confines of the course, not to mention the fairways, cost him more than one medal play championship."—O. B. Keeler, The Bobby Jones Story.

Despite Keeler's diagnosis, Hagen terrorized the British in medal play at the Opens. In 1921, Hagen made his second foray in the British Open at St. Andrews. He lost to local expatriate Jock Hutchison, but in 1922 Hagen's blowsy 300 was enough for the first native-born American to take the Blighty crown. (COURTESY THE BETTMAN ARCHIVE.)

nails to hang the players' clothes, Hagen gathered Duncan and Mitchell to constitute a committee of three. They marched into the offices of the tournament directors and announced that unless the conditions were rectified they would quit the scene. The assembled dauphins surrendered, partially. Permission to use the clubhouse was granted but only to the trio of protestors.

During the French Open he continued his mind games. Against Abe Mitchell, one round, he outdrove his foe by a few feet. Casually, he selected a brassie for his next shot. Mitchell, hitting first, took the hint and went for the brassie, which crashed his ball into a row of trees crossing the fairway. Hagen slipped his brassie back in his bag and drew forth a 2-iron, which he hooked around the trees. He gained a stroke on Mitchell here, which cost Abe an opportunity to join Hagen in a playoff against a French hero named Lafitte.

Lafitte apparently preferred to play in a leisurely fashion, so when their playoff match began, Hagen quickly hit his shots and then chased after them as if he had a train to catch. On one hole he climbed an uphill tee and belted his drive before the puffing Lafitte could even complete the ascent. Lafitte then drove into the rough. Hagen won easily.

On his second trip abroad, Hagen fared somewhat better, finished a respectable 6th in the British Open. The third time out in 1922 established Hagen as a force that could not be denied. His 300 wasn't a pretty score but it was still good enough for a margin of 2. He promptly endorsed his prize check worth about 300 dollars over to his caddie, boarded his rented Rolls-Royce to motor all the way down the coast, where he shipped out on an ocean liner bound for the U.S. and the pots of gold now awaiting his claim.

At home, the press trumpeted his fame. Grantland Rice paid homage to him in the *American Golfer:*

Then up spake Walter Hagen
A Homebred bold was he.
And who will stand at my right hand
And hold the bridge with me?

Then Sarazen* straight answered.
His keen blade ringing true.
Lo, I will stand at thy right hand
and pull the Homebred through.

Hagen embarked on an unending series of tours, exhibition matches, and tournaments that carried him to all corners of the planet. He partnered with trick shot expert Joe Kirkwood,† an Australian, for nine years of globe hopping with a *Boston American* sportswriter, Dick Harlow★ as their manager. He averaged more than 125 exhibitions a year and he performed on just about every golf course in the U.S. The operation asked no guarantees; it depended on the buck or two admission charge. As the treasurer, Harlow stuffed the dollar bills in a suitcase; whenever the bag became too heavy they opened an account at the nearest bank. Years later Hagen would hear of deposits in his name at long-forgotten sites.

A 1926 dream match pitted him against the majestic game of golf's other titan of the 1920s, the amateur Bobby Jones. Their confrontation was to be a seventy-two-hole affair in Florida, but Hagen trounced Jones 12 and 11 with a superb demonstration on the greens, taking only 53 putts over the first thirty-six holes. In one stretch of nine holes, he required only 7 putts, having chipped in twice.

Oddly enough, Hagen never won another U.S. Open after his 1919 victory, while he repeated at the British Open in 1924, '28, and '29. However, the circumstances for his 1928 triumph in the event were anything but propitious.

Hagen snuck aboard the S. S. *Aquitania*, bound for England, through a cargo door to avoid a process server armed with a warrant covering back alimony and a right to arrest the golfer. For all the money he earned, Hagen was frequently tapped out.

Indeed, the 1928 sally was an opportunity to recoup his finances. Toward that end, Harlow arranged a big money battle against huge Archie Compston, who towered over Hagen.

The American began partying from the moment he boarded the vessel and continued in London. Harlow, desperately anxious for his client to take the 500 guinea purse—2,500 dollars in U.S. currency—hired a hulking detective from Scotland Yard to ensure Hagen got to the tee on time. There had been some bad press on an earlier excursion after Hagen kept Abe Mitchell and 3,000 fans waiting in another match. The British press laughed heartily at Hagen and his bodyguard through cartoons and feature stories. The publicity-conscious Harlow only regretted he could not convince the detective to wear a deerstalker cap à la Sherlock Holmes. But punctuality proved no help as Hagen caught the British giant at the wrong moment. Compston fired a 67 in the morning round while the best Hagen could manage was 72, leaving him in match play down four holes. But in the afternoon, Compston went berserk, banging through the course in 66, with a 30 for the last nine. Hagen faded and when the day ended he was down 14.

On the second day, Compston continued the rout; adding another 4 to his lead during the morning's play. When they halved the first hole after lunch, the match was over, 18 down, 17 to play, the worst loss ever suffered by Hagen. The British press lapsed into an orgy of American bashing. Headlines blatted:

Hagen's Ghost Is Laid

The Rout of Walter Hagen

Compston, The "Lion Tamer"

Walter Hagen Submerged

---

* Gene Sarazen★ won the U.S. Open in 1922.

† Kirkwood supposedly engaged Hagen for an Australian tour with a guarantee of 16,000 dollars. But when the gate for the expedition fell well below expectations, Hagen reportedly pulled out the contract and said: "Do you know what I think of this scrap of paper Joe? Just this!" He ripped the document to shreds. Hagen insisted Kirkwood forget the 16,000-dollar obligation and the pair would split expenses and income equally. It was a typical Hagen gesture.

George Duncan was the winner of the 1920 British Open, the first since the guns of August boomed in 1914. Hagen salvaged some of his rep by whipping Duncan in the French Open of 1920. (COURTESY RAY DAVIS.)

America Gets Its Own Medicine

The Eclipse of Hagen

Hagen Takes His Physic

The *Morning Post* chortled:

Such a signal victory as that accomplished by Archie Compston in his match with Walter Hagen, deserves more than passing celebration. It is an event that must be dear and refreshing to a British golfer's heart.

The loser read it all in the Rolls back to London and accepted his defeat with good sportsmanship. "I was outplayed. Compston was too good."

The winner, taking a leaf from the attitude of his victim, boasted: "I will play anyone, anywhere for anything."

Although unruffled on the surface, Hagen resolved to exact retribution. After going through his little black book to find, "who is going to share my sorrow with me tonight," he informed Harlow and the detective, "Archie was good, but I can beat him any old time."

His opportunity lay in the 1928 British Open, and he uncharacteristically buckled down for a week of practice, restricted diet, and reasonably decent hours. He absolutely drubbed the field, including Compston. The same newspapers that had trilled over Hagen's thrashing now bleated about his supremacy.

The London *Times* observed:

The way in which Hagen accepted his smashing defeat at the hands of Compston opened the eyes of many people to his good qualities. Many a man can take a beating in the spirit of a good sportsman, and yet, for awhile at any rate, will have the spirit crushed out of him by that beating. Not so Hagen; it only goads him to further effort. No one else is quite so richly blessed in the matter of temperament. He is a terrible, great golfer.

The forerunner of Colonel Blimpism, raised at the ceremonies attendant upon Walter Travis's win in 1904 had been exorcised. During the 1928 Open, the Prince of Wales, later to become Edward VIII (who abdicated and was reincarnated as the Duke of Windsor), followed Hagen's round on the final day. He presented the cup to the victor:

Overseas entries have added keen competition to our open championships. We are getting a little jealous, but we always want the best man to win. We hope the overseas golfers will continue to come until, as they say in America, we are able to "put one over" on them.

In succeeding years, Hagen frequently golfed with the speaker, both as a Prince and as a Duke, but it is not true he once directed, "Hold the pin, Eddie." (He had called out the instructions to the caddie.)

The following year, the Haig had no intention of entering the British Open; what more could he prove? But a Briton, George Duncan, committed the error of whipping him a few weeks before the 1929 classic and Hagen was duty bound to take his revenge at Muirfield. The elements disapproved; the rain pelted down the first day on the early starters like himself, but he trekked to a 75 even after bogeying the first four holes. He refused to allow the mistakes to distract him. The next day he recouped with a 67, a record for the Open, lifting him from eighteenth to second. Storms again ravaged the play but, while none of the other top five finishers could break 75, Hagen scored one in the morning and another in the afternoon for a winning total of 292. More wormwood and

On the cover:

LIFE

BEN HOGAN TELLS HIS SECRET

THE AMAZING WORLD OF INSECTS:
13 PAGES IN COLOR

HOGAN APPLIES SECRET;
WHAT IS IT? SEE PAGE 60

20 CENTS

AUGUST 8, 1955

Ben Hogan was the cover story for the August 8, 1955 issue of Life *magazine.* (COURTESY
YALE JOEL)

The Lum Hat was used to measure the amount of feathers to be used in stuffing a golf ball. Also pictured are some of the various tools which were used in making vintage wood clubs.

ADDRESSING THE BALL

Facing page: Left to right: Sterling silver martini shaker with four goblets, in a unique golf motif, from the 1920s; A bronze knickered golfer, circa 1920; Golf Illustrated, *published in England in 1911;* The Complete Golfer *by Harry Vardon, 1905;* The Badminton Library of Golf *by Horace G. Hutchinson, 1890; A British clock, made in 1895, with thistle, crossed clubs, and ball; A commemorative plate from the International Ryder Cup Matches at the Greenbrier, 1979; Spoons: Horace Hutchinson Souvenir (center) and other spoons with golf club motifs.*

Above: A page from the supplement to Black and White, *August 24, 1895.*

PICTORIAL
REVIEW

AUGUST·1931

TEN CENTS

MARLENE DIETRICH—IN P

An intimate close-up of the internationally popular

BY CORINNE LOWE

Gossard
Corsets and Brassieres

The Gossard Line of Beauty

No matter how loosely draped her raiment, how much fashion conceals the figure, correct carriage, proper poise, and comfort itself, demand proper corseting—Gossard corseting.

No matter what the occasion or the costume, whether gowned for social function, or an afternoon at golf, she must retain the natural line of womanhood's identity—the Gossard line—that rounds from armpit in at the waist, and then sweeps over hip downward.

No matter what her age, or the style of the moment, if a woman would be graceful, she *must* have that youth-line which Gossards give and preserve.

No matter where she lives, the modern woman will find a good store that features Gossards—an expert corsetiere, who knows at a glance how she should be fitted, what Gossard model she should wear, that the Gossard Line of Beauty, the youthful figure line, may be preserved.

The H. W. Gossard Co., Chicago, New York, San Francisco, Toronto, London, Sydney, Buenos Aires

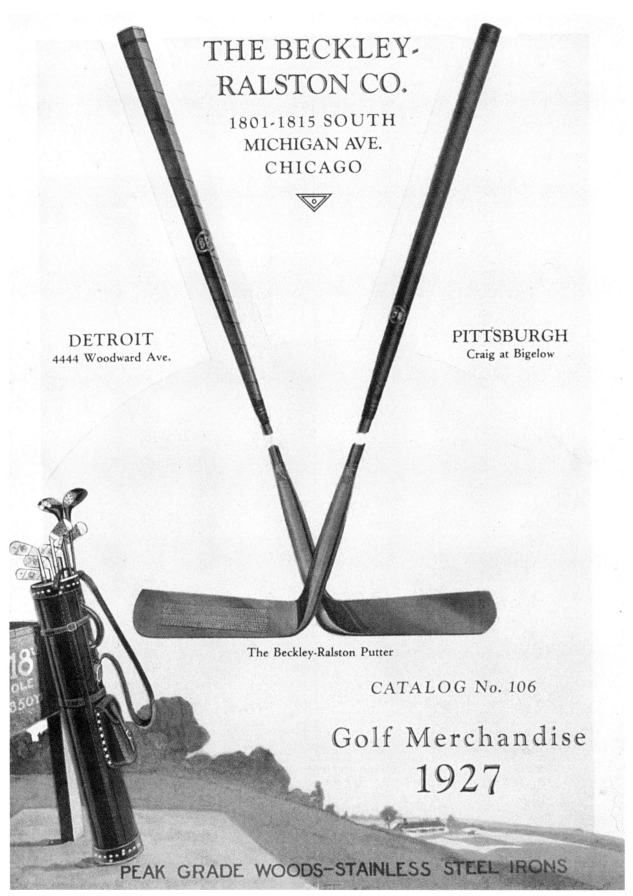

THE BECKLEY-RALSTON CO.

1801-1815 SOUTH MICHIGAN AVE. CHICAGO

DETROIT
4444 Woodward Ave.

PITTSBURGH
Craig at Bigelow

The Beckley-Ralston Putter

CATALOG No. 106

Golf Merchandise
1927

PEAK GRADE WOODS—STAINLESS STEEL IRONS

Preceeding spread, left page: Left to right, from the top: An issue of Pictorial Review, *August, 1931; Golfball teapot, cast in silver, circa 1895; Straw hat with golf club hatpins, circa 1915; Ladies golf tee carrier, circa 1925–1930; Automated score counter, circa 1925–1930; Reusable scorecard, circa 1925–1930; Cricket bag with six ladies' golf clubs, circa 1920.*

Right page: A page from The Ladies Home Journal, *May, 1924.*

Above: An advertisement for the Beckley-Ralston putter, in Golf Merchandise, *1927.*

gall for the locals as no Briton cracked 300.

British golf writer Arthur Croome of the *Morning Post* identified one source of Hagen's success:

> He makes more bad shots in a single season than Harry Vardon did during the whole period 1890–1914 during which he won six open championships. But he beats more immaculate golfers because three of "those" and one of "them" count four and he knows it.

From the moment Hagen won his first British Open his star lit up the golf sky and also cast a pretty bright glow over the entire Jazz Age. He was now "Sir Walter" or "The Haig," and he lived the role. He brought a noisy style to the golf wardrobe—alpaca sweaters, silk shirts, boisterous cravats, and argyle stockings that shouted attention for his black and white shoes for which he paid the unheard-of price of 100 dollars a pair. A handsome, five-foot ten-inch, 175 pounder, he wore his jet black hair plastered to his skull. His drink in the Prohibition era of bathtub gin remained scotch and he consumed amounts that leveled many who tried to match him.

He traveled in chauffeured limousines. He golfed with the likes of the Emperor of Japan as well as the Prince of Wales and with American royalty like John D. Rockefeller.

He occasionally hung out with Babe Ruth. They were much alike in their joie de vivre—a polite term for intensive boozing and wenching, punctuated sometimes with a stunning earthiness. Henry Clune wrote, "I'm afraid Walter was as ill-suited for the restraints and ordinances of the conjugal state as a pirate." Ruth and Hagen were known for their generosity to their pals, picking up checks, treating one and all as equals, even though frequently they could not remember names—the Babe referred to everyone as "Kid" while Hagen called them "Junior." Hagen later enunciated a philosophy that served them both: "You're only here for a short visit. Don't hurry. Don't worry. And be sure to smell the flowers along the way."

But their greatest similarity lay in their contributions to their chosen sports. Ruth was a prime mover in the resurrection of baseball following the scandal in which eight players on the 1919 Chicago White Sox were identified as part of a plot to fix the World Series. Hagen made golf fans even out of those who followed the game only in newspapers. Perhaps even more importantly, he refused to accept the social distinctions country clubs and their members applied against golf pros. Almost single-handedly he lifted the golf professional from the untouchable caste.

Gene Sarazen, who battled Hagen any number of times, recognized what The Haig had done for him and the others:

> Golf has never had a showman like him. All the professionals who have a chance to go after the big money today should say a silent thanks to Walter each time they stretch a check between their fingers.

When the modern generation of professionals gave Hagen a testimonial dinner in the late 1960s at a club in Michigan, Arnold Palmer, Hagen's clone on the course, minus the gamesman routines, said: "If it were not for you, Walter, this dinner would be downstairs in the pro shop and not in the ballroom."

From across the ocean, Henry Cotton, who played a somewhat similar role there, noted:

> . . . he released the professional from the attitude which had relegated him to a po-

The Prince of Wales presented the 1928 British Open trophy to Hagen. They golfed together several times. "He was not the pushy type and never sought an invitation. With the then–Prince of Wales tagging in Walter's footsteps, somehow he didn't have to."—Grantland Rice, The Tumult and the Shouting, 1954. (COURTESY RAY DAVIS.)

Joe Kirkwood persuaded Hagen to travel the world for exhibitions and to safari in Africa. (COURTESY RAY DAVIS.)

Hagen could hardly resist an opportunity to flirt, even if it meant climbing aboard a camel. (COURTESY RAY DAVIS.)

Joe Kirkwood and later his son, Joe, Jr., developed a show-biz turn based on trick shots. (COURTESY RAY DAVIS.)

The Haig graces the scene at Winged Foot, Mamaroneck, New York. "He was the finest short-iron player the game has ever known. He was a magnificent putter. He had courage and unquestioning faith in himself."—Gene Sarazen, Thirty Years of Championship Golf, *1950.* (COURTESY THE BETTMANN ARCHIVE.)

sition "below the salt" in the golfing hierarchy. His bland indifference to what people expected of a professional's subservience to the members (amateurs)* of golf clubs, his ability . . . to combine in his greatest years an extremely social life with phenomenal playing when he most needed it, and his whole lifestyle, which presupposed that "Sir" Walter was the object of adulation even in the presence of his friend the Prince of Wales, seemed to bring a fresh current of air through the stuffier corridors of the game.

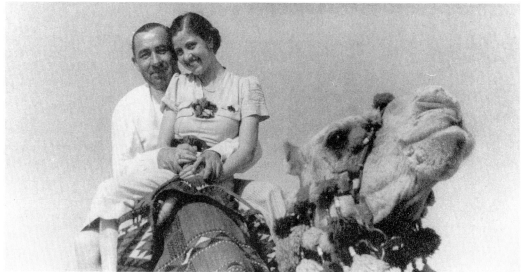

---

*As late as the 1970s, some British authors listing entries and results for Open tournaments applied the honorific "Mr." to amateurs, while denying it to the professionals.

(Left) "I'm going to miss at least seven shots in every eighteen holes so if I'm going to be angry, I might as well start right on the first tee." —Walter Hagen. (COURTESY RAY DAVIS.)

(Right) "During the last three holes of the 1919 U.S. Open, which The Haig won for the second time, he smiled at a pretty girl on the sixteenth tee, struck up a conversation with her on the seventeenth fairway, and made a date with her as he walked off the eighteenth green. After The Haig, nobody would take golf too seriously." —Charles Price. (COURTESY RAY DAVIS.)

"There has never been anybody with Hagen's ability to rise to the most tremendous situation; to produce according to the difficulty of production; to meet the toughest problem with the coolest head, the steadiest nerves and the most masterful shots. Neither golf nor any other sport has produced a champion with so invincible a reserve of nerve, gameness and sheer cold determination as Sir Walter. He was the greatest competitive athlete I have ever encountered. And one other thing. Walter never forgot for one instant what he owed the public. I have seen many a lesser champion become snobbish in the moment of opulence and glory, but never the old Haig. Winning or losing, he was just the Old Haig himself." —O. B. Keeler, The Bobby Jones Story.

No longer a threat to the new crop of professionals, Hagen performed in a 1939 exhibition with Johnny Farrell, 1928 U.S. Open winner, and two outstanding women players, Glenna Collett Vare (hat) and Marion Hollins. (COURTESY RAY DAVIS.)

9

Ladies on the Links

An entry in the complaints register for England's Worcestershire Golf Club in 1881 said: "I noticed a lady in the clubhouse at the weekend. I urge the Secretary to see that this does not happen again." And, though men and boys certainly dominated the public notice of competitive golf at the time of Ouimet's deed, women had been digging divots for almost as long as the males. In 1867, following the line that perhaps began with Mary, Queen of Scots, a group formed within the sacred precincts of the Royal and Ancient, calling themselves the St. Andrews Ladies Club. The *St. Andrews Gazette* took notice of their achievement a few years later:

> Its remarkable success has led to the introduction and culture of golf as a female recreation in England and elsewhere. . . . Of course the wielding of the club assumes a mild form under the sway of the gentler sex and has never as yet extended beyond the simple stroke of the putting green.

One of the first historians on women's golf, and herself a prominent player, Issette Pearson wrote *Our Lady of the Green* in 1899. She backed the *Gazette* statement that the 500 or so distaff members restricted themselves to the putter. In addition, her research indicated women created their own organizations at Westward Ho!, Musselburgh, Carnoustie, Troon, and other well-known early hives of golf.

As soon as 1890, a bare two years after Jock Reid and company permanently planted the seeds of golf in the States, "Albion," writing in *Outing*, made the case for women in the sport. He paid tribute to archery and croquet, "the pioneers that made a breach in the walls which that awful per-

sonage Mrs. Grundy had raised up to separate the sexes in outdoor sports," and credited tennis as stimulating new interest in outdoor games for "our girls." Noting that "Baseball, cricket, and even football, have been tried by the fair sex, but never can become popular with womenly women," Albion believed that the slowness of croquet and archery and the other extreme of hard-fought tennis battles could yield to "a splendid medium . . . in the grand old game of golf." Within a couple of years, Florence Boit had begun setting flowerpots in the Wellesley Lawns as a female Johnny Appleseed of golf. By 1893, a course "for women only" had surfaced in Morris County, New Jersey.

Their game was a milder copy of the more furious efforts of men. Lord Wellwood in 1890 placed a limit of 70 or 80 yards to drives by women:

> . . . not because we doubt a lady's power to make a longer drive, but because that cannot well be done without raising the club above the shoulder. Now we do not presume to dictate, but we must observe that the posture and gestures requisite for full swing are not particularly graceful when the player is clad in female dress.

In the United Kingdom, by 1893, Issette Pearson, then a member of a Wimbledon club, spearheaded a movement that resulted in the Ladies' Golf Union. The first eighteen-hole championship was held over the short, 2,132-yard course at Lytham. The longest hole measured only 337 yards. The distances may seem slight, but the wonder is they could swing a club at all. The prescribed uniform of the day called for blouses with high-necked, well-starched collars and ties, military-style jackets, long tweed skirts covering layers of petticoats, and heavy leather boots. A stiff boater-type

9 2

Beatrix Hoyt lines up a putt in 1898. Following her three straight wins in 1896–1898, she abandoned competition with no more worlds to conquer. (COURTESY RAY DAVIS.)

hat or even a great bonnet topped off the outfit. On windy days, women were expected to don a binding, elasticized garment beneath the skirt to prevent petticoats flying up and an unseemly display of ankles.

There were thirty-eight entries at Lytham. Lady Margaret Scott, who had learned the game playing with her father and brothers on a course laid out on the family estate, lifted the club above her shoulder and, despite her garments, whipped Pearson 7 and 5. The pair met again the following year in the finals of what became known as the British Ladies' Championship, with Scott again the victor, as she was also in 1895. Having won three consecutive championships, Lady Margaret quit competitive golf.

Horace Hutchinson observed her on the links and declared: "I had never seen a lady able to play golf at all as Lady Margaret played the game. She had all the crisp and well-cut approach strokes at her command."

In the same year that Scott captured her third title, American women organized their first championship, contested at Meadow Brook, Long Island. The Americans chose medal play for their first championship and the winner, Mrs. Charles S. Brown, managed to beat all comers with a tidy 132

for eighteen holes. She received a silver pitcher to mark her effort. The level of play might be gauged from a contemporary account: "Mrs. Brown did not start off with very good prospects as she took 11 strokes to make the first hole. The second she made in 4 and the third in 9."

The competition achieved a note of respectability the following year when the USGA assumed responsibility for regulating the championship. A writer at the time suggested the USGA became convinced women were part of golf after Robert Cox, an Edinburgh member of Parliament contributed a handsome trophy.

At the turn of the century, women introduced subtle changes that enabled them to score respectably. Skirts were shortened to above the ankle; blouses lost some of their frills and starch; it was no longer *de rigueur* to balance a bulky hat on the head while swinging a club, although coiffeurs remained covered.

Few women, around the turn of the century, could join golf clubs on their own; membership was through a male member of the family. And, in a tradition that continues in some parts of the U.S. today, men enjoyed other advantages. For example, the Chicago Golf Club rules declared:

Harriot Curtis became U.S. female champion in 1906. (COURTESY RAY DAVIS.)

Margaret Curtis, sister of Harriot, surpassed her sister with amateur titles in 1907, '11 and '12. (COURTESY RAY DAVIS.)

Thursday, women [had] preference in securing caddies; Monday, Tuesday, Wednesday, Friday and Saturday mornings they [had] equal privileges with men. On Saturday afternoons [the work week for men at the time often included that day's a.m. hours], Sundays and holidays women [had] no standing on the regular course, [could not] be furnished with caddies and [had to] give way to all matches.

Still, America fielded a formidable champion. Beatrix Hoyt in 1896 at age sixteen began a string of three straight titles as U.S. Ladies' Champion. She had been tutored by Willie Dunn at Shinnecock and it was her precision with the irons that provided her margin over other women, many of whom frequently outdrove her. Hoyt stroked well enough to score occasionally in the 80s, although her medal scores in the three championships never fell below 92. Defeated in match play during her 1899 title defense, Hoyt retired from tournament combat. Indeed, competitive women's golf in the early days suffered from rapid turnover, as that era did not encourage a career as an amateur golfer and of course there were no professionals.

There were signs, however, that women were beginning to attack the game with a high seriousness. A Halifax, Nova Scotia, minister, the Rev. W. J. Ancient, in 1903, scolded his parishioners from the pulpit, denouncing women who came to church appearing humble and sincere on Sunday but on Monday, out on the links, not only smoked but "swore like troopers." A group of women golfers forthwith demanded an apology, but the Rev. Ancient refused to retract his aspersions.

A pair of sisters, Harriot and Margaret Curtis, between them won four U.S. Ladies' Championships from 1906 to 1912. They were among the first, in 1905, to attempt a repeat of the American victory of Walter Travis over the best of the British. The expedition failed and the defenders became the conquering attackers a few years later as Dorothy Campbell, the tall and plump 1909 British Ladies' titleholder, scored a double with the American honor that same year and returned in 1910 to

successfully defend her championship. She added to her North American conquests with the Canadian Ladies' Open championships in 1910, '11, and '12. And after marriage to J. V. Hurd in 1924, Campbell at age forty-one invaded the States for a stunning win in the national championship.

World War I halted British women's golf as effectively as it shut down play by the men. In the United States, golf continued until the country entered the fray and all national competition went on hold for 1917 through 1918.

The British women's heroine, immediately upon the resumption of competitive golf, was Cecil Leitch. There was nothing dainty about her approach to the game; she took a wide stance and a hefty swing, banging out balls more in the fashion of men. Leitch had crowned herself best of the women in 1914 and in the decade after the Armistice notched titles in 1920, '21, and '26. British star (Ladies Golf Union champion 1931–33) and writer Enid Wilson acclaimed:

> Miss Leitch was the first of the Amazons. Her swing was graceful, but more powerful than had hitherto been seen in women's events. In particular, her crisp shots with the iron clubs set a new standard for her sex.

In the United States, the most formidable woman player was a childhood friend of Bobby Jones, the willowy Alexa Stirling. She, too, had learned the game from a silent, Scotland-bred pro, Stewart Maiden, at the East Lake Country Club. Stirling and Jones played golf together as children and as young adults. Three times she held the American championship and was also runner-up thrice.

As the Roaring Twenties began, women golfers no longer suffered from the handicap of tightly restrictive clothing. Skirts now ended a couple of inches below the knee, and comfortable, loose blouses and jackets allowed the upper body freedom of movement. Most of the players still wore hats, but these were small, light, and hugged the head.

The tiny competitive circuit became a

battle ground for a pair of titans representing Great Britain and the United States. First on the golf scene was Joyce Wethered,★ who, in 1922 at age twenty-one, won the first of her four British championships, besting Cecil Leitch, who the year before overcame Wethered in the finals. After Bobby Jones played a round with Wethered at St. Andrews, he said with a mix of gallantry and tribute:

I have not played golf with anyone, man or woman, amateur or professional who made me feel so utterly outclassed.

It was not so much the score she made as the way she made it. [Leo] Diegel, Hagen, [Macdonald] Smith, [George] Von Elm and several other male experts would likely have made a better score, but one would all the while have been expecting them to miss shots. It was impossible to expect that Miss Wethered would ever miss a shot—and she never did.

Enid Wilson compared Wethered with the previous best female Briton: "Miss Leitch brought power into women's golf; Miss Wethered brought power combined with perfection of style and a hitherto unknown degree of accuracy."

There were those who argued that, at her best, Wethered could have played in the number four or five slots on the British Walker Cup teams. Henry Cotton wrote:

In my time, no golfer has stood out so far ahead of his or her contemporaries as Lady Heathcoat-Amory [Wethered's married name] . . . I do not think a golf ball has ever been hit, except perhaps by Harry Vardon, with such a straight flight by any other person. . . . Curiously, both she and the great Harry seemed to allow the shot to drift slightly to the right when it could not be described as dead straight.

A more succinct appraisal came from Scottish pro Willie Wilson: "Good swing? My god, mon! She could hit a ball 240 yards on the fly while standing barefoot on a cake of ice."

According to Cotton she was superb at the shot-saving, pitch-and-run. "It was these low-flying shots, played with a mashie more often than not, which intrigued me. They were played with such a beautiful touch, and had been well calculated before hand. They were not just guesswork."

Having carried off the palm for three British championships between 1922 and

Dorothy Campbell took a pair of crowns, 1909–1910. (COURTESY THE BETTMANN ARCHIVE.)

Dorothy Campbell Hurd, having added a husband and some poundage, came back to victory in 1924. (COURTESY RAY DAVIS.)

1925, and with a trunk full of other titles and golf honors, at age twenty-four Wethered temporarily stowed away her competitive clubs.

Her American counterpart, two years younger, was Glenna Collett Vare.★ She began to build her reputation with her first U.S. Ladies' title the same year of 1922 and over more than a decade tucked away that same championship a record five times.

A native of Providence, Rhode Island, she was behind the wheel of an automobile at the advanced age of ten and her interest in the more active sports made Collett, in the language of the twenties, a "tomboy." Baseball was her first passion and she was good enough to star on her brother Ned's team. The horrified adults first tried to steer her towards the more respectable tennis, at which she became quite proficient. But at age fourteen, her father carted her along over the Metacomet Golf Club links. Intrigued by the game, Glenna begged for a chance to hit a ball and, given her chance, smacked it far down the fairway. That led to more strokes, most of which fell well below the level of that first effort, but the adolescent was addicted.

Her father, an enthusiastic sportsman, indulged his daughter with proper lessons and equipment. In her first summer of play she chopped 20 strokes off her initial rounds to even out at about 130, a large reduction but hardly the stuff of tournament golf. One afternoon, she watched a Red Cross benefit that featured a mixed foursome match with Alexa Stirling and Elaine Rosenthal as the female members and the boy wonder Bobby Jones, only one year Collett's senior, and Perry Adair, another adolescent prodigy from Atlanta. Rosenthal set a woman's course record that day with an 80 and the brilliant iron work of Stirling was equally impressive. Collett returned home inspired and on her very next nine holes she banged out a 49.

Twice a week she took lessons from the good-humored Alex Smith and, to ensure a layoff did not stale her skills, the Collett family traveled south in the winter to where Smith was in residence at a country club. Smith's major contributions to her art were

a compact putting stroke and a reduction in her backswing with irons. Undoubtedly he tutored her on the woods, the brassie and spoon on the fairway and her driver, although she had from the first moment at Metacomet shown an innate talent getting off the tee. Like so many young golf phenoms, Bob Jones certainly included, Glenna could be brilliant one round and then spray balls all over the countryside like any duffer.

Just as her play climbed several notches overnight after watching Stirling and Rosenthal, so too did Collett's tournament fortunes zoom sharply after a resounding defeat. Beaten in the opening round of the national championship by Cecil Leitch's sister Edith, a gloomy Collett followed the minute women's circuit (strictly amateur, of course) to the Berthellyn Cup tournament at the Huntingdon Valley Country Club near Philadelphia. For the first round, she drew the awesome Cecil herself. Collett conceded defeat inwardly but determined at least to put on a respectable show. Instead of striking out for winning holes, she plotted a strategy of playing within herself, in effect trying only to halve holes rather than gain a lead. And indeed the pair stroked along dead even for the most part until they arrived at eighteen with Collett, to her astonishment, 1 up. All she needed to beat the Englishwoman was one more half. She took it, knocking in a 10-foot putt.

That single win stoked her confidence. An emboldened Collett loosened up and boomed out her shots, assured of the results. She went on to win the Berthellyn Cup, and those who followed the fortunes of female golfers immediately tagged her as the one to beat. And she did not betray the faithful, running off with the North and South and then the Eastern. It looked as if her closest competition would need a 3-stroke handicap to compete with Collett. So superior did she become that in 1924 she won fifty-nine of her sixty matches.

Whatever her accomplishments as a player, Collett may have contributed even more to the sport by making it attractive to women. World War I had destroyed some

A childhood pal of Bobby Jones and, like him, a pupil of Stewart Maiden in Atlanta, Alexa Sterling toured with Jones on behalf of the Red Cross during World War I. She also notched three amateur championships, 1916, 1919, and 1920. (COURTESY RAY DAVIS.)

of the taboos on female behavior; the 19th amendment to the U.S. Constitution, ratified in 1920, awarded the vote to women. The segment of the generation to spawn flappers, consumers of bathtub gin and speakeasy hooch, and challengers to conventional mores came from affluence—the sophisticated inhabitants of cities, resorts, and golf clubs. Collett, physically attractive and exhibiting what were then the prized feminine attributes of graciousness and good humor, became a role model for the active but virtuous woman. Golf for women not only achieved respectability but was now also the popular pastime for those who could afford the investment in equipment, lessons, and club membership.

With Collett as the idol of America and Joyce Wethered the doyenne of British golf, it was inevitable that the twain should compete. There were two memorable confrontations.

In 1925, Collett embarked on a European campaign. Victorious in the French Championship, she now entered the lists for the British Ladies' Championship at Troon. In the third round of play, Collett came up against Wethered. The Briton recalled:

. . . the match anticipated between her and myself was worked up to such a pitch beforehand that, when the day came, one of two things was almost bound to happen. Either we should rise to the occasion or one of us would fall under the strain of it.

For the first nine holes, the prediction of the pair meeting great expectations was fulfilled. After eight holes they were dead even with both women having enjoyed 1-up status briefly. On the ninth tee, it was the American who slipped, topping her drive and enabling the defending champion to turn for home with a lead that increased to 2 after Collett misplayed another shot.

On the eleventh hole, Wethered, to the amazement of onlookers, bolstered her reputation as impervious to all distraction. The *Times* of London noted: "Miss Wethered holed a long curly putt for a three, characteristically enough with an engine snorting on the line behind her."

Actually, she noticed the train quite clearly:

It was puffing smoke in clouds behind the green in a way that could not very well be

"Lady Heathcoat-Amory, in the days when she was Joyce Wethered, was a great golfer, for she hit the ball as far as the average scratch player, and with feminine grace. . . . Lady Heathcoat-Amory hit the ball a long way from the tee, could play a spoon or brassie from the fairway as straight as most professionals could play a short iron shot, and her chipping and putting were beautiful to watch."
—Henry Cotton, Country Life, *1948.*
(COURTESY THE BETTMANN ARCHIVE.)

Known for her acute accuracy, Joyce Wethered plays one of her rare bunker shots. (COURTESY UPI/ BETTMANN NEWSPHOTOS.)

Joyce Wethered relaxing over a round with her soon-to-be spouse, Captain John Heathcoat-Amory. (COURTESY THE BETTMANN ARCHIVE.)

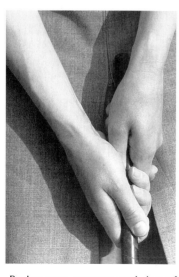

By her own account and that of those who witnessed her on the course, the grip Wethered exerted on her mind meant far more than how she held a club. (COURTESY THE BETTMANN ARCHIVE.)

ignored. However, I was too well acquainted with the ways of a Scotch engine driver not to know that he was determined to wait to see the hole played to a finish before he continued with his goods to Ayr. Knowing this, there was little to be gained by my waiting. Besides, it was just possible that a train was not an unlucky portent. Whatever may be the truth of the supposition the putt made me 3 up and almost decided, I think, the result of the game.

Indeed, the match ended 4 and 3 after the fifteenth hole. Collett had played excellent golf, being only 1 over par on a windy day. But Wethered had 4 birdies and not even par golf could compete against such scoring.

While Wethered limited her golf, Collett returned to England in 1927 for another crack at the United Kingdom championship but was ousted in the fourth round. The tournament is notable as the first in which a foreigner, Frenchwoman Simone de la Chaume, usurped the line of British queens.

Two years later, Collett came back for her third assault. The drama surpassed that of 1925 as she met Wethered in the finals at St. Andrews. Naturally, the press and the fans blathered about the international bragging honors at stake, particularly as the home favorite had come out of semi-retirement to play. Wethered dismissed the talk as pure bosh.

It has often been attributed to me that I entered for this event in a purely patriotic spirit, with the expressed intention of preventing any of the American invaders from winning our championship. I must really protest against this rather pretentious statement. The fact that Glenna Collett and I actually met in the final lent some color to the rumor, but I feel I should never be justified in entering for the sole purpose of hoping to prevent some other particular player from winning. A championship in my opinion is an event originally instituted solely for private enterprise and for the best player to win and it seems to me a pity that it need necessarily be converted into an international match on a larger scale.

What gave some credence to the notion of Wethered as the country's paladin was her emergence from the sheltered life of a titled woman to the hurly-burly of a tournament with an international cast. But to Wethered her return meant she could relax.

. . . I was able to enter after an interval with much less expected of me than usual. There could be no justification for such remarks as, "Of course you will do well," which in a game like golf spell ruin if they are believed for one moment. I was prepared for anything or everything to happen, however disastrous or extraordinary. It created an enchanting sense of freedom to feel that the well-meaning friends who come up after a bad shot and say, "That really wasn't like you!" would not this time allow themselves to be so easily shocked.

At St. Andrews I did not . . . feel I needed be weighed down by any responsibilities that might be thrust upon me. I was no longer a regular player in competitions. The moment had merely arrived when I could take part in an event to which I had looked forward for years.

In fact, her relaxed attitude seemed to have afflicted the guardians of the tournament. During her first round match the gallery washed over the fairways.

Eventually flag-wavers appeared and shooed the spectators away. Wethered played only well enough to beat her foes but not to her satisfaction. Collett's route was similar—good, rather than spectacular golf brought her to a repeat match against the Briton.

This time the American's game caught fire. Collett covered the first nine holes of the match in 34 and her opponent called it, "the finest sequence of holes I have ever seen a lady play." That string buried Wethered, for when the pair walked off the ninth green she was down a massive 5. When they turned for home, matters failed to improve as they halved 10 and 11.

In spite of Wethered's protests, the locals were taking her defeat very hard. Supposedly, in the midst of the match, the streets of the town were all but deserted. The only humans visible were a postman forced to perform his duties and a solitary visitor, oblivious to golf and intent only upon photographing a cathedral. As the stranger passed the mailman he heard an agonized mutter, "She's 5 doon!"

On the twelfth hole, both women reached the green in 2. Wethered then stubbed her first putt, leaving her woefully short. She missed again and only got down in 5. If Collett could can the second putt, somewhere between 3 and 4 feet, she would go 6 up, for a near-insurmountable lead. She stroked smoothly and the ball spun towards the cup, only to trickle to one side. The lead stayed at 5.

"There is almost always a quick reaction when an important chance is missed," remembered Wethered. "Nothing can be so heartening to the player who is behind, and the mistake encourages a feeling of strain and uncertainty in the leader."

Given a reprieve, Wethered promptly began to press Collett. On the thirteenth hole, Wethered dropped a 12-foot putt and picked up one of her deficit. Collett's pace slackened slightly and, when they ended the first eighteen holes, the margin between the pair was reduced to two holes.

The two women seemed to reverse roles now. Wethered now had the hot sticks. After they completed the first nine holes of the afternoon, she (astonishingly) stood 4 up, a reversal of an unthinkable 9 from where she had been at the same point during the morning round. She recalled:

One might imagine from the psychology of the game that the excitement of the match was probably over, and that all would end quietly on a green four or five holes from home. From any likelihood of such a peaceful ending I was rudely awakened by Glenna doing the next two holes in three apiece and winning them abruptly.

Now the Englishwoman felt the pressure. She recalled how some years before she had thrown away a similar lead in a match at Troon. Although she won a subsequent hole she also dropped another one and they came to the fifteenth with her lead still a bare two. Collett dropped her third shot within 7 or 8 feet of the hole while her opponent lay more than twice that distance away. To Wethered it appeared likely her lead would be cut in half. She struck the ball "rather hard as the putt was uphill; and then the hole gobbled it up." She had managed to tie Glenna and retained her slim margin. And after they halved 16, the Briton was dormy* two. When Collett got in trouble on the seventeenth, the match ended; Joyce Wethered again was the British champion.

Oddly enough, Wethered never made a bid for the U.S. title. Her countrywoman, Dorothy Campbell Hurd, had been the first woman to be champion of both countries and, not until after World War II, in 1947, would an American female successfully invade the United Kingdom.

The rivalry of Wethered and Collett was renewed with the Curtis Cup. In 1930, Glenna Collett captained a squad of American women who crossed the Atlantic to meet a British team. The matches had no official sanction but both the USGA and the British Ladies' Golf Union were intrigued by the idea. The agreement to supervise such competition received a tremendous boost when the golfing sisters, Margaret and Harriot Curtis, donated a trophy inscribed: "To stimulate friendly rivalry between the women golfers of many lands."

As it turned out there were only two takers, the British and the Americans. But the Curtis Cup wrought a renewal of the battles between Collett and Wethered. When the first teams collided at Wentworth, England, the meeting of Lady Joyce Heathcoat-Amory and now Glenna Collett Vare was inevitable. And the results were the same; the American was whipped 6 and 4. However, the overall quality of the

Glenna Collett strides down a fairway alongside defending champion, Mlle. Simone de la Chaume of France, during the British Ladies Amateur at Hunstanton in 1928. The French woman won her own country's championship six times along with a flock of other tournaments. She married the best-known French tennis player of the times, Rene Lacoste. (COURTESY ACME NEWSPICTURES.)

---

* Sometimes spelled "dormie," the term means a player is as many holes up as there are holes to play. It comes from the Latin *dormire*—to sleep—via the French *endormi*. Incidentally, one is always "dormy up" and never "dormy down."

American play was superior and the visitors walked off with the first Curtis Cup. With competition scheduled every two years, the U.S. retained the Cup in 1934 at the American Venue of the Chevy Chase Country Club, tied at Gleneagles, Scotland, in 1936, and won again at Manchester, Massachusetts, in 1938 before World War II brought a ten-year hiatus.

"The female Bobby Jones," Collett defended her U.S. Amateur title in 1929 at Oakland Hills. Altogether, she amassed six of these crowns along with doubles in the Canadian Amateur and the French Amateur. (COURTESY PGA.)

Glenna Collett tees off at the Greenwich Country Club, Greenwich, Connecticut, while her husband-to-be, Edwin H. Vare, Jr., keeps his eye on the ball. (COURTESY RAY DAVIS.)

10

The Golf Boom

By 1916, golf was a game dominated by players who demeaned anyone attempting to make a living at it, thus, stirring increased dissatisfaction among the working stiffs. So zealous were the partisans of the pure amateur that the USGA even removed the peerless Francis Ouimet from the ranks of the nonprofessionals because he founded a sporting goods company. Subsequently, wiser heads prevailed and Ouimet was reinstated after he entered the army. The USGA responded more to patriotic fervor than the hail of criticism, including some from Walter Travis who had been judged a pro because he engaged in golf course architecture.

The true working pro suffered more than the snubs that barred him from the clubhouses. He was expected to play with members for nothing—time spent that might have earned income for him through giving lessons or repairing equipment. The clubs reserved for themselves the income from the sale of balls and clubs, while the professional worked for a pittance.

In 1916, professionals in the U.S. came together to form the Professional Golfers' Association of America. This was fifteen years after the founding of its British counterpart. (J. H. Taylor served as first chairman of the London association and James Braid was named first captain.)

The PGA in the U.S. was formed to aid its members, and while the headlines belonged to a few people like Hagen and Jim Barnes, the foundation of the organization then, as now, were the teaching pros, most of whom even then worked at country clubs and never teed off in a major tournament. The PGA was expected to represent its members, to help them perform better, to increase their sources of revenue, and also to act as an authority to

govern and sponsor tournaments for professionals.

Among the early features of the PGA was its own monthly publication, *The Professional Golfer of America.* In its pages, the pro received information on course maintenance (many pros then doubled as greenskeepers) tips on teaching techniques, discussions on golf clubs and balls, ways to display pro shop merchandise, reports on tournaments. More dubious was the advice in the late 1920s to jump into the surging stock market. While it was not a union suited to bargain on wages and hours, the PGA could and did lobby for manufacturers to distribute pro-shop-only items.

Even as it developed these programs, the American PGA created immediate attention with its own tournament, held at the Siwanoy Country Club in Mount Vernon, New York. Welcome support came from Rodman Wanamaker, the Philadelphia department store scion with a vested interest in the promotion and sale of golf equipment, who donated a cup. Long Jim Barnes, an émigré from Cornwall, finished first, 1 up on Jock Hutchison, a Scotland-born pro and naturalized American. The victor also pocketed 500 dollars from the total purse of 2,580 dollars and received a diamond-encrusted medal. It is a measure of the times that newspapers gave equal coverage to the pro-am tournament before the actual PGA event.

With the entrance of the U.S. into the Great War, the PGA tournaments for 1917 and 1918 were cancelled, but the organization, along with the Western Golf Association and the USGA, put on many exhibitions designed for war relief.

When the PGA resumed its contest in 1919, Barnes repeated his victory. A six-

Long Jim Barnes chewed on a flower, but the lanky émigré from Cornwall carried off the honors in the very first PGA championship in 1916. The tournament was cancelled by World War I in 1917–1918, but when revived in 1919 Barnes repeated. (COURTESY RAY DAVIS.)

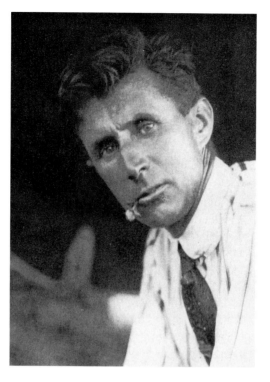

foot four-inch native of Leland, England, professional at age fifteen, Barnes immigrated to the U.S. in 1906 when he was nineteen. He was among the few to win both the U.S. Open (1921) and British Open (1925). Barnes's victory in the American championship was one of the more lopsided; he beat out Hagen by 9 strokes. Furthermore, it was the first U.S. Open ever followed by the nation's chief executive —President Warren G. Harding, accompanied by Vice-President Calvin Coolidge, observed the final round and handed Barnes his cup.

By 1921, Sir Walter was fully asserting himself in the PGA's championship. The tournaments were match play (until 1957) and that sort of contest fitted Hagen even better than his plus 4s and cardigan sweaters. One on one meant the occasional bad shot cost him only a single hole rather than boosting his total score, and he could focus his psychological warfare on the opponent of the moment.

Over the space of 1921 through 1927, Hagen captured the Wanamaker Cup five times. He won it so often, he treated it as carelessly as if it were one of his own possessions. After winning at Olympic Fields in Illinois in 1925, Hagen returned to New York. Hagen handed the cup to a cab driver and instructed him to deliver the trophy to his hotel. The cup never arrived.

When Hagen carried off the PGA honors in 1926 and 1927, no one noticed the absence of the Wanamaker award; certainly not Hagen. When he finally lost in 1928, the authorities sought to present the cup to Leo Diegel. Hagen confessed he had no idea of its whereabouts. Since it had been missing for three years and Hagen of course could not produce a receipt from the taxi driver the insurance company declined to pay. The PGA bought a new cup for its winners. But in 1930, a porter cleaning the cellar of the Detroit company that manufactured clubs bearing Hagen's imprint found a locked, unmarked case. In it lay the missing Wanamaker Cup.

The PGA tournament drew the biggest names in golf and contributed to the popularity of the game in America, but there were other individuals and forces at work that helped boost golf. Certainly, golf benefitted when a string of U.S. chief executives spent afternoons out on the course. The first president to become associated with golf was William Howard Taft, who heaved his near 300 pounds around the course, and declared: ". . . golf is in the interest of good health and good manners. It promotes self-restraint and, as one of its devotees has well said, affords the chance to play the man and act the gentleman." Political cartoons frequently resorted to golf metaphors to make their points, a technique repeated more than forty years later when Dwight Eisenhower occupied the White House.

A Washington sportswriter, Maury Fitzgerald, caddied and watched a number of the American presidents play. Fitzgerald remembered Taft on the course after he left the White House and was named to the U.S. Supreme Court.

Chief Justice Taft was a big, fat man, as everybody knows. But he was not the jolly caricature of a fat man that's so popular. He was all concentration when he played and seldom spoke to his caddie. He also had another peculiarity. He never played in anything but striped trousers and I always had the feeling that he was on his way to sit in on a case and had sneaked a few minutes of golf.

Fitzgerald recalled Woodrow Wilson as "dour and uncommunicative." Wilson used a cloth bag (a "Sunday bag" in the parlance of the day) with only five clubs and played in his regular street shoes.

The favorite of the caddies came on the heels of Wilson. Warren G. Harding, whom Fitzgerald knew as a U.S. Senator, was definitely from the "good ol' boy" strain. Said Fitzgerald:

> He was the most pleasant man I ever met—always telling jokes. And once he knew you, he never forgot your name. We used to get sixty cents for eighteen holes but Harding always gave two dollars. And he was the best golfer of the three presidents.

Historians regard Harding as a president who preferred a good time to the onerous duties of his office. But at least he had the good sense to accompany himself on the course with two of the foremost literary proponents of golf, Granny Rice and Ring Lardner.

In the 1921 U.S. Open, Barnes walloped Walter Hagen by 9 strokes and his victory in the 1925 British Open made him among the first to have triumphed on both sides of the Atlantic. (COURTESY RAY DAVIS.)

Barnes accepts the emblem of his victory in the British Open. (COURTESY RAY DAVIS.)

Fitzgerald had no comments on the golf style of the tight-lipped Calvin Coolidge, but the parsimonious Coolidge was known to carry on prolonged hunts for lost balls.

Presidents on the links gave prestige to golf, even as some in government continued to equate it with the work of the devil. The Federal Director of Prohibition Enforcement in Minnesota denounced the sport, which he claimed:

> ... encourages idleness, shiftlessness, and neglect of business as well as family responsibilities ... deprives many wives of their husbands and children of their fathers ... tempts hundreds of young men into extravagance that sometimes leads to crime.

Such bluenoses were swept aside. Charles Merz in *The Great American Bandwagon* equated golf with a new frontier for the bored, frontierless world, one in which plus 4s replaced the cowboys' leather chaps and the argyles fancied by Walter Hagen served as "the warpaint of a nation." Just as show biz signed up baseball players of the day for turns on the stage and before the cameras, golf invaded the performing arts. A play called *Follow Through* had a golf motif and, in one silent movie, the hero conquered the girl by knocking a brassie shot into the cup on the final hole. Tin Pan Alley tunesmiths incorporated the language of golf into their ditties, though with minimal success.

Golf prospered through the evolution of the U.S. economy. The work day and week were slowly shrinking, allowing more leisure time. One of the greatest obstacles to the spread of the game, travel to the country club or course, yielded to the incredible growth of the automobile.

Henry Ford introduced his Model T in 1908 but it was six years later that he innovated the assembly line that cut the cost of cars to prices within the reach of a mass market. Half a million Americans bought "tin lizzies" in 1916; after a brief hiatus because of the war, the total reached 2 million in 1923 with a price below 300 dollars by 1925. When Ford switched to his Model A in 1927, the company could count a total of 15 million Fords since the first of the flivvers. To these figures must be added the millions produced by other manufacturers.

The effect upon golf is easily grasped from a description of plucky golfers headed for St. Andrew's before the advent of the automobile. Members had their choice of trolley cars or trains to the Chauncey railroad station, which still left them a long, uphill hike. Usually, they rendezvoused with the St. Andrew's four-horse stage coach or its horse-drawn bus. As trains neared Chauncey, golfers queued up by the exits, hoping to be among the first hauled to the

"Edward Ray of England, is open golf champion of the United States because he stood the gaff best—he finished first of the half dozen leaders because he cracked least under the terrific strain of the bitterest finish ever witnessed.... Somewhere in his huge system the big oxeyman carried the ultimate ounce that supplied the final punch— the single stroke by which he led Harry Vardon, his partner in the quest...."—O. B. Keeler, Atlanta Journal, *August 15, 1920.*

Ted Ray, loser in the great play-off with Francis Ouimet, extracted some revenge with his stunning win in the 1920 U.S. Open. (COURTESY RAY DAVIS.)

clubhouse. Frequently, the more youthful members jumped off several hundred yards from the peak of the climb in consideration of the straining beasts pulling the coach or bus.

Consider the saga of Francis Ouimet's three streetcars plus a long trek to reach the public course in Boston a few years later. Even in 1914, Walter Hagen rode a smelly, cinder-belching train from Chicago to the Midlothian Club. Within a half dozen years the automobile bore Sir Walter to the jousts. True, instead of a Model T, he preferred the likes of a hired Rolls or Austin-Daimler when abroad and at home such motor car classics as a Chalmers, a front-wheel drive Cord, a Stephens-Duryea, a Chandler painted with orange and black checks, a red Lozier, a Pierce-Arrow and the more prosaic Cadillac, all of which he equipped with a chauffeur.

Arthur Sweet, golf editor of the *Chicago Daily News,* in 1930, whose very job bespeaks the growth of the game, pointed to the growth over a twenty-year period from 40 to 208 courses catering to the Chicago area. Some of the spreads lay fifty miles from the Loop. Sweet noted that where once a country club was always situated adjacent to the railroad line the automobile had freed golf courses from that limitation. By the 1920s, golfers on winter vacations already were motoring south, pausing to sample fairways and greens enroute.

The 1920s introduced big, fast money to the United States and the sports world. The so-called "Golden Age of Sports" dawned with Babe Ruth and the rise of the New York Yankees. Harold "Red" Grange packed 80,000 people into stadiums to see his Illinois football team and almost single-handedly Grange brought enough customers through the turnstiles for the newly born National Football League to survive. Bill Tilden and Helen Wills Moody gave American tennis international cachet. In the boxing ring, Jack Dempsey and then Gene Tunney started the million-dollar gates.

According to an editorial in *The Professional Golfer of America,* it was an item about a boxer, early in the decade, that pushed professional golf into the big money. The story told of Battling Siki, a Senegalese fighter given to wearing a silk hat, collecting 50,000 dollars for a series of exhibitions in the U.S. The figure impressed Jack O'Brien, sports editor of the *San Antonio News.* A few years later, O'Brien recalled:

... if he could draw down that much money, then it was high time to make a worthwhile purse for men who had spent their lives perfecting themselves in the game of golf.

At that time, the first prize for the national open was approximately $500 [the PGA itself did offer a slighly more substantial reward] and there were no winter prize tournaments. It took me nearly a year to sell the idea of a $5,000 purse to the merchants of San Antonio.

O'Brien organized and conducted the first Texas Open in 1922. He publicized it as the "gladsome giggle" and advertised:

The prizes won't be cups, they're useless nowadays, but will be those silver discs produced at Uncle Sam's factory. The king will be crowned with 1,500 cool iron men, the place man putting 750 smackerinos in his kick and the show entry bulging his wallet with 500 bucks.

Thus began the tradition of a winter tour in the sunshine states. Three years later the Los Angeles Junior Chamber of Commerce fronted 10,000 dollars for an Open. By 1928, the winter circuit of Texas, California, Oregan, Hawaii, and Arkansas was doling out a total of 77,000 dollars, which rates about a fourth-place finish in a big 1990 tournament. But for the pros of the 1920s, it meant a chance for income during the months when many courses closed down.

The figure for golfers in the States in 1913 was set at about 350,000. A decade later, it was pegged at 3.5 million. Interest in the game was strong enough for an aging Harry Vardon to make his third tour of the U.S. in 1920, and for him and his companion Ted Ray to receive 12,000 dollars apiece. Grantland Rice informed the public through the *Literary Digest* that some golf pros banked as much as 10,000 dollars a year through lessons, sales of balls, clubs, and exhibitions in 1921. Hagen and Jim Barnes raked in 1,000 to 1,500 dollars per exhibition. For lesser lights, the price of a lesson ran from a dollar and fifty cents to two dollars and fifty cents. Rice asserted 1,500 to 2,500 golf pros averaged 2,500 dollars, which compared favorably with the annual salaries of the average baseball player, perhaps 600 of whom, including 350 major leaguers, received 2,500 dollars or less.

A more dubious indication of golf's fascination surfaced in a story by Hugh Fullerton, the newspaperman who broke the Black Sox scandal in baseball. In 1925, Fullerton spoke of heavy wagering. He reported one amateur championship at the Chicago Golf Club drew bets of 50,000 to 100,000 dollars, with half a million resting on the clubs and balls of the finalists. In 1920, when Chick Evans met Francis Ouimet in the championship round of the U.S. Amateur, partisans of the East and West engaged in a fury of betting on favorite sons, with Chicago's Evans topping Boston's Ouimet.

The USGA, labeled by Fullerton "the highest hatted body in America," took steps to prevent gambling at tournaments under its aegis, and so did the Western Association and the PGA. Bookmakers continued to frequent the sites of major golf tournaments during the 1930s and newspapers solemnly reported their comments on the odds and wagering, even though gambling was illegal. The bookies disappeared after World War II, but not until thirty years later, when the Internal Revenue Service stuck its aquisitive nose into the tents of those promoting Calcutta pools,* was bigtime gambling finally curbed.

In Great Britain, the path of golf was far less green. The war wiped out much of a generation that would have supplied a fresh crop of players and left a shattered econ-omy. Vardon and Ray came to the U.S. for a successful tour. Ray captured the U.S. Open at Inverness in Toledo with a 295 and Vardon, now fifty years old, managed to stagger home in a quadruple tie for runner up, 1 stroke behind, along with Jack Burke, Sr., Leo Diegel, and Jock Hutchison. The affair could easily have ended in a five-way tie. Ray had started his final round with a neat 35 but the air had seeped from his balloon almost all the way home and he was 4 over after seventeen. However, on the final 322-yard hole, the bulky Briton harnessed all of his considerable mass into a titanic drive that left him perhaps 20 yards from the pin. His chip dropped to within four feet of the cup. At this moment, he was informed that if he sank the putt, the Open was his. O. B. Keeler, who became Bobby Jones's Boswell, wrote:

> He handed his club back to his caddy, removed the habitual pipe from his mouth, and while the assembled thousands fairly sweated blood with anxiety, he calmly refilled his pipe, lighted it, puffed away two or three times, took back his putter from the caddy, and without any more to-do, sent down the putt that made him champion.

The USGA rewarded Ray with 500 dollars in cash plus a gold medal and a silver bowl.

At forty-three, Ray was then the oldest man ever to win the U.S. Open, but his age was more symbolic of the plight of British golf than of a weakness in the States. *Golf Illustrated*, while celebrating the triumph, recognized the vulnerability of the Union Jack and cautioned against assertion of bragging rights.

> From a national, perhaps one might suggest an insular, point of view, it is extremely gratifying to our pride and our belief in the supremacy of British golf, but it is to be sincerely hoped that our Press will refrain from making too big a song about the success of our two professionals.

The feat of winning the Open champi-

---

* Gamblers bid for the golfer of their choice with the auction receipts pooled and then distributed to those "owning" the winners.

onship of the States in 1920 is an infinitely bigger thing than was the victory of Vardon in the event twenty years ago, and the task was undoubtedly more difficult than that which he and Vardon failed to accomplish seven years ago at Brookline, as the general standard of play in America, particularly in connection with professional golf, has improved muchly in the past few years. There are in the country at the moment more good-class players who originally learnt their game on British links, and moreover they have a whole host of home-bred golfers who play the game more than passing well. Each succeeding season the best of these dangerous homebreds is being added to. They have probably not yet unearthed a Vardon, a Braid, or a Taylor, but the time is probably not far off when they will.

One of those individuals who "originally learnt his game on British links" was Jock Hutchison. He was born in St. Andrews, and then quit Scotland for the economic opportunities golf offered on the other side of the Atlantic. After his near miss at Inverness, Jock Hutchison entered the British Open the following year as an American and became the first, albeit foreign born, U.S. citizen to hold the British Open championship.

Hutchison accomplished the feat in spectacular fashion. He aced the 142-yard eighth hole, and then on the 303-yard ninth walloped a ball off the tee that rolled onto the green, rimmed the cup, and stopped 3 inches away, coming close to an unprecedented pair of successive holes-in-one. On the final day, he needed a par-busting 70 to tie the front runner, amateur Roger Wethered. In the playoff, Hutchison humbled the amateur by a 9-stroke margin.

In a move sourly reminiscent of the reaction to Walter Travis in 1904, the Royal and Ancient promptly banned the deeply slotted clubheads used by Hutchison. But the weapons of the game were on the verge of a major change. The first patent for steel-shafted clubs was issued in 1910. In 1926, the USGA declared them legal; three years later the Royal and Ancient lifted its bans.

A worse misfortune than Hutchison's triumph was to befall the United Kingdom's hopes, as a "homebred" in the person of Walter Hagen began his rampage through the Opens there. Perhaps the most symbolic case of the shift in golf power is that of Tommy Armour.★ He grew up in Scotland, spent four bloody years serving with the British Expeditionary Forces in France, and mustered out as a tank corps major. He had survived, but barely, losing the sight of his right eye in a gas attack, engaged in hand-to-hand combat in which

Jock Hutchison, among the last of the British-born pros to become a naturalized American, was the first U.S. citizen to take the British Open, 1921. A year earlier he captured the USPGA title. (COURTESY RAY DAVIS.)

he strangled a recalcitrant German officer with bare hands, retained eight chunks of shrapnel in his left shoulder and suffered such grievous wounds that doctors thought he might never walk again, let alone play golf.

Part of his rehabilitation cure sent Armour out onto the golf course. There, he parlayed super hand-eye coordination—which had given him a reputation as the deadliest man with a machine gun in the tank corps—and the sight of a single good eye into superlative play with irons. Oddly, he always thought of himself as a finer wood player, using the far-less-predictable hickory shafts for much of his career. Putting was his nemesis; undoubtedly the loss of an eye handicapped him when he judged the topography of greens. Over the years, the stress of putting became more pronounced. Henry Cotton called him, "Three-putt Tommy." As age withered the jet black hair of his youth, he became known as "the Silver Scot."

Unlike most of his contemporaries and predecessors, Armour entered the pro ranks from a family of some means and with considerable education. He had been a

(Right, top) *Not only did President Warren G. Harding play the game (as shown here), but he and his vice-president, Calvin Coolidge, joined the gallery for the finals of the 1921 U.S. Open.* (COURTESY RAY DAVIS.)

(Right, bottom) *During the 1920s, the Prince of Wales (who became the briefly reigning Edward VIII), a pal of Walter Hagen, and his brother, the Duke of York (who became King George VI), took instruction from pro Sandy Herd (far left).* (COURTESY RAY DAVIS.)

(Below) *Maurice Chevalier, the French songman, put the Gallic stamp of approval on golf.* (COURTESY RAY DAVIS.)

U.S. royalty that favored the links included film idol Douglas Fairbanks, Sr. Observing the swashbuckling drive are (left to right) George Van Elm, 1926 amateur champion, Leo Diegel, winner of the PGA in 1928 and '29, and motion picture executive Joseph Schenck. (COURTESY RAY DAVIS.)

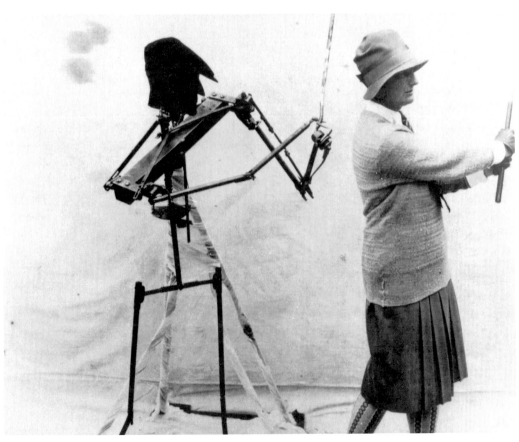

The golf rage created mechanical marvels to analyze the golf swing. (COURTESY RAY DAVIS.)

university student when he enlisted, played classical music on the violin, was literate, and articulate—sometimes painfully so to those who offended his hair-trigger temper. His friend, Clarence Buddington Kelland, a popular author frequently serialized in the *Saturday Evening Post*, described the tall, brooding Scot has having "a mouth like a steel trap, a nose like a ski jump, hands like fins of a shark, and

eyes which indicate that he would enjoy seeing you get a compound fracture of the leg." He added: "He is as temperamental as a soprano with a bullfrog in her throat."

Armour was part of a group of Britons to follow Vardon and Ray to the U.S. The group also included Cyril Tolley, a vet who languished in a German POW camp for thirteen months, and Roger Wethered, whose sister would prove more famous

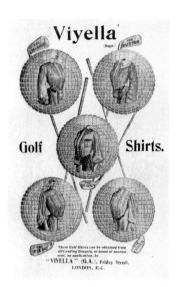

Fashion ads promoted golf styles.
(COURTESY RAY DAVIS.)

than he in golf. On his first visit, Armour, who had taken the French amateur championship earlier, was the only Briton to even qualify for the U.S. Amateur, and he fell in an early match.

Two years later when Armour arrived on American shores it was to become a resident. He entered the pro ranks in 1924 and landed a job at the Congressional Country Club near Washington, D.C. In 1927 he journeyed to Oakmont, outside of Pittsburgh, for an Open that some claim covered the toughest course ever to determine the championship.

Balls skittered and rolled endlessly over huge greens shaved so close the ground should have bled. Almost 300 traps pitted the landscape and, to further punish trans-

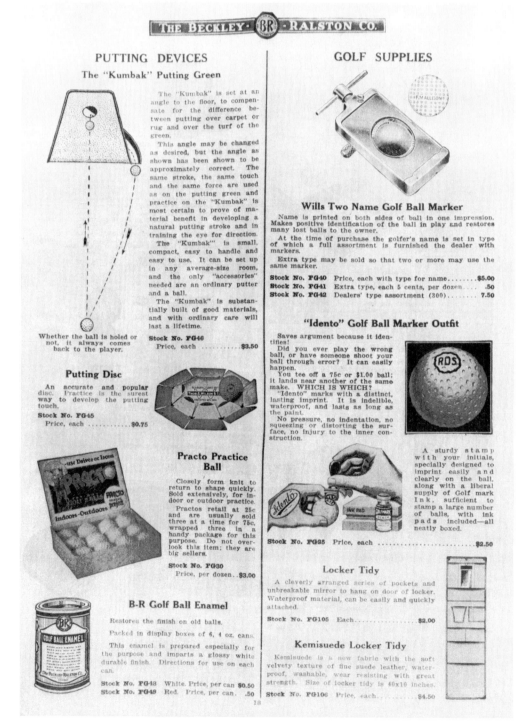

Golfer's aids were popular even as far back as the 1920s, as this page from a Beckley-Ralston catalog shows. (COURTESY RAY DAVIS.)

gressors, the rakes gouged deep tracks. Under these conditions, Armour shot 301, the highest total any champion scored since 1919 and a total unreached by any winner since Armour. He was 9 over par but his 71 in the second round was the only sub-par card in the entire tournament. The great Bobby Jones, defending his 1926 title, could never get beneath 75. Armour added the Canadian Open to his 1927 laurels and three years later capped his professional tournament play by winning the PGA.

After Armour quit tournaments he established himself as the foremost teacher of the game. His reputation as golf's most knowledgeable pedagogue grew. Through his pro shop, he sent clubs bearing the Armour label around the world. He was a master of the indirect hard sell. Kelland explained the technique:

You come into the shop and meet Mr. Armour. He does not fall on your neck in raptures of joy. There is little if anything of the effusive in his make-up . . . he peers at you with basilisk eyes calculating the strength of your sales-resistance and estimates your possibilities as a customer and as a human being. He snaps off a few Scottish consonants and then walks over to your golf bag and picks out your driver. . . . He waggles the club; he grips it; then he holds it out in front of him with a gesture so eloquent that you begin to shrivel inside your clothes and to wish you had gone to Chicago instead.

. . . his tanned, angular face takes on an expression of such utter scorn—mixed with a trifle of sorrow—that you feel exactly as if you had been caught stealing a blanket off a baby's bed on a cold night. He puts your driver back in the bag gently—so gently—and then walks away with dragging step, as if there were things in the world too terrible for the human mind to consider.

Following a few off-hand remarks, according to Kelland, "You walk out of the shop with three new woods, a full set of irons and a putter—and a date to take a number of lessons from Mr. Armour at an unpleasantly early hour."

Armour's shift of nationality figured in the beginnings of team competition. Until 1921, golfers from Britain and America competed against one another as individuals. Charles B. Macdonald had attempted in 1913 to create team tournaments from amateurs representing their nations, but even as the Royal and Ancient mulled over the idea, the guns of August boomed, blowing away any chance of that kind of fight. When hostilities ended, American and Canadian amateur squads matched pitches and putts in 1919 and 1920, but it was the

Walter Hagen led the winning first U.S. Ryder Cup team in 1927 at the Worcester Country Club, Massachusetts. The Americans included Johnny Golden, Joe Turnesa, Johnny Farrell, Al Watrous, Leo Diegel, Wild Bill Mehlhorn, Al Espinosa, and Gene Sarazen. The losing Britons fielded George Duncan, Archie Compston, Ted Ray who served as captain, Fred Robinson, F. Gadd, Charles Whitcombe, Arthur Havers, Abe Michell, Herbert Jolly, and Aubrey Boomer. (COURTESY RAY DAVIS.)

The Walker Cup competition, the amateur counterpart to the Ryder Cup, preceded the professional tournament by five years. Among the Americans in 1925 were Bobby Jones, George Van Elm, and Francis Ouimet. (COURTESY THE BETTMANN ARCHIVE.)

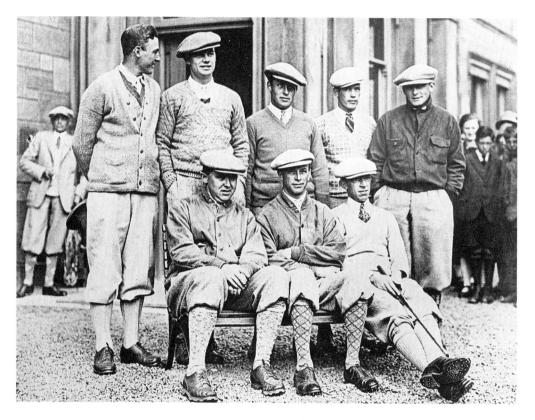

Baseball and golf met on a country club bench, from left to right, pitcher Rube Marquard of the Boston Braves, Gene Sarazen, the incomparable Babe Ruth, and Johnny Farrell. (COURTESY RAY DAVIS.)

USGA that established a pattern for team tournaments. It invited the golfing nations to send amateur groups to compete for a trophy in the States. The only response came from England, which fielded Cyril Tolley, Roger Wethered, Ernest Holderness, and Tommy Armour. The victorious U.S.

team consisted of Bob Jones, Chick Evans, and Francis Ouimet.

George H. Walker, president of the USGA, donated an International Challenge Trophy, which newspapers dubbed the Walker Cup. Subsequently, the international team matches, which became limited to the two original countries, took the name of the trophy. Originally held annually, the meetings became biennial after 1924.

The Anglo-American team competition concept spread to the pro ranks. An unofficial series of matches was played in 1926 in Britain. The locals, led by Abe Mitchell, George Duncan, and Ted Ray, now forty-nine-years old, by a score of 13–1 walloped the visiting Americans, including home-bred Hagen, but also numbering the naturalized fellows from Great Britain, Jim Barnes, Tommy Armour, and Australian born Joe Kirkwood. Naturally, the results enchanted citizens of the United Kingdom, since visitors from the States had begun to dominate their Open and had been invincible in Walker Cup confrontations. A wealthy seed merchant, Samuel Ryder, who employed Abe Mitchell as his private pro, donated a gold cup that cost 750 British pounds, close to 4,000 dollars in U.S. currency and obviously a very valuable bauble.

Unlike the case of the Walker Cup, the Brits held their own in the Ryder competition for four years, starting in 1927. However, after 1935 it was all USA except for a brief reversal of form in 1957. Not until the Americans began to face all European squads in 1979 did the competition even out.

The spirit of individual achievement in the Olympics, the principle espoused by Baron deCoubertin, founder of the modern games, had already eroded in favor of us against them. The Walker and Ryder Cups, along with the subsequent Curtis Cup for women, institutionalized the phenomenon of national golf rivalry. Sportsmen might grumble about the intrusion of chauvinism but the opportunity to root for standard bearers also built further interest in the sport.

In the United States, the perfect target for adulation strode to center stage. Robert Tyre Jones, the one-time boy wonder from Georgia, embodied irresistible ideals. He was clean cut and utterly free of any commercial taint in his sporting endeavors. Even his name, one of the two most common in the land, marked him as the quintessential American hero.

While Jones's father was not originally a golfer, the gift of athletic ability was within him. He had given up an opportunity to play baseball for the Brooklyn Dodgers only because Bob's grandfather refused to accept a career in baseball as suitable for a graduate of the University of Georgia. The mysterious combination of genes that

Tommy Armour came home to Scotland for the 1931 British Open. "He is full of imagination, a bundle of quivering nerves kept fiercely under control, and this is the kind of temperament that either breaks a player of games or makes him terribly formidable. As a striker of the ball, except sometimes when it is dead at the holeside, Armour is truly magnificent."—Bernard Darwin, Country Life, *June 12, 1931.)* (COURTESY UPI/BETTMANN NEWS-PHOTOS.)

The stamp upon his U.S. citizen-ship papers was hardly dry be-fore Armour shot his way to the U.S. Open title in 1927. He added a PGA championship in 1930. (COURTESY UPI/BETTMANN NEWSPHOTOS.)

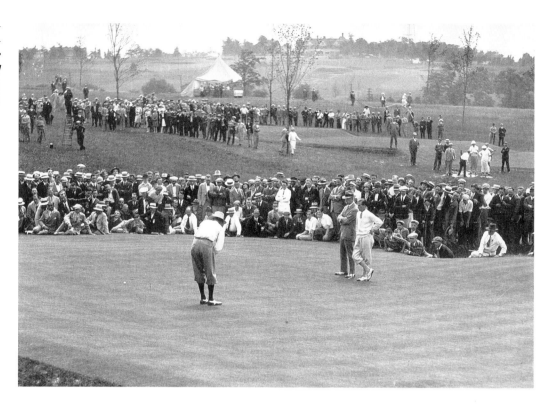

"That guy Armour was and is an artist. His shots were for the picture books. At every stage of a shot he was so gracefully and firmly in balance nothing but an earthquake could tilt him."— Herb Graffis, Esquire, *January 1946.*

A kilted Earl of Airlie presents the British Open Cup to expatriate Scot Tommy Armour after he triumphed at Carnoustie in 1931. (COURTESY WIDE WORLD PHOTOS.)

creates sports superiority coursed through Bob's body. But for a start there seemed little with which to work. Bob Jones (he did not care for the diminutive Bobby and some press accounts referred to him as "Rob") was a sickly, Georgia-born kid. In an autobiography he wrote:

> I started out with an oversize head and a spindling body and legs with staring knees, and some serious digestive derangement which caused my parents and six or seven doctors a deal of distress. Dad says I didn't eat solid food until I was five years old. . . .

The family took up residence at a boarding house one summer outside of town, "in a big house about a mashie pitch from what was then the second fairway of the East Lake golf course of the Atlanta Athletic Club." The six-year-old and a friend, fascinated by the game at East Lake, created two holes for themselves on the dirt roadway, just as Francis Ouimet had done only a few years earlier. Jones insisted his quickness to play a shot, including a putt, dates back to this childhood initiation, The neighborhood kids organized their own six-hole tournament, which Jones won. The three-inch high cup occupied a prominent place

among the hundreds of trophies and medals subsequently kept on display in his home.

When Jones's parents took up golf, their small son accompanied them, "beating the ball along," with a single cut-down club. He met the pro, Stewart Maiden, so newly arrived from Scotland that the boy could not understand a single word of his dialect. Instinctively, the youngster began to follow Maiden on the course, watching him perform and then unconsciously adopting his techniques.

At age nine he took his first genuine title, a junior tournament sponsored by the Atlanta Athletic Club. At thirteen he began winning competitions against some of the better amateurs in the South, and he was merely fourteen, a short five-foot four-inch stocky 165 pounder, when he teed off in the summer of 1916 at the National Amateur on the Merion Cricket Club grounds. Dressed in his first pair of long pants, the Georgia adolescent, accustomed to the coarse Bermuda grass greens of his region, was astounded by the swiftness of the greens at Merion. During a practice round he tried a 30-foot putt and, to his dismay, the ball galloped across the green, down a fairway, and into a stream. He promptly led the first qualifying round with a 74.

His first opponent was the former national champion, Eben Byers, a member of the group that had entered the British Amateur of 1904. Both players were given to spectacular tantrums and spectators were bemused by the seesaw battle of rant and thrown clubs. Players behind them joked about what appeared to be a juggling contest. Byers eventually hurled one offending stick over a hedge and refused to permit his caddie to retrieve it. Years later, Jones laughed that he won because Byers ran out of clubs first. The boy wonder played excellent golf to take his second match, but he finally fell to the defending champ, Bob Gardner.

While the spectators and press marveled at his proficiency, they also criticized his lack of self control. However, his achievements were sufficient for him to be recruited for exhibitions to raise Red Cross money once the U.S. entered World War I.

Over the next half-dozen years he appeared in a number of major tournaments, was a member of the Walker Cup squad that beat the British, won a few lesser titles, but always finished behind the leaders in the majors. He continued his education at Georgia Tech and Harvard. Perhaps the most important event during this period was a loss at the 1921 British Open. Coming off his Walker Cup win, Jones was encouraged by his early play. But when the typical stew of wind and rain spattered play in the third round, Jones skied to a 49 for the first nine. On the tenth hole he double bogeyed; on the short eleventh he faced the prospect of a dropping 3 more to par. Jones picked up his ball. Almost instantly, the nineteen year old was shocked by his own behavior. At that moment, says Herb Wind, Jones matured, resolving never again to permit his short fuse to fully burn. However, years passed before commentators accepted his change of heart. Keeler explained:

W. C. Fownes, USGA President handed Armour his 1927 cup. (COURTESY THE BETTMANN ARCHIVE.)

The sports writers loved to depict him as a hot-blooded southerner long after he had taken their criticisms to heart and had mastered his emotions, so far as any outward symptoms were concerned.

A fierce foursome: (left to right) Johnny Farrell, Armour's Open champ successor in 1928, Leo Diegel, the silent Harold McFadden, and Armour. (COURTESY WIDE WORLD PHOTOS.)

Jess Sweetser, a Yalie, like Bob Jones stuck to the amateur ranks over his golf career. In 1922, Sweetser drubbed Jones in the national championship semi-finals, 8 and 7. Along with Jones he became a mainstay of the early Walker Cup squads. (COURTESY RAY DAVIS.)

Keeler argued that the seven years of famine from 1916 to 1923 helped Jones immeasurably:

> Jones, beaten year after year, acquired needed seasoning under the black shadow of depressing fortune. It was there he discovered the jewel in the toad's head of defeat.

Jones himself agreed he always learned more from his losing efforts. Seven years wandering the tournament wilderness without victory provided ample time in the classroom.

His era dawned at the 1923 U.S. Open at the Inwood Country Club on New York's Long Island. He appeared to have the title in hand when he completed his final eighteen but Bobby Cruickshank, a tiny Scot, birdied the last hole to create a playoff. The pair went through seventeen holes only to remain tied. The pressure seemed

to afflict both for their drives on the 425-yard, par-4, eighteenth. Cruickshank topped and hooked the ball, which knifed through the rough before coming to rest on a roadway. His lie meant he could not hope to carry the moat guarding the green. Jones sliced his drive, leaving him a narrow vista of the green, 190 yards distant.

Jones was away; discretion suggested a safe shot setting himself up to compete with his opponent on the chip and putts. And there was always the possibility that Cruickshank could add to his troubles. Grantland Rice described the scene:

> The ball was . . . resting in loose dirt amid the rough. He took the gamble of a champion at heart, slashed into the ball with a mid-iron and as it soared upward against the dark gray sky, heavy with the threat of an approaching storm, he saw his dream coming true upon the trajectory of a ball that was headed straight for the fluttering flag. The ball struck 10 feet short and stopped just 7 feet beyond the cup. . . . The long hike was over at last. The weary slogging march was ended. His 1,263rd stroke through four championships and a playoff had turned the trick at twenty-one, with greater years still ahead.

Actually, the crowd on the perimeter of the green broke into cheers almost instantly as they perceived the exquisite flight path of the ball. The dour Stewart Maiden, following the fortunes of his star pupil, snatched the new straw hat from his head and mashed it down on the brow of Jones's caddie. The hapless Cruickshank then pitched into a trap, flubbed his out badly enough to require 2 putts. Jones finally had a major title.

In 1926, Jones qualified for the British Open using a new driver he named Jeannie Deans, after a Scottish heroine.* He

---

* Jones also personified his putter as "Calamity Jane." Stewart Maiden's brother gave him the original in 1920, and Jones believed the wood-shafted club was probably made around 1900. In 1926, Spalding supplied him with half a dozen copies for his own use. He gave several away but substituted one for the original, whose head "had become too light from continued polishing." Curiously, the shaft of the first Calamity Jane had been cracked and Jones wrapped it in several spots to preserve it. The people at Spalding, like the proverbial tailor in Hong Kong who replicates a suit down to the old cigarette holes in the model, also added wrappings to the new versions. The original Calamity Jane disappeared but the one used by Jones for much of his career is now at the USGA's Golf House in Far Hills, New Jersey.

turned in rounds of 66 and 68, easily defeating the field. Bernard Darwin wrote:

> After a reverential cheer at the final green, the crowd dispersed, awestruck, realized that they had witnessed something they had never seen before, and would never see again.

Although Hagen had mounted two successful invasions of the British Open in 1922 and 1924, Jones returned to far more acclaim. As the liner S.S. *Aquitania* steamed into New York harbor, a hundred rooters from his home state packed the decks of a municipal boat, the *Macom*, sounding Rebel yells while a band thumped out "Glory, Glory to Old Georgia" and "Dixie." From the dock Jones marched in a three-mile parade with the cops halting all traffic, ticker tape streaming from the towers of Manhattan. At City Hall, Mayor James J. Walker, in the words of the *New York Times*: ". . . bade him welcome . . . and felicitated him warmly on his victory. No prince that has visited New York received a more royal welcome."

The best, however, was yet to be. A year later he successfully defended his British Open title and then met Chick Evans in the finale in the U.S. National Amateur in Minikahda in Minneapolis. On the ninth hole, a 512-yard dogleg up a steep slope, he walloped two of the most prodigious woods ever seen. According to Keeler,

> Bobby played a spoon second with an eighth of a mile carry, or more, that stopped two feet short of the cup, toward which it trickled straight as a ruled line and wanted only a grasshopper's kick added to the silken swing of Bobby Jones to have rolled in for a deuce.

Almost a double eagle, it was the first eagle recorded on the hole and Jones was 5 up after the morning's eighteen. On the twenty-sixth hole, as rain spattered the gallery, Evans accidentally moved his ball. Smiling, he picked up, conceding Jones's inches-away putt and a lead of 8–7. Said the loser, "It was worth a good drubbing to see such a marvelous exhibition of golf."

The peak, of course, was 1930. When Jones sailed for England as a member of the Walker Cup team, his wife accompanied him. Also on hand to see the matches were the reigning celebrities of the period, vaudeville's Sir Harry Lauder, the art and antique world's Sir Joseph Duveen,

Lighthorse Harry Cooper learned the game in Texas playing on sand greens. Grantland Rice endowed him with the nickname because of his swift play. (COURTESY THE BETTMANN ARCHIVE.)

Left to right are Grantland Rice, the golf promoting newspaper and magazine writer, J. Victor East who became a pro and outstanding maker of clubs, and Bobby Jones. East was known to apply a stethoscope to shafts in an effort to divine the quality of wood fibers. (COURTESY RAY DAVIS.)

and the film stars Maurice Chevalier and Douglas Fairbanks, Sr., who was a golfing companion of Jones, Hagen, and Evans.

The famous elbowed for position among a gallery of 15,000 as Jones captured the British Amateur title in eight matches. At the British Open, Keeler became the first man to broadcast a sporting event across the Atlantic Ocean, through the facilities of the BBC and NBC. On the final day, Jones held a 1-stroke advantage, with Leo Diegel, MacDonald Smith, and Archie Compston in close pursuit. Compston, the Briton who once humiliated Hagen to the delight of the homefolks, pressed Jones, firing a 68 to the visitor's 74 to lead by 1 as they headed for the final eighteen.

Jones continued to spray shots. His drive on the second hole slewed to the right and was saved from disaster only by conking the convenient head of a tournament steward. From the relative safety of a bunker, Jones then pitched onto the green and a 20-foot putt gave him a bird. But on the eighth hole he appeared to have thrown away any chances. He was green high after two, but a simple run-up shot never even reached the target. A poor chip left him still 10 feet from the pin after 4 strokes. He swatted his putt 12 inches beyond the cup. Annoyed, he tapped at the ball without looking and missed to leave himself a horrid 7. "It was the most inexcusable hole I ever played. An old man with a croquet mallet could have got down in two. I will

play that hole over a thousand times in my dreams," he said.

The gods took pity. His two nearest foes, Diegel and Compston, frittered away their opportunities, and Jones returned to the U.S. with both of the major British events in hand. He went directly to the Interlachen course for the U.S. Open. Once again he opened up a gap between himself and the top professionals. He received another smile from Dame Fortune when, on one hole, he sought to carry a small lake. His half-topped spoon produced a line drive with no hope of clearing the far bank. The ball smacked the water 20 feet from shore, skittered into the air before spanking the lake once more, then bounded up to safety just shy of the green. Some insisted a lily pad saved Jones; others explain the phenomenon in terms of a skipping flat stone. Buoyed by the escape from disaster, Jones was 5 up after fifty-four holes, but a final 75 almost cost him the tournament. However, a 40 footer on the last hole ensured a 2-stroke margin.

On the eve of the year's U.S. Amateur at Merion, the normally unflappable Jones became obsessed with what some termed the "Impregnable Quadrilateral," and which Keeler dubbed the "Grand Slam."

It is the first tournament in which I have ever played that I could not sleep at night. There is something on my mind that I cannot shake off. I go to sleep all right from fatigue, but about midnight or later I wake up and have to get up. I have always been able to sleep. There was only one night, no, two when I remember I did not sleep. One was at Worcester in 1923, the night before the playoff but the heat contributed to that. The other was at the British Amateur Championship at Muirfield in 1926. I sat in the window and marvelled that I could see cattle in the distant fields at 11:30 o'clock in the long Scottish twilight. There is something bearing down on me in this tournament that was never there before.

Erratic appropriately describes Jones at Merion initially but medal play mitigated the potential consequences of a 39 on the front nine and he followed with a dazzling 33 coming back. Having shot a record-tying 142 in the qualifying heat, Jones zipped through five opponents with a minimum of difficulty. Most satisfyingly, in his last match he sacked and burned Jess Sweetser 9–8, to revenge an 8–7 loss to him in 1922.

Francis Powers of the *Chicago News* drew from Grantland Rice's recent apostrophe to the Notre Dame backfield: "There goes another race by the Four Horsemen of the Apocalypse over the fairways of Merion, and this time their names are Jones, Jones, Jones, and Jones."

In November, Jones, twenty-eight years old, announced his retirement from competitive golf. He had won every major event he could enter and climaxed his achievements with what was officially now the Grand Slam. In later years, as the domination of the sport shifted to the professionals, the Grand Slam would consist of the Masters, the British Open, the U.S. Open, and the PGA Championship. But Jones was the only player to capture his form of Grand Slam in a single year.

Fans greet conquering hero Bobby Jones aboard his ship as he sails home from England. "He was the only celebrity I ever knew who was prepared to accept as gracefully as possible every penalty there is to be paid for fame and publicity."—Paul Gallico. (COURTESY THE BETTMANN ARCHIVE.)

Charles Price on
BOBBY JONES

The first thing you have to understand about Bobby Jones is that he was an amateur, not a professional. Yet his colossal career was largely made by beating the pros at their own game. Jones won seven of the last eleven open championships he played in, both in America and Britain, and in three of the other four he was runner-up. No pro before or since him, let alone another amateur, has come close to making such a record.

The second thing you have to understand about Jones is that his career was as brief as it was brilliant. He won his first national championship in 1923, when he was twenty-one, his last in 1930, when he was twenty-eight. Then he quit, retiring from the championship scene forever.

The third thing you have to understand is that Jones was not just a tournament player. In those eight years, he played in only seven tournaments that had no major titles attached to them. More accurately, Jones was a championship golfer, a national championship golfer—indeed, an international one. What's the difference? Well, tournament golf is like walking a tightrope that is a few feet off the ground. You have to watch your step. *Championship* golf is when they raise the rope to 60 feet. A *national* championship is when they take the net away.

There is no way of explaining the golf Jones played except to say that he was a genius at the game. Jones played no more golf than the average dentist, perhaps eighty rounds a year. He detested practicing, went months at a time without picking up a club, and more often than not played in only two championships a year.

At the peak of his career, when Jones must have known as well as everybody else that he was the best golfer in the world, he regarded the game as nothing more or less than what it is—a game. "My wife and my children came first," he would write in later years, "then my profession [Jones was an attorney]. . . . Finally, and never in a life by itself, came golf."

Yet in those last eight years of competition, Jones won a record five United States Amateurs, a record-tying four U.S. Opens, all three of the British Opens he entered, and one of two British Amateurs. In 1930 he won each of those championships in a single cataclysmic season for what has come down to us in history as the Grand Slam. That is a record that can never be broken and will be tied, as Herbert Warren Wind wrote back in 1946, "about the time women are breaking the 4-minute mile."

Jones played the worst golf of his career in the 1927 U.S. Open, finishing in a tie for eleventh at Oakmont Country Club, near Pittsburgh. The championship

(Top, left) *The boy phenom raised money for the American Red Cross through golf exhibitions during World War I.* (COURTESY THE BETT-MANN ARCHIVE.)

(Top, right) *Even as a six year old, Jones did not restrict his back swing.* (COURTESY RAY DAVIS.)

was won by Tommy Armour. Several weeks later, Armour got together with Jones for some friendly games. They played two-dollar nassaus, nothing higher. As Armour himself would tell the story, Jones won so often that he quietly started to give Armour 1-up a side.

Years later Armour was asked how he could take 1-up from an amateur when he was then Open Champion. Armour bristled. "Because," he said, "that's how goddamn good he was."

There were surprisingly more talented pros in the twenties than we tend to concede today. Besides Armour, there was Gene Sarazen, who won the U.S. Open before Jones, and half a dozen others of what are now called "majors." Additionally, there were dozens of splendid shotmakers who won several national titles, perhaps only one, or who were a constant threat without winning any. Walter Hagen, for example, won eleven national championships in addition to so many tournaments that even he lost count.

Yet none of them could win a championship Jones entered.

Turn to any record book for the years 1923 through 1930, and you will find Jones's name on every page. It was not Jones against this man or that man but Jones against the whole field. When somebody else won a championship, the news was not that he had won but that Jones hadn't.

The only men who beat Jones head to head in a championship were those who did not expect to, who never won anything of consequence before or afterwards. A pro could carve a whole career out of beating Jones just once. And two of them did, plus an amateur who turned pro immediately thereafter. They then settled down in plush club jobs, each to be known for the rest of his life as the man who once beat the one and only.

Jones could get into scoring streaks during which no pro could stop him. For amateurs like himself, those streaks could be staggering, leaving them to wonder if they were playing the same game. The 1928 Walker Cup Matches were played at the Chicago Golf Club the last week in August. Jones had played very little golf that summer. So he went to Chicago a few weeks early to play his game into shape over three courses he had never seen before. The first was Old Elm, where he broke the course record the first time he played it. A few days later he broke

The fourteen-year-old Jones already had brawny forearms. At this tender age he debuted in the National Amateur. (COURTESY RAY DAVIS.)

the course record at Chicago. The following day, he broke *that* record and tied the old one the day after. A few days later, while playing in a local invitation tournament—which he won—he broke the course record at Flossmoor, despite having played the first seven holes in 2 over par. He finished 3, 3, 3, 3, 3, 3, 3, 4, 3, 4, and 4. After three more rounds, someone added up his last dozen rounds. They came to this: 69, 71, 69, 68, 68, 68, 67, 68, 67, 70, 69, and 67.

It should be kept in mind that Jones played with hickory shafts, using a ball that was at least 30 yards shorter than today's, all over courses that were in atrocious condition by current standards, and before dozens of changes were made in the rules, such as cleaning the ball on the green, which in themselves made scoring immeasurably easier. What's more, Jones was then two years away from his best golf.

In the singles of the Match that followed those rounds, Jones faced Phil Perkins, then the British Champion. Jones won, 12 and 11. Two weeks later, in Boston, Perkins worked his way clear to the final of the U.S. Amateur, only to find that he had to play Jones again. Jones won this time, 10 and 9. Perkins soon after turned pro. He couldn't see any future in amateur golf with Jones around.

Right there is the chief reason Jones seldom played in amateur events. He was embarrassed by the margins he won by. Jones went into the Grand Slam two years later having played thirteen matches at thirty-six holes in the U.S. Amateur—quarter-finals, semi-finals and finals. Those he won were won by an average margin of 9 and 8. In other words, he could be expected to win one of every three holes he played without losing any.

Jones never took a formal golf lesson in his life. He had put the basics of his game together as a boy by imitating Stewart Maiden, the Scottish pro at East Lake, his home club in Atlanta. But Jones's swing as he matured became distinctly his own, the quintessence of what professionals taught but often couldn't bring off themselves, what with its grace, its panther power, its balletic balance. Bernard Darwin, the British golf sage, would write that it had "a touch of poetry."

Jones's game was so polished in every department that few experts could agree on what the brightest part of it was. Certainly, he was one of the game's supreme putters. The Old Course at St. Andrews, Scotland, was the stage for some of Jones's most scintillating performances. It has immense greens, some so large they serve two different holes. Jones once sank a putt on one of these double greens that was later measured off at 100 feet.

To tie pro Al Espinosa for the 1929 U.S. Open at Winged Foot—a playoff he would win by 23 strokes—he holed a downhill putt of about 12 feet with a violent left-to-right break. Grantland Rice, the sportswriter and an expert on golf, wrote it was "the greatest single putt I have ever witnessed." In honor of that event years later, four pros who were all former Open Champions tried to duplicate the putt, just for laughs. None of them could.

At the Chevy Chase Golf Course, site of the U.S. Open in 1921, Jones was a collegiate dandy, still full of promise, but the smile hides a temper he had not yet learned to control. "I was paired with Bobby Jones and we were both great club-throwers at the time; we'd miss a shot and throw the damn club away. So we made a bet on the first tee that whoever threw a club had to pay the other ten dollars—this was 1921 and ten dollars was a lot of money. Jones started off his round in a big way. I think he had a birdie on one and a birdie on three, and when we came to a dogleg to the left, he tried to cut the dogleg and go for the green. His shot wasn't too good and as we watched the ball sail out of bounds, I looked over at my caddie and said, 'Here comes ten dollars.' Then Jones dropped another ball and put that one out of bounds too. With a big smile I leaned over to my caddie and said, 'Here comes twenty dollars!' He finished the hole with a 7 or 8. And from then on, Bobby never threw another club and neither did I."—Gene Sarazen, in The Squire, *by John Olman.*

That same year in the third round of the British Open, Jones was so disgusted with his performance, he picked up and left; it was the last time he ever quit in mid-tournament. (COURTESY UPI/BETTMANN NEWSPHOTOS.)

Not a big man—he stood five feet nine inches and weighed 175 pounds—Jones always played well within himself, depending for his best golf on the technical perfection of his swing and uncanny timing, as though he had some metabolic metronome within him. But he could hit towering drives and fairways woods when called for. The sixteenth hole at the Olympic Club, in San Francisco, is 603 yards long. Jones reached the green in 2 the first time he played it.

For all his length off the tee and his delicacy on the greens, not to mention the way he could rifle iron shots, Jones's favorite shot was from sand, a shot he played with a niblick, or 9-iron, the sand wedge not to come along until just after

Probably the best-educated top golfer in the history of the game, Jones held degrees from Georgia Tech, Harvard, and Emory University Law School. (COURTESY THE BETTMANN ARCHIVE.)

he retired. In some movie shorts he made in Hollywood in the early thirties, he demonstrated the shot by playing six balls in succession. Not one of them was left more than 3 feet from the hole. What is really remarkable about the demonstration, though, is that Jones half buried each ball before he hit it by tapping it into the sand with the toe of his shoe.

Jones's genius for golf was evident off the course as well as on, what with the syllogistic reasoning he brought to the game. It had become a truism in his day that if a putt was never up to the hole it could not possibly go in. The thought seemed obvious enough but, after mulling it over, Jones rejected it as sophistry. "Of course," he was to write years later, "we never know but that the ball which is on line and stops short would have holed out. But we do know that the ball that ran past did *not* hole out." Thereafter, Jones played his putts to "die" at the hole. Such philosophical hairsplitting might have seemed ridiculous to a tournament golfer. But Jones was a *championship* golfer, and his disdain for the commonplace helped make him so.

Jones had a knack for reducing the game to its least common denominator. Asked what went through his mind when he was playing a shot, Jones replied, "Hitting the ball. If I thought of anything else, I couldn't hit it."

Asked if his best shots were brought off consciously or subconsciously, Jones said, "Neither one. I hit them with blind instinct. Some of the shots I read about in the newspapers the day afterwards I couldn't even remember playing."

While not an intellectual in the European sense—and certainly not an egghead in the American sense—he had an educated mind as well as an inquiring one. After graduating from high schol at sixteen, he got a degree in mechanical engineering from Georgia Tech. He then entered Harvard to get a degree in English literature. After a boring year in Florida real estate, he entered law school at Emory University. During his second year, he took the bar exams just to see how tough they were. He passed them, and so quit school to practice.

With this background, foreign as it then was to the pros, some of whom hadn't even finished high school, and from the way he savaged both amateurs and pros alike, Jones could have been the most disliked golfer of his day. Actually, he was the most genuinely liked and admired, and would remain a lovable legend in golf for decades, even after his death. Jack Nicklaus, who wasn't born until ten years after Jones had retired, would say that Jones was somebody special to him.

What endeared Jones to other golfers was that there was nothing calculating or priggish about his behavior. He smoked to excess on the course, drank corn whiskey off it, swore magnificently in either place, and could listen to or tell an off-color story in the locker room afterward. He was self-effacing, affectionate, and loyal to his friends, all of whom called him Bob, which he much preferred to "Bobby," a name perpetuated by the press. Perhaps his closest friend was his father, who was not a tournament player although he played consistently in the seventies. Bobby would forever remain nostalgic that he had won the championship at East Lake when he was thirteen by defeating his father in the final.

Jones was famous for his modesty, which he did not wear on his sleeve. At Harvard he was ineligible for the golf team, since he had already matriculated at Georgia Tech. So he served as the team's assistant manager. He was then the U.S. Open Champion.

Perhaps the only traits that surpassed Jones's modesty were his thoughfulness and integrity. On the night before his Sunday playoff with Al Espinosa for that U.S. Open at Winged Foot, Jones, a Protestant married to a Catholic, secretly requested officials to postpone the starting time for an hour so that Espinosa might have time to attend mass.

At four national championships Jones called penalty shots on himself for minor breaches of the rules. In the 1925 Open Championship at Worcester, Massachusetts, he insisted on penalizing himself a stroke when his ball accidentally moved slightly as the blade of his iron touched the grass. No one else possibly could have seen the ball move, not even his caddie, and officials tried to argue him out of the penalty. But Jones insisted. That stroke put him into the playoff that he lost to a now forgotten pro named Willie Macfarlane, and eventually prevented him from becoming the only man to win five U.S. Opens. When Jones was praised afterward for throwing the book at himself, he became indignant. "There is only one way to play the game," he said. "You might as well praise a man for not robbing a bank."

In his day, Jones was considered the ultra-athlete, somebody better at his sport than any other athlete was at his, this at a time when there were a lot of athletes to choose from: Jack Dempsey, Red Grange, Bill Tilden, Babe Ruth, and Ty Cobb

Only twenty-five years old, Jones drove from the first tee in the rain at St. Andrews to defend his British Open title in 1927. (COURTESY UPI/BETTMANN NEWSPHOTOS.)

among numerous others. Yet Jones remained unaffected at a time when flattering headlines were being made by athletes who had not a fraction of his talent, some of whom were a good deal more unsavory than even the uninhibited journalism of that period cared to report. When Jones spoke in public, his thoughts were measured, his words selected, his tone of voice modulated, and so the image of him that was projected through the newspapers was impeccably true to life, not larger than it.

With his boyish good looks and apple-pie personality, he enraptured the public of two continents. If possible, he was even more popular in Britain, especially in Scotland, than he was in America. Twenty-eight years after he had retired, among much pomp and ceremony, he was made a Freeman of St. Andrews, a title not awarded lightly and then usually only to scholars and statesmen. Jones was the first American to have been so honored since Benjamin Franklin.

Parades up Broadway are usually reserved for victorious generals, political leaders, pioneering aviators, and others for monumental accomplishments. Bobby Jones remains the only one to have been given two such parades, the first in 1926, when he became the first golfer to win both U.S. Open and the British Open in a single season. The other came after he had won both the British Amateur and British Open in 1930—when he was only halfway finished making the Grand Slam.

While it is generally regarded as a unique string of championships won in a single season, actually to Jones the Grand Slam was more a metaphysical adventure than anything. He was trying to take an age-old game to places nobody had ever taken it before, into the unexplored, to its outer spaces, toward its

Shrouded by umbrellas, the St. Andrews gallery watches a Jones putt. (COURTESY UPI/BETTMANN NEWS-PHOTOS.)

Jones holes out for his 1927 British Open championship before 12,000 spectators, who swept him onto their shoulders and bore him about the course.

"It is no easy matter to follow in the train of encomiums which have greeted the second successive victory of Mr. "Bobby" Jones in the British open golf championships. At this state, it seems stilted and commonplace to congratulate him, although indeed, we do offer him all the felicitations that can be put forward by a people who hail him as the greatest golfer of his generation. What the British nation desires most to express is that it likes him not only for the super-skill with which he plays the game, but for the spirit in which he plays it. The British race, having been self-nurtured and self-developed by an innate love of adventuring and pioneering, admires any man who enters its strongholds in the role of invader, but it is not slighting the champions of golf or any other sport or pastime who have come from abroad fired by an ambition to win here to say that Mr. "Bobby" Jones is the most popular enemy we have ever known."—The Professional Golfer of America (quoting unnamed British magazine), 1927. (COURTESY UPI/BETTMANN NEWS-PHOTOS.)

fourth dimension. Not only was the term Grand Slam unthought of but the whole concept of winning those four championships in one year undreamed of. Hence the second parade up Broadway when the Grand Slam was only half consummated. The public would not even imagine that after what Jones had done he could then go on to win both the Open and Amateur Championships of this country as well.

Unknown to the public, Jones had decided to retire from competition after the 1930 championship season, regardless, a decision he told only to O. B. Keeler, the kindly newspaperman from Atlanta who covered all twenty-seven of the major championships in which Jones had competed since a boy of fourteen, during which he became Bobby's uncle-confessor. Jones chose 1930 because the United States Golf Association would pay his travel and hotel expenses to play in the Walker Cup Matches in late May that year. Jones was nowhere near as wealthy as the public thought. It would be financially unfeasible for him to play in those four championships again in the same year.

The Walker Cup Matches that year were scheduled for Royal St. Georges, at Sandwich, hard by the Atlantic in the south of England. They would be followed by the British Amateur, scheduled for St. Andrews, which gets its often fierce weather from the North Sea. In May, both events were being played somewhat earlier than usual. Jones therefore decided to whip his game into shape by playing in two tournaments he ordinarily wouldn't. They would feature the top pros in America, just the sort of competition he would need to put an edge on his game.

The first event was the Savannah Open, played in late February. Jones broke the course record in the first round with a 67. The following day, Horton Smith, who had won seven tournaments on the winter circuit, broke Jones's record with a 66. The day after that, Jones broke Smith's record with a 65. But he eventually lost the tournament to Smith by hitting his drive out of bounds on the next to last hole. That would be Jones's last defeat.

The second tournament was the Southeastern Open, played in Augusta, Georgia, a few weeks later. When Jones reached the sixteenth tee in the final round, he was leading the field by an almost unimaginable 18 strokes. A par 3, the sixteenth had created a traffic jam. There was a gang of players waiting to tee off when Jones got there. To kill time, he sat under a tree to chat with some of them. When at last it was his turn to play, forty-five minutes later, he found that his

Cyril Tolley lost to Jones in the final match of the 1930 British Amateur, the one major the Atlantan had never won, to set the stage for Jones's Grand Slam. (COURTESY THE BETTMANN ARCHIVE.)

"The red badge of courage always belongs upon the breast of the fighter who can break and then come back with a stouter heart than ever before.

"This crimson decoration of valor came to Robert Tyre Jones, of Atlanta, Georgia, twenty-one-year-old amateur, when he rode at last to the crest of the open golf championship of the United States. . . ."—Grantland Rice. (COURTESY RAY DAVIS.)

concentration had snapped. With an insurmountable lead, he carelessly finished with a double-bogey, a par, and another double-bogey. Still, he won by 13 strokes.

As captain of the American squad in the Walker Cup Match, Jones paired himself in the foursomes—alternate shots with one ball—with the most erratic member of the squad. With Jones's steady shotmaking, they nevertheless won, 8 and 7. In the singles, Jones put himself in the number-2 position so that Jimmy Johnston, the winner of the Amateur Championship the year before, in which Jones was upset in the first round, might have the honor of playing first. Jones won his match against Roger Wethered, a former British Amateur champion, 9 and 8.

Like anything so stupendous, the most difficult thing about the Grand Slam was getting it airborne. The British Amateur that followed the Walker Cup would prove to be the most obstinate championship Jones ever won. Before it was over, he would extract from it every possible bit of drama. Keeler called Jones's win at St. Andrews "destiny." Jones preferred to say it was due to "luck."

In the very first round, Jones started against his opponent, a thoroughly unknown Englishman named Sid Roper, with a birdie 3, a par 4, a birdie 3, an eagle 2, and a birdie 4. This barrage left even the sophisticated galleries of St. Andrews bug-eyed. Although Jones was 5 under for five holes, he still stood only 3 up. And Roper seemed not the least bit shaken.

On the eighth hole, Roper laid Jones a stymie, meaning his ball lay between Jones's and the cup. (The stymie would be abolished in 1952.) Jones couldn't negotiate a chip over it, and so Roper became only 2 down. But he ran out of holes on the sixteenth green, and the match went to Jones, 3 and 2.

In the fourth round, Jones was up against Cyril Tolley, who held the reputation for being the longest hitter in Britain, amateur or pro, and who was defending champion. The match came as close to spoiling the Grand Slam as anything later would. The wind was blowing at such force off the River Eden that it tore the sand out of the bunkers and turned the Old Course's outsized greens into skating rinks. Still, every man, woman, and child came out to watch. The town of St. Andrews itself was all but deserted.

By the time Jones and Tolley got to the seventeenth tee, all-even, each had been 1 up three different times. The seventeenth at St. Andrews, the Road Hole, is one of the most bizarre holes anywhere in golf, and one of the most strategic. To begin with, you had to drive to the left of a barnlike building known as "Auchterlonie's drying shed," where a well-known clubmaker dried the sap out of his hickory shafts. (Today, a hotel sits on the same site.) If you were long enough, and brave enough, you could carry the shed by aiming directly at it, thereby shaving off some of the hole's 461 yards. But you would be flirting with out-of-bounds on the right. This is the route both Jones and Tolley safely chose, Tolley slightly the longer.

The flagstick was in its most inaccessible position, behind a deep pot-bunker that guards the left-front of the two-tiered green. Behind the green lies the road the hole is named after and behind it a stone wall. Both are played as hazards. With the wind behind him, Jones at any cost didn't dare play a shot that would land him in the bunker, on the road, or against the wall. So he decided to play to the left of the green toward the eighteenth tee, a shot he had never seen anyone try before. Neither had anybody else.

After asking the stewards to wave back the gallery, he hit his mashie-iron, or

(Pages 132–133) *New York City gave Jones a tickertape parade when he returned home from his wins of the British Amateur and British Open in 1930. It was the second such reception in the Big Apple, which had honored the golfer similarly in 1927. Beside him in the car is his wife, Mary.* (COURTESY UPI/BETTMANN NEWSPHOTOS.)

At the Merion Cricket Club on the outskirts of Philadelphia, Jones received from Findlay Douglas, president of the USGA, his National Amateur trophy, marking the completion of the Grand Slam. (COURTESY RAY DAVIS.)

4-iron, precisely as he wanted, only to have the ball hit a bewildered spectator. But it came to rest almost exactly as he had planned. He was now in a position to pitch back to the green, safely out of reach of all hazards.

Tolley then tried to play safely to the right of the green. But the shot didn't come off, leaving him just short of that dreaded pot bunker. He then played an exquisite pitch over it that stopped only two feet from the cup, a shot he would later declare to be the finest of his career. Jones in turn pitched eight feet from the cup and holed the putt. Tolley sank his 2 footer. And so they marched to the eighteenth tee, still all-even.

The eighteenth hole at St. Andrews is 354 yards long. The wind that day was behind Jones and Tolley, and it was so strong that both were able to drive within 30 feet of the green. Jones elected to play a pitch-and-run through the Valley of Sin, a huge swale that stood between him and the flagstick. He left the shot 25 feet past the hole. Tolley in turn played a standard pitch, leaving himself about half that distance. Neither could hole his putt, and so the match went into extra holes.

The first hole at St. Andrews shares the fairway with the eighteenth and lies parallel to it, going in the opposite direction. So the wind was now in their teeth. After both hit drives as far as could be expected, Jones bore a long-iron 12 feet from the flagstick, a magnificent shot under the circumstances, and one that apparently shook Tolley a bit. He hit a slack second shot that stopped short of the Swilcan Burn, the narrow creek that fronts the putting surface. Tolley pitched over it, 7 feet from the cup for his par.

Jones lagged his putt, as he always did, and laid Tolley a stymie that couldn't possibly be negotiated. And that was the match. Jones was so exhausted by the desperate urgency of the struggle that he felt as though he had fought a battle "with broadswords."

Jones would have more anxious moments before reaching the final, all against Walker Cup teammates. Jimmy Johnston, the U.S. Amateur Champion, took him to the eighteenth green, where Jones, 1 up, was left with an 8-foot putt for a halve and the match. Coming to that final green, Jones had the eerie feeling that, come what may, he could not lose this championship. He knew before he stroked that 8 footer that it could not stay out. And it didn't.

Jones won his semi-final match against teammate George Voigt on the final green after having been 2 down with only five holes to play, again mainly with pressure-packed putting. In the final, Jones once again was up against Roger Wethered, who was no match against someone as determined as Jones, who could handle the Old Course the way Shakespeare might a crossword puzzle. Jones closed out Wethered on the thirtieth green.

Fifteen thousand spectators then swamped Jones in an effort "to see what made him tick," as Keeler would write. Jones had to be escorted by constables clear to the clubhouse of the Royal and Ancient Golf Club, which stands directly behind the first tee, a mile and a half away. A band had been set to play him in, but it never got to sound a note, so complete was the pandemonium.

Jones would go on to win the British Open at Hoylake, simply enough for him, by breaking the seventy-two-hole course record by a clean 10 strokes, leading the field from start to finish. It was plain to see that if anybody was going to stop Jones from winning a championship that year, it was not going to be Jones himself. He became the first man in forty years to win both the Open and Amateur Championships of Britain in the same year, prompting New York City to give him that second parade up Broadway.

The U.S. Open that year was played at Interlachen, in suburban Minneapolis, which was in the middle of one of the worst heat waves in its history. Several contestants had to stop play after dizzy spells, and one of them fainted. Jones was so drenched in perspiration after the first round that he couldn't unknot his necktie, de rigueur for national competition at the time. O. B. Keeler had to cut it off with a penknife.

Jones won this third leg of the Grand Slam by becoming the first man in the history of the Open to break par for seventy-two holes. Despite numerous water hazards and knee-high rough, Jones spun off 7 birdies in the first sixteen holes of the third round, knocking his second shots only inches from the flagstick. He might have waltzed away with the championship if an unfathomable incident had not occurred on the next-to-last hole.

The putter he dubbed "Calamity Jane" was given to Jones by pro Jimmy Maiden in 1920. According to Jones, the head was probably forged around 1900. In 1926, Spalding turned out half a dozen copies of the club and Jones handed several to friends and replaced the original "because it had become too light from continued polishing." (COURTESY RAY DAVIS.)

Interlachen's seventeenth was, and so remains, the longest par 3 in Open history, 263 yards to a green bordered by bunkers. Walter Hagen was the only man to birdie it all week. After getting a birdie on the sixteenth, Jones pushed his shot to the seventeenth green with a brassie, or 2-wood, wildly to the right. There were 15,000 spectators in Interlachen that day, at least three-fourths of whom were fighting each other to see Jones. None of them, however, saw where his ball ended up. Some thought it ricocheted off a tree into an adjacent lake, but couldn't be sure. Wherever it bounced, it was never found, although 200 people looked for the five minutes the rules allow.

This hand-crafted replica of a small post office, a tribute to Jones, was built by a Duluth, Georgia, postmaster in 1976 for the U.S. Open Golf Championship at the Atlanta Athletic Club. Postmarks during the Open bore the legend, "Calamity Jane Station, Georgia." (COURTESY RAY DAVIS.)

Jones was allowed a drop and played another ball. What with the penalty, he made a double-bogey, cutting his lead from a comfortable 3 strokes to an uneasy 1. On the last hole, a par 4, Jones purposely left his shot to the green short of the flagstick, about 40 feet, to avoid going over. He then stroked the putt in his usual molasses style. While it was still rolling, 10 feet from the hole, he started walking towards it. He knew it was in. And it was.

Jones did not wave his cap or shake his fist in the air. He simply smiled bashfully. He did not act as a man beating incalculable odds, although he actually was. Nor was he showing how good he might be or realizing how lucky he could get. This was a man walking toward an unnamed destiny, nonchalantly because he now knew it was preordained.

Jones was, of course, an immense favorite to win the U.S. Amateur, which, by historical coincidence, would be played at the (then) Merion Cricket Club, outside Philadelphia, where Jones had made his debut in championship golf fourteen years before when he was but a boy. The real problem for Jones at Merion turned out to be just getting there. One afternoon that summer, while playing a friendly round at East Lake, Jones was caught in a violent thunderstorm during which lightning bolts narrowly missed him as he ran for the clubhouse. One bolt exploded a double chimney of the clubhouse as Jones was passing underneath it, blasting bricks and mortar 300 feet away, the debris from which tore the shirt off his back and left a 6-inch gash on his shoulder.

Not three weeks later, Jones was walking along a sidewalk in downtown Atlanta on his way to a luncheon engagement when a runaway car mounted the curb and crashed into the very spot from which he had made a split-second broad jump. And, only days before the championship, he had unthinkingly tried to catch a blade in midair that had slipped from his razor. Luckily, he only scratched his hand.

At Merion, Jones stonewalled the field, winning the medal and never having to play past the fourteenth hole in any of his matches. In the final, he stood 8 up against Eugene Homans on the eleventh green. Jones was away, and putted 10 inches from the cup. Before Homans's putt to keep the match alive had gone half way to the hole, he knew it wasn't in. Smiling, he walked towards Jones with an outstretched hand. The Grand Slam, yet to be named such, was now a new chapter in golf's ancient history. Twenty years later, the Associated Press would vote it "the supreme athletic achievement of the century."

The gallery was the largest the USGA ever had for any championship—18,000 —certainly a record anywhere for a single match. For a moment, there was a churchlike silence among them. Then everyone, it seemed, clapped, howled, shrieked, and roared at the same time. The clubhouse was 600 yards away, and it would take a cordon of fifty marines to get Jones there unhurt by a delirious crowd who wanted to shake his hand or simply touch him, just to see if he were

The Jones grip. (COURTESY THE BETT-MANN ARCHIVE.)

During World War II, Major Robert Tyre Jones served in the U.S. Army. (COURTESY RAY DAVIS.)

real. "It was," said the *New York Times* in an editorial, "the most triumphant journey that any man ever traveled in sport."

In Merion's smallish clubhouse—despite Prohibition still in legal but not realistic force—champagne, corn whiskey, or bathtub gin was in everybody's hands. Jones's father was lost in the crowd, yelling, "Where's my boy? Where's my boy." For a caddie, Jones had drawn from a pool a nineteen-year-old named Howard Rexford, who waited in a corridor, wrapping his whole body around Jones's clubs, refusing to let anybody so much as look at them until Jones came out of the locker room. Although Jones had never asked him for any advice, young Howard had been touched by how thoughtful Jones had been toward him. When Jones finally stepped out of the locker room, he shook Howard's hand and thanked him, as though he could not possibly have won the championship without his aid, Rexford would recall.

Howard could feel some bills in Jones's hand. Without looking at them, he stuffed them into his shoe and took off on a dead run through the woods that line the eighteenth fairway. Out of breath, he then sat down and removed his shoe. There were ten twenty-dollar bills folded over, ten times more than he had ever earned in one week. Overcome by Jones's generosity and overwrought by the history he had been a party to, he began to sob.

In the retirement that soon followed, Jones dug into his law practice with a vengeance. He also became a vice-president of A. G. Spalding & Bros., the sporting goods firm. Using his engineering background, he designed for Spalding the first matched set of steel-shafted clubs. They sold steadily for forty-one years. His movie shorts, nine in all, proved so popular that he was asked to make nine more. They are selling to this day, in videocassettes.

In one of his few public appearances after illness invalided him, Jones sat for a TV interview. (COURTESY PGA OF AMERICA.)

But his most ambitious project was founding the Augusta National Golf Club. Two years after it opened, the club inaugurated the Masters Tournament, which was originally meant to be just a gathering of Jones's old fairway friends. Jones reluctantly decided to play as host, refusing to accept any prize money. But his name was still magic to golfers everywhere. So, in time, the Masters blossomed into one of the four major events on the golf calendar, although it is not, strictly speaking, the championship of anything. That's the only reason Jones would play in it.

Jones competed in the Masters haphazardly, having known from the outset that he could not bring back his old game unless some title was on the line. He last played in it in 1948, when he was stricken with a mysterious ailment that slowly paralyzed him. It took eight years to diagnose, when a specialist in New York City declared it to be syringomyelia, an extremely rare disease of the central nervous system. Jones was not expected to live much past the fifty-four he then was. He lived to be sixty-nine.

When Jones retired in 1930, the *New York Times* ran an editorial that ended in blank verse. Those words were even more apt at his death. "With dignity," the *Times* said, "he quit the scene on which he nothing common did, or mean."

11

Depression, Divots, and Drives

One golfer of extraordinary note spanned both the ages of Hagen and Jones and remained a competitive factor over four decades. Gene Sarazen is a model of the American success story, the sickly kid, born of immigrant parents, who grew up to become a giant in his profession. His father, Federico Saraceni, educated enough in Italy to have studied for the priesthood but then forced by familial impoverishment to emigrate and hammer at the trade of carpenter, embittered by the vicissitudes of life and speaking broken English, regarded the diversion of golf as suitable only for dilettantes and the despised idle rich.

Eugene, who arrived in 1902, had contributed to the family income from the ripe old age of four, first scavenging scrap, then peddling the *Saturday Evening Post*, picking fruit for three cents a quart, and lighting gas lamps for the town of Harrison, New York. He was eight and living in Harrison when he first became acquainted with golf. According to him, his mother remarked that a neighbor's son held the post of pro, caddie master, and greenskeeper at the nearby Larchmont Country Club. "He makes a lot of money," said Mrs. Saraceni, "and he needs boys to carry the sticks for the rich people."

The opportunity was too good to be dismissed, despite Papa Saraceni's disapproval. The fruits of the first day at the club amounted to forty-five cents, a quarter for caddying eighteen holes plus a munificent twenty-cent tip. By age eleven, Gene knew the difference between a jigger and a mashie and had moved on to the greener fields of the Apawamis Club, even closer to home.

This was 1913, the year that Francis Ouimet astounded the golf world with his defeat of Vardon and Ray. For the likes of Gene Saraceni, this event conjured up a particular version of the American dream, the humble caddie who rises to supremacy at golf. Gene honored the achievement of the native-born hero by adopting his interlocking grip. Ouimet's victory also affected the attitude at places like Apawamis to the extent the club held a one-day tournament for caddies, hitherto barred from the course on pain of immediate dismissal. In true Horatio Alger style, Gene should have astounded watchers with a brilliant performance; by this age Bobby Jones was already ready to challenge the best adults. The carpenter's son, who played hooky from school in order to compete, shot a dismal 105 for a last-place finish. The results, however, did not diminish his ardor for the game.

At age fifteen, with the United States entering World War I, he abandoned school for jobs in the war plants at Bridgeport, where the family had moved in a desperate effort to escape financial ruin. A near-fatal case of pneumonia and pleurisy altered his life. Death was banging on his door, when a surgeon successfully employed a new and risky operation. When Gene recovered, doctors warned he was too weak to return to his vocation of an apprentice carpenter. Golf suited his health needs and fulfilled his passion.

He began his full-time career at Beardsley Park, a local municipal nine-hole course, doing odd jobs—caddying, applying his woodworking skills to club repair—and, above all, practicing. He improved so much that the pro Al Ciuci recommended him for an assistant pro job at the private and affluent Brooklawn Country Club.

No longer was he Eugene Saraceni. After reading and rereading a brief newspaper account of a hole-in-one he had scored, he chalked up a blackboard with possible names that rang more like those of Chick Evans, Walter Hagen, or Jim Barnes. The winning choice was Gene Sarazen. And at Brooklawn he honed his game until it was sharp enough for him to enter increasingly tough competition.

He promoted himself to better pro slots, first in Indiana and then in Pennsylvania. At eighteen he qualified for the National Open in 1920, tying for 30th in the tournament that went to Ted Ray. He improved to 17th the following year and earned some ink for the 1921 PGA as the upstart who ousted Jock Hutchison.

While he surprised the experts with a victory in the Southern Open in New Orleans, when he qualified for the Open in Skokie, Illinois, in 1922, the twenty-year-old

Sarazen stood a bare five foot five at a flyweight of 115 pounds. He seemed no threat to long-hitting Wild Bill Melhorn, Bob Jones, and other luminaries.

However, Sarazen had visited the Skokie layout a month before the tournament began. He decided the key to scoring lay in avoiding the rough off the tee. Back home, he spent his practice time working on his driving and, during the week prior to the Open, he focused intensively on the greens, memorizing the contours, the pattern of the grain, the speed.

He fired a 2-over-par 72 for his opening round and a 73 on the second eighteen placed him only 3 behind the leader. Sarazen slipped on the third round to 75 as his putting betrayed him. Now he was 4 down to Melhorn and Jones. Before teeing off for the finale, with the brashness of youth he informed his partner, Johnny Farrell, "This is no time to be timid—I'm going for everything."

And on the first two holes he appeared

"In all his play, Sarazen's boldness and confidence are apparent. Like Bob Jones, he prefers to shoot for the pin, no matter what lies between or beyond. He regards a golf course in much the same light as an opponent. Old Man Par himself can be beaten. ... The fact that he doesn't always beat the old fellow discourages him not a whit." —O. B. Keller, The Wheeler Syndicate, 1923.

Young Gene Sarazen glows with the aura of a champion after the 1922 Open victory at Skokie. (COURTESY RAY DAVIS.)

to have written himself a prescription for disaster. He scrambled to par the first one, then bogeyed the second. Lying 25 feet from the cup on the third, however, Sarazen smacked the ball boldly, for a bird. He followed that with a 15 footer for a second par buster on the fourth. Confidence welled up and caution fled as Sarazen attacked with booming drives, stroke-cutting approaches to the greens that enabled him to walk off the ninth green with a flaming 33, despite the second-hole bogey.

The pace slackened as he played the final nine. He scored par for the first eight holes but needed a par 5 on the 485-yard eighteenth to finish ahead of Melhorn, already in the clubhouse with a 290. Prudence counseled he should avoid risk. But his caddie reminded Sarazen that Jones and another contender were on the course behind him and he could not discount their chances. Sarazen heeded the advice and, against the wind whistled a 250 yarder off the tee. But he was still a long way from the green: The Scylla of water lay to the left; Charybdis of out-of-bounds to the right. The caddie proposed caution. Sarazen recalled:

> I heard somebody say Jones and Melhorn were right back of me and I said, "Oh hell, give me that brassie." I shot right for the green and put it about 12 feet from the hole. On the seventeenth, Jones hit out of bounds and I won by a stroke.

The victory further popularized golf. Increasing numbers of Italian Americans had begun to arrive in the U.S., and the ethnic background of the winner gratified those still struggling to acclimate themselves in a world that was not always friendly. Sarazen himself had been snubbed because of his background but that served only to toughen his resolve. And for millions of others, Sarazen ratified the only-in-America, poor-boy-makes-good theme.

He quit his job as a club pro, took to the road for exhibitions, and climaxed his year by copping the PGA and then challenging and beating Sir Walter in a seventy-two-hole match, 3 and 2. The Haig had declined to enter the PGA that year and,

since he was the only heavyweight he hadn't beaten, the cocky Sarazen called him out. Promoters hyped the match as the "World's Golf Championship," which was not so far off since between them they held the major titles open to professionals. On the final day, Sarazen could barely hobble about the course because of a bellyache; when the match ended with his victory, he was rushed to the hospital for an acute appendicitis operation.

On the dark side, Sarazen exemplified the too-much-too-soon syndrome. He entered into a ten-year-long decline, with few bright moments. One exception: he did retain his PGA title in 1923, knocking off Hagen in a weird sudden-death playoff hole for the title. The hole chosen was a short par 4, dogleg left with trees abutting the angle cut in the fairway. Hagen played a solid drive to midfairway, leaving himself a routine pitch. Sarazen pressed his luck with a drive aimed at cutting the distance but which hooked badly into the woods. The ball could easily have caromed out of bounds or chosen an unplayable lie. Instead it was found still in play, at the edge of the trees, albeit in a swatch of deep rough. Sarazen dug into the ground with a niblick and the ball bounced onto the green, 2 feet from the cup for a sure birdie. Even the unflappable Hagen flapped. He promptly squibbed his pitch into the bunker and not even a magnificent out that almost found the cup could save him. Sarazen sank his putt for the winning bird.

Much later Herb Wind asked Sarazen how he had the temerity to challenge Hagen and resist Sir Walter's cool, intimidating presence.

> I don't think I had enough sense to know what pressure was. I was young, and, like most kids, I had lots of confidence when I was hitting the ball well. I knew that Hagen could play magnificent recovery shots, and I knew how good he was on the greens, but I figured I was a better shotmaker than he was. I felt I could beat him by outplaying him from tee to green.

From then on, Sarazen slid down the slope in a bumpy ride. Hailed as the new

Inspired by observing airplane lift, Sarazen created for himself a sand wedge. The club at left is a mashie niblick with a ⅜-inch wide sole— the bottom of the clubhead. (COURTESY PGA WORLD GOLF HALL OF FAME.)

U.S. hope to win the British Open, he busted out early, failing even to qualify for the last thirty-six holes. Not until 1932 would Sarazen win another major event. As he finished out of the money in a string of tournaments, the confidence of outplaying people from tee to green oozed away. No longer did he simply step up to the ball and take his stroke. An endless series of experiments with grips, backswings, foot placement, and the like gave him a new look each month, with the same dreary results.

As he approached his thirtieth birthday and the 1930s dawned, Sarazen analyzed his misfortunes and concluded his troubles all arose from his poor play in the bunkers. While he pondered the problem he happened to be learning to fly an airplane.

> I used to pal around with Howard Hughes; we played a lot of golf together. Hughes was a good golfer, about a 3 handicapper. . . . when I took off in the plane I pulled the stick back and the tail went down and the nose of the plane went up. Something flashed in my mind, that my niblick should be lowered in the back. So I had Wilson send me seven or eight niblicks. I went downtown in New Port Richey and bought all the solder I could get my hands on and put it on the clubs. What I did was put a flange on the back of the club and angled it so the flange hit the sand first, not the front edge, which was now raised [a fraction of an inch]. It was just like the airplane when it took off. Now I could hit behind the ball and explode it out. . . . in those days we played out of the sand with a regular niblick . . . and you had to chip the ball. You couldn't explode it, because the front edge of the club was sharp and would dig too much. Hagen was a terrible exploder. So was Jones.*

He tinkered feverishly at a machine shop near his home, attaching his gobs of solder to the underside of niblicks, to which, for good measure, he added a few more degrees of loft. Trial and error at a local course developed the tool Sarazen desired. He spent hundreds of hours practicing and reached a level where he was willing to bet even money he could get down in 2 from a lie in the bunkers.

He was not the first man to hit on the notion; various other experimenters including Bob Jones, Walter Hagen, and Horton Smith had all sought relief from bunker misery with altered niblicks, some of which the USGA banned as illegal.

Sarazen's innovation consisted in the delicate balance of a sloped flange designed to allow the front edge of the club face to remain above the ground at the moment of impact. The club slid through the sand rather than digging into it. Until Sarazen's innovation, golfers usually tried to sort of scoop the ball cleanly, which frequently resulted in a shot that flew over the green or, if the club bit, moved the ball only inches. A second aspect of his bunker tactics lay in the stroke Sarazen tailored to fit the newly designed weapon.

Unfortunately, Sarazen, like millions of others, had booted all of his hard-earned gains in the Crash of '29.

> I was absolutely flat in 1930, '31. All my securities were worthless. . . . I had my eye on the British Open in 1932 and Mary, my wife, said I had my game just right and I ought to go over. I said, "How could I? We don't have any money to spend, a thousand dollars." "You're going to go," she said. "You've improved your sand shot and your grip. You should win." So she got me the tickets.

Sarazen toted his sand wedge to the wars of the British Open in 1932. Fearing the overseers of the Royal and Ancient might react as they did with Travis's Schenectady putter, Sarazen literally kept the sand wedge under wraps until tournament play began. It was an immediate success, not only because, in his memory, he never failed to get down in 2 from the traps but perhaps because that had restored his confidence. The closest loser at the British Open, 5 strokes back, was Macdonald

---

* Golf authority Charles Price rejects the assertion that Jones was poor at extracting himself from bunkers.

Smith,* golf's perennial bridesmaid, a fellow who won more than fifty tournaments but never an Open championship.

The win at Prince's Golf Club was something of a sentimental triumph for Sarazen. In 1928, when Sarazen lay becalmed in the golf doldrums, he had journeyed to England with Walter Hagen for another try at the Open there. Hagen ordinarily employed a professional caddie, Skip Daniels, who even then, with failing eyesight and a limp, knew the British championship courses down to the last tuft of grass. In the sort of generous gesture typical of Hagen, he offered to let Sarazen have Skip Daniels for the tournament at Royal St. George's Golf Club.

Sarazen and the thin, rumpled caddy with his soiled, checked cap, faded string tie, and worn celluloid collar hit it off extremely well. Sarazen was in contention until the second round when he ignored Daniels's advice. He had hooked his drive on a hole known as the Suez Canal in honor of a watery ditch that crossed the fairway. When Daniels pulled a short iron from the bag, Sarazen scorned safety. "I can make the green with a full brassie poke."

Daniels demurred: "If you topped a brassie out of this bristly rough, you'd land in that big ditch. Better take this niblick, lob one up short of the hazard and play it safe for a 5."

That was not the Sarazen style. He ordered the brassie in place of the niblick. The ball traveled a mere 20 yards, leaving him still in the rough. Daniels tried to comfort him: "Don't let this upset you, sir. You made the braver choice in gambling for a 4. It was just bad luck that you caught the ditch. Forget it, sir. We'll make it up."

But Sarazen paid full price for his rashness. He finally reached the fairway on the next shot, but his score for the hole was a 7, 2 over par, and the margin that separated him from the eventual winner, Hagen.

At Princes in 1932, Sarazen strokes toward his British Open honors.
(COURTESY THE BETTMANN ARCHIVE.)

Before Sarazen left, he apologized to Daniels, admitting his error in not taking the sage advice. The caddy consoled him: "We'll try again, sir, won't we. Before I die, I'm going to win an Open championship for you."

When Sarazen first arrived at the Sandwich course in 1932, he brought along a young caddie, for Daniels was now barely sighted. But the new hand failed to work out and Sarazen recruited Daniels, promising to accept his counsel. Largely on instructions from the caddie, Sarazen had vanquished the tough eighth hole easily. It involved a blind shot over a well-trapped ridge 80 yards or so before the green. He carried the ridge the first two rounds with his brassie but on the third and fourth encounters, with a mild wind behind, Daniels chose the spoon. The results were a pair of eagles, crushing the field. When

---

* In the magazine *The American Golfer*, Tommy Armour, a close friend of Smith who lost the Open at Carnoustie to Armour by finishing 5–6–5, wrote: "If we all played golf like Mac, the National Open Championship could be played on one course every day in the year and never a divot mark would scar a beautiful fairway. He has the cleanest twenty-one-jewel stroke in golf. He treats the grass of a golf course as though it were an altar cloth."

Sarazen received his trophy, he asked permission for Daniels to stand beside him on the platform. And as a final gesture to the caddie, Sarazen gave him his camel's hair coat. His last vision of Daniels was of the caddie, pedaling his bike across the moors, the polo coat flapping in the wind. Daniels had helped Sarazen to the British Open, and as he prophesized, he was dead within a few months.

Braced by the win, worth only 100 pounds in cash but more in eventual rewards from equipment manufacturers and exhibition sponsors, Sarazen now embarked upon a rampage along the tournament trail. At the Fresh Meadow course at Princes, Sandwich, two weeks after Sarazen's victory in the Open, several golfers trampled par as the field headed for the final eighteen. Sarazen's first rounds were an out-of-the-money 74 and 76. He came to the tee to start his last round needing a 68 to win over Bobby Cruickshank and Phil Perkins. Gene went out in a torrid 32, leaving the ostensible leaders only the hope of a collapse over the final nine. Sarazen continued to blaze away—4, 4, 3, 4, 3, 3, cooling off to par the last three holes and card a 66.

After this performance, no less a student of the game than Bob Jones said of Sarazen:

Sarazen has ever been the impatient, headlong player who went for everything in the hope of feeling the timely touch of inspiration. When the wand touches him, he is likely to win in a great finish as he did at Fresh Meadow and Skokie, or in a parade as he did at Prince's, but if it touch him not throughout the four rounds, the boldness of his play leaves no middle ground. When he is in the right mood, he is probably the greatest scorer in the game, possibly, that the game has ever seen.

The sand wedge changed the approach to one of the hazards of golf. There were other technological innovations that influenced play in obvious and in subtle ways. Manufacturers had continued to experiment with the makeup of the ball. Liquid cores* from various substances replaced the old solid cores because of superior restitution—the speed and capacity to return to its

Sarazen putts at Merion in the 1934 Open. He finished second. Even today, Merion retains the basket-tipped flag sticks.

"There is a subtle difference between bravado and braggadocio. Sarazen's cockiness is defined by the former term and Walter Hagen's arrogance by the latter. Gene has the knack of boasting without giving hearers the impression that he is a swashbuckling fire-eater. There is a quiet, ingenuous matter-of-factness about Sarazen's boasts that disarms listeners."—George Trevor, New York Sun. (COURTESY WIDE WORLD PHOTOS.)

* Shortly after the introduction of the Haskell ball, some wizard invented balls with compressed air at the center. They performed nicely, except that occasionally, when smacked with a driver, they exploded. On at least one occasion, a ball blew up in a golfer's pocket.

round self after having been knocked, for an instant, into ovoid shape. Balls of different sizes and weights dove, fluttered, rolled, and sailed according to their innate whims and the fancy of individual golfers. The "improvements" transformed the standard courses of less than 6,000 yards into almost a series of drive and pitch holes. Chick Evans decried the emphasis on distance.

> ... the men who build the golf courses and the men who love the variety of shots of other days lament the untoward influence. The pride of golf has been that it included in its championship competitions players with an age-range of fully twenty-five years. . . . But the present-day ball is for the slugging youth. With it he can out-date any course in a few seasons and even spacious America will soon have to grudge the room he demands. The fine second shot is a thrill of the past and the variety that really distinguished the good player from the poor one has been lost. We all know the lusty youth who carries only a driver, a slotted club and a putter.

To students of golf, this seemed like the Babe Ruth syndrome, the long ball that changed the strategy and tactics of a game. Meanwhile, the governing bodies wrestled with the problem of standards.

In 1929, the USGA issued a decree. It would approve only balls of 1.68 inches in diameter with a weight of no more than 1.55 ounces. Officially, the balls began falling on fairways in January 1931. They were a disaster. The pros derided them as balloon balls while the hackers discovered that, because of their airy quality, mishits traveled farther into the rough or out of bounds.

A year later, the USGA changed the specifications to the current dimensions of 1.68 inches in diameter and a weight of 1.62 ounces. The Royal and Ancient, mindful of the windswept nature of Britain's courses, opted for a slightly smaller ball—1.62 inches in diameter but the same weight as the American.

Still, the danger of an excess of rabbit vexed authorities. The USGA solved that menace in 1942, with a rule that restricted the initial velocity of a ball to 250 feet-per-second (plus 2½ percent at 70 degrees F at sea level). Cores today consist of silicone, whose viscosity is such that they appear solid but instead are fluid. The advantage of the silicone core is extremely limited compressibility, which arrests the shock of club impact.

While the great minds of golf pondered the infant science of aerodynamics, a modest invention of a mundane nature stupendously enhanced the game. Along with tycoons, physicians and dentists had flocked to the game. Fittingly, it was one of their ilk who, disturbed by the messy, unhygienic and time-wasting business of molding tees from the sand box, revolutionized the ritual of the drive. Dr. William Lowell, a New Jersey dental surgeon, noticed his hands and fingers turning rough and chapped, undoubtedly from the act of swishing a handful of coarse sand in a bucket of dirty water in order to form the tee. According to legend, Dr. Lowell, while working on a patient, became distracted. His eye fell upon a flag stick mounted on the wall. Without further ado, he grabbed it, donned his hat and coat, leaving behind an astonished patient. Back home, Dr. Lowell whittled away at the flagstick until he produced a 2-inch peg, the first golf tee, which he painted red. He quickly tried out his invention, decided it was an idea whose time had come, and after some trial and error, produced an effective design. Others had tinkered with tee-like devices, but Lowell's was the first successful commercial one. In fact, on December 12, 1899, one George Grant received patent 638,920 for a tee.

Initially, fellow club members derided Lowell's device, arguing golf rested on tradition and that such frippery would never be accepted. However, Lowell persevered, and he secured a patent that included specifications of color. He mortgaged himself to the limits and incorporated the Reddy Tee Company. By its second year the firm grossed 300,000 dollars, largely through an order for a billion tees from the five and dime giant, F. W. Woolworth. At the other end of the fiscal pole, John D. Rockefeller, now in his eighties, placed an order. When Walter Hagen started to walk about the

In 1933, Johnny Goodman became the last amateur to win the U.S. Open. He also fired low score for the 1937 amateur title. (COURTESY RAY DAVIS.)

courses with a tee lodged behind his ear, tens of thousands of golfers followed suit. Dr. Lowell's tale, however, lacks a happy ending. His patents proved hard to defend and others copied the idea and competed for business. He died penniless some thirty years after that sudden stroke of genius.

The most significant change in equipment, however, was the development and acceptance of the steel shaft during the 1920s. Wooden shafts, almost exclusively of hickory, were extremely susceptible to torsion from the force of the swing, leading to a change in the attitude of the clubhead between the moment of address and the actual collision with the ball. Wet weather, temperature extremes and age warped and decayed hickory and the subtle differences in the stock of wood at the factory inhibited production of matched clubs.

Steel shafts finally were legalized by the USGA in 1926 and the Royal and Ancient approved them three years later. The problems of torsion during the swing disappeared. The metal was largely impervious to climate and time. And most important, it was now possible to mass produce perfectly matched sets of clubs.

Less agreeable, the new shafts brought an incredible proliferation of clubs designed to cover every possible shot. The old guard moaned the loss of true tests of human mettle, the full, three-quarter and half-strength shots all with the same club. Walter Hagen's bag now held as many as twenty-eight sticks, including such irons as a 5, 5.5, 7, and 7.5. Considering what else Hagen toted in his bag—a clock, an umbrella, a ball cleaner with brushes, a thermometer, a tee case, a wind gauge, a caddie whistle, a rule book, an extra sweater, and a change of shoes, one must pity his caddies. In fact, in 1934, when Lawson Little★ entered the British Amateur at Prestwick, his caddie demanded extra pay for the load he was expected to tote. In 1936, the USGA decided a full quiver amounted to fourteen sticks, announcing, "The multiplicity of clubs tends toward mechanization of the game."

By this time, however, a full bag was the least of the sport's troubles. Golf, like every other endeavor, staggered under the weight of the Great Depression. Roughly a quarter of the 4,500 U.S. country clubs operating in 1929 folded as members could not afford the dues and notes against the property became due. The purses for tournament pros, which had been steadily climbing, shrank and the number of events dropped.

When President Franklin Delano Roosevelt and his "Brain Trust" devised the National Recovery Administration to cope with the deflated economy, the PGA assured General Hugh "Iron Pants" Johnson that it would cooperate to the utmost. George Jacobus, president of the PGA, wrote to the twenty-five sectional groups that made up the organization, calling upon them to support the code for dealing with caddies, greens workers, and the like. Jacobus also expressed a willingness to press manufacturers to eliminate what he termed "unfair trade practices which have been cutting into the pro's business."

The U.S. Supreme Court declared the entire NRA out of bounds. But the PGA continued to attempt to ameliorate the blows of the Depression. The organization created its own unemployment relief fund, which offered quick, small loans to cover rent, food, or transportation in emergency situations.

In this bleak time, Bobby Jones chose to swim against the economic undertow. He decided to create a new golf club in Augusta, Georgia, one designed to meet his notions of proper challenges. The notion had been percolating in his mind for several years. In 1929, shortly before Wall Street drove into the deep rough, Jones had traveled to Pebble Beach on the West Coast for the National Amateur. To the shock of all, a twenty-one year old from Omaha, Johnny Goodman, the fifth of ten orphaned children, ousted Jones in his first match. The loser had arrived by Pullman from Atlanta while the winner was so stone-broke he rattled from Nebraska to San Francisco aboard a cattle car.

Instead of folding his tent and slipping away to his home, Jones explored the local courses. He delighted particularly in

While the Augusta National course still lay under construction, its creator experimented with a drive from one of the proposed tees. (COURTESY UPI/BETTMANN NEWSPHOTOS.)

Cypress Point. Taken with the beauty of the layout, which preserved all of the natural glory without sacrificing the challenge to the golfer, Jones complimented the architect, Alister Mackenzie, and approached him about collaborating on a new course in Augusta, Georgia.

The 365-acre, gently rolling site was a pre–Civil War indigo plantation turned into a nursery copiously garlanded with magnolia trees, cork trees, huge pines, and flowering shrubs. Jones, along with New York banker Cliff Roberts★ who vacationed in the area, formed a holding company and sold the idea of a national membership—no more than thirty people from the Augusta area would be allowed. In those parlous times it was possible to set the initiation fee at 350 dollars and dues at sixty dollars a year.

Aside from retaining the scenic wonders of what would be known as the Augusta National Country Club, Jones and

Mackenzie agreed the design principle should be a test of strategy rather than one based on penalties. At Augusta, players could choose options for attacking the course. The notion was to reward daring; the greens for par 5 holes could be reached in 2, but the woes of bunkers, water and rough awaited anyone who simply swung a mighty club without accuracy. The fairways were disarmingly wide and, whereas some courses were cratered with as many as 200 or so traps, the Jones-Mackenzie blueprint sprinkled a mere twenty-two. However, the huge greens, where pin position could drastically toughen the demands on a player, increased the importance of that aspect of the game.*

While Mackenzie more than satisfied Jones with his approach, the foremost golf architect of the first three decades of American golf, Donald Ross,★ overcame his chagrin at being snubbed, and flattered the creators of Augusta by redrafting plans

---

*During the early 1930s some students of golf questioned whether putting skills should possess high values. They argued the weak player who could putt had an advantage over the person who mastered all the strokes except those on greens. Gene Sarazen went so far as to propose doubling the diameter of the cup to 8 inches and some experimental rounds used the oversized hole. But the idea never was accepted.

The home of the Masters sits for an aerial inspection during its early years. (COURTESY FRANK CHRISTIAN STUDIOS.)

for the Number Two Course at Pinehurst Country Club in North Carolina with imitations of broad fairways, limited rough, a few well placed bunkers, and expansive greens.

Pinehurst and Ross exemplified how far golf had come in just thirty years. Originally, James Walker Tufts, a Boston pharmacist who became a tycoon through his American Soda Fountain Company, said he "planned Pinehurst with an eye to bettering the condition of fellowman and affording northern invalids an opportunity to enjoy an unexcelled health resort at moderate expense."

Tufts bought the 5,000 acres in 1891 for a

buck an acre and the locals silently chortled. Bob Harlow described the property in its virginal state:

> The sand barrens were regarded as good for nothing but to hold the earth together. Water and fertilizer filtered through the sand and left no trace. When it rained a close listener could hear a sizzle; the rain had struck Hell. Crows were reported to carry their rations when flying over these sand dunes.

In 1897, a handful of guests arrived with the basic implements of golf. Three years later, the management recognized the desires of the clientele and brought in Donald Ross from Scotland to act as golf pro.

Ross built a nine-hole course, which not only temporarily satisfied the urge for a pastime but also acted as a fire break.

Ross soon evolved into a golf architect, starting at Pinehurst where he created five of the more than 600 courses he designed in the States, a strong antidote to the shoddy layouts of Bendelow. When Harry Vardon toured the U.S. in 1900, Pinehurst was one of his stops. At that time, the greens consisted of hard-packed sand.

Ross basically believed, as Jones did, in the strategic rather than the penal approach. He used bunkers sparingly; his greens tended to perch on the crown of a slope. He plotted his layouts to offer a variety of holes with an exceptional number of interesting shots, suited to the fairly good and even accomplished player.

The Jones-Mackenzie inspiration saw its first golf in the autumn of 1932. Instant admiration followed. Golfers approved the test of their skills and the beauty of the landscape with its azaleas, flowering dogwoods, camelias, magnolias, and majestic pines. Talk of holding the U.S. Open there reached the ears of the members. But they decided they'd rather put on their own golf gala.

Invitations went out to all past winners of the U.S. Open and U.S. Amateur who were still active, plus twenty other worthy golfers. Of the eighty-eight asked, seventy-two golfers accepted bids for a March date in 1934. The stars included Hagen, Ed Dudley, the Augusta pro, Craig Wood, Paul Runyan,★ and Horton Smith.★ Jones, who had retired from tournament play in 1930, reluctantly agreed to play. The four-year layoff from competitive action, however, doomed him to a curiosity, well behind the leaders. Horton Smith finished at 284, 1 better than Wood.

The success of the tournament and the impeccable cast earned it instant fame and its current title of The Masters.

Paul Runyan and Horton Smith graced the pro tour during the 1930s. The diminutive Runyan (who never tipped the scales at more than 125 pounds) began, as a boy, to sneak away from his father's Arkansas dairy farm to caddie at the Hot Springs Golf and Country Club. His dad considered the sport "frivolity," and never ac-

The master of the Masters congratulates the first winner of his tournament, Horton Smith. (COURTESY UPI/BETTMANN NEWSPHOTOS.)

(Top, left) *Jones eventually passed on the management of the Masters to a former New York banker, Cliff Roberts.* (COURTESY RAY DAVIS.)

(Top, right) *Starting out as a pro at Pinehurst, Donald Ross developed into the foremost golf architect of the first three decades of the twentieth century.* (COURTESY RAY DAVIS.)

cepted it as a vocation. But Runyan brought home 45 to 90 dollars a week hauling bags, and shagging balls for pro lessons. "I wasn't a good player right from the start. I had to work for it. I was not a natural. All the kids in the caddie pen beat me, until I just dug it out and became better."

Indeed, he advanced to apprentice pro and soon was able to deposit 500 to 700 dollars a week in his boss's till while on a salary of 75 or 80 dollars a week. He won the state open four times between 1920 and 1930, and as an assistant, found ample time to hit 600 balls a day.

I recognized early that I had to be very good at the short game or I wasn't going to go anywhere. All my playing career I was made fun of for my small size and being a short hitter . . . I lived with being an unorthodox player . . . I swayed way back behind the ball intentionally and lunged past it to get more leverage. I never learned to hit it far.

While Runyan deprecated his stroke, others discerned quality. Horton Smith counseled: "Watch Paul's unhurried swing. It's as lazy as a Spanish siesta, as delicately fashioned as a flower petal."

He set out on the minuscule pro tour over the 1930–31 season after the members at Metropolis, a suburban New York club, put up 3,500 dollars for his expenses. The train ticket that carried him from New York to Florida to California, and then back through the southwest to Louisiana, Florida, and finally home, added up to 202 dollars plus an extra 8 dollars a night for a berth. He won 4,700 dollars that first year, and his sponsors graciously refused their share of the profits. Soon he was banking as much as 14,000 dollars a year, a small fortune during the Great Depression. His 6,767 dollars in tournament gold topped everyone for 1934.

Twice he won the PGA (1934, 1938), on the second occasion outplaying Sam Snead in the finals. The matches were at Shawnee-on-the-Delaware with temperatures hovering around 100° with a wilting 90 percent humidity. Runyan kept himself fresh and strong with soaks in tubs of cold water before play. Snead outhit him by close to 50 yards every drive, but Runyan killed him on the par-5 holes, pitching up close enough to birdie while Snead struggled to pars.

Horton Smith didn't smoke, drink, or cuss, which stamped him as a man apart from the likes of Barnes, Hagen, and Jones. He also was one of the few professionals with a collegiate background (two years at Missouri State Teachers).

As a twenty-two-year-old stripling, Smith blazed around the circuit in 1929–30, capturing seven of nineteen tournaments, finishing second in four others to earn about 20,000 dollars. The "Missouri Rover," "Joplin Jigger Juggler," or "Joplin Ghost" (how the writers struggled to create color for the tour!) outshot Bob Jones at the Savannah Open, just before Jones made his successful bid for the Grand Slam of 1930. Shortly after Savannah, Jones revenged himself upon Smith with a 13-stroke whupping at the Southeastern Open.

Smith repeated his 1934 Masters victory in 1936. Although these are his only two major titles, he finished at the top of the list in thirty tournaments recognized by the PGA, and in '36 his paltry 7,662 dollars topped all money winners.

Al Barkow, in "Golf's Golden Grind" (a history of the tour), labels Smith the one player of his era with "organizational and public-relations talent. . . . he showed sponsors that at least one pro knew how to say thank you." He personally typed out letters of appreciation while aboard trains after finishing a tournament. Other recognized his genius, and he became chairman of the tournament committee in 1933, eventually becoming president of the PGA after a distinguished career during WWII as a recreation specialist.

Older masters of the art gathered at Augusta in the persons of Sarazen, Jones, Hagen, and Armour. (COURTESY FRANK CHRISTIAN STUDIOS.)

12

The Tour Takes Off

Haphazard scheduling, slow payment of prize money, and poor promotion bedeviled the circuit followed by tournament professionals during the 1920s and early 1930s. While Walter Hagen traveled in limousines, dined on prime cuts, quaffed fine scotch whiskey, and enjoyed the hospitality of the rich and famous, most of those on the road struggled to meet their expenses, staying in cheap rooming houses, skimping on meals and doubling up in cars to save a few bucks. Jack O'Brien's Texas Open suggested a vista of jackpots, but as hard times struck the world in the 1930s, sponsors became increasingly scarce and some reneged on the payoff. To protect themselves, the pros sometimes conspired to share the pots equally, no matter who won.

Tommy Armour's wife, Estelle, had joined forces with two other spouses, Josephine Espinosa and Nellie Cruickshank (wives of Al and Bobby, respectively) to scare up sponsors. The trio succeeded in arranging a couple of gigs but they lacked the expertise and peculiar talents necessary to build a tour and soon lost heart.

In an effort to maximize their opportunities, the golfers engaged a Newark, New Jersey, newspaperman and golf addict Hal Sharkey to provide management. Sharkey arranged for some geographical logic to the· sequence of tournaments, sought out potential backers, negotiated with hotels to offer cut rates for the pros, and called on his press contacts to build interest. Sharkey brought improvements but bickering over details soured him on the job. Players gravitated to the tournaments with the biggest prize, pulling out of others even after their appearances had been advertised. Neither the sponsors nor the golfers wanted to pay Sharkey what he felt he was worth. He quit.

A Chicago sportswriter, Francis J. Powers, lasted one year before the PGA hired Bob Harlow for 100 dollars a week, a good salary during the Depression but in Harlow's case only a fraction of his income since he continued to manage Hagen and arrange exhibitions for several other golfers like Paul Runyan, Horton Smith (who had become head of the PGA tournament committee), and Ed Dudley. He also filed a syndicated column for about a hundred newspapers.

Harlow knew how to approach businesses, country clubs, radio stations, and newspapers for the promotion of tournaments and exhibitions. When Horton Smith suddenly surfaced in 1929 as a prime player, Hagen and Harlow engaged him for a series of 100 exhibitions. Remembered Smith:

> We played as many as five or six exhibitions a week. . . . [One time] we played thirty-three consecutive days across Illinois, Missouri, Oklahoma, Texas, Kansas, Nebraska, Colorado, Utah, and Idaho.

Harlow, a minister's son who learned at his father's knee the arts of proselytizing and fund raising, knew how to beat the bushes to flush out sponsors and money. He negotiated with Chambers of Commerce, instructing communities on how to fund a tournament through donations from local businesses anxious to see their towns publicized and dinners where Walter Hagen would gossip about his experiences. Harlow introduced show biz to the tour, publicizing his wares with snappy patter.

He brought some order to the chaos of the circuit, added tournaments, taught officials at country clubs such rudiments as the need to schedule starting times. (Formerly, every player simply showed up at the first tee.) Local papers received advance notice of pairings, sparking fans to come out to see their favorites. Harlow assiduously cultivated the press, whom he supplied with releases, bulletins, and refreshments.

Considerable bickering continued to roil relationships between those who toured and the bulk of golf pros who remained at home tending to their country club members. A proposal that the tour players tithe ten percent of the pot to finance a manager like Harlow drew a negative vote from the men on the circuit, as did a suggestion each individual pay a buck whenever he entered a tournament. And the stay-at-home guys resented the notion of their dues supporting those on the road.

Wiser heads recognized the symbiosis of teaching and touring pro. A nontour PGA official in 1930 counseled:

I believe that the [PGA] should be vitally interested in every phase of golf. Personally, I feel that the tournament golfer is a great asset to golf. As it has been said, it is a stimulation to the interest in golf and if interest in golf is stimulated it will redound to the advantage of every professional in the country.

And of course as club professionals taught members the arts of the game, the audience for tournaments grew. The local pro was also in an excellent position to work with Harlow to develop a tournament. The mutual benefits derived by teaching and touring pro continue today.

Harlow even managed to brighten the dismal outlook of Depression-forced cutbacks. He triumphantly announced "fewer and better tournaments" for the 1934–1935 season. Total purses for events ran as low as 1,500 dollars (California Open at Lakewood) with top money of 6,500 dollars for the tournament at Glendale. A Harlan, Kentucky, event, sponsored by the area's businessmen and coal mine operators during a period of bloody labor union strikes, offered 2,500 dollars for competition over a nine-hole course hacked into the mountains and surrounded by slag heaps. Coal miners, unfamiliar with the sport, watched with some amazement. After a pro had sunk a hole-in-one, one spectator leaped to his feet, shouting, "Home run!"

Apart from the PGA's own championship and the USGA-run U.S. Open, the two-year-old toddler at the Augusta Na-

When the U.S. Ryder Cup Team of 1933 dined, among those at the table, at the extreme right was the newly appointed director of the professional tour, Robert Harlow. (COURTESY RAY DAVIS.)

tional Country Club, through the shine of the Jones sponsorship and the luster of its entries, had achieved national significance. The Masters now offered 5,000 dollars in rewards. And in 1935, a blow by Gene Sarazen thrust that already prestigious event to the golf forefront.

Sarazen had been one of the few top players not to have entered when the tournament made its 1934 debut. In the final round, a year later, he arrived at the par-5, 485-yard, fifteenth hole, 3 strokes behind Craig Wood. Paired with Walter Hagen, Sarazen blasted a 250-yard drive that deposited the ball in a sloppy patch looking directly at the pond guarding the green. In the distance, they heard a faint cheer as Wood birdied the final hole. Hagen remarked, "Well, Gene it sounds as if it's all over." Sarazen casually asked his caddie what it would take to beat Wood. Nonplussed, the bag toter mumbled he needed four birdies. Hagen giggled at Gene's temerity.

Because the ball lay almost submerged, Sarazen chose a 4-wood rather than his spoon. He laid into the ball with a hefty swing and the ball screamed off more like a baseball line drive than a conventional high arc. It easily soared over the water before setting down on the front edge of the green. The ball bounced once, then glided swiftly, dead on the flagstick. It slowly decelerated before gently plopping

into the cup. The double eagle served as the equivalent of the three birdies Sarazen had needed to draw even.

The shot, which for golfers bears as much fame as Babe Ruth's alleged called home run in the 1932 World Series or Bobby Thomson's ninth inning homer to win the 1951 playoff, was, according to Sarazen, witnessed by perhaps two dozen people. But the obervers included the two most famous individuals in the sport. For aside from Hagen, Bob Jones happened to have wandered out to see the twosome at work.

Sarazen kept his cool, shooting par on the final three holes to tie Craig Wood. A reporter described Wood's reaction: "He looked like a man who had won a sweepstakes and then had lost the ticket on the way to the payoff window."

Whatever the initial effect, Wood proved no match for Sarazen in the thirty-six-hole playoff. Gene scored an even par 144 while the unlucky Wood could only manage a 149. Sarazen's headline-making work endowed the Masters with enormous publicity and further cachet with the public.

For all of Sarazen's heroics, however, the tournament game's cast of characters was changing. Walter Hagen was well past his prime. Sarazen would continue to be a factor but he too would surrender his titles to younger men. Bob Jones had retired, removing the greatest amateur ever to tee off. Johnny Goodman, who beat

Fred Corcoran (left) built up the PGA circuit, and then performed similar duties for the distaff side, all the while giving the likes of Sam Snead, Ted Williams, and Babe Didrikson Zaharias, the benefits of his personal management. Joe Dey (right) directed the USGA for many years before moving over to the PGA. His contributions to the game brought overseas recognition in the form of election as captain of the R & A in 1975. (COURTESY RAY DAVIS.)

him at Pebble Beach, stuck around long enough to become the last amateur to win the U.S. Open in 1933. But from now on, the professionals would dominate tournament golf, and the competitions for those who played only for cups and medals would decline in public favor, both in the U.S. and in Great Britain.

As a consequence of the growing strength of the pro tournament tribe and the conviction of some who believed Bob Harlow wore too many hats, the PGA replaced Harlow with Fred Corcoran,★ as a fulltime employee.

Corcoran was no new kid on the golf block. Born in Cambridge, Massachusetts, in 1909, he started to caddie as an eight-year-old at the Belmont Country Club. At the advanced age of twelve, he became caddie master and at the venerable age of fifteen, the club's directors put him in charge of the golf program. He was still in his teens when he was appointed executive secretary of the Massachusetts Golf Association. He supervised competitions, handled publicity, and achieved renown with his scoreboard, an elaborate, multicolored crayon system that provided hole-by-hole information on tournament progress. The USGA itself took note of this accomplishment, signing him up to serve as its official scorer for the major USGA tournaments, played by both men and women.

Corcoran's stroke of genius on behalf of the pros was his notion to sell cities on the value of a big tournament. He demonstrated to the business segment that the front money would be more than covered through the bucks spent by the seventy-five to one hundred pros eating, drinking, and sleeping in the neighborhood, and from gate receipts. Corcoran persuaded the U.S. Sun Belt that it could attract both visitors and business to the communities through publicity generated by hotshot golfers competing in warm sunshine while the rest of the nation shivered and shoveled snow.

He was a peerless engine of puffery. Corcoran stuffed newspapers with anecdotes and statistics, albeit not always accurate ones.

The modest circuit developed by Harlow grew from less than twenty tournaments to a more robust twenty-eight events. In 1936, the pros fought over a total of 150,000 dollars. A year later, with Corcoran running the show, the figure zoomed to 175,000 dollars. Horton Smith led in dollars won for 1936 with 7,884.75, but in 1937, Lighthorse [a nickname given by Damon Runyon because of the speed with which he took his strokes] Harry Cooper pocketed almost double, 13,573.69 dollars. The amounts, even that of Cooper, would put a 1990 tour player at the very bottom of the list, but with 20 million Americans unemployed, these wages of golf were certainly respectable.

It was not easy. Corcoran's annual reports to the PGA listed tournaments cancelled for lack of sponsorship, and big events like the Los Angeles Open sliced the 1920s total of 10,000 dollars in prizes to little more than half. By 1939, however, the 10,000 dollar affair again fattened the game and Corcoran boasted about the 500,000 spectators drawn to tournament golf.

In the pages of *The Professional Golfer of America*, Corcoran exhorted professionals to join the winter tour. He stressed the advantages of the experience for the young player in the way of "education, contacts, competitive poise and self-discipline." He candidly reported that the chances of an unknown youngster breaking into the money list was extremely slim. However, Corcoran advised that the fifteen-week adventure might involve an outlay of only 1,000 dollars. "A player may make the trip stopping at the better hotels at a cost between two or three dollars." Caddie fees ran about a dollar to a dollar fifty and entry fees to tournaments with 5,000 dollar purses were five dollars. There was an added charge of one dollar per 1,000 above that. All told, Corcoran figured a player could get by for roughly ten dollars a day and, if accompanied by his wife, the cost "may be conservatively in the neighborhood of twelve to fifteen dollars."

The picture may have been a bit rosy. Raising the 1,000 dollars was beyond most would-be tour candidates and, on Corcoran's budget, the meal money was skimpy

and the travel facilities on the tatty side. However, he was also somewhat of a seer. He saw the outbreak of World War II as an ill wind redounding to the good of domestic pros. With Europe in conflict, Americans would be forced to vacation at home, following the sun in the winter months and inevitably swelling the tournament galleries. He was quick to act on his insight, talking promoters into raising purses. And in less than ten years, the players were battling for slices of a 750,000 dollar pie.

One of the first individuals available for Corcoran's pumpery was an awesome former amateur from the American West, via U.S. army overseas posts, Lawson Little. An army brat, Little became acquainted with golf in San Antonio and as a prepubescent played a few times on nine-hole courses in the Philippines while his father was stationed there. Still in short pants when the family took up station in Tientsin, China, he discovered the eighteen holes maintained by foreigners in the Russian concession. His experience there supplied good fodder for Corcoran.

Chinese burial customs are such that there were countless graves all over the golf course. The caskets were placed near the surface and covered with soil. . . . Many golfers found that shifting winds and rotting coffin wood produced some interesting surprises. It happened to me, the day I played. The course scorecard included the sentence, "Ball may be lifted and dropped from an open coffin." I was looking for a lost ball, guessed that it had gone into a nearby coffin and reached in. My hand landed on a pile of human bones.

When the family returned to the States, Little took up golf in earnest, with instruction from club pros. But perhaps the greatest influence on Little was Tommy Armour, who in 1927 entered the Oregon Open, a tournament in which the seventeen-year-old Lawson also played. Upon finishing his rounds, Little would rush back to the course to study Armour at work and soon adopted his closed stance.

A husky, handsome, near six footer with a shock of dark wavy hair, Little may well have been the greatest match player ever,

including Hagen and Jones. As an amateur in 1934 he won both the British and U.S. Amateur titles and the following year successfully defended the pair. Sandwiching a Walker Cup series between these feats, Little rattled off thirty-two consecutive match play victories. Hagen's best was twenty-two and Jones only fourteen. (In more recent years, Michael Bonallack won the British Amateur three straight and knocked off twenty-four opponents in a row.)

Little turned pro in 1936. But Little disappointed those who figured he'd grind up the pros. Two nongolf interests may have interfered with his performance. He probably outshot Hagen in his consumption of martinis and he knew easier ways to make money than by breaking par. Jack Burke, Jr., who toured with Little, recalled:

We were the only two guys traveling together on the Tour then who didn't fight in the morning to see who got the sports section of the paper first. Lawson didn't want it. You just handed him the financial page and he'd be happy for hours. Maybe after breakfast, driving out to the course or something, he'd casually ask you who was leading the tournament. I don't know how the man played as well as he did. He never practiced. Sometimes he didn't even finish a practice round.

No one who saw him on a course was likely to forget his martial appearance, striding down the fairway like a conqueror surveying the territory he ruled. His study of the financial pages was paralleled by his exceptional knowledge of the rule book, which he seemed to have committed to memory.

He appeared to have no weakness to his game, with total mastery of the putting arts and the ability to recover from errant shots. He smote such monstrous drives that his nickname became "Cannonball." For all of that, he never dominated the pro ranks. Periodically, Little topped the class in tournaments but his one major victory came in 1940 when he beat Gene Sarazen in a playoff for the U.S. Open.

Certainly, the competition along the play-for-pay trail had become tougher. Among

"Lawson Little was the greatest match player in the history of golf. Indeed, it would be difficult to construct an argument that says he wasn't. In 1934, he won the British Amateur and then the United States Amateur. The following year, he won them both again. . . . To Bernard Darwin, who even then had been writing about golf for half a century, Little was a 'man of destiny.' In a word not usually bandied about by Cambridge men, Darwin summarized his game as 'colossal.' " —Charles Price, Golfer at Large. (COURTESY ACME NEWS-PHOTOS.)

(Top) *Little erupts from a trap. His long hitting earned him the nickname "Cannonball."* (COURTESY UPI/BETTMANN NEWSPHOTOS.)

(Bottom) *Willie Turnesa, a pro's son and one of six golfing brothers, won the 1938 and 1948 U.S. Amateur titles before joining the play-for-pay gang.* (COURTESY RAY DAVIS.)

He caddied at the Homestead Hotel course in Hot Springs, bearing huge bags so much wider than his shoulders that he draped them around his neck. Spare moments, when not sneaking onto the local "Goat Course" reserved for hotel employees, the boy practiced in a pasture, barefoot. Golf faded as an enthusiasm in high school where Snead entered everything—baseball, football, basketball, track, and tennis. His interest revived after he won a couple of schoolboy driving contests, although a loss as a senior forced him to restructure his grip: "Somehow I felt I should figure out such things for myself and so I never took a golf lesson from anyone—not that they were being offered in those days."

A career as a soda jerk and short-order cook ended when a job opened up as a "flunky" in the pro shop at The Homestead. Snead progressed to apprentice pro and golf-club repairman until, at age twenty-three in 1936, he entered the Cascades Open. His first place put 358.66 dollars in his pocket for a few moments before assorted creditors cleaned him out. But the golf manager of the Greenbrier had seen Snead smoke a few drives and offered him the post of pro. Snead's life in golf started in earnest.

One year later, Snead teed off at the Hershey (Pennsylvania) Open. In one of his several autobiographies, *The Education of a Golfer*, he emphasizes a critical piece of philosophy picked up there during a practice round. On the first tee, conscious of his hayseed appearance, his puny eight-club bag, he embarrassed himself with two out-of-bounds drives, and the other pros snorted about the caliber of player allowed in the tournament. Encouraged by George Fazio, Snead tried one more time and reached the green, more than 300 yards off. He settled down to shoot a 67, including the penalties for his first two swings.

"The lesson was that no matter what happens, never give up the hole."

In 1937, Snead joined forces with Johnny Bulla, splitting all expenses evenly, gulping cheap hamburgers, "squeezing nickels until the buffalo groaned." They badly needed an infusion of cash from the Oak-

the more formidable was Harry Cooper, British born, Texas raised, and schooled on the sand greens of that state. Like Craig Wood, he was destined to runner-up status for the major tournaments. Apart from the diminutive Paul Runyan, who twice won the PGA title (1934 and 1938), Olin Dutra, as burly as Runyan was slight, hammered his way to a 1932 PGA championship and a 1934 U.S. Open title. Denny Shute was the tenth consecutive American to annex the British Open in 1933 and he served as PGA champ in '36 and '37.

Corcoran found a fit subject for his puffery in a southern strong boy, Samuel Jackson Snead, a natural athlete with such flexibility he could high kick to toe a ceiling or pluck his ball from the cup without the need to bend his knees. The self-styled peckerwood remembered his first drive at age seven outside a Baptist church in Ashwood, Virginia. He fashioned a driver from an old head, which he affixed to a buggy whip. When Sunday Bible class ended, the boy walked down the road, swinging at rocks and dried up horse droppings. One rock even sailed through the church window.

land Open to remain on the tour. When they signed on for the tournament, he was so little known that the scoreboard listed him as "Sneed."

On the sixteenth hole of the last round, very much in contention, Snead practiced what he'd learned at Hershey. Instead of surrendering to a situation with a potential of double or triple bogey, he dug in for a saver, losing only a single stroke to par.

At the eighteenth, the word was a bird would guarantee a tie for the top money. Snead surveyed a mild dogleg left, par 5,

with trees and a ravine to the left. The right side lay wide open.

"Jackson, for the Lord's sake, keep it up the right," begged Bulla, addressing his buddy by his middle name.

"I think you're wrong," answered Snead. "I'll shave it left." The appalled Bulla demanded, "What for?" Snead always had a touch of the gambler. He figured he could stay within the margin for error and gain a better angle to the green. And he performed exactly as planned, following the successful drive with a 2-wood to the edge

On the grind in the 1930s, Johnny Palmer and Clayton Heafner load clubs and spiked shoes into the trunk before hitting the road. " 'We used to figure 160 dollars a week was the break-even figure,' Byron Nelson remembers. 'So if you shot 74 you loaded it and yourself into somebody's Graham-Paige or Essex and drove until the connecting rod made a double bogey. Air travel? That was a fantasy, something you saw in the movies for a dime.' "—Dan Jenkins, The Dogged Victims of Inexorable Fate. *(COURTESY RAY DAVIS.)*

of a bunker, a popshot over the trap to 4 feet from paydirt and an easy putt.

Photographers, reporters, and the crowds all sought a piece of him, but Snead did not understand that he actually had won, that Corcoran, using his primitive scoring and communication system, knew Snead's 270 was unbeatable.

Corcoran, of course, plugged the rural rube angle in the stories. And it was after this event that one of the more celebrated tales of Sam's ingenuosness arose. Henry Picard showed Snead his photograph in the *New York Times,* and Snead wondered: "How in the world did they ever get that? I never been to New York in my life."

There are those who believe that Snead was never so unknowing. Whatever the truth, the legend took root, particularly as from that moment on Snead started winning tournaments. No pro ever matched the stretch of his career, from the 1930s into the 1980s (as a senior). He amassed three Masters titles, three PGA championships, three Canadian Open crowns, and in 1946 captured the British Open. When he did not win, he was frequently second. The one major that somehow escaped him was the U.S. Open.

To his job for the PGA, Corcoran soon added the personal management of Snead. After a few years, Corcoran would expand his agentry to baseball's Ted Williams. Corcoran's two hats and some of his decisions eventually disturbed some players. And a decade or so later, a dispute with pro Dick Metz ended with Corcoran on the

wrong end of a punch in the nose, for which Metz received a brief suspension from the PGA.

Seeking to promote the hillbilly past of his boy Sammy, Corcoran had him play a few practice holes barefoot. The stunt outraged Gene Sarazen, who never forgot the low esteem for pro players during his youth. He confronted the tour's wagon master:

> Is that your idea of publicity for the Masters, making a Huckleberry Finn out of Snead? What we need these days is Masters, not barefoot boys. Can you imagine Walter Hagen playing barefoot on this course?

Corcoran fired back that Sarazen was no slouch at publicizing himself:

> I'm tired of hearing that story about how you bought yourself a loaf of bread and went trudging out to the course to win the Open in 1921. This is another day.

Sarazen served as something of a self-appointed keeper of golf morality. He doggedly traveled the high road, scorning the lucrative Agua Caliente Open because the Mexican authorities permitted pari-mutuel betting on the tournament. He also performed ambassadorial duties. During the mid 1930s, Sarazen, following in the footsteps of Hagen, journeyed to Australia to promote golf. He found a most receptive audience for his discourses:

> They couldn't get enough of the theory to play the game. Why in five lectures I gave in one department store in Sydney, the total attendance was more than 7,000. People came 150 to 200 miles just to watch the play and hear the lectures and stayed to listen again and again to pick up every point.

Sarazen prophesized that the Aussies would eventually achieve golfing prominence.

But while Sarazen campaigned abroad, the long-hitting and dapper Snead continued to flourish. The Corcoran fanfare, coupled with his genuine skills, made Snead the prime gate attraction.

Olin Dutra clubbed his way to the PGA championship in 1932, and the U.S. Open title in 1934. (COURTESY RAY DAVIS.)

Nick Seitz on
SAM SNEAD

Golf is proudly and prosperously known as "the game of a lifetime." I can remember the day a few of us, no doubt avoiding typewriter deadlines, sat around and concocted the slogan. It grew out of an admiring bull session about Samuel Jackson Snead, the Methuselah of the fairways, who had just become the only professional golfer ever to win in six different decades. Snead was the exemplar of the game in our lifetime.

A touring pro for more than fifty years, he was a central figure in establishing the booming PGA Tour in the 1930s and the booming Senior PGA Tour in the 1980s. He is the only man to shoot his age on the regular tour and is its oldest winner. At age sixty-two, he finished third in the PGA Championship.

I first saw Snead play at the Masters years ago. He was past one or another of his several primes, and I remember thinking how wonderful it was that the Masters, alone among the American major championships, still invited all its past winners to play, even if they weren't necessarily competitive. We could tell our grandkids we saw the great man play. There he was wearing a jaunty straw hat and walking to his ball like John Wayne at the climax of a movie. His swing blended power and grace like no other. How could I have guessed then that I would have the delight of reporting on Sam and getting to know him over the course of another thirty years?

Now I am trying to adjust to the idea of tournament golf in the 1990s without Sam Snead. What do we do for continuity, for soul, for a raconteur whose racy stories can enliven the dullest of social functions, if they occasionally send a shocked corporate wife scurrying for the powder room?

Snead, then seventy-six, told me of his impending retirement from the senior tour when I encountered him by chance in the Roanoke, Virginia, airport near his birthplace and lifelong home in the hill country. He was on his way to do an exhibition in Florida and said, "I can't play tournaments because I can't see well enough out of this bad eye to putt. I can make 10,000 dollars for a day putting on a clinic and playing a round of golf, plus what I can pick up in bets."

Sam then spun a couple of stories that cannot be repeated in a family sports book, grinned leeringly, and ambled off to catch the 8 millionth plane of his career. Finally at the end of the tournament road, he still relished the thought of playing golf—especially with a little betting action on the side.

Sam Snead, with apologies to the Internal Revenue Service, may have earned more money in pickup games than he made playing tournaments. He is the eternal gamesman.

As a strapping farm boy, Snead would bet that he could drive the green on a 330-yard par-4 hole, and do it, hitting not a driver but a 3-wood. Barefooted. "The swing started getting complicated when I put shoes on," he said later. "Playing barefooted is a great way to develop good rhythm and tempo."

At the sumptuous Greenbrier resort, where Snead was the head pro for much of his life, he once won a substantial wager by breaking 80 using only a putter and a club he fashioned from a tree limb. Of course he had neglected to mention that one of his early jobs in golf was making clubs.

One day an older Sam was losing a bet to a young Bobby Cole during a practice round at the Augusta National before the Masters started. At the famous thirteenth hole, a par 5 that can be reached with 2 robust shots, Snead was working on Cole to try a dangerous drive cutting the corner of the dogleg.

"Son," drawled Sam, "when I was your age I used to just take it up over those trees and have me a middle iron left to the green."

Cole jumped at the bait. He smashed a tremendous drive that climbed and soared—and hit a tree and dropped into the creek.

"Sam," Cole wondered incredulously, "how in the world did you ever hit it over those trees?"

"Son," said Sam from behind his best cat-that-swallowed-the-whole-golf-course expression, "when I was your age those trees were only half that high."

What's the most money Sam won on a golf bet?

"It started with a little old five-dollar nass, which has always been my basic bet," he said. "A friend of mine approached me in Boca Raton and said he'd like a game. I said I was booked up till Tuesday. This was Saturday. Sure enough he comes back Tuesday with another fellow.

"I told them my fee to play a round was 100 dollars plus the cart or caddie. They agreed, and we played a five-dollar nassau. With all the presses, I ended up winning forty-five dollars, and we went in the clubhouse for lunch. 'Tell you what I'll do,' I said. 'I'll forget the 100 dollar fee and we'll play this afternoon for a little more.'

"They were all for that. My friend was a 5-handicapper and his buddy was also a 5, and we picked up a car dealer who was an 8. We played another eighteen that afternoon and I won about 700 dollars.

" 'Don't go away,' they said. 'Let's play some more.' "

"So I canceled my lessons for the week, and we went on a tour of Florida courses: Palm-Aire, Pompano, Fort Lauderdale Country Club, Tamarack and a couple of others. I gave them all their full handicaps and kept beating them every day. It never seemed to discourage them—they just kept pressing and raising the ante. The worst round I had was a 67, and I set four course records that week. I won 10,000 dollars in seven days, and it all started with a 5-dollar bet. This friend

(Opposite) "Slammin' Sammy—as he became known to idolatrous millions—became one of the game's captivating personalities. He traveled the world. He wore silk suits, cashmere sweaters, and fifty-dollar shoes, but city polish never wore off on him. He remained the perpetual hillbilly, completely devoid of affectation and full of droll backwoods humor. Every time his familiar straw hat (covering a balding pate) appeared on the course, crowds congregated. Even when he was not competitive, Sam always attracted a huge gallery. People loved to watch him hit a ball."—Will Grimsley, Golf, Its People, History and Events. (COURTESY FRANK CHRISTIAN STUDIOS.)

As an eight year old, Snead toted a canvas bag in the hills of Virginia. "Barefoot, with that swamp stick, I could hit for twenty fence posts, about 125 yards. If the ball sliced it fell into some mucky bottomland. By trying different grips and different stances, I got so it would sail both far and fairly true."—Sam Snead, The Education of a Golfer. (COURTESY PGA.)

In his first days, Snead played without his later trademark hat.

"No golfer in history could have been more richly endowed in these [purely physical gifts] than Snead. He was blessed not only with great strength but with remarkable suppleness that made possible an effortless turn of the shoulders and body without any loss of control or balance, and a marvelous sense of rhythm. The result was a natural swing, matchless in its grace and beauty and power.... there have been many swings that were a delight to watch but there has never been one more beautiful than Snead's"—Pat Ward Thomas, The Golfer's Bedside Book. (COURTESY AP/WIDE WORLD PHOTOS.)

"A lean, tan mountaineer from West Virginia won the Oakland Open Golf Tournament today by shooting 270 in a seventy-two-hole play," reads the photo caption for this shot of Snead's first PGA victory in 1937. (COURTESY AP/WIDE WORLD PHOTOS.)

of mine lives out in Idaho now, and I still see him every once in a while. We're still friends because he could afford to lose that much."

The most pressure Snead ever felt in a money match was in the 1930s in Cuba. L. B. Icely, then president of the Wilson Sporting Goods Company that Snead represents, lured him into it, as Snead unwinds the story.

"A well-known sportsman named Tommy Shevlin had gone on a drinking spree in New York City with a rich Cuban named Thornwald Sanchez. Sanchez claimed that his pro at the Havana Country Club, Rufino Gonzales, could beat anybody in the world on his home course. Shevlin said he'd put up 5,000 dollars that Gonzales couldn't. Shevlin called Mr. Icely for advice, and that's how I got the offer. I'd never been to Cuba before. When I arrived, everybody there had money on this match. What started as 5,000 dollars must have grown to 100,000, which was a lot of pesos back in the '30s.

"Shevlin asked me how much I wanted to bet. I said I didn't want to bet anything. I'd never even seen this guy Gonzales before. He told me to bet 250 dollars so he'd feel better. I said okay.

"I played a practice round with Gonzales before the match and shot a 65. P. Hal Sims, the famous bridge expert, was there and told me, 'Don't play with him anymore. Don't show him what you've got.' But after that one round, I knew where I could beat him. I had the edge on the par 5s, which I could reach in two and he couldn't, and on one long par 4, where I could cut across the dogleg and knock it on.

"But this Gonzales was no easy pigeon waitin' to be plucked. He was very straight off the tee and a magician with the putter. When I got to the course the day of the match I saw all these rough-looking hombres around the first tee. It was explained to me that they were Batista's boys, and that the dictator himself was betting on Gonzales. That's all I needed to hear. I already was jumpier than a cat burglar at the Policeman's Ball.

"We played a thirty-six-hole match, and it was decided on those long holes. I shot 69–68 and Gonzales had 71–71. Batista's boys pressed in pretty close to us as we walked back to the clubhouse, so I wasted no time collecting my winnings and hightailing it out of the country. 'Good luck,' I said to Gonzales. He had to face the hometown fans.

"Back in Miami, the first person I ran into was Mr. Icely. He asked me how I was feeling. I told him the next time the stakes were that high he should send Jimmy Demaret, who would make a prettier corpse than I would."

Most golfers have trouble believing me when I say that Sam can enjoy a low-budget match with friends as much as a big-money match or tournament. A thrill of my hacker's life is winning two dollars from Sam by scrambling for a net par on the last hole when he was needling me furiously. He paid, grudgingly, but refused to sign the two bills for souvenirs.

"I love competition," he says. "I truly play just as hard for five dollars as I do for 50,000 dollars. It may be hard to understand, but it's the way you have to be. I have to play for a *little* money to get my interest up, but I don't care *how* little. Competition keeps the blood flowing."

Late in his tenure on the senior tour the amazingly supple Snead was betting people he could kick the top of a seven-foot doorway—and taking their money.

His stupefying loose-jointedness and flexibility kept Snead's ethereal swing long and fluid for half a century. "He's the greatest athlete in the history of the world and has the greatest swing ever," chirps Chi Chi Rodriguez. The lasting image is one of effortless power.

Says Bob Toski, a fine little player who became a top teacher, "I've played with Sam a lot, and I learned early on that I couldn't watch him swing and play my own game. He hit the ball so purely and so far I'd be coming out of my socks trying to drive it out there with him. He always called me Mouse, and when he'd notice that I wasn't watching him he'd step back from the ball and say 'Come on, Mouse, watch me swing.' "

Tom Watson, the leading golfer of the 1980s, looks forward to playing in the Masters because he can watch Snead, who has continued to tee it up in an honorary starting group, on the practice range. "He was my father's swing model and he is mine too," says Watson. "When my tempo goes off, I picture Sam's smooth swing in my mind."

Cashmere should be so smooth. Sharp-eyed experts will tell you Snead's languorous-looking swing isn't mechanically perfect, because his clubface doesn't stay square throughout and his leg action has never been the liveliest, but his classic tempo lets him compensate with awesome ease. His strength allowed him to swing well within himself, and his long arms generated an extra-wide arc.

Snead is probably the only self-taught superstar of modern times. Even Ben Hogan and Byron Nelson sought out teachers before it became fashionable. (Today's tour pro is accompanied by a retinue that includes an instructor, a psychologist, a full-time caddie, and a few other support systems.)

Sam bristles, though, at the common suggestion he is "a natural." He said he's probably hit 2 million practice shots in his lifetime and thought seriously about every one of them. He also claims he's given as many golf lessons as any teacher in the country. He's always been his own best teacher.

"My swing looks natural because I've worked to keep it simple," he says. "That's why it held up so long. I've tried to eliminate jerks and hitches and extra movements. I've built it from results back. . . . results dictate form. That's why it's an easy swing for people to copy. If a person wants to build a house economically, he looks for a building site that doesn't need much clearing and modifying. That's the way my swing is."

Sam's way with a simile or metaphor is enchanting. I've heard him talk about wanting his swing to feel "oily," or say he wants to swing as smoothly as "warm molasses pouring out of a jar."

The Slammer has amazing sensitivity for a husky, powerful man. He says he can feel the hair on his ham-size hands. Joe Phillips, the Wilson tour representa-

"... [The] clubface never touches the ball in any explosion shot—that you simply are playing a divot of sand out onto the green. Personally, I don't see a golf ball in a trap. I think of it as an extra big grain of sand I want to flip out of there. I aim an inch or two back of the ball and generate plenty of hand speed and fast wrist action at impact with the sand. The biggest 'grain' in the trap (the ball) is bound to travel farthest if you don't stop the shot and follow-through until your hands are at least shoulder-high at the finish."
—*Sam Snead*, The Education of a Golfer. (COURTESY PGA.)

"To be able to scramble from trouble . . . is the key to winning golf." —Sam Snead, The Education of a Golfer. (COURTESY PGA.)

The country boy's home club in White Sulphur Springs, West Virginia, honored him with a carriage parade when he was named Golfer of the Year. (COURTESY CHASE-GREENBRIER PHOTO.)

Snead also demonstrated talent with a trumpet. (COURTESY PGA.)

tive for much of Snead's career, says Sam is the only player he's ever seen who could feel the difference between a driver swingweighted D-1 and another swingweighted D-2. The difference is the weight of a dollar bill. Is it any wonder Snead could shape a golf shot any way you wanted it?

Sam's golf and fishing buddy Bob Goalby tells the story of Sam doing a clinic a few years ago. "Sam had been sitting on his bag for fifty minutes waiting his turn to hit," says Goalby, "and you know how stiff even a young person can get that way. I was the announcer and when I finally called him up he took a 3-iron out of his bag and told the crowd he had five balls and was going to call his shots and do something different with each one. He didn't even take a practice swing. He hooked the first one from right to left. He faded the second one from left to right. He hit the next one low. He hit the next one high. And he hit the last one dead straight, which is the hardest shot in the game. He called every shot. Gardner Dickinson just shook his head and said Sam was born warmed up."

Snead's main mechanical swing key is to make a full turn on the backswing. "Turn and burn!" he'll exhort a 12-handicapper like myself. "Turn and burn!"

He says, "A long swing is the one that lasts. If you're short when you're young, you'll never get the club back far enough when you're older. I always worked hard on keeping my swing long. The longer your backswing, the better chance you have for slowing down your tempo."

No matter how long and sound a player's swing, golf is a game of continual correction. Says Dr. Cary Middlecoff, the two-time U.S. Open champion, "People always talk about Sam's great talent, and he had great talent, but in the last twenty-five years that he played professionally he developed a remarkable ability to fix his swing in the middle of a round. If he started duck-hooking, you could bet that he'd have it stopped in a hole or two. His mental alertness is a major reason he was able to compete for so long."

If Snead had a weakness, it was his putting. A good enough lag putter, he was doubtful from 4 feet even in his best days. Putting kept him from ever winning the U.S. Open, I suspect. (It is the Open, America's premier tournament, that somehow seems diminished by this quirk of record, rather than Sam.) Four times he was runner-up.

One night I was driving Sam from a social function back to his hotel and the touchy subject of the Open arose. Sam said he always had trouble with the

In the late 1940s, Snead presents the best known black golfer of the times, former heavyweight champion Joe Louis, with a phonograph record of golf tips. (COURTESY ELI SILVERBERG.)

"I'm only scared of three things—lightning, a side-hill putt and Ben Hogan."—Sam Snead, in Inside Golf, by Bob Chieger and Pat Sullivan. It was Snead's misfortune to win eighty-four PGA titles, every major except the U.S. Open, and still fall under the shadow of Ben Hogan. (COURTESY UPI.)

"super-fast, tricky greens." He said he felt he had to try to keep from 3-putting rather than try to make his first putt. Normally an aggressive putter, he was on the defensive in the Open. It went against his personality and his game and he abhorred it.

Later, when his nerves were letting him down on the greens to the point he couldn't beat players he was accustomed to beating, Sam developed a novel croquet style of putting that virtually took the twitchy little muscles of the hands and wrists out of his stroke. The putts began falling again. Then came the bad news. The U.S. Golf Association, the rulesmaking body, banned croquet putting; a player no longer would be allowed to straddle the line of a putt.

"I was crushed," says Snead. "I figured I was finished, unless I could find a way to sidestep that new rule."

He literally did.

"I remembered an old-timer I'd seen over in England who would bet that he could out-putt anyone. He must've been seventy-five. He putted the same way I'd been putting except he didn't straddle the line. He faced the hole but put his feet together to the side of the line and putted sidesaddle. It didn't take me long to get the hang of it. I'd pitched horseshoes by the hour out behind the barn when I was a kid, and I just put that movement into my putting. It kept me going."

There were those who scoffed and giggled at Snead's sidesaddle method. No one copied it. He paid no heed. It may have looked peculiar, but it worked. Sam's courageous willingness to experiment and adapt extended his already prodigiously long tournament life, vanity be damned.

As a weaver of colorful stories, Snead takes a rumble seat to nobody else in sports. Taking him to dinner is tantamount to bringing your own entertainment. He always looks classy in a jacket and tie for dinner, by the way, belying the hillbilly image he never discouraged. But he won't try to pick up the check and belie his reputation of being super-frugal. His late manager Fred Corcoran liked to say Sam had a reach impediment when it came time to pay a tab.

One after-dinner story reminds him of another, which reminds him of the afternoon at the Masters when he was being pestered by large flies that didn't seem to be bothering anyone else. "I asked the caddie what kind they were, and he said 'Dem flies are de kind you see in de back of horses.' I asked him if he was saying I'm a horse's arse. He said, 'No, but dem flies don't seem to know de difference.' "

Sam called a time-out here to cleverly fashion a fetching doll from a cloth napkin for a pretty waitress. He is a man of many and mysterious talents. He autographs it for her, and she blushes with delight and leaves.

The next couple of Snead stories also would have caused her to blush, with embarrassment. Then Sam tells about a lesson he gave a 20-handicapper. The man, whose hand-eye coordination left something to be wanted for Christmas, asked how Sam was able to put all that backspin on his long-iron shots. Sam asked the man how far he could hit a 3-iron.

"About 150 yards," was the reply.

Snorted Snead, "Then why in hell do you want backspin?!"

Which reminded him of the one . . .

My lasting impression of Sam will be of the old impressionist's lastingness. He played so well for so long. I asked him once what his secret was, and he replied, "No pushups, no swimming and no sex after Wednesday." He sounded entirely serious.

He's always been a man of strict moderation in his personal habits. If he drinks alcohol, it is no more than a beer or a light gin-and-tonic before dinner, two at the most. "Stay away from food made of sugar and flour, and you can eat what you want," he maintains. He's been going to bed early as long as I've known him.

Certainly his big swing and his competitiveness helped him endure, and his health held up unusually well. Most tellingly, though, Snead simply loves to play golf. He has played nearly every day of his adult life with undiminished enthusiasm. He has played with the other greats of his extended time, with the near-greats, with the mediocre, and with the weekend basket cases, and he has relished every single hour of it. That's how he lasted, he agrees.

Which reminded him of a story, of course. His memory is uncanny. The longest he ever went without playing was a few days on an African safari. He was

The yips—"that ghastly time," according to Tommy Armour, "when with the first movement of the putter, the golfer blacks out, loses sight of the ball, and hasn't the remotest idea of what to do with the putter or, occasionally, that he is holding a putter at all"—the paralysis that afflicts most golfers with the advance of age, drove Snead to extreme remedies. The authorities objected to his croquet stance but accepted a side-saddle style. (Left photo COURTESY CLARK'S PHOTOGRAPHY; right photo COURTESY MIAMI METRO DEPARTMENT OF PUBLIC-ITY & TOURISM.)

with a friend named Gordon Fawcett, who brought his clubs without letting Sam know. Sam soon missed his golf, and out came Fawcett's clubs.

Unfortunately he had not brought golf balls. Snead determined that dried elephant droppings made a playable substitute. The two laid out a mini-course in a jungle clearing and played—you guessed it—a five-dollar nassau.

"I had to give Gordon strokes," recalls Sam, "but I beat him anyway because I insisted on playing winter rules. I could reposition the dropping so I'd hit it on the firmer side. Gordon never caught on, and his shots kept disintegrating when he hit 'em."

Samuel Jackson Snead could almost always find a way to beat you at this narcotic game of a lifetime.

13

The Texas Trio

For all of his triumphs, Sam Snead endured considerable travail from a trio of nemeses, all of whom hailed from Texas. The first fellow to bedevil Snead was tall, shambling Ralph Guldahl★ —a Gary Cooper with golf clubs. As a shy, rumpled twenty-one year old, Guldahl suddenly drew notice at the 1933 U.S. Open at the North Shore Country Club in Glenview, Illinois. Johnny Goodman, the poor boy who rode the cattle train to the 1929 U.S. Amateur at Pebble Beach, ousted Jones, then fell before Lawson Little. His card left him 7 strokes behind the leader, Tommy Armour. But a brilliant 66 and a sub-par 70 on the morning of the final day put Goodman at 211, 6 strokes better than the tyro Guldahl.

Goodman started his final round in the afternoon, par, eagle, birdie. Certain he had blown away any contenders, he shifted his strategy to a defensive approach. Goodman promptly lost his touch, dropping 6 strokes to par over the next half-dozen holes. Teeing off about an hour later, Guldahl, 9 behind after Goodman's sensational start on the final nine, ignited from tee to green. He actually stood even with the faltering Goodman after the fourteenth hole. Only his sloppy putting kept him from routing the leader.

Goodman, somewhat settled down by his playing partner, Mac Smith, restored order to his game over the last few holes and posted a final-round 76. Under these circumstances, Guldahl arrived at the par-4 eighteenth hole needing a par to tie, a bird to win. He drove well enough but his approach shot with a 3-iron faded into a bunker. Guldahl grimly blasted out and the ball stopped a mere 5 feet from the cup. Ralph took aim, tapped the ball, and missed. After he holed out, the chagrined Guldahl succumbed to a mild tantrum and fired the ball into the ground. Guldahl had been done in by his putter long before that miserable shot; over the last two rounds, he had taken 35 and 36 putts, hardly the stuff of champions.

Guldahl's failure left Johnny Goodman the winner by a single stroke; he was also the last amateur ever to win the U.S. Open, further testament to the growing dominance of the pros. Six years previously, R. T. Jones had been the last of the breed to win the British Open.

Having flashed across the golfing sky, Guldahl appeared to be a dying star rather than one newly born. He vanished from contention for more than two years. Disheartened by his lack of success, Guldahl quit the game to sell cars. Fortunately, he was no more successful at this vocation. After a pair of Hollywood types, comedian Robert Woolsey and actor Rex Bell,★ played a couple of rounds with Guldahl, they advanced him 100 dollars, enabling him to enter the True Temper Open in Detroit.

Guldahl returned to the wars in 1936, much improved through some tinkering

Ralph Guldahl enjoys his relatively brief celebrity. (COURTESY UPI/BETT-MANN NEWSPHOTOS.)

---

*Lloyd Mangrum was able to join the tour on the strength of 250 dollars from a now-forgotten matinee idol, John Boles. Just as the great industrialists and financiers had discovered golf some twenty years earlier, the show-biz world, particularly the Hollywood colony, had taken up the game with the advent of Walter Hagen. Douglas Fairbanks, Sr., thought nothing of sailing to England for the sole purpose of observing Sir Walter in his British Open jousts.

The film world financed a string of clubs. Warner Brothers film studio even contracted with Bobby Jones to star in a series of two-reelers, "How to Play Golf," in which Jones was shown instructing the likes of Fairbanks, W. C. Fields, James Cagney, Loretta Young, Edward G. Robinson, and Warner Oland, the first actor to play the Chinese detective, Charlie Chan.

with his grip under the tutelage of Olin Dutra, and having discovered the art of lagging the distant ball close enough to the cup to avoid the dreaded 3-putt and occasionally rack up a spectacular bird. In 1936, he failed to cop a major tournament; his best win was the Western Open. Still, he finished second among the leading money winners for the year with a princely 7,682.41 dollars, a scant 200 dollars less than number one Horton Smith, and he earned the Radix trophy for the lowest average score for the tour.*

High noon arrived at the 1937 U.S. Open held at Oakland Hills near Detroit. Most of the gallery focused upon the Slammer, who'd won several tournaments earlier in the season, including the very first Bing Crosby★ pro-am. He'd cured some driving problems with a club bought from Henry Picard for five dollars and fifty cents, and which he repaired constantly over a period of years; copies of the driver never seemed to give Snead the same feel.

Snead made all the seers happy in the first round with a course record of 69, 3 better than par. He slacked off the next round but regrouped to break par with a 70 and 71 the final day. When the official at the eighteenth green blatted to the gallery, "Sammy Snead, a 71 for the round. Total 283," the Virginian marched towards the clubhouse as the front runner.

Guldahl had been trudging toward the nearby tenth tee and heard Snead's score announced. It dawned on Guldahl that he had an excellent chance to beat Snead. When the final round started they had been tied at 212 but Guldahl, after plodding along at a par rate, suddenly crashed through at the eighth hole, at 491 yards a short par 5, most vulnerable to long hitters like Guldahl. After a hefty drive he smacked a 2-iron that left him looking at 35 feet of green between his ball and the cup. Fortified by his newly acquired command of the long putt, Guldahl devoted little time to studying the task. He stroked the ball firmly and

---

*A year later, the honor for the lowest stroke average became known as the Vardon Trophy.

it took the appropriate break to the right before falling into the cup for an eagle 3. He followed that triumph with a birdie on the 215-yard ninth with a 1-iron to the green, on which he canned a 10 footer. On this pair of holes, Guldahl had carved 3 strokes off par.

The news of Snead's total put a spring in his step, for now even a 1-over par 37 for the final nine would make Ralph a winner. To his playing companion, Lighthorse Harry Cooper, Guldahl remarked, "If I can't play this last nine in 37 strokes, I'm just a bum and don't deserve to win the Open."

The brave words must have stuck in his throat, for Guldahl posted bogeys for the next pair of holes. Self destruction appeared imminent. Now par for the remaining seven would only tie him with the leader. He came to the 555-yard twelfth hole, a tricky par-5 affair, yet one of the few opportunities to save strokes. He drove solidly, but his second shot veered off line and might have obliterated any chance had it not bounced off the foot of an onlooker. Instead of ricochetting into the heavy rough, the ball trickled into a smooth trap by the green. Still, he was in deep trouble. The pin lay to his extreme left, 40 yards off, close to the edge of the green, and behind a fairly steep mound that sloped toward the cup.

Bob Jones was on hand and he recalled Guldahl's predicament:

It was a wee pitch of about 40 yards and I really didn't see how any golfer could stop that ball anywhere close to the hole. A running shot was absolutely out of the question and a pitched shot that landed on the reverse slope would very likely go clear off the green beyond.

Guldahl played the finest controlled niblick pitch I have ever seen. He sent the ball up with a world of control, to drop just short of the crest of the slope, bounce once and again, and then just barely wriggle over the crest and trickle like a perfectly gauged putt down to stop a foot from the hole, for a birdie 4.

The coup on the twelfth seemed to inspire the Texan on the next hole as his pitch on the par-3, 142 yarder halted within a foot of the cup, giving him another bird. With Cooper now counseling him not to be hasty, he scrambled to pars the rest of the way for a 2-stroke victory.

The new Open champ, however, could not capture the hearts and minds of the golf faithful. They pursued golfers who exuded elan, played to the gallery, or supplied the basic stuff out of which publicists could manufacture colorful anecdotes. The dour Guldahl, drably dressed, reacted to his triumphs only by a nervous habit of running a pocket comb through his thick hair, a gesture not even the redoubtable Corcoran could transform into hot copy.

Yet, Guldahl continued to win the big ones while his more celebrated competitors finished as also rans. In 1938, at the Cherry Hills Country Club in Denver, Guldahl beat his closest challenger, Dick Metz, by 6 strokes to join the select group of Willie Anderson, Johnny McDermott, and Bob Jones as U.S. Open winners in consecutive years. Reporters seemed more interested in interviewing an obscure California pro, Ray Ainsley, who set a new unofficial record of 19 strokes on a single hole after he repeatedly slashed and splashed at his ball when it landed in a gurgling brook. Ainsley's dubious achievement eclipsed the 18 set in 1919 by Willie Chisholm, who struggled futilely with a ball trapped in a ravine at Brae Burn Country Club.

In 1937, Guldahl had also taken the second of what would be a trio of consecutive Western Opens and finished runner up in seven other tournaments, including the Masters. And, in 1939, he came to Augusta to record one last great win. He'd been the bridesmaid the two previous outings. On both occasions, on the final day, the twelfth hole proved a Waterloo where he fell into the drink of Rae's Creek.

For Sam Snead, the 1939 Masters had a touch of déjà vu. Just as at the 1937 Open, Snead was home at 280 as Guldahl reached the final turn, this time needing an unthinkable 3 below par 33 to beat Sam. He started with the tenth, picking up his first bird with a deft 4-iron to a yard or so of the cup. On the thirteenth hole, a 490 yarder where his tormentor, Rae's Creek, ambled along the fairway before cutting directly in front of the green, soggy footing caused Ralph to sky his drive a short 220 yards. That left him a side-hill lie and needing a good 230 yards to clear the water. Instead of playing safely short with an iron to guarantee at least the necessary par, Guldahl drew his spoon and attacked. The ball soared in a high arc, descended just beyond the creek to the edge of the green and then gamboled to within 5 feet of the cup. Again, where Ralph had hoped for a bird, he had struck an eagle.

Ahead now, the phlegmatic Guldahl had turned river boat gambler and savaged the water-guarded fifteenth with another miraculous spoon. The birdie earned here made the difference for, on 17, the go-for-broke style cost him a bogey. He finished at 279. Although he was favored by bookmakers to take a precedent-shattering third Open in 1939, he was barely a factor. Within a few years he faded swiftly from the tournament scene.

However, a pair of Texas colossi had now stridden onto the stage to contest with Snead and others for honors. John Byron Nelson, Jr.,★ was built along the lines of Guldahl but Ben Hogan, a pint-sized, scrawny, natural left-hander seemed hardly the stuff from which golf champions are molded.

Nelson and Hogan, both born in 1912, more or less grew up together, caddying at the Glen Garden Club in Fort Worth and developing a natural rivalry. Nelson recalled his first real round when he was twelve.

I shot 118, and I don't think I counted when I whiffed it. I actually hit it 118 times. But I went from 118 that year to 79 the next. I just fell into it, and started hitting the ball. . . . the pros weren't interested in teaching juniors and you didn't just go up to them and get them to help you. They weren't approachable, most of them. So . . . when I got interested I got every book that was around and watched good players and started piecing together my own game.

His opportunities to play increased when the caddie master awarded him a junior membership at the club in 1928, saying,

"There are few golfers who themselves don't get the jitters playing for the Open title. The few who don't are nearly always the winners, and the coldest blooded, least jittery man of them all is Ralph Guldahl."—Henry McLemore, United Press, June 7, 1939.

Guldahl finished seventh in this Open, yet had one of his better years, taking four tournaments, including the Masters. (COURTESY UPI/ BETTMANN NEWSPHOTOS.)

"Byron Nelson is the only caddie who doesn't drink, smoke or curse. He should have it." And, as he grew older, Nelson became friendly with the professionals at Glen Garden and received some valuable advice.

Like so many players from the 1920s, however, he had to restructure his game when steel replaced hickory shafts. Where control of the wooden-shafted clubs demanded exquisite tuning of hands and wrists, steel, which did not yield to torque, allowed golfers to look to their legs for power. Nelson's legs became a launching pad for belting balls. And to correct another flaw, Nelson developed his unique, ramrod-straight left arm technique. He recalled:

I was still pronating the way you had to do with hickory because of the torque in the shaft, which would open the clubface. But steel didn't have the same torque, and I would hook the ball around a house. I had to stop the hook, so just by trial and error I found that the more I moved laterally through the ball and kept the club and hands going in front of the ball, the straighter it would go.

Nelson turned pro in 1932, making his debut in a tiny Texarkana tournament graced by a total prize package of 500 dollars. Times were hard enough so that some better-known players like Ky Laffoon and Dick Metz entered. For the one-day affair Nelson packed a small bag, toted his sticks aboard a bus for the 200-mile trip, declared himself on arrival as a professional, and paid his five dollar fee to begin his pro career. He finished third and collected seventy-five dollars.

"That Nelson was not a great putter—he was more in a league with Vardon, Cotton, and Hogan than with Hagen, Jones, and Locke—does even more credit to his driving and iron play. Nelson's first round in the 1937 Masters more or less symbolizes his tee-to-green excellence. During that eighteen holes at Augusta National, he hit every par-3 green in one shot and all others, including the four par-5s, in two. He 1-putted only two greens, yet shot 66. The two 1-putts were from 2 and 3 feet."—Dick Aultman, In Celebration of Golf. (COURTESY UPI/BETTMANN NEWSPHOTOS.)

Nelson is credited with innovating a "one-piece, upright, left-side dominant, flex-kneed swing." His trademark was the dip to his body and the added power generated by the weight shift forward. (COURTESY UPI/BETTMANN NEWSPHOTOS.)

Recommended by a friend, Nelson secured the post of pro at the Texarkana Country Club. He received sixty dollars a month, not from salary but from lessons and sales of equipment. However, his expenses amounted to a mere seven dollars a week for room and board with a local family. Most importantly, few members showed up before noon, allowing Nelson ample time to practice, although he had to shag for himself.

The father of Louise Shofner, his fiancee, agreed to lend Nelson 650 dollars to try the circuit. The initial foray returned minimal results. By the time he had worked his way back to Texas barely anything remained of the grub stake. When he stepped onto the tee for the Texas Open at San Antonio, the florid sendoff of the starter so flustered Nelson that he dribbled a 100-yard drive. Luckily, he recovered with a fine brassie and iron to make par. In Al Barkow's oral history "Gettin' to the Dance Floor," Nelson recalled: ". . . the thought popped into my head, you dunce, if you can miss it that bad and make a par, if you ever hit it right you're going to make a birdie."

He scored well enough for second place with a saving 375 dollar reward. He motored to Galveston for another runner-up slot and now the prospects as a touring pro brightened. He married Louise and in 1934 trekked westward to follow the sun. Even though they scrimped, the nut amounted to about 160 dollars a week. One memorable occasion, Nelson led after three rounds of a tournament at Niagara Falls when he learned he would play the final eighteen paired with his idol, Walter Hagen. The Haig dropped one of his favorite psychological bombs on his worshipper, showing up two hours late—in those times the officials indulged the high and mighty like Sir Walter. Nelson was unnerved enough to falter for a horrendous 44 on the front nine but saved himself from humiliation with a 35 back. He pocketed a 600 dollar prize and cautioned his wife: "We've got to hide this six-hundred dollars before we hit the road. Since we're rich, we're bound to get robbed. But if we hide it, maybe they won't get it all."

By no means prepared to risk all as a circuit rider, Nelson accepted a job as an assistant at the Ridgewood Country Club in New Jersey under George Jacobus, who served as PGA president for many years. Jacobus encouraged Nelson in his approach to the steel-shafted clubs and the younger man responded with more consistent play. He won a number of tournaments in his new home state, climaxing the season with an impressive victory in the 1936 Metropolitan Open over Henry Cooper, Denny Shute, and Henry Picard.

Nelson declared himself a prime player with his performance in the 1937 Masters. He opened with a 66 but, on the third day, tottered to a 75 while Guldahl, never far off the pace, blazed a 68 for the lead. Guldahl led by 4 strokes with only seven holes remaining. However, when Ralph managed to water himself on thirteen and fourteen, Nelson exploited the opportunity. He birdied the twelfth with a 2 and then chipped in for an eagle on thirteen, the very same holes that a year later would see Guldahl rack up a bird and an eagle and go on to victory. However, in Nelson's year, the combination of Byron's feats and Ralph's failings added up to a 6-stroke shift. The eagle, along with a pair of earlier birds and a string of 5 straight pars, led Nelson to a course record of 32.

He had most definitely arrived. Nothing bespoke his prominence more clearly than his nomination to the Ryder Cup squad that demolished the Britons seven matches to three with two halved.

Lord Byron, the inevitable nickname given him by Arthur Daley of the *New York Times*, transferred his base to the pro post at the Reading (Pennsylvania) Country Club. He entered the 1939 U.S. Open over the Spring Mill Course of the Philadelphia Country Club. Once again, the odds makers and the gallery favored Sam Snead. The Slammer had already notched a trio of victories and narrowly lost out to Guldahl's sprint at the Masters.

As play began for the final eighteen holes, Snead was only 1 stroke behind Johnny Bulla and tied with Clayton Heafner, Denny Shute, and Craig Wood. Bulla and Heafner quickly shot themselves out of contention. Nelson, 5 behind the leader

"Lawson Little was the big star that year and I was the most unknown of all the unknowns in the tournament [Sacramento Open], so they matched me with Little in the first round. Although I was pretty scared, I decided I'd have to teach him who I was on the first hole. His tee shot was a beauty, but I took me the biggest-headed driver in my bag, teed the ball way up high and I really lit into it. I must have passed his drive by 20 or 30 yards. They had a circle around the green as a restraining line for the crowd and I put my second shot inside the circle." —Byron Nelson.

[Some months afterwards, says Nelson, Little told him:] "Before our match in the Sacramento Open, I was going around asking everyone, 'Who's Nelson?,' and everyone said that you were just a long, hungry kid from Texas. But those first two shots of yours opened my eyes."—Arthur Daley, New York Times, *October 12, 1944.* (COURTESY ACME.)

Bulla, crafted a nifty 68 to come in at 284. Snead, after a shaky start, steadied himself and, when he arrived at the seventeenth hole, all he needed was a pair of pars for a 282; even one bogey would not deny him the title. Snead immediately surrendered a stroke on seventeen when he flubbed a 5-foot putt.

In those days scoreboards were not scattered throughout the courses and Snead knew nothing of his advantageous situation. Faint cheers from out on the course reached his ears, leading him to believe that Shute and Wood, playing behind him, were making a charge. Snead concluded he needed a birdie on the par-5 eighteenth to win. Gambling, Slammin' Sammy lived up to his name with a prodigious wallop for his drive. Unfortunately, he hooked into deep rough, 275 yards from home. He reasoned a good, stout brassie could drop him close enough for a putt-saving chip and his birdie. But in his eagerness, he topped the ball and, in true duffer fashion, it careened, squiggled, and then died in a steep bunker, a long 110 yards from the green. Snead rashly opted to recover with an 8-iron, rather than the safer 9 or sand wedge. The ball not only failed to clear the overhang of the bunker but it also wedged itself into a crack between some freshly implanted sod.

Flustered, Snead flailed away and tore the ball loose, only to have it stop along the edge of another bunker some 40 yards from the green. The lie forced Snead to plant his feet on the fairway, in what he later described as a baseball stance. He awkwardly swiped away and knocked himself 40 feet past the cup. A long putt left him 3 feet out and he promptly missed the shortie. He staggered off eighteen with an awesomely awful 8 for 286.

Nelson, however, was not home free. Denny Shute came to seventeen needing only pars to win. Like Snead, he bogeyed seventeen, and his par on eighteen only tied him with Byron. Craig Wood, the unlucky fellow overcome by Gene Sarazen's miracle at the 1935 Masters and undone in a playoff for the 1933 British Open against Shute, teed off on eighteen, requiring a birdie to tie the leaders. Unlike Snead, he

pulled it off and the stage was set for a three-way playoff.

In the shoot-out, Shute folded early. But Nelson and Wood stayed within 1 stroke of each other throughout the afternoon. Both carded 33 for the front nine. At the seventeenth hole, Nelson held a single-stroke lead. However, when he 3 putted while Wood sank a birdie their standings were reversed. Both men drove well on the last hole. Wood then appeared to destroy himself with a vicious hook. In a bizarre twist, the ball conked a spectator on the head. Read a newspaper account:

> . . . Flattening him as effectively as though impaled by a right cross from Joe Louis. The victim apparently semi-conscious was carried from the course on a stretcher. . . . The ball caromed off the man's cranium almost to the fairway, giving Wood a clear shot for the hole.

Wood exploited his break with a superb pitch to within 4 feet of the cup. Nelson's fine third stroke left him twice the distance off. But he rammed his putt home and when Wood, inexplicably, missed, the round had ended in another tie.

The following morning they teed off again. It was over early. Nelson birdied the third hole and on the dogleg fourth, he ripped a 1-iron over a corner hive of bunkers. The ball landed at the front of the green. Its momentum carried it uphill beyond the cup before it succumbed to gravity and then slid backward, coming to rest between pole and hole for an eagle. When Nelson then ran off a string of pars there was no way Wood could make up the deficit. After a double playoff Byron was now the U.S. Open champion. He won 1,000 dollars in cash and another 2,000 dollar bonus from the equipment company he represented.

The third of the Texas-bred golf giants lacked the size or the early promise of his contemporaries. Nelson's former caddie mate, Ben Hogan, like Byron, first sought fortune on the tour in 1932. The previous year, in search of an amateur victory, he had sold his watch in order to pay his caddie. His career encountered considera-

Frequent runner-ups along the tour were Vic Ghezzi (left) and Craig Wood. In 1941, Ghezzi held the USPGA title while Wood won the Masters. In the 1933 British Open at St. Andrews, on the fifth and 530-yard-long hole, Wood exploded a drive that must have been seized by an errant jet stream for it carried to a bunker 100 yards from the pin, traveling 430 yards according to no less an observer than Bernard Darwin. (COURTESY RAY DAVIS.)

bly more bumps and detours than Nelson's. From the start he was handicapped by the need to play right-handed. Hogan was a natural lefty and, even today, southpaw golfers are relatively scarce. Furthermore, Hogan's size made him the butt of other caddies until he fought them to a truce. And when he did embark on the circuit he was a David among the Goliaths, like the burly Guldahl, the willowy Nelson, the lithe Snead, and the solid Little.

Before this challenge, he squirmed under the burden of second best to Nelson. At the annual Christmas tournament for caddies in 1927, however, Hogan surprised everyone with a 39 for nine holes. Byron managed to tie only with a last green, 30-foot putt. When Ben fired a par 4 on the first playoff hole while Byron bogeyed, the smaller youth thought he'd won. But those in charge decreed a full 9 to determine the winner and Nelson's 18-foot putt on the final hole decided in his favor.

The family was painfully poor, but when Hogan dropped out of high school to con-

centrate on golf, his mother gave Ben's brother, Royal Hogan, forty dollars to buy Ben a set of clubs for Christmas. The adolescent Hogan worked on his game, hustled odd jobs, picked up a few bucks from the frequent local gambling action, and occasionally snookered marks with sucker bets. In one con, he would practice his drives while a caddie pal would brag he could catch the ball barehanded. Ben was accurate enough and the caddie adept enough to snag seven out of ten for a winning bet.

He put together seventy-five dollars and struck out for paydirt on the winter tour, starting in Los Angeles. He finished thirty-eighth, good for eight dollars and fifty cents. His money lasted only a month before he left the gang at New Orleans and retreated to Fort Worth. The next year he played in the Agua Caliente Open, where he earned nothing for his troubles but managed to win fifty dollars at the Phoenix Open.

Back home again, Hogan analyzed his situation. He could point to some good scores over a single round but he lacked

the consistency demanded for tournament wins. He concluded: "There's no such thing as one good shot in big-time golf. They all have to be good—and for seventy-two holes."

He became a demon for practice, hitting shots endlessly. Meanwhile, he earned a dollar any way he could—as a laborer in the oil fields, a mechanic for a bank and a hotel, and even as a croupier at a dice game.

At twenty-four, he stood a bare five foot eight and weighed a slight 135 pounds when he qualified for the 1936 Open at Baltusrol. When Tony Manero walked off the eighteenth green, waving in triumph to the gallery, Hogan was long gone, having failed to make the cut after two rounds.

Still, by the end of that year, with his wife, Valerie, working, they had saved 1,450 dollars, enough to finance a second-hand car and allow a sustained effort on the circuit. While his fellow Texan, Nelson, won the Masters and the Open, Hogan failed even to qualify for either. He took his losses hard.

Although Byron had already set his name in sports page headlines, he and his wife remained close friends of the Hogans. Sometimes they traveled together to save a few dollars.

Already so totally immersed in the play when on the course that he regarded all golfers as foes, Hogan enjoyed some off-the-links comradeship, duck hunting with Nelson and another Texas star, Jimmy Demaret.★ And Nelson, on one occasion, when he ordered a pair of drivers made, gave one to Hogan.

The absolute bottom of the pit yawned in 1938 when Hogan played in a tournament at the Claremont Country Club in Oakland. He and Valerie had eight dollars left and their diet consisted of oranges. Snead came across Hogan in the parking lot, smashing his fist against a brick wall.

"I can't go another inch. I'm finished," groaned Hogan. "Some son of a bitch stole the tires off my car."

But he was back on the course the next day. Perhaps inspired by adversity, as he frequently seemed to be, Hogan scored well enough to come in second behind Harry Cooper and earn 380 dollars. It was enough to replace the missing tires and continue on the trail. He failed to win a single tournament that year. Nevertheless, Hogan ranked 15th in earnings and in 1939, again without one victory, he pushed himself to 7th on the money list.

Not until March of 1940 at the North South Open in Pinehurst did Hogan win. Immediately he went on to victories in tournaments at Greensboro and Asheville to complete a North Carolina triple. The total for the three triumphs was 3,400 dollars and, although he was an also ran in the Masters, PGA, and U.S. Open, his 10,655 dollars still led the pros for the tour.

Across the Atlantic, one professional challenged the American claim to superiority. In 1924, Henry Cotton had left the amateur clan at seventeen, a year after his countryman Arthur Havers had captured the nation's Open. Following Havers, however, eleven long years passed before another Englishman, in the person of Cotton, would claim the British Open title against the best from the U.S.

In the first round of the 1934 British Open at the Royal St. George in Sandwich, the invaders from America reeled from the sharpshooting of Cotton and half a dozen of his countrymen. Cotton scored a 67, 3 better than fellow Briton Fred Taggart. Five more Englishmen came in at 71, along with a pair of foreigners, the Gaul, Marcel Dallemagne, and the Yank, Denny Shute, who was the defending champion. The weather seemed partial to locals. While Shute played his round before the rain fell, the heavens pelted Americans Gene Sarazen, Mac Smith, Joe Kirkwood, and the U.S. Amateur champ, Bob Sweeny. Then the downpour halted long enough for Cotton and most of the homebreds to take the field.

Cotton appeared to have routed all comers when he carded a fantastic record 65 in his second round. (The achievement was memorialized by the Dunlop sporting goods firm with a new ball labeled "65," which the company continued to market forty years later.) He "slipped" to a par 72 his third time out, giving him a huge 11-stroke lead.

"The answer to Hogan is, I fancy, that if Hogan means to win, you lose."—Henry Longhurst, Round in Sixty-Eight, *1953.* (COURTESY FRANK CHRISTIAN STUDIOS.)

Scheduled to finish that afternoon, Cotton suddenly experienced difficulties:

After a light lunch and rarin' to go, I found that the start had been postponed for a quarter of an hour to allow the stewards better to control the crowds. This shook me and I sat alone in a hut by the first tee, while friends tried to ward off well-wishers. I had suffered from ulcers which later caused a lot of trouble, and by the time the stewards called me to the first tee, I had severe stomach cramps.

Coming home I began with three 5s and had three long holes to come. The crowd anticipated the most appalling "blow-up" in championship golf. I continued to struggle and feared a fourth consecutive 5 at the thirteenth, but blessedly, I holed a 10-footer for a 4. The tension relaxed and I played as I had been playing all week, returning a 79 for a total of 283, equalling Gene Sarazen's record at Prince's in 1932. But I had missed a short one on the eighteenth and would otherwise have broken the record. It was a marred victory but it was a victory, and for the first time since Arthur Havers' triumph, the British Open trophy was back where it belonged, and by 5 shots after all.

Cotton was gratified by the

. . . enormous encouragement that the old brigade gave me. James Braid, J. H. Taylor and Ted Ray always seemed to be there to egg me on and Harry Vardon . . . now hardly able to walk . . would sit at the "Maiden" and watch us pass.

Although Walter Hagen had supposedly destroyed the restrictions foisted upon pros,

Cotton was forced to borrow a camel's hair overcoat from writer Henry Longhurst for the presentation of that cup. "My jacket was in my car, which I used as a changing room as usual, for the clubhouse was out of bounds then for professionals."

The win by Cotton presaged his ascendancy to glory. For he dominated European tournaments over the next five years, repeating as British Open champion twice more—in 1937 when he also captured the German and Czechoslovakian Opens and in 1948 when he copped his third British Open at age forty-one.

Cotton's victory in 1934, rather than an aberration, marked a temporary hiatus in U.S. possession of the British Open trophy. The best of the Americans began to stay home to compete in the more lucrative tournaments in the States rather than spend the nearly three weeks required for the round-trip voyages to England to play under the unique conditions of British courses and weather for a lesser pot.

Largely unnoticed by the press during these heroic struggles was the birth of a singular event. The PGA decided in 1937 to add years to the tournament lives of an aging cadre of stars. The organization created the very first annual Seniors' Championship, competing for a trophy contributed by Alfred S. Bourne and a reasonably substantial (for those days) purse of 2,000 dollars. The winner of the fifty-four-hole tournament at Augusta National was Jock Hutchison, the Scotland-born winner of the British Open at his native St. Andrews in 1921. Thus began what is today a major circuit for professionals who have passed age fifty.

Michael McDonnell on
HENRY COTTON

T he transformation of the professional sportsman from gladiatorial freak to millionaire performer has been a long and sometimes painful campaign, not always fought on the field of play itself. Moreover, the champions of this cause have an historical importance beyond their particular sports because they, like the games they represent, reflect changing moods and values within society itself. Their priceless contribution was that they themselves prodded the process along.

Perhaps the history of sport itself can be told through such heroes whose excellence lifted their pursuits just a little higher, leaving them better than before. Such a rule applies only to the great men whose very names epitomized their sport to a public that had no other interest.

One such was Sir Henry Cotton, knighted by Queen Elizabeth the Second for his services to the game of golf only a few days before his death in 1987. But the fact is this famous Englishman performed a much greater service to professional sports in general and to its practitioners in particular.

From the outset, it is important to understand the social period in which Cotton emerged as a supreme sportsman, if only to appreciate the enormity of his task and the magnitude of his triumph over the bias and prejudice that dogged anybody of that era who attempted to play sport for a living.

He was born in the early part of the twentieth century, when English society was divided sharply into distinct social classes and when sport itself was perceived to be in its most noble Corinthian form when pursued for its own sake, without thought of remuneration. The other side of this coin was that somehow sport seemed to lose part of its merit when there was a pay packet involved and that, in this form, it was nothing more than a trivial vocation available to the lower classes who were good enough, but not good for much else.

On reflection, the overt distinctions were quite hurtful and to the modern conscience intolerable. In cricket, for example, the amateurs were known as "Gentlemen" while the paid ranks were collectively branded as "Players." In golf, the amateurs were referred to as "Mister." The pros were called by their surnames—as one would a servant of the day. They were accorded respect for their skill of course but such appreciation did not open all doors. They were still, after all, working class. Most of them had been caddies. The profession itself had grown from the ranks of blacksmiths and carpenters of the nineteenth century.

Golf pros remained therefore confined to the servant class. They were not allowed into clubhouses, although a suitable nail was always to be found in a nearby shed, on which they could hang their coats during play. They knew their place and they never questioned the outrageous values that permitted them, as it were, only half a life.

At least, that is, until Henry Cotton came along. He turned the system and its values upside down so that it could never be the same again. And without question, he set an image for the professional sportsman that led eventually to the millionaire status and prestige that is now commonplace to them. And there have been few of them to ever exhibit the personal class and style that Henry Cotton brought with him.

The irony of it all was that he came from the right side of the tracks. He was from the privileged class. His father was an affluent engineer and he and his brother Leslie attended an expensive fee-paying school in London. Thus Cotton, an extremely intelligent and articulate student, was expected to join his peers in the legal, medical, or business professions.

But he had other ideas. He chose golf and wanted to play it for a living. In this respect he had joined the working classes. But therein lay the problem. How could he be banned from clubhouses by people of his own class? And how would his new-found colleagues in the lower orders treat one of the toffs who claimed now to be one of them?

It is a tribute to his skill and dedication that Cotton was able to win both battles—or, rather, that by the time he had finished his own lifetime of fame and fortune, there was no division to be seen and, if anything, the professional golfer had become the archetypal hero of clean-cut sportsmanship.

Cotton would have achieved nothing away from the fairways without supreme skill on them to make himself noticed. He needed the cash from his successful golf to afford the Rolls-Royce and chauffeur parked defiantly outside the clubhouse from which, as a professional, he was occasionally barred.

He also needed enormous stature and nerve to have criticized sponsors for not providing enough prize money—as he did when accepting the French Open trophy one year. His rule was a simple one: "I have worked hard to become the best there is. I expect to receive the same treatment and courtesy accorded to a lawyer or a doctor or any man at the top of his profession."

Indeed, he had paid a high physical price for his success. Hours of practice putting had left him stooped and his right shoulder drooped slightly, as though he were permanently in the position to make a shot. Even so, he was, at times, slightly dismissive about the skills required for golf.

He felt the golf swing was not natural movement and that, therefore, it could be learned and practiced to a high standard, even by those who had no "eye for a ball" but were prepared to apply themselves diligently to the task. That said, he had been an outstanding schoolboy cricketer with all the essential reflex skills until he turned to golf.

There is no doubt that he was influenced in his outlook by what he discovered on his first visit to the United States in 1928 when he was twenty-one years old

At Carnoustie, in 1934, Henry Cotton retrieved the British Open championship to the delight of his countrymen and women. It was the first British victory in the tournament in eleven years. (COURTESY UPI/BETTMANN NEWSPHOTOS.)

and determined to learn what made the American golfers so superior. What he saw clearly affected his own attitude and laid down an inflexible dogma for the rest of his career. He witnessed, for example, how the successful sportsman was accepted totally in his own right. He learned too from Walter Hagen that it was possible to make a handsome living solely from playing golf, provided you were

Lips pursed, Cotton extricates from a bunker during a 1933 match at Purley Downs. (COURTESY AP/WIDE WORLD PHOTOS.)

good enough and, more importantly, had a personal style and elegance. It was clear to Cotton that the great American had turned golf into a performing art, and that was how he saw it too.

True enough, Cotton himself had the looks and sophistication of a matinee idol. He became the darling of cafe society, on first name terms with the rich and famous, and a familiar figure in all the luxury resorts around the world. He spoke French, Spanish, and Portuguese fluently, was an avid oil painter, and throughout his life had a knowledge and curiosity for the world around him that stretched far beyond the golf course.

When the Duke of Windsor, living in exile in Paris after the Abdication, wanted to assess whether public opinion would allow him back to live in Britain, Cotton was asked to arrange an apparently casual game of golf for a much more important purpose. He partnered the former king against two senior figures from the British establishment who, between shots, relayed the message from England that the time was not right for such a return. Sadly, it never was. But Cotton had earned another footnote in history.

Yet, throughout his career Cotton found himself in conflict with officialdom and at times with his fellow professionals. He walked out of one tournament because he calculated he could not earn enough prize money to pay his expenses for the week.

He refused to play for Britain in one Ryder Cup match when officials would not permit him to stay on in the United States and play in other events. Prior to his major breakthrough in 1934 when he won the first of three British Open titles, he had in fact fled from Britain to live in Belgium.

There were good reasons for such a move. He needed to escape the pressure of being acknowledged as the best golfer in Britain—most certainly of world class—but unable to deliver the ultimate proof with a major title. He was acclaimed as the homegrown hero who could end the American domination of Bobby Jones, Walter Hagen, and others in the British Open, yet his own fickle temperament seemed constantly to undermine his chances. His playing skills were not in question but his psychological vulnerability was painfully apparent.

Even his first victory at Royal St. George's in Kent showed the best and worst of Henry Cotton. He had opened with a record-breaking 65 and was so far ahead of his rivals at the start of the final round, it seemed to be merely a lap of honor for the adoring crowds.

"When anyone asks me who is the greatest striker of a golf ball I ever saw, my answer is immediate. It is Henry Cotton.... He developed an immense strength in his hands, and they became the focal point in his essentially simple swing. As the ball flew straight at the flag, you felt that, if you hit it in that fashion, it could hardly do anything else. He could do almost anything with a golf ball on purpose and would have made a great trick-shot artist. We often used to challenge him to take his driver from a bad lie on the fairway, simply for the aesthetic pleasure of seeing the ball fly away as though fired from a rifle, and I remember once at Bad Ems seeing him knock a shooting stick out of the ground with a 1-iron shot at a range of 20 yards. We christened him 'the Maestro,' and he deserved it."—Henry Longhurst, The Sunday Times. (COURTESY UPI/BETTMAN NEWSPHOTOS.)

Even the U.S. press took notice as Cotton, in 1934, blazed a record 132 for the first thirty-six holes of the British Open, breaking his own best score for eighteen with a 65. (COURTESY AP/WIDE WORLD PHOTOS.)

Not so. As he waited alone in the starters tent to tee off, he began to feel ill. By the time he had played nine holes he had taken 40 strokes and looked hell-bent once again on throwing it all away. But somehow the crisis passed; he regained control of his nerves and finished with a 79 to win the title by a comfortable margin.

At last Cotton had proved his worth to others, and himself. He was the new hero and of course he looked the part. His lifestyle was star quality. For a time he lived in a suite in Claridges. He later had a home in London's fashionable Eaton Square and employed a full staff of butlers, maids, cooks, and gardeners. He married Isabella Moss, an Argentinian heiress who was to become the major influence in his life both on and off the course. Without question, she lived for Henry and his golf. They met when he did a tour of South America and she booked lessons with him for a month. From that moment on, they were inseparable until she died in 1985, two years before her husband.

But what Cotton also did as his fame spread was to broaden the appeal of golf and take it to the most unlikely places. He topped the bill in a chain of British vaudeville theatres, performing trick shots into the audience. He began to write his own column in a 5-million circulation newspaper. He penned numerous books without the services of a ghostwriter. He made instructional films, became a TV commentator, designed golf courses, as well as serving as a PGA official and being captain of the Ryder Cup team in postwar years.

Throughout his life he was a man of unlimited enthusiasm and energy, always trying new ideas and equipment. He is even credited with popularizing the golf glove in Britain by wearing it whenever he played. His quest for knowledge once prompted him to position a couple of inflated balloons under his sweater to understand the swing problems of a lady pupil.

Cotton believed in the supreme importance of strong hands because he declared they had to "find the ball" in the downswing and they dictated the strength, shape, and flight of a shot. He himself perfected this strength to such a degree that he could hit a succession of drives one-handed, without the need to re-grip the club. Even in the final years of his life, when he lived at Penina in southern Portugal—on the championship course he designed and to which hundreds of enthusiasts made regular pilgrimages to learn from the man they called The Maestro—he still propounded the doctrine of strong hands.

By then he had devised a simple routine to give even beginners some feeling of the way the golf swing is controlled by the hands. He acquired a collection of old car tires and simply instructed his pupils to take up to 100 short and rapid swings at them with a club. The strain imposed on wrists and forearms is almost unbearable, but the exercise is priceless. Moreover it is the lazy golfer's way to practice because it gives the hands a "live" feeling without hours of pre-match toil on the range.

My own view is that it was this kind of strength—both physical and of the spirit—that saw him to what many consider his greatest Open triumph when, in savage weather conditions at Carnoustie in 1937, he outplayed all the outstanding American golfers of the day who had turned up to play in the Ryder Cup match.

In the final round, as he trailed the Whitcombe brothers, the course was virtually unplayable in the relentless rain and as huge pools began to gather on the greens, officials cut one new hole and pondered on the prospect of abandoning play.

Bernard Darwin, writing in *Country Life* magazine, recalled "all through the afternoon the authorities were on tenterhooks and if anybody had lodged a formal appeal against the conditions, I think it must have been upheld."

Even so, Cotton picked his way brilliantly through these newly formed watery hazards to return a 71, only 1 stroke outside the then course record, and waited to see if his distinguished rivals, among them Byron Nelson, Ed Dudley, Sam Snead, Ralph Guldahl, and Denny Shute, could catch him.

The Hon. Michael Scott presented the 1934 trophy to Cotton, who led from the first round. His 283 tied the record previously set by Gene Sarazen. (COURTESY AP/WIDE WORLD PHOTOS.)

Cotton had made immense preparations for this moment. Earlier in the year, he had spent a full week at Carnoustie getting to know the course. Then, during the championship, he and some friends completely took over a small hotel so that his concentration would not be distracted in off-duty hours by the public.

When he came to the seventy-second hole with the out-of-bounds fence on the left and the two burns cutting across the fairway, it occurred to him to play short of the second stretch of water guarding the green. Instead, he hammered a 2-iron deliberately towards the right-hand greenside bunker and away from trouble, fully prepared to accept the penalty of a trap shot rather than the disaster of being out of play.

The strategy paid off, because he nipped his 3rd shot from the hard, wet sand and left the ball short of the hole to take 2 putts and win the title by 2 strokes. By his own admission, it had been one of the finest rounds of his life, made more fulfilling because he had beaten the acknowledged best players in the world.

What might have been was then thwarted for Cotton—as it was for his generation, by World War II—although, with exquisite timing, he managed to win the German Open in the late summer of 1939. He then drove across Europe to catch the last cross-channel ferry to England. In his haste, he forgot to pick up his winner's check. After the war, he received a reminder from the German Golf Federation. The check was still in their office awaiting collection.

During the war Cotton served for a time as an officer in the Royal Air Force, but regularly took time off to play exhibition matches to raise money for the Red Cross (and always bought a ticket to get into his own show). Curiously enough, until his knighthood, Cotton's only civil honor was the Order of the British Empire for these efforts in raising food parcel money for prisoners of war.

It remains a mystery why the Grand Old Man of Golf had been ignored in this way for so long (some said it was because he chose to live abroad) and, indeed, when the honor eventually came he was eighty. At first, he confessed, he was not really interested personally but then decided he would accept it for the game itself. He was after all golf's first knight.

Cotton's lack of recognition is even more difficult to understand in view of the succession of achievements credited to him long after he had won his last Open in 1948 (after an eleven-year span when he was forty-one years old).

He felt it was time to broaden even wider the appeal of the game and to bring more players into it. Thus, along with several influential friends from the golf trade, he established the Golf Foundation so that thousands of youngsters could learn how to play. Some of the outstanding players from subsequent generations—among them Tony Jacklin, Peter Oosterhiuis, and Nick Faldo—all benefited from tuition through the Golf Foundation, which paid local club professionals to teach the game to newcomers.

Nor did Cotton consider his job complete after merely instructing them how to play. He embarked on a program of providing areas where the newcomers could play. He designed golf courses throughout the British Isles and in Europe and then advocated what he called "primitive golf courses"—basically mown areas of grassland on which beginners could learn to hit the ball before moving on to more established centers.

For a man who had been such a great player and performed the game at its highest level, he never tired of watching other people play—no matter what their handicap. However, once he had stopped competitive golf in the early 1960s he was reluctant to play in public.

He was persuaded, however, to make an appearance in the 1977 Open at Turnberry and, although he was rapturously received by the fans, he vowed not to do it again. He explained: "The public expect me to be as I was—not an old man lucky to break 80. I should leave them with good memories of me."

There is one glaring omission in the catalog of achievements listed against Henry Cotton's name. He never scored a major victory in the United States. His only triumph came in the White Sulphur Springs Invitational, Virginia, just after the war.

He came close a number of times in the U.S. Open, although some critics argued that he was never able fully to make the transition from the traditional small (1.62-inch diameter) British golf ball of which he was the undisputed master to the larger (1.68-inch diameter) American ball in use on the U.S. tour. In any case, he professed no wish to pursue a career in the United States and therefore never stayed long enough to make the necessary adjustments in playing and living styles.

Essentially he regarded himself as a European player and must be judged within that context. Indeed it is part of his huge legacy to the game that his ideas, attitudes, and schemes eventually brought about the renaissance of British golf and, in so doing, shifted the balance of power within the game itself.

He exerted headmasterly influence over professionals who followed him and even donated a Rookie of the Year prize out of his own pocket to young professionals he considered worthy of the accolade (although there were some years when the prize was not given because Henry did not think anybody was good enough). In their times, all the players of promise were spotted by The Maestro and included Tony Jacklin, Nick Faldo, and Sandy Lyle. In fact, Jacklin himself paid handsome tribute to Cotton when he said: "What I admired about Henry was that he refused to allow the pros to be treated shabbily in any way; to be put down. He did that for all of us."

And yet there was an extraordinary paradox. For all his fame and achievement, he remained genuinely a man of deep humility. At the height of his success when he was one of the best-known and loved personalities in Britain, I visited him at his mansion in Eaton Place and he said: "You know, I don't regard any of this as really mine. I've just got the use of it for the duration."

He was a deeply religious man despite a notorious habit of shocking dinner party guests with a repertoire of impish but rude jokes. He was a convert to the Roman Catholic faith observed by his wife, Isabella, whom everybody knew as "Toots" (a nickname legend suggests was bestowed on her by Walter Hagen himself).

Though not a Catholic at the time of his 1934 Open win, he nevertheless visited a local church in Sandwich every day, unbeknownst to anybody but his wife. He explained: "It wasn't to ask for anything like winning. I didn't even pray as such. I just wanted to be somewhere away from the pressure and the attention where nothing was expected from me. I discovered an astounding tranquility. Maybe that was the greatest gift of all that week although I lost it for a while in the last round."

There was one other private moment at that championship. All week, an elderly gentleman had stood at a short hole to watch him play. But, on the last day, the man was absent, too ill and confined to his bed at a nearby hotel. Cotton knew he had been there and, when he had made his winner's speech and the crowds departed, he took the cup to the hotel and knocked on the old man's door. Without a word, he handed it over. The old man wept. So, too, did Cotton as he watched Harry Vardon reunited with the cup he had won five times in an illustrious career.

Both men sensed the moment and that there was much to be done before the younger man's own journey would be complete. That mission has now been accomplished.

Throughout his life, Henry had a sense of fun and an awareness of the ridiculous that never allowed him to take any predicament too seriously. Hospitalized the day before Christmas Eve 1987, he acquired a joke golf club, which he wore as though the shaft were sticking through his head. When the astonished doctor entered the room, Henry said: "To tell you the truth doctor, I don't think those pills you are giving me are doing any good at all!" The next day, he was dead.

14

The War Years

The outbreak of World War II shut down all competitive golf in Europe. Fighting off food shortages, Great Britain reverted to the nineteenth century and sheep grazed on the fairways of St. Andrews. Many other courses once again became agricultural fields. Others were chewed up and desecrated with abandoned buses and similar refuse to hinder airborne invasions by the Nazis. One club posted tongue-in-cheek regulations:

1. The position of known delayed action bombs will be marked by red flags placed at a reasonably but not guaranteed safe distance.

2. A ball removed by enemy action may be replaced as near as possible to where it lay or if lost or destroyed another ball may be dropped, not nearer the hole, without penalty.

3. Competitors during gunfire or while bombs are falling may take cover without penalty.

It required more than a stiff upper lip to maintain any tournaments. And, as in World War I, Britain's golfers disappeared into the armed services ranks.

The U.S. golf establishment had a natural affinity with the land where the modern game originated. It was not surprising that a committee composed of Bob Jones, Grantland Rice, the heads of the USGA, PGA, and Western Golf Association sponsored a special British War Relief tournament. Such affairs, which grew to include Finnish War Relief, the United Service Organization, the Red Cross, and other funds, were to become a staple of the war years, before and after the entrance of the U.S. With Pearl Harbor two years off, golf actually boomed in the U.S. as the arms industries revived the depressed economy.

Ben Hogan, still unable to capture any of the three most prestigious affairs in the country—the Open, the PGA, and the Masters—continued to tote the most prize money to the bank in 1940, '41, and '42. Sam Snead, runner-up in the 1940 PGA to Nelson, tucked away that title in '42. He drew the biggest galleries as he plundered the regular circuit and, thanks to Corcoran's ancillary promotions, socked away many more dollars than Hogan whose earnings basically came from tournaments.

Byron Nelson, after his 1939 win in the Open, could not repeat it at the Canterbury Club in Cleveland a year later. Instead, tragicomedy and high drama featured other stars. Snead was only 1 stroke down as he began his final round but this time he blew up over a series of holes, carding a horrendous 81. When thunderclouds began gathering, a mob of players rushed to the first tee to play their last eighteen. The gang ignored the advice of a marshal and a reporter that they risked disqualification if they played out of turn. Among the crew was the popular Ed "Porky" Oliver. When he ambled off the last green with a 287, he had tied Lawson Little.

Meanwhile, out on the course, the aging Sarazen, winner of the Open eighteen years before, plugged away. His 38 for the first nine left him needing a 34 to tie the leaders. It was a formidable challenge over a layout that included a 615-yard par 5, a 230-yard 3 and a 441-yard 4. When he birdied two of the early holes he was on target. He canned a sharp-breaking 8 footer to preserve par on sixteen but he would need to play scratch golf on seventeen and eighteen where he'd bogeyed on several earlier occasions. Doom loomed as his pitch on seventeen left him 30 feet from the pin. Undaunted, he rapped it home. On the last hole, Sarazen lay 50 feet away after his second stroke. He very nearly pulled off a bird that would have won had the ball not ended perhaps 8 inches from victory. When he tapped it in, he had his tying 72.

It seemed to be a three-way draw but the officials now disqualified Oliver for his offense. Although both Little and Sarazen argued Porky should not be penalized, the authorities were adamant. The playoff was too much for Gene, however, and the thick-chested Little beat him 70 to 73 for his first major title.

The victor over Snead in the 1940 Masters, Jimmy Demaret, was another Texan but radically different in personality from the likes of Guldahl, Nelson, and Hogan. Guldahl had never overcome his shyness and when he lost his stroke he vanished. Nelson and Hogan traveled with their wives, making them less accessible to the public and press and neither man radiated the bonhomie favored by reporters or fans. But Demaret resembled Hagen in his eagerness to "smell the flowers." He claimed The Haig was his boyhood idol:

I try to pattern my tournament psychology after Walter's relaxed but determined attitude on the links. Like Hagen I make it a rule to forget golf once a round is on the scoreboard. I never take the game home with me at night.

Demaret, like Hogan, was lefthanded. He took up the game when hardly more than a toddler and, at age nine, became caddie master for a nine-hole course used by army officers at Camp Logan shortly after the Armistice in 1918. By age thirteen he had a job as assistant pro.

An excellent all-around athlete in high school, Demaret thought of trying for a baseball career. A talk with Hagen, who had abandoned an opportunity as a major leaguer for golf, convinced Demaret to stick with the links. His big break came from one of his golf pupils. Orchestra leader Ben Bernie took lessons from Demaret and in return allowed Jimmy to sing with the band. Demaret's voice sounded good enough for occasional gigs but Maestro Bernie, joined by a nightclub owner and an oilman, decided Demaret merited an audition on the golf tour. They chipped in for a 600 dollar stake, much of which disappeared into the pockets of a pool shark. However, Demaret debuted at the Los Angeles Open in 1935 and collected enough to continue.

His fondness for partying endeared him to the lustrous of the silver screen. He later told Dan Jenkins:

We knew everybody in Hollywood. It was pretty impressive to be hanging around Bing Crosby and folks like that all the time. And there were an awful lot of dandy little old gals around. We didn't know who they were. They had different names then. But we realized later that they were Susan Hayward and that kind of thing.

While Gene Sarazen strove to give the calling dignity, Jimmy Demaret associated with a raffish crew. Lloyd Mangrum, with the mustache and demeanor of a riverboat gambler, used his skill at cards to keep himself afloat. Once, when he arrived in New Orleans for a tournament flat broke, Mangrum took up residence in the city jail for two days. Ky Laffoon, who spat tobacco juice while stalking the course, had played caddie for the famous hustler Titanic Thompson.*

---

*Born Alvin Thomas, Titanic, contrary to his legend, did not earn his nickname for an escape from the steamship disaster by the ruse of wearing a dress. But he perfected the golf hustle as a means of fleecing rubes and suckers. Ed Dudley, an excellent teacher and pro, and later a PGA president, schooled Thompson in golf strokes. Advance agents like Herman Keiser, 1946 Masters winner, and Bob Hamilton, 1944 PGA champ, would spot a mark, a well-heeled wisenheimer whose brag exceeded his skill. Titanic, a natural southpaw, would arrive and play an awkward round righty. Then when the target brayed about his victory, Thompson would boast, "Why I could beat you left handed." The fool and his money soon parted, for Titanic was good enough to outshoot even Byron Nelson on one occasion. In addition to Laffoon, Thompson also employed Clarence Yockey, a 105 pounder, in the role of a tiny caddie who could beat the man chortling over his defeat of Thompson. Yockey, of course, was a pro-caliber player despite his size.

In a more sinister role, Thompson was a principal in the rigged card game that led to the murder of gambler Arnold Rothstein in 1928, and one biographer, Carlton Stowers, insists Thompson murdered at least five people.

Demaret's wardrobe shouted to the galleries. He packed a rainbow of slacks—multicolored, plaid, checked, striped—and polka-dot jackets. Eventually, he owned some 500 hats and, while real men shrank from anything brighter than gray, Demaret ordered bolts of pastel fabrics to be tailored into his outfits. Demaret led the golf fashions towards comfort and freedom of movement, although no less a staid character than Byron Nelson had shattered precedent at the 1939 Open when he appeared in a short-sleeve, open-necked shirt, now standard for the course.

According to Al Barkow, Jimmy displayed his own unique style.

Demaret had technique and mannerisms that were the stuff of pantomime. He walked with short, quick, rhythmic steps, like someone treading over a fairway of unbroken eggs, his buttocks shimmying from side to side. . . . In preparing to play a shot, Demaret pranced up to the ball from behind it, his head tilted like someone lining up a billiard shot, his body slightly angled to the left of his line and the club spinning constantly in his hands.

For all of that he was an excellent golfer. Midway in size between Nelson and Hogan, Demaret exploited blacksmith's sized forearms to give him long straight drives. And, although he eschewed practice, he played a consistently fine all-around game. He hit low line drives—he called them "snake rapers"—that avoided wind problems.

On the first day at Augusta in 1940, he carded a genuine astonisher. After a pedestrian 37 going out, Demaret turned for home. On the tenth hole, his 1-iron left him 3 feet off to set up a birdie. On the eleventh hole he dropped a 30 footer for a second bird. He parred 12 and then when he faced Rae's Creek for the thirteenth he played short and safe with his second shot. But after his subsequent chip put him 2 feet from the hole, he smacked the ball into the cup to register his third bird. The fourteenth was a routine par and on fifteen the gods apparently decided to frown. The ball carried the pond in front of the green but just barely and imbedded itself in muck and water.

Demaret removed both of his fancy shoes, took a stance in 2 feet of water and blasted away. The ball exploded onto the green, close enough for him to sink a fourth birdie. When he 1 putted again on sixteen he was now 5 under. He duplicated the feat on seventeen and missed a seventh birdie on eighteen by bare inches. His total for the back nine added up to a record-shattering 30. Twenty-seven years later, a venerable Ben Hogan would match the mark and then another nineteen years would pass before an aging Jack Nicklaus in 1986 would equal the score. Oddly enough, the same day that Demaret knocked off his 30, Lloyd Mangrum outshot him for the early lead with his own, still uneclipsed 64 for eighteen holes.

Mangrum and Demaret stood even after the second day, with Lloyd shooting a 75 to Jimmy's 72. The screws tightened after the third round when Demaret's 70 lifted him 1 stroke ahead of Mangrum while Sam Snead crept into the fight with a 69, putting him only 3 behind. In the finale, however, Snead slipped slightly going out, then collapsed with another hole reminiscent of his 1939 Open disaster as he watered himself twice on the eleventh. When the last putt had fallen, Demaret had coasted in with a 4-stroke margin.

As the U.S. plunged into World War II, the major golf events—the PGA, U.S. Open, and the Masters—were cancelled, but some local tournaments and exhibitions continued. Golf courses themselves became part of the war effort. The Congressional Country Club in Maryland served as a training site for the Office of Strategic Services, predecessor to the CIA. Augusta National, with no masters tournaments, became a turkey farm. The Wykagyl Country Club in New Rochelle, New York, sprouted "Victory Gardens" on its first two holes and beef cattle grazed on the fairways of Baltusrol in New Jersey.

Jimmy Demaret stowed his many-hued duds in favor of navy blue and Hogan, Snead, Little, and hundreds of other golf pros entered the military ranks. The one titan of the game who remained to play was Byron Nelson, since a condition similar to hemophilia barred him from the services.

In place of the celebrated tournaments came the "Hale America Open." It was sponsored by the USGA, which had adopted the slogan, "Keep 'Em Swinging for War Relief and Defense." The event, held only in 1942, drew 1,500 entries. Hogan, playing out of Hershey, Pennsylvania, outscored Mike Turnesa and Demaret by 3 strokes with a 271.

There was one major exception to the decline in tournaments. The ubiquitous Corcoran had come across an amateur who confided, "I have a friend who will put up more money than you play for on the entire circuit." Not one to pass up an opportunity, Corcoran met with George May back of the eighteenth green during the USGA amateur championship at Winged Foot.

At a banquet celebrating the 1940 Chicago Open at the Tam O'Shanter Club in Chicago, May, the president and principal owner, announced the prize money for the following year would be bumped from 5,000 to 11,000 dollars, setting it a notch above the 10,000 offered by Los Angeles and Miami for their opens. He further surprised the audience by declaring admission prices would be slashed to the level of grandstand seats at the ballpark (a dollar and ten cents or so).

What May produced in 1941 was unprecedented in golf. It combined top-notch golfers with a carnival atmosphere. Some 300 pros competed for the extravagant first prize of 2,000 dollars and to excite the hordes of the unsophisticated, May arranged for the players to shoot from the front tees. Low scores, he reasoned, would impress the rubes. Those who came to gawk—and the four-day affair drew 41,000 with a mob of 23,000 present the final Sunday—feasted on hot dogs, beer, soda pop, just as if they were at a baseball game. If bored by golf, they could wander to the swimming pool to see an aquatic show, pause in the clubhouse to gamble on slot machines, or wait until the day's play ended and then dance in the outdoor pavilion.

May toted the idea a step further in 1942 when America was already at war. Capitalizing on the jingoism infecting the land, May now called the tournament the All-American Open. He created a pair of simultaneous competitions, one for professionals and one for amateurs. The USGA, already aghast at his pitchman approach, sought to discourage amateurs from entering. But May won them over by promising 10,000 dollars of the profits to Army Emergency Relief. May even invited nonwhite golfers to play, making the Tam O'Shanter the first big U.S. event to break the color line. Out on the course, the promoter continued to whip things up in ways that would have shamed Fred Corcoran. When Byron Nelson faced a 12-foot putt to break the course record, May, on the spot, offered a 1,000 dollar bonus if he sank it. Nelson missed.

In spite of his largesse, the former Bible salesman offended some of his star attractions. He had programs printed up that sold for a quarter identifying players by numbers—numbers he expected the golfers to wear. Quite a few of the pros considered the stunt undignified and a mini-rebellion erupted. May stuck to his guns, and even disqualified Joe Kirkwood, Jr., for failing to conform. Some participants, though, made their point by fastening their numbers to the seats of their pants.

Despite the growing shortage of gasoline, attendance zoomed to 62,000. May did even better in 1943, to the dismay of most of golf officialdom. Over the next ten years, he would fight a running battle with guardians of tradition. When he tried to boost the prize for an amateur to 500 dollars in war bonds rather than the limit of 100 dollars, he was rebuffed by the USGA. His chief weapon remained oversized purses, temptations the pros—whatever their misgivings about the ambience—found difficult to resist. Sleight-of-hand, or perhaps mouth, might describe even this aspect of May's machinations. The prizes trumpeted in his ads and by accomplices in the press were the face values of war bonds and stamps. Byron Nelson won 13,462.50 dollars for the 1944 All-American Open, but only a churlish, less than 200-

"Byron and Ben had about a year in which to prove who was the better golfer—from August 1945, when Ben was discharged from the Army, until August 1946, when Byron went into semi-retirement on the ranch he had bought in Roanoke, Texas. Their year of grim-faced competition proved that a steady diet of tournament golf does a terrific job on the nerves of men who act nerveless, that 275 and not 288 approximated par for four rounds on a circuit course, and quite a few other things about modern professional golf, but it did not prove who was the better golfer, Hogan or Nelson. It would be unfair to either golfer to say that the other had demonstrated even a slight superiority. When Hogan did something remarkable, Nelson invariably came up with a a matching performance and vice-versa."—Herbert Warren Wind, The Story of American Golf. (COURTESY FRANK CHRISTIAN STUDIOS.)

percent American would have remarked that the cash value was closer to 10,000 dollars. May was not unique in this patriotic cash-in. Other tournaments also awarded prizes in war bonds.

While the Tam O'Shanter tournament flourished during the war years, the golf crowd coped with shortages that severely crimped play. When gas rationing cut auto travel, clubs like Tam O'Shanter, Bon O'Link, and Baltusrol in New Jersey arranged for horse-drawn coaches to meet players at nearby train stations. Some clubs used buses to haul members to the links.

With rubber and its kin in very short supply no new balls were manufactured. Clubs scoured the bottoms of their ponds and streams to retrieve long-abandoned balls. In Bulawayo, South Africa, they tested wooden golf balls. Spalding advertised to the pros:

War-Flite Golf Balls. Volunteered by you and your members . . . mobilized from the nation's lockers. . . . And whipped into fighting shape by Spalding's exclusive reprocessing method. Fresh reinforcements to back up the game *and your job.*

The company offered top of the line Hurricane and Pursuit models and the less expensive, Bomber and Recruit

Wilson Sports Goods bought ads that featured soldiers amid the heat of battle juxtaposed with a pipe-smoking golfer. The copy, under the headline, "Patriots of Golf," declared:

Golf had a *place* in this all-out war. And it will continue to have a place as long as there are men who need diversion, relaxation and outdoor exercise to keep them fit for their wartime duties.

The golf professional who sees in the physical benefits of golf the means of keeping businessmen and workers fit and able, and *who keeps them playing* is aiding the war effort. He too *is a patriot.*

The golf professional who stimulates the interest of "Juniors" and establishes classes to teach golf, with its fine training, rhythm and times, *is a patriot.* He is

helping to build future fliers, gunners and officers. . . .

Ed Dudley, as president of the PGA, had contacted President Franklin D. Roosevelt about the place of the game during the war. The White House, which had blessed baseball as an aid to homefront morale, responded that golf should continue as a booster for civilian spirits.

Not a few GIs were entertained by troupes of golfers who put on demonstrations at hospitals and military camps. As in World War I, the sport was also used for the physical rehabilitation of victims of the war. But there remained the haughty few who believed golf was a rich man's pastime. The imperious New York Parks Commissioner, Robert Moses, declined to allow soldiers to play free at one of the courses under his jurisdiction, remarking: "The average American soldier regards golf as a game for toffs and gentlemen, and doesn't know a divot from an inscription on an attic tomb."

The few top pros not in uniform, Nelson, Harold McSpaden, Olin Dutra, and Jimmy Thomson, teamed up with the show biz golfers Bing Crosby and Bob Hope★ to play exhibitions that raised money for the Red Cross and various military service organizations. An ersatz Ryder Cup competition using an American team captained by Hagen and challengers led by Bob Jones brought in 35,000 dollars for the Red Cross. In place of the classic events were tournaments known as the Victory Open and the Red Cross Open. And in a flush of patriotic fervor, the North South Open at Pinehurst admitted only men in service or those over age thirty-eight, the limit for the military draft. Hogan, on leave, won the tournament in 1943 but in 1944, forty-eight-year-old Bobby Cruickshank, who had escaped a German prisoner of war camp in World War I, beat out Joe Kirkwood, Joe Turnesa, and Gene Sarazen, all well over the age limit. *The Professional Golfer of America* printed a growing list of members in the service, which by the time of V-J Day totaled more than 500. Scattered through the pages were a series of black-edged boxes with the names of those who had lost their lives.

From a golf standpoint, the single most outstanding phenomenon of the period was the win streak achieved by Byron Nelson as the peace finally arrived. Nelson had won six tournaments in 1944, averaging a brilliant 69.67 strokes over the seventy-eight rounds of testing play.

When his 1945 run began, he was up against stiffer opposition. Sam Snead, sent home by the Navy after twenty-six months because of back problems, took tournaments at Portland and Richmond as 1944 ended, and then snapped up the Los Angeles Open by a single stroke margin over Nelson.

Byron recouped with a stunning performance at the Corpus Christi Open. His score on those baked-hard Texas fairways was 264, which did not qualify for the record book only because, with winter rules in effect, Nelson enjoyed preferred lies. At New Orleans, the next stop on the tour, he outshot Jug McSpaden in a playoff. But then Snead usurped his reign with victories at Gulfport, Pensacola, and Jacksonville. When they made the turn for Miami, Snead had won six, Nelson four, over the winter circuit, starting from December 1944.

Winning a four-ball tournament in Miami with his pal McSpaden, Nelson started his march through the record book. The next win was at the Charlotte Open and it required a double playoff before Snead fell. At Greensboro, Nelson whipped Sammy Byrd, a refuge from major league baseball outfields. The Durham Open made it four in a row and on the final stop of the winter circuit in Atlanta, Nelson fired a 263, but the course was considered too short for a record. Craig Wood's 264 for four rounds continued as the official best.

In June, Nelson and Snead went head to head in a sideshow, a medal and match play series. The Slammer outshot his rival 143-144 in thirty-six holes at Fresh Meadows on Long Island. Nelson evened matters with a 4 up, 3 left for thirty-six holes the next day. Back on the trail, Nelson won his sixth consecutive tournament at the Montreal Open, 10 strokes ahead of the

nearest foe, McSpaden. Jug then challenged Nelson with three rounds of 66 at the Philadelphia *Inquirer*'s Invitation and still finished second as Byron whizzed home with a last round 63. In the Chicago Victory Open, losers McSpaden and Laffoon could come no closer than 7 strokes behind. Snead was not on hand anymore, due to a wrist broken during a softball game.

After V-E Day in May, the PGA restored its championship for a July date. Nelson contended at match play for a change. Weariness sagged his shoulders and he faced a huge field. "I feel like I'm one-hundred years old," he told a friend. After turning back Sarazen, Nelson confronted Mike Turnesa who banged out a 68 on the front nine. With only four holes left, Turnesa

"The wonder of this mild-mannered and humble Texan is that he can be topped by specialists in practically all phases of the game. He appears to do no single thing better than someone else you might name, yet none of the specialists can be called a better golfer. There is nothing freakish about his personality and less about his game. You cannot single out any phase of it as better than another. Nelson is deadly serious about life and golf, but wholly without delusions of grandeur of his own importance."—Arthur Mann, Colliers, *August 1945.* (COURTESY UPI/ BETTMANN NEWSPHOTOS.)

held a commanding 2-up edge. Nelson bird-ied thirty-three and thirty-four to pull even. Turnesa battled back with a bird on thirty-five and Byron squelched him with an ea-gle. They halved the finale with pars. "I was 7 under par," whined the noticeably unhappy Turnesa. "I don't see how *anyone* can beat him." Indeed, Denny Shute, Claude Harmon and then ex-ballplayer Sammy Byrd all fell before Nelson. For the 204 holes he played, Nelson trimmed 37 off par.

He rested from his labors for a week before attending the George May extrava-ganza. Ben Hogan was back from the air force but he and Sarazen could only scrape to a tie for second, 11 strokes worse than Nelson, who battered par by 11. That made it ten in a row and when he entered the Canadian Open, Nelson captured his elev-enth consecutive victory.

Of course it had to end. And in the Memphis Open, amateur Fred Haas cracked an 18-under-par 270 for the first big tourna-ment win by an amateur since 1936. Nel-son wound up fourth. But for the year, Byron counted a total of nineteen triumphs

worth 63,335 dollars in war bonds and stamps.

Byron, however, paid a price for his accomplishments. He was overgolfed, hav-ing in 1943, for example, appeared in 110 exhibition matches at military hospitals. By the end of 1945 he was a patient at the Mayo Clinic in Minnesota, where doctors blamed his acute gastrointestinal pains on his obsession with his game. Seemingly calm, Nelson simmered inside, throwing up in his room before appearing on the first tee. He flung an occasional club and minor squabbles with colleagues even in-duced him to blows.

In 1946, Nelson was the favorite as the National Open resumed at the Canterbury Country Club in Cleveland. Golf fans, so long denied an opportunity to see the best in the game, flocked to the site. Marshals could barely contain the mob of 12,000 on the last scheduled day. Nelson started out 2 strokes behind Hogan and Vic Ghezzi. He posted a morning round of 69, which included a 1-stroke penalty after the un-ruly hordes jostled his caddie, causing him

Demaret (left) and Johnny Palmer laugh it up after tying in the regu-lation seventy-two holes of the Tam O'Shanter World Cup of Golf in Chicago in 1949. Demaret col-lected the winner's share of the pot in the playoff. (COURTESY ACME.)

An exuberant Jimmy Demaret flings his club in the air to celebrate his 283 in the 1957 U.S. Open at Inverness, Toledo. Unfortunately, Dick Mayer fired a 282. (COURTESY BETTMANN/UPI NEWSPHOTOS.)

Ed "Porky" Oliver, a runner-up in several majors, toured for service agencies during WWII. His bulk and prowess at the table supplied fodder for one-liners by Demaret and Bob Hope. (COURTESY RAY DAVIS.)

to step onto Nelson's ball. Still, as the afternoon play began he held a 1-stroke lead over Ghezzi and Lloyd Mangrum, wounded during combat in Europe. When Nelson came to the final three holes he needed only to par them for a victory. He parred sixteen, a birdie putt ticked the cup on seventeen but did not fall and then on eighteen he hooked both his drive and second shot, enabling both Ghezzi and Mangrum to tie him.

The trio set out the following morning for the playoff and the agony, at least for Nelson, continued. Another three-way draw, with 72s. Forced to play another eighteen in the afternoon, Nelson's stress was obvious. He did not slide clubs back into the bag; he slammed them home and on the seventeenth hole, his bogey eliminated his chances. Purple Heart vet Mangrum outlasted Ghezzi and became the first postwar U.S. Open champ.

After then losing in the PGA quarterfinals to Porky Oliver, Nelson turned away from the tournament circuit, content to make an occasional appearance over the next few years. Temporarily lost in the shuffle was the friendship with his fellow former caddie, Hogan. Some believe Hogan resented the assumption of Nelson's golfing superiority, which a few observers derided as having been at the expense of

weaker foes. But, in truth, Nelson's scoring over championship courses was as good as that seen during the prewar years and immediately after.

Peace restored the country clubs that had enlisted in the war effort. As the postwar American economy boomed in response to the pent-up demand for consumer goods, the tide swept up golf. Inflation and the Tam O'Shanter influenced pots with the U.S. Open, for example, boosted from 8,000 dollars in 1946 to 10,000 dollars a year later. And that was hardly the top of the scale. The San Antonio Open, the Richmond Open (California), and something called the Esmeralda Open equaled the Open purse. Many other promotions, learning from George May, offered more. May more than met the competition, bumping his prizes to 30,000 dollars.

The tournament gold now often meant less than the potential exploitation of the title. As National Open winner, Mangrum collected only 1,500 of the 8,000 dollar total, but he received 5,000 dollars from Wilson Sporting Goods for endorsing its gear, 3,000 dollars for other testimonials, and a hefty 10,000 dollar deal from George May to represent the Tam O'Shanter while on the tournament trail. The pro tour, for the more successful at least, had become a golden road.

(Top) *At the Women's Western Golf Tournament in 1943 (left to right): Beatrice Gottlieb Martel represented the Women's Auxiliary Army Corps; Seaman first class Ruth McHenry was a Coast Guard SPAR; Lt. Margaret H. Cecil putted as a Navy WAVE Sgt.; Ferne Wait of the Marines rounded out the foursome.* (COURTESY RAY DAVIS.)

(Bottom) *"George S. May was a singular character. Whether you liked it or not, you had to admit that he was largely responsible for turning professional golf into the 'spectator' sport that it is in the United States and thus, by inference, influencing its character all over the world."—Henry Longhurst,* The Best of Henry Longhurst.
Celebrating with May is Ted Kroll, beneficiary of the 50,000 dollar check awarded for a win in 1956. (COURTESY UPI/BETTMANN NEWSPHOTOS.)

15

The Postwar Boom

Demaret, Snead, and Middlecoff won their share of tournaments during the post–World War II decade but Ben Hogan, an economy-size golf Colossus, bestrode the scene. In 1946, his first full season back on the circuit, he won thirteen tournaments, even though he muffed two opportunities in major events. At the Masters, Hogan was 12 feet away from the cup, needing only to get down in 2 strokes to tie. He 3-putted. At the U.S. Open, he arrived at the final hole needing a 5-footer to turn the three-way tie for the lead into a foursome. He missed.

Then, in February, 1949, came the ghastly accident. On fog-shrouded, two-lane U.S. 80, between Kent and Van Horn, Texas, a Greyhound bus pulled out from behind a semi. A concrete abutment denied Hogan any chance to turn his Cadillac off the road. At the penultimate moment, he threw his body in front of Valerie. The bus rammed the Caddy, driving the steering wheel through the space Hogan had occupied just before he dived to his right. The steering wheel still caught him in the shoulder, and the car's engine, jammed backwards, hammered him in the stomach and pinned his left leg. It took an hour to extricate the golfer and Valerie, who, although bleeding, was not seriously injured.

At the hospital they toted up the damage—broken ankle, broken collar bone, broken rib, fractured pelvis, massive contusions of the left leg, and a bladder injury. In spite of the injuries and the need to wear a waist-high cast, he appeared to be recovering well. But two weeks after the crash, just as he was scheduled to be discharged, the battered blood vessels in his leg began throwing off clots. One lodged in a lung; it seemed only a question of time before he would suffer a fatal embolism. The AP transmitted his obituary for

quick use. He desperately needed an operation by a surgeon who practiced in New Orleans. Hogan's life seemed forfeited when bad weather grounded all commercial flights between New Orleans and Texas. Valerie prevailed on the Air Force to pick up the doctor and fly him to El Paso. The procedure ended the threat of clots but Hogan suffered through months of agony. Medical experts predicted he would never walk unaided, much less play golf.

He returned to golf as the 1949, nonplaying, U.S. Ryder Cup captain. His ordeal hardly mellowed him. Hogan grimly argued about the grooves on a clubface used by a Briton. Ten months after the crackup he played his first rounds. Riding a golf cart, he carded a 71 and 72.

A record gallery of 9,000 showed for his first competitive test, the Los Angeles Open. He angered the press with a request to the sponsors to ban cameras. The prohibition lasted eight holes before officials rescinded it. With a 69 on the second round added to his opening 73, he was tied for third. The effort cost him enormous physical discomfort. To boost circulation, he bound his legs in elastic bandages. He limped every step and between shots rested on a folding seat. At night he soaked his aching body in hot baths. Rain washed out a day, affording a critically needed rest. He responded with a pair of 69s and zoomed ahead. Sam Snead, still on the course, heard Hogan's score and remarked to his playing partner, "Looks like we need a couple of birdies." He promptly knocked home a 14 footer on the seventeenth and not even a spectator falling out of a tree on eighteen prevented Snead from dropping a 15 footer to tie. A suffering Hogan snapped, "I wish he'd won it out there."

Because of rain and the start of the Crosby, the playoff was postponed a full

"The new king, Ben Hogan, was a hard man—a hard man to know, a hard man to beat. He hated to lose and drove himself harder than any of the pros to develop a game that would win for him. In his warmup sessions before a tournament round, Hogan was not content to get the feel of his clubs in a leisurely twenty minutes of practice. He put more concentration into his warmup than many pros put into their rounds on the course, cracking each shot down the practice field as if the outcome of the tournament rode with the flight of that ball. When a tournament round was over, were it a 66 or 72, Ben was out on the practice field again, pumping each shot for all he was worth."—Herbert Warren Wind, The Story of American Golf. (COURTESY UPI/BETTMANN NEWSPHOTOS.)

week. When the two did meet, Snead easily defeated Hogan, 72–76. But within a few weeks, Hogan savored his revenge, winning the Greenbrier Invitational. His blazing 259 whipped hometown hero Snead by 10.

The climax of the Hogan Saga came at Merion in the Open. The format still called for thirty-six holes on Saturday and he started that morning 2 behind. Hogan got off in a rush before it appeared fatigue would defeat him, as he missed several short putts. At the final hole, 458 yards from the pin, he needed a par.

Said Jimmy Demaret:

If there was ever an obvious spot for Hogan to blow a tournament, it was there on the eighteenth. His lead had evaporated entirely. But this is the kind of spot in which Ben's iron discipline asserts itself. He walked up to the tee for the last hole of the tournament in perfect control. He slammed a long drive and then a whistling iron shot to a good spot on the green. He knocked in his second putt, a tough one to make for a par and a tie.

Hogan spent much of the night in another hot tub. He took the field against Lloyd Mangrum and George Fazio on Sunday and his deft 69 collected his second Open title. Convinced he could survive the rigors of the tour, having been named PGA Player of the Year, Hogan now chewed up courses and the opposition. In 1951, he notched his third National Open triumph over an Oakland Hills course that scalded the most intrepid. Hogan commented, "I'm glad I brought this course, this monster to its knees."

He made the conquest pay a bonus, raising his exhibition fees to 1,000 dollars an appearance. Snead hiked his price, undoubtedly advised by Corcoran, who sensed a tide that could lift their boat. "If Hogan's worth a thousand, I oughta be worth eight hundred," declared Snead.

Hogan bore off the Masters in '51, and, in '53, repeated in that event and added a fourth U.S. Open to his laurels. But his appearance that year in the British Open at Carnoustie provoked a teapot tempest.

Sam Snead bested Mangrum in the 1949 Masters. (COURTESY UPI/ BETTMANN NEWSPHOTOS.)

Mustachioed Lloyd Mangrum earned medals and battle wounds during WWI before returning to tournament combat. Mangrum once snarled, "Try playing for money when you haven't got any." (COURTESY UPI/BETTMANN NEWSPHOTOS.)

A pair of forty-two-year-olds squared off in a 1954 playoff for the Masters. Snead squeezed by with a 70 to the loser's 71. (COURTESY FRANK CHRISTIAN STUDIOS.)

After several practice rounds he discovered the championship used the back tees set deep in the gorse and heather. He did his usual homework, walking the course at night, in reverse, checking distances and making note of useful visual references. He memorized the shapes of greens, the placement of bunkers. And he grumped about conditions freely.

Among his remarks:

"The bunkers were put in like a man throwing rice at a wedding. It looks like they took a handful of bunkers and threw them out over the course. . . . I guess they mow the greens once a week, maybe, and the fairways once a month. Usually they let goats in on the fairways and they never touch the rough . . . I've got a lawn mower back in Texas. I'll send it over."

Then the "wee ice mon" performed deeds to match his mouth. Using the smaller ball, he boomed out unprecedented 300-yard drives, followed by impeccable irons and precision putts. His 68 on the final eighteen was the record for a single round on the course; his 282 the best by 8 strokes over any previous tournament at Carnoustie.

The local press forgave him his trespasses. "Hail to the greatest golfer of our time," said the writer in the London *Daily Herald*. "And who shall say he is *not* best of all time?" inquired Leonard Crawley in the London *Daily Telegraph*. Bernard Darwin was seventy-six that year and announced: "I am happy to have lived long enough to see Ben Hogan play golf."

Like Bob Jones twenty-three and twenty-seven years before him, Hogan received a New York City ticker tape parade.

While Ben Hogan thus reigned over the men's tour, the environment and the structure of the tournament game made some giant steps. Golf in America, and the world, expanded rapidly, starting in the 1950s. A booming economy and more recreational hours boosted all sports, but golf above all. As one of the nation's most popular presidents, Dwight Eisenhower's ferocious appetite for golf gave the sport a tremendous lift. He installed a pitch-and-putt green behind the White House, broke away from

Herb Graffis (left) devoted his journalistic career to golf and penned a definitive history of the PGA. With him is Henry Poe, a PGA president. (COURTESY RAY DAVIS.)

President Dwight Eisenhower, the most enthusiastic golfer ever to occupy the White House, gesticulates to the press while Japanese Prime Minister Nabusike Kishi loosens up on the first tee at the Burning Tree Golf Club. (COURTESY UPI/BETTMANN NEWSPHOTOS.)

Ike delights as his grandson David demonstrates an interest in the game. (COURTESY UPI/BETTMANN NEWSPHOTOS.)

PROFESSIONAL GOLFER

PGA — THE PROFESSIONAL GOLFERS' ASSOCIATION OF AMERICA

APRIL 1975

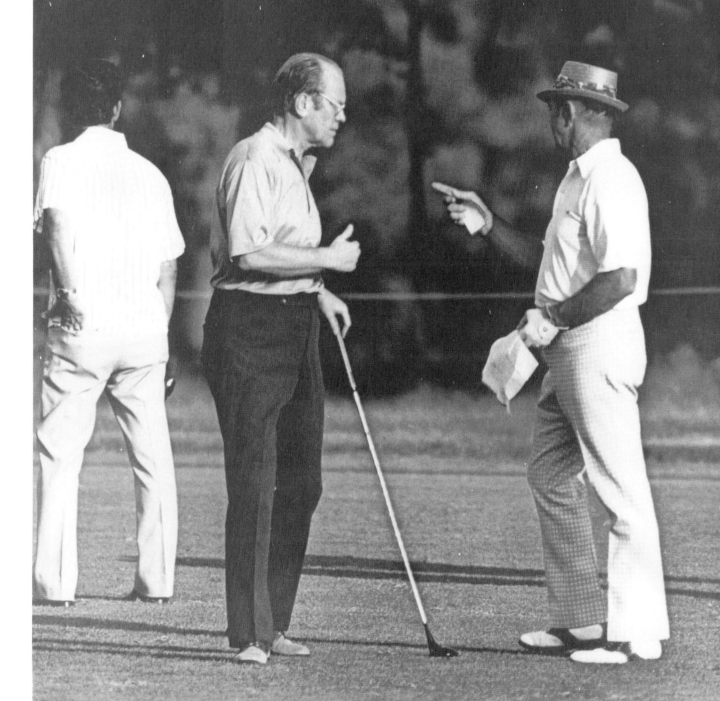

official business for afternoons at Burning Tree Country Club, and vacationed at Augusta National. He played rounds with Ben Hogan, Cary Middlecoff, and the North Carolina amateur Billy Joe Patton. His love of golf endowed the sport with a spirit that attracted the masses. Herb Wind wrote: "Ike's undisguisable relish for golf made the 3-wood seem as traditionally American as the old fishing pole."

In his time, Ike could count maybe 5 million fellow travelers on the courses, certainly a sharp boost from the 1 million of thirty years earlier. And to accommodate the swelling population seeking battle with "Old Man Par," the total number of golf courses had climbed to well over 5,000. Four years after Eisenhower left office, the National Golf Foundation reported the number of golfers stood at 8 million and regulation size courses totaled more than 7,000.

The popularity of golf was also fueled by technology like the development of the electrically powered golf cart. The vehicle made the game accessible to the aging and even the infirm. Furthermore it sped up play, making it possible for more rounds per day.

Golf had long engaged the fancy of the press. Working stiffs like Bernard Darwin, Ring Lardner, Granny Rice, Henry Longhurst, Herb Graffis,★ Herb Wind, and Charles Price covered and played the game and the nonworking press, including P. G. Wodehouse, Robert E. Sherwood, and later George Plimpton and John Updike, produced golf literature with information and high style.

Sherwood shared with the audience of *Colliers* his impressions of the types he swore inhabited the courses. He depicted one "Joe Primble" who:

> ... takes golf far more seriously than Jim Barnes.... His business, his home, his wife, his innocent little children—have all been forgotten in the mad pursuit of a diminutive gutta-percha globule across six thousand yards of greensward.

Then there was "General Spofford," who "treats a golf ball much as he would a buck private in his command. He orders the pellet to move forward 200 yards and when it fails to obey ... proceeds to explode."

Herb Graffis came out of Logansport, Indiana, hardly a hotspot of golf. He reached his majority in the first days of World War I. After a brief stint in trade journalism dealing with public utilities and oil fields, Graffis fled to the sports beat. But although he wrote on many different activities in what Red Smith called "the adult toys department," Graffis had a lifelong infatuation with golf.

Convinced there was an audience for specialized publications, he founded the *Chicago Golfer* in 1923, followed up with *Golfdom* in 1927, and then a national monthly, *Golfing*. In 1934, with his brother Joe, he set up the National Golf Foundation, which compiles authoritative information on the game and furnishes would-be investors with appropriate data. In the midst of these efforts he found time to contribute a column to the Chicago *Times* and assist Tommy Armour in writing some instructional books.

The enthusiasm of the better writers percolated to the taste buds of a larger and larger audience. A newstand shelf of magazines devoted only to the game—*Golf Magazine* (to whom Graffis sold his publications), *Golf Digest*, *Golf World*, and later *Golf Illustrated* and *Golfiana*, plus the huge circulation of the weekly *Sports Illustrated*—cooked up savory reports of tournaments, techniques, gadgets, and personalities that widened the appetite for golf.

In 1930, Ted Husing, one of the pioneers of sports broadcasts, showed up at the National Open at Interlachen in Minneapolis wearing plaid knickers and bearing a knapsacklike affair that contained a shortwave transmitter. In 1927 an effort had been made for local radio to cover the Los Angeles Open. But Husing was employed by the Columbia Broadcasting System; this was network radio aimed at the entire country. Unfortunately, Husing started his broadcast of the final day at 4 P.M. By that hour Bobby Jones, en route to the Grand Slam, had already posted his winning score. The

Lew Worsham's 104-yard eagle-deuce wedge shot in the 1963 World Golf Championship earned him 62,000 dollars. Commenting on TV, Jimmy Demaret said: "He's hit it fat ... It will probably be short ... It just hit the front edge of the green ... It's got no chance ... It's rolling but it will stop ... It's rolling toward the cup ... Well, I'll be damned!" (COURTESY RAY DAVIS.)

(Opposite) *After Eisenhower, the most notorious White House golf addict was Gerald Ford, here getting the word from Sam Snead.* (COURTESY PGA OF AMERICA.)

listening public was deprived of a stroke-by-stroke account of the victorious round. However, this marriage of radio and golf was enlivened by some banter among Walter Hagen, Horton Smith, Gene Sarazen, and others, who, although prepped by the broadcast producers, preferred to ad lib.

Radio actually had little impact upon golf and vice versa. But in the late 1950s, television wallowed in both football and golf. Golf was relatively inexpensive to cover and well suited for television, although TV did not truly represent the actual play of the games. George May, ever glad-handed when opportunity knocked, beamed his tournament over national TV in 1952 and viewers saw Lew Worsham's incredible chip worth 62,000 dollars. The USGA arranged for national TV coverage of its 1954 Open at Baltusrol. Golf shows multiplied on TV until hardly a weekend passed without some tournament on display. The great electronic eye now hardly misses a stroke,

with cameras at every vantage point and instant replays. Television even came to dictate tee times that ensured the winning moments do not escape the camera.

In its formative days during the 1950s, *Sports Illustrated* exploited golf as the one sport it believed (erroneously) attracted both a large, well-heeled audience and the ad dollar. Both Herb Wind and Dan Jenkins wrote on golf for *SI* and George Plimpton's best seller, *The Bogey Man*, began as an article for the magazine.

Marketing experts quickly divined the sport's vast commercial possibilities. The communications moguls and advertising sales meisters were players themselves and they conspired to seduce the public into a love affair with golf. The clubs and balls, the clothing, the shoes added up to 2 billion dollars in sales as the final decade of the twentieth century began.

Two of the best salesmen for the sport made their marks in the entertainment

(Opposite) Bing Crosby was an early sponsor for the professionals, and his tournaments (first at Del Mar and then Pebble Beach) became fixtures. After his death, the family kept the Crosby going for several years before relinquishing it to corporate backing. (COURTESY RAY DAVIS.)

Even the normally dour Ben Hogan (center) relaxed in the ambience supplied by the crooner. (COURTESY UPI/BETTMANN NEWSPHOTOS.)

Bob Hope, here with Dutch Harrison, boosted the game with wartime relief tours, volleys of jokes on radio and TV, and through his own tournament at Palm Springs. (COURTESY UPI/BETTMANN NEWSPHOTOS.)

world well before World War II and continued to promote the sport long after. As a caddie in his hometown of Tacoma, Washington, Bing Crosby associated himself with golf even before puberty's magic transformed him into a crooner. By the early 1930s, when he had already achieved fame as a singer and was starting his movie career, Crosby had knocked his handicap down to a 2. He even played a match in the 1950 British Amateur, intentionally letting the contest get away, according to Herb Wind, because he thought the crowd scene around him unseemly.

In 1937, he welcomed a hardy band of traveling pros and show biz golf fanatics to an eighteen-hole pro-am at the Rancho Santa Fe Country Club near San Diego. Crosby invited sixty-eight professionals in-

cluding Sam Snead, Dutch Harrison, Henry Picard, Denny Shute, and Paul Runyan. What made the event something special were the sixty-eight amateurs, featuring Fred Astaire, Richard Arlen, Zeppo Marx, and William Frawley. Sam Snead gained the professional honors but all hands had such a good time, with barbecued steaks and some tuneful crooning from the host, that Crosby continued to throw similar bashes. In 1947, he moved the party to California's Monterey Peninsula and by 1958, the Bing Crosby National Pro-Am, popularly known as the Crosby Open, had become the premier West Coast event. After his death in 1978, while playing golf, his family operated the event briefly before surrendering sponsorship to AT&T.

Bob Hope, whose *Road* films with Crosby

The putter collection of Horton Smith. Smith was the winner of the first Masters Tournament in 1934.

1

2

3

4

5

Preceeding spread: The background photo is of the 18th hole, course #2, at the Pinehurst Golf Club, at dawn. The players pictured are: 1. Arnold Palmer. (COURTESY RICHARD MEEK, SI) 2. Tom Watson. (COURTESY RICHARD MACKSON, SI) 3. Jack Nicklaus. (COURTESY NEIL LEIFER, SI) 4. Arnold Palmer. (COURTESY JAMES DRAKE, SI) 5. Nancy Lopez. (COURTESY UPI/BETTMANN NEWSPHOTOS)

Above: The cover of The Poster, a supplement to Modern Advertising, No. 24, Vol. IV, July, 1900. Illustration by Starr Wood.

Right: From top: Board game, "Ladies on the Links," 1920; Cover of Harper's Weekly, 1905; President Dwight D. Eisenhower's personalized golf ball, golf shoes, and golf umbrella; Golf knickers, circa 1930; Photograph of champion golfer Gene Sarazen; Golf glove used by Arnold Palmer to win the 1962 British Open; Golf tees from the early 1930s; Sand tee mold, circa 1920.

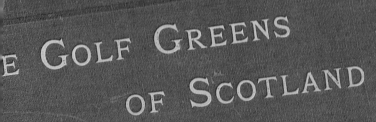

CLUB HOUSE. *(From a photo by Fred T. Palmer, Eastbourne.)*

ST. GEORGE'S GOLF CLUB.

> "A land that is thirstier than ruin;
> A sea that is hungrier than death;
> Heaped hills that a tree never grew in;
> Wide sands where the wave draws breath
> All solace is here for the spirit
> That ever for ever may be
> For the soul of thy son to inherit,
> My mother, my sea."
>
> *The North Sea—SWINBURNE.*

HAPPY is the Club that has no history.
The St. George's Club has no history; has not, so to speak, passed its
pleasant youth, with all that age's promise of a bright future. What a
contrast this to its situation, lying as it does in a corner of the world which
means with memories! Sandwich Bay has suffered many vicissitudes. In the
beginning of our island story, and for
many following centuries, it was
famous as a place of ships, the coign of
vantage to invader and marauder, the
harbour of the earliest missionaries,
and, after the rise of England as a sea
power, the gathering place of her
fleet when war danger threatened.
Nature the while was slowly working
a sea change. The silting of the bay
began by the drift of choking sand
creeping from the east, and by the
sea ceasing to carry away the alluvial
deposit of the river. Roman Rutu-
piae became shipless, and Sandwich,
"the settlement on the sand,"
taking its place, arose as the port

AMATEUR CHAMPIONSHIP CUP.

(From a photo by Martin-Jacolette, London.)
Mr. Ralph Chaton,
Captain 1896-97.

of London. Although often the centre of war, it grew and
prospered. Where war and rapine had failed, the faithless sea
prevailed, and slowly driving the river ever farther from the
town, left it inland and lonely, with nothing to recall its early
greatness save here and there architectural beauty. Towards

C 2

Preceeding spread: Bottom book: The Golf Greens of Scotland, *by John Smart, illustrated by Walter Colour, 1893; Top book: pages 10–11 of* British Golf Links, *Horace Hutchinson, editor, J. S. Virtue & Co., Limited. London, 1897; Sheepskin golf cub grip, circa 1930; Golf balls, starting from top left: Gutta ball mold with mesh pattern; Smooth black gutta ball before molding (1862), and a bramble pattern ball; A present-day Top-Elite; A ball specially made for the Straton Country Club, Vermont; A rubber core, circa 1905; A production-line ball, called the Kro-Flight, made by Spalding in 1925.*

Above: Resident trophy from the Tin Whistle Men's Golf Organization, one of the first golf clubs to establish a tradition of excellence on the course at Pinehurst, North Carolina; The Walter Hagon Ryder Cup Jacket, from the first Ryder Cup match, 1927; The Calamity Jane putter given to President Eisenhower by Bobby Jones; Masters Medal won by Arnold Palmer on April 12, 1964; Time magazine with Ben Hogan on the cover, January 10, 1949.

Shell Oil's "Wonderful World of Golf" dispatched Gene Sarazen and Jimmy Damaret to Scotland as broadcast hosts for an eleven-match series played over world-famous courses. (COURTESY RAY DAVIS.)

rated the balls. The code, written by the Royal and Ancient back in the eighteenth century, forbade a golfer from aiming for a stymie.

In practice, however, players often deliberately created a stymie. Confronted with stymies, a golfer could either calculate the effects of a carom and hope to bounce off into the hole or loft his ball over the obstacle. During the 1920s, the USGA briefly banned the stymie but reinstated it. The joint decree in 1951 permanently killed it.

The management of golf also responded to the demands of the times. Fred Corcoran, increasingly involved in the care and feeding of his personal clients, Ted Williams, Stan Musial, Sam Snead, and Babe Zaharias,★ resigned his post as tournament director for the PGA and accepted a role as counselor to the Ladies Professional Golf Association. In Corcoran's wake, the men's tour saw a series of administrators come and go as the PGA and the tour experienced growing pains. Among the disputed issues were the scheduling of tournaments, required appearances in PGA

sponsored events, and the split of the burgeoning TV cash.

Temporary peace arrived in 1969 when Joseph C. Dey,★ a former sports writer for the Philadelphia *Evening Bulletin* and the executive secretary of the USGA since 1934, accepted the office of Commissioner of the Tournament Players Division of the PGA. Dey had considered life in the ministry before becoming a journalist, as which he reported Bob Jones's win of the 1930 U.S. Amateur that completed the Grand Slam. In his USGA post he had been largely responsible for unifying that organization's rules with those of the Royal and Ancient.

A significant step, masterminded by Corcoran and Dey, moved the Women's Open under USGA jurisdiction in 1953, giving the female championship both respectability and stability.

Well before Dey came on the scene, however, the PGA wrote new rules to control the multiplying number of tournaments and maintain high standards in the face of the ever-larger numbers who wanted to play for the tour money. Gone were the days when a Byron Nelson or Ben Hogan simply showed up at a tournament site, declared himself a pro, slapped down a five-dollar entry fee, and then teed off in the tournament. To play for pay in a PGA sanctioned competition, the individual now had to pass muster with the organization.

Today, to become a bona fide member of the PGA, an individual must spend five years as a head professional at a recognized course or club or serve as an assistant to the chief pro at such a place, participate as an "approved player" in a minimum of twenty-five tournaments under PGA rules, or combine any of the three for five years. To ensure that only the very best golfers appear in its sanctioned events, the PGA instituted a Qualifying School. Only upon completion of the program is the individual entitled to an Approved Tournament Player's card, without which he cannot enter PGA events.

The rules thus protect the public and tournament sponsors against unqualified entries. The PGA also educates and polices the professional staffs at country clubs and public courses. It is not enough to have a clean shirt, pressed slacks, and shoot a reasonably good score. There is a full program designed to ensure that apprentices or assistants learn the basic skills of their trade. Toward that end the PGA conducts classes in how to operate a pro shop, from inventory control to proper salesmanship. There is instruction in techniques for teaching the sport, the methods to communicate information about stance, grip, stroke, and strategy—either one on one or through group clinics. The PGA-qualified pro is expected to know the quality of golf gear on the market, and how to fit swing weight, shaft stiffness, loft, and lie to the needs of the individual customer. The PGA programs also instruct novices in the arts of club repair, from cracked driver heads to frayed grips and bent shafts. Even psychology is part of the lore—how to talk to golfers who become discouraged, how to settle arguments about the rules.

One learns the golf ropes at short clinics run by organizations like *Golf Digest* as well as at the PGA itself through its National Golf Club in Palm Beach Gardens, Florida. There is also on-the-job training as an apprentice for the well-schooled PGA pro. For those desiring to know it all, the PGA recommends golf-management curriculums at Ferris State College in Michigan or at Mississippi State; these include two six-month internships at golf courses. The five-year programs at these institutions produce a Business Degree with a major in golf management.

Tom Callahan on
BEN HOGAN

Legend isn't enough; phantom is better. To golf, Ben Hogan has been something of a living ghost—the most coveted invitee to all the game's great gatherings who never comes to any of them but is always there. The National Open (the preferred old name for the U.S. Open) especially evokes Hogan: He won four officially, although some statisticians say five. At Merion, Pennsylvania, in 1950, he won quite a lot more than a golf tournament. But the plainest truth, apparent to anyone who has ever brushed by the PGA tour in autumn or spring, is that every tournament evokes Hogan. Every golfer recalls him, particularly those who never saw him. Every conversation includes him.

When someone questions the severity of the cut or slope on a Masters green, Tournament Chairman Hord Hardin responds, "Hogan would have found a way to play it." Not Jack Nicklaus, who maintains a rack of six green coats on the premises. Nor Arnold Palmer, who has collected four Augusta jackets. But Hogan, who nearly never shows up to model either of his two championship blazers at the annual reunion.

Once, during the mid-seventies (his own mid-sixties), he did. It was the year that Mr. Cliff Roberts, the octogenarian massah of the plantation, committed suicide out on the course—he shot himself near Ike's Creek. The devoted curator of Bobby Jones's holy relics, Mr. Cliff was something of a stone monument himself, and Augusta National beseeched Hogan to come pay his final respects. That kind of death rubbed an old hurt in Hogan, and, though under no circumstances would he stay around for the tournament, Ben agreed to attend the champions' dinner. That afternoon, he materialized like Brigadoon in the press barn. The few writers who were loitering there could not have been more astonished if Babe Ruth had strolled in with his arm around Grantland Rice.

Hogan's appearance was calculated, of course. But not everybody detected his real purpose, and no one minded it. "By the way," he said after a cordial few minutes of small talk, casually getting to the point of his visit. "My name has been bandied about in that 'Legends' television tournament coming up." (More than a few network hints were being dropped that Hogan was thinking of playing.) "Let me tell you something, I would not put my game on public display," he said firmly. All the same, Hogan could not deny the report that he had recently shot his age—sixty-four—at Shady Oaks Country Club in Fort Worth. An emboldened reporter wondered how close Hogan had ever approached to shooting a perfect round. Without laughing, Ben said, "A perfect round would be

18. I . . . almost . . . dreamt . . . it . . . once. I had 17 holes-in-one and lipped out at 18. I . . . was . . . mad."

For at least one of the writers, the only competitive glimpse of Hogan had occurred there at Augusta in 1967, when Hogan was fifty-four. The pain in his knees then made him wobble like a short-legged table. With a 30 on the back nine, birdieing the entire expanse of Amen Corner, he shot a 66 the third day to come within a couple of strokes of the Masters lead. "I apologize to everyone for taking so long to putt," he said afterward. "I still freeze some, but I'm trying. I can hear people in the gallery saying, 'Why doesn't that man go ahead and putt?' I wish I knew the answer." He confided, "There's a lot of fellas that have got to fall dead for me to win." The next day, Hogan shot 77 and disappeared.

"Those steel-gray eyes of his," one friend once remarked with a slight shudder. *"He looks at you like a landlord asking for next month's rent."*—Will Grimsley, Sport.

In this instance, he cans the final putt at the 1942 North-South Open for the first prize money, a grand total of 1,000 dollars. (COURTESY UPI/BETTMANN ARCHIVE.)

Even the dour Hogan could be persuaded, in his early days, to pose for photographers after he was victorious—in this case, at the Oakland Open. (COURTESY TOMMY MCDONOUGH, OAKLAND TRIBUNE.)

It is amazing enough that, more than three decades removed from his glory, a smokey apparition of five-feet eight or nine inches, 135 or 140 pounds, could still be the hugest figure in a sport. But Hogan has found a way to become both the most adamant absence and pugnacious presence in golf. His way has to do with integrity—as players of every stripe know, this is the first fundamental of golf—accompanied by a curt style and cold standard that once moved Hogan to hang up the telephone on Gary Player.

In the famous story only half-told some years ago, Player related how the accumulated misery of battling his career-long hook ultimately prompted him to place an intercontinental telephone call from Brazil to Texas. If only he could discuss his swing with Mr. Hogan for a few minutes, Player reckoned that everything would be all right. With the possible exception of Hogan himself, the world's most peripatetic South African could honestly say that he had practiced harder and taken fewer shortcuts than any other golfer in history. But Player was in the middle of this speech when Hogan interrupted him to inquire bluntly, "Are you affiliated with a club manufacturer?" Taken aback, Player muttered, "Dunlop." At which point Hogan said, "Call Mr. Dunlop," and slammed down the receiver.

For years, a journalist rewrote and retold this story merrily, until, one day, the listener was the old saloon singer and former eminent amateur golfer Don Cherry, who had joined the writer's threesome as an anonymous fourth. After about seven or eight holes, it occurred to all that the stranger hadn't missed any fairways, hadn't missed any greens, and had 2-putt everything. "You want to give me your name one more time?"

Laughing wonderfully, Cherry recalled a practice round long ago in Houston during which young Gary Player was effusively admiring Hogan's driver. He hefted it, and waggled it, and exclaimed how perfectly it fit in his own hands. At the end of the round, as related by Cherry, Hogan magnanimously presented it to the young man. In those days Player represented Shakespeare equipment. Overnight, Gary had the Hogan driver repainted all black, in the Shakespeare style. *Are you affiliated with a club manufacturer? Call Mr. Dunlop.* "The thing about Hogan," Ken Venturi says, "is that he doesn't bother to explain himself to Player, to you or to anyone else. That's great, I think. That's Hogan."

Sam Snead, Hogan's historic rival (the great contemporaries Hogan, Snead, and Nelson were all born in 1912) describes Ben with traces of both esteem and vinegar. Long after the others had withdrawn, Snead remained a visible entity in his Panama hat, though throughout the 1980s he was seen better than he saw. "In

In the early days, at the Oakland Open they knew him as "Little Ben Hogan." Second prize money of 380 dollars in the 1938 tournament enabled Hogan to remain on the tour. (COURTESY TOMMY MC-DONOUGH, OAKLAND TRIBUNE.)

When Hogan returned to the tournament wars after military service, among his steadiest challengers was Cary Middlecoff. (COURTESY PGA OF AMERICA.)

pro-ams," Sam confessed at a stop on the senior tour, "my partners like me to line up their putts for them. But what they don't realize is that I have to walk all the way to the hole now just to tell if a putt is uphill or down." Also, yip-ridden for so many years, Sam had long since taken to putting the way a flamingo plays croquet. "You have time to smoke a whole cigarette waiting for Hogan to take the putter back," Snead passed along a report, not too sorrowfully, "but do you know something? If Ben were guaranteed to win another National Open just by putting side-saddle, I'm sure he'd still refuse to be seen publicly in that awful-looking position. As much as winning meant to him, that's his pride."

Waves of younger players, particularly the Texans lucky enough to have encountered Hogan in his sixties on fairways and seventies on practice tees have been awed by the sight alone but even more amazed by the lore. John Schlee, who, as no one remembers, finished second in the 1973 Open to Johnny Miller's 63, did hardly more than glance up once, and there he was. "This little guy in a white cap asked me for a game. Then there he was attending the pin for me. I thought, 'If they could only see me now.'" Young or old, no golfer has ever been more moved by history than Ben Crenshaw, who speaks of Hogan in hushed tones:

"He would pick a target score, form a game plan, and never deviate. He wouldn't just outshoot the field, he'd outthink the world. What's so incredible to tournament golfers today is that they know the understanding and discipline it takes to pass up all the risky chances, to take all the necessary ones. I don't think

At the 1953 British Open on the Carnoustie links, Hogan tired the locals with jibes about the course. But the "Wee Ice Mon" captured the fancy of the gallery with his sterling play.

"There were, to begin with, certain local patriots disposed to speak of him as 'Your man Hogan,' and to murmur that he might do all manner of things on American inland courses, but let him wait till he comes to play over the great Carnoustie course in a Carnoustie wind. Yet even those more parochial critics were soon convinced, for they knew golf and were too honest not to admit that here was such a play as occurs only once in a generation or indeed once in a lifetime."—Bernard Darwin, Country Life, *July 1953.* (COURTESY UPI/BETTMANN NEWSPHOTOS.)

anyone's more dedicated than Mr. Hogan to the things he believes in. He's not quite the cold, aloof person everyone thinks either. There are a lot of little unknown kindnesses. But the hard way he learned it, that's the way he thinks others should go about it too." Hogan is apt to hand you back your iron and say, "I dug it out of the ground: now you can do the same." Crenshaw considers this a compliment.

Hogan's father, a Texas blacksmith, shot himself to death over a stack of bills in the living room. Ben was nine. His brother's given name was Royal. His sister's was Princess. He was just Ben. A shy child, Hogan was attracted to caddying by the wages (sixty-five cents a loop) more than the card games and fistfights or even the golf. By way of initiation at the Glen Garden Country Club in Fort Worth, the caddies blindfolded their twelve-year-old applicant, rolled him down a hill in a barrel, paddled him purple, and made him fight their best boxer. He survived.

"There'd be about ten or fifteen caddies," he recalled once, "and while we were waiting for the golfers to come out, we played 'drive for a chase.' Somebody would have a driver and we all had a ball, and the shortest hitter had to pick up all the balls. I was always the shortest. That's probably what got me going. I began copying the good players and I started hitting a much longer ball. You learn how to take care of yourself and how to think when you're out on your own. I was too old for thirteen."

Lanky Byron Nelson, the champion caddie of Glen Garden, had to make a 30-footer on the last hole to tie the little upstart Hogan in the nine-hole caddie tournament of 1927. On the first extra hole, Ben made a 4 to Byron's 6 and presumed he had won. But, after a lengthy discussion, officials decided a full nine-hole playoff was called for, and Hogan was beaten, 41 to 42. In 1928, the members decided to honor one of the caddies with an honorary membership to the club. It went to Nelson.

"I caddied until I was sixteen," Hogan picked up the narrative, "and then went to work in the golf shop. On weekends I polished clubs until three in the morning. Boy, I'd look at those clubs and they were the most beautiful things—Nickels and Stewarts, all made in Scotland. I got my own set of mongrel clubs out of a dime store barrel for a dollar apiece."

In a way almost too harsh and torturous to be watched, he came to love the game as no one ever had. "It is a curious sort of love," cringed Red Smith, "that makes a man go white about the lips and freezes his features into a death mask." After a decade as a pro, Hogan was still winless. He and his wife, Valerie, his childhood sweetheart, prized the moderate finishes and spare checks that kept them going. Learning everything the hard way, Hogan was thirty-four before he took his first major championship, the same age as Palmer when Arnie won his last. Not allowed to count the U.S. Open–like Hale America Tournament in 1942 (after which he paused to fight a war), Ben was thirty-six when he finally won a certified Open.

In three attempts from 1948 to 1951, he took three National Opens. But the year Hogan laid out—literally—set up the most dramatic comeback in the memory of any sport. On a foggy highway near Waco, Texas, a barreling bus pulled out to pass a truck and left Hogan's car, and Hogan too, in pieces. The first fear was that he wouldn't live, the next was that he wouldn't walk. But he came back 100 yards at a time, then a quarter-mile. But would he be able to recall his greatness? With bones shattered, nerves torn, muscles ripped, how would he find the way back?

In practice rounds prior to the accident, his habit had been to tee off three

times at certain holes, hooking one, slicing another, and driving a third down the middle. Therefore, wherever he might end up during the tournament, he always knew the way back. To the squeak of a rubber ball clenching and relaxing in each fist, Hogan limped back to the Los Angeles Open, all the way to a playoff with Snead, and then actually seemed glad to lose it. "I can't afford the satisfaction," he said. "I still have a great distance to go." The final 200 yards or so, he negotiated famously with a 1-iron at the 1950 Open at Merion, near Philadelphia. That got him into another playoff, and this time his creaky legs carried him to the championship against which all others will forever be measured.

That particular 1-iron disappeared from Hogan's bag before his playoff with George Fazio and Lloyd Mangrum. There is no evidence that he ever struck another 1-iron of any make. It took about thirty-two years and several changes of owners and grips to wend its way back to him. Of course, when the iron was improbably found, identifying it was easy. There was a worn area about the size of a dime precisely on the sweet spot. "My long lost friend," Ben murmured.

Regarding clubs, he is the industry's standard of quality. If HOGAN irons are slightly off, the price is not slightly reduced—the clubs are slightly destroyed. His loyalty is not to a company but to an ideal. "He has the highest standard of everything," Ben Crenshaw says, "of friendship, of work, of going to the store, of picking up a pencil, whatever small thing it is." Before Hogan had his own label, back when he was a MacGregor advisor, company executive Bob Rickey tried

(Opposite) Like Bobby Jones, Hogan also enjoyed a hero's welcome home in New York City after conquering the British competition. (COURTESY UPI/BETTMANN NEWSPHOTOS.)

New York went so far as to temporarily assign a street name in his honor. (COURTESY UPI/BETTMANN NEWSPHOTOS.)

everything to coax him away from Titleist golf balls toward MacGregor's own brand, including setting up hillside demonstrations with one of those 5-iron catapults that purport to be the only unbiased judges of ammunition. "If I couldn't hit it better than that machine," Hogan muttered, "I'd quit."

When he stopped hitting it better than a machine, he did quit. His concentration was going so fast, he was nearly noticing the holes-in-one struck by his playing partners. The final score includes sixty-nine U.S. tour victories, four Opens, two Masters, and two PGAs in its match-play era. He won the only British Open he ever saw (and became the Wee Ice Mon of Carnoustie, Scotland). Fourteen straight times he finished in the top ten of both the Open and Masters. His top four finishes in those tournaments numbered 18. In the storied summer of 1953, when Hogan was forty, he won the Masters, the U.S. Open, and the British Open. Because he had to qualify for the British, Hogan was forestalled by overlapping dates from trying for the modern Grand Slam. Anyway, his legs would never have stood up to thirty-six-hole days of PGA match play. At that, no one has ever come so close to the Slam.

In 1955, Hogan seemed to have a record fifth Open in hand when an obscure pro from Davenport, Iowa, Jack Fleck, improbably tied him and then won the playoff. Hogan had rationed every ounce of his strength just to last seventy-two holes, and as Fleck made his birdie 3 to force an extra 18, Ben declared too honestly in the smallest voice, "I wish he'd made a 2." With one hole remaining

(Opposite) Home in Fort Worth, the golfer and his wife, Valerie, feasted on the tribute of Texans. (COURTESY PGA OF AMERICA.)

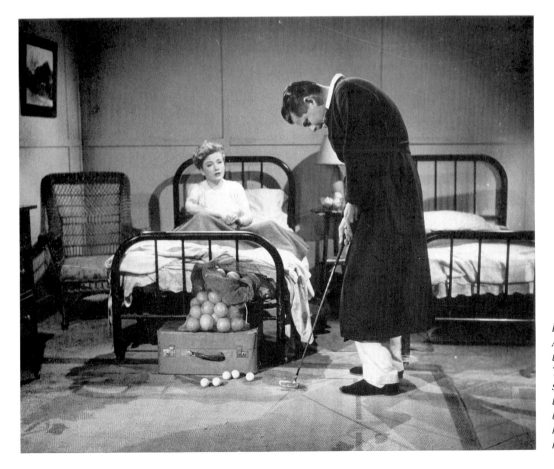

Hollywood cast Glenn Ford and Anne Baxter in the lead roles of the film biography, Follow the Sun. *This hotel room putting-practice scene recreated the moment when the despairing Hogan was advised by Valerie on the way to win: "Just hit the ball a little closer to the hole."* (COURTESY 20TH CENTURY FOX.)

in the next day's playoff, Hogan trailed by only a stroke, but a hooked drive ("A hook," he used to say, "is like a rattlesnake in your pocket") and a deep lie in the rough settled it. Lining up a last 30-foot putt that didn't matter, Hogan put Jim Murray in mind of "a woman doggedly cooking a good meal in a bombed-out house." He steadied, steadied, steadied over the ball and then rolled the putt resolutely into the cup. He tipped his cap.

He might have won the fifth Open at Denver in 1960, when Arnold Palmer became Arnold Palmer, but Hogan acted sorrier for the twenty-year-old amateur, Jack Nicklaus. "That kid I played with today," he said, "should have won by 10 shots." Declining ever to be used, Hogan has gruffly avoided cooperating with Jack's annual Memorial Tournament. The special format, every year on Memorial Day weekend, calls for the stuffing and mounting of one of golf's greatest legends, living and dead. Bobby Jones was the natural first honoree at Muirfield Village near Columbus, Ohio. Hogan was going to be the second.

But the Wee Icemon never cometh. Snead, Nelson, and a stream of others have taken their turns gracefully. Believing eulogies to be a scarce honor for the living, Hogan begs to point out that he's still kicking. He and Valerie have never had any children. They have always had each other. "I don't play," he says. "I hit some balls almost every day. I do my own shagging. I go out in a cart on a little nine out at Shady Oaks, where I am a member, and I am out there by myself most of the time, so I can hit any kind of shot I want to. I will hit half a bag of balls and then go pick them up myself. Get a little exercise. Bring them back. Do the same thing over again."

"Drive for a chase," the caddies used to call it. The shortest hitter has to pick up the balls.

Jack Fleck, an unknown armored with Ben Hogan model clubs, astounded the golf world by tying the master at the end of seventy-two holes of the 1955 Open at Oakmont. Worn down, particularly after the thirty-six holes of the final day, Hogan slipped to a 73 in the playoff, while Fleck carded a winning 69. (COURTESY WIDE WORLD.)

"Ben even has his toenails going for him."—Arnold Palmer. Despite a somewhat flatfooted stroke, Hogan constructed a biochemical engine that packed enough power for him to match or surpass people several inches taller and fifty pounds heavier. (COURTESY RAY DAVIS.)

A fairly wretched movie was once made of Hogan's life. It was called *Follow the Sun* and starred Glenn Ford and Anne Baxter. A musty old museum piece, almost nothing in it was especially true, except a short speech delivered by the real Granny Rice in a scene set at a banquet after the limping Hogan lost his L.A. Open to Snead. Young sportswriters have been known to search out the obscure film just to lay eyes on that famous newspaperman and hear his actual voice. Demonstrating both sentimentality and economy, Rice says of Hogan, "Courage never goes out a fashion. His legs simply weren't strong enough to carry his heart around."

So Hogan never goes out of fashion. Even at Jack's tournament, he is present in the locker room despite himself. Everywhere, in every clubhouse, in every season, an uncompromising little man in a white linen cap still leads the tour in respect. He should have been given a royal name, too.

Even as they slipped toward their retirement years, old rivals Hogan and Snead continued to draw crowds for exhibitions. (COURTESY UPI/BETTMANN NEWSPHOTOS.)

One final shot at the U.S. Open in 1960 at Cherry Hills eluded Hogan as a desperate gamble sank him in the creek. (COURTESY DAVID C. SNYDER.)

16

The Babe of Golf

Harry Vardon, along with Taylor and Braid in Great Britain, and Walter Hagen, with some help from Gene Sarazen and Tommy Armour, in America—in spite of a momentary diversion by Bobby Jones—ineradicably stamped men's golf with professionalism. But the women's game fielded only amateurs right through World War II. It wasn't that the female stars lacked skill. Joyce Wethered and Glenna Collett, for example, lacked only the power of the best men; otherwise they demonstrated equal proficiency. But the ethos of the times, which reluctantly permitted only the most determined and persistent women to enter professions like law or medicine, adamantly set itself against them earning by the sweat of their brows.

Just as Jackie Robinson broke the color line in baseball through a unique combination of talent and personality, so it was that professionalism in women's golf teed off in the person of a special woman. Born Mildred Didrikson,★ the Babe was another of those ubiquitous Texans who lit up the links. As a twenty-year-old, one-woman track team and star player on the Golden Cyclones basketball squad, the Babe headed the female contingent of U.S. Olympians entered in the 1932 Games in Los Angeles. Limited by the rules to only three events—at the National AAU meet two weeks before, she had won five contests, tied for first in another, and took a fourth in one—Babe received two gold medals for the javelin and high hurdles,

and was dropped to second on a technicality in the high jump.★

In the press box on the final day of the Olympics, Grantland Rice sang her hosannahs. Braven Dyer, sports editor of the Los Angeles *Times*, was on the scene:

> Granny was always loud in his praise of Babe, and on this day he told all of us in the press box he simply couldn't think of any sport that Babe couldn't master. [Westbrook] Pegler was a skeptic and he said, "What about golf?" Granny said, all right, golf. He sent word down to the field for Babe to come up and see him. She trotted up to the press box immediately. I think Babe probably would have done anything for Granny Rice in those days, it was a case of absolutely mutual admiration. So when Granny said to Babe, "When do we play golf?" She said, "Tomorrow."

Dyer, Pegler, Rice, and Paul Gallico met her the next day at the Brentwood Country Club. She borrowed some equipment and then shot a 52 going out and 43 on the back nine, hardly the stuff of legends. However, Rice ignored the performance and wrote:

> She is the longest hitter women's golf has ever seen, for she has a free, lashing style backed up with championship form and terrific power in strong hands, strong wrists, forearms of steel. She has as fine a swing as either Helen Hicks or Glenna Collett Vare and it came naturally to her after a few rounds, just as everything else comes naturally.

*Oddly enough, the very first Olympic gold medal earned by an American woman was for golf. At the 1900 Games in Paris, Margaret Abbot of Chicago came in first.

(Right) *In the 1932 Olympic Games at Los Angeles, Mildred Zaharias sprinted and leaped to victory in the high hurdles.* (COURTESY UPI/ BETTMANN NEWSPHOTOS.)

(Below) *Babe climbed to the top of the awards' stand for gold medals in the high hurdles and javelin. She also claimed a silver in the high jump.* (COURTESY UPI/BETT-MANN NEWSPHOTOS.)

That was sheer puffery. At this point, her swing had far more affinity with a baseball bat than a golf club. Some years later, she would add to the legend with a claim that this was her very first experience with golf. Actually, she had played perhaps a dozen rounds in previous years. The genuine truth was she could indeed hit balls impressive distances, on occasion knocking out 250-yard drives.

Her exuberant and frequently boastful ways annoyed the ayatollahs of U.S. amateurism. They soon discovered reasons to ban her from competitions under their control. She decided to take up golf seriously and studied under a driving range pro, Stan Kertes, in Los Angeles. Kertes, whose pupils included Al Jolson, Burns and Allen, the Marx Brothers, Harold Lloyd and other Hollywood notables, offered free lessons, buckets of balls, and practice space. In *Whatta-Gal*, by William Oscar Johnson and Nancy P. Williamson, he recalled:

> She hit a few for me. Her grip was wrong, she held it like a bat. I had the hardest time getting her to use her fingers on the

shaft instead of her fist. Babe used to hit a thousand, fifteen hundred balls every day. Her hands would blister up and bleed. She wore tape on them all the time. Babe would hit eight or ten hours a day. We'd work until eleven o'clock at night.

Later, she received further instruction from a Dallas pro, George Aulbach, and then from Tommy Armour. By 1934 she was on the amateur circuit, such as it was, for women. Her presence at the 1935 Texas state championship was not welcomed; Peggy Chandler, a member of the Texas Women's Golf Association sniffed: "We don't need any truck driver's daughters in this tournament."

Life followed bad movie art; who should the Babe face in the thirty-six-hole final but the snobby Mrs. Chandler. It is a measure of the limited appeal then of women's golf that the gallery numbered only a few hundred. The "truck driver's daughter" —actually Ole Didrikson was a seaman and odd-jobs carpenter—banged out an eagle on the first hole, while her detractor took a bogey 6. And after twelve holes the upstart led by five holes; a seemingly insurmountable lead.

At this point, Babe's game collapsed and she began thrashing about the woods, rough, and traps when not muffing putts. By the twenty-sixth hold of the match, Peggy Chandler had grabbed a three-hole advantage. However, Didrikson settled down to draw even as they teed off on the thirty-fourth. She boomed out one of her 250-yarders but it rolled into a ditch. Her opponent dropped her second shot at the green's edge. Babe smacked a 3-iron that bounded beyond the green and then slid into a watery rut, leaving just the top of the ball visible. When Chandler neatly chipped to within two feet of the cup for a sure bird, Babe was in deep trouble. She peered at her ball, pulled out a sand wedge and addressed the problem. The club cleaved the puddle and a small shower of mud and water spattered the green as the ball hopped into the air. Backspin slowed its progress as it rolled inexorably toward the cup, then dropped for an eagle. The spectators roared and rushed forward in

congratulations, knocking her down in the mud.

Back on her feet, 1 up, she halved thirty-five and then won the final hole. It was a popular victory in the press but brought down the wrath of the Texas golf establishment, which complained to the USGA that since Babe had been declared a pro by the AAU she should be barred from any amateur competition. Stuffed shirtism prevailed. A USGA committee banned her in "the best interest of the game."

The Western Open and a Texas Open created by some friends of hers were the only opportunities for a woman professional to make a few dollars competing. Most of Didrikson's income during the late 1930s came from exhibitions, particularly a series with Gene Sarazen. When Joyce Wethered came to the U.S. in 1935, Babe played her head-to-head twice. The night

When Babe played golf, "The sound was not that of a woman hitting a golf ball; it was the noise made at impact when the club is wielded by a good man player.... When a woman swings the club it sounds 'whoooooosh, plop!' A good man player sounds 'whizz, tok!'"—Peter Dobereiner, The World of Golf. (COURTESY RAY DAVIS.)

(Above) *"The Babe practiced sixteen hours a day each weekend. On weekdays she was on the course at 5:30 A.M. for a three-hour session. Then she went to her regular job. Most of her lunch hour was spent chipping balls onto a leather chair in her boss's office. After work she took lessons for an hour and practiced until dark. 'I'd hit golf balls until my hands were bloody and sore,' she once grimly explained. 'Then I'd have tape all over my hands and blood all over the tape.'"—Arthur Daley,* New York Times, *September 30, 1956.* (COURTESY RAY DAVIS.)

(Opposite, top) *"I loved Babe. She was good to play with, fun to be around. She was very witty and kept the gallery laughing all the time. Wisecracks all the way around. Very uninhibited. She was a little crude, and some things she said shocked me a little because I was just the opposite, but the gallery loved her. There will never be another like her."—Betsy Rawls, quoted by Al Barkow,* Gettin' to the Dance Floor. (COURTESY RAY DAVIS.)

before the first encounter, a manufacturer made Didrikson a generous offer if she would use his clubs. She agreed, although it meant playing a crucial match without ever trying them out. She scored a dismal 88 to Wethered's 78. The results were not significantly different the second outing as the Briton carded a 77 to her 81.

In 1940, two years after she married wrestler and promoter George Zaharias, she renounced her professional designation and applied to become an amateur. To qualify, she could not play for money for three years, a restriction made simpler by the lack of tournaments during World War II. But she shaped her game in exhibitions that aided War Bond sales. She won the 1943 Los Angeles Mid-Winter tournament in 1943 and further flabbergasted the stodges of golf as the sole female entry in the 1944 Southern California Open. Shortly after the war ended, she captured her third straight Western Women's Open, having finally won back her amateur standing a year earlier.

While the new Mrs. Zaharias had endured very slim pickings, several other women amateurs had come to the fore. Patty Berg,★ a chunky Minnesota girl, was, like the Babe, known as a tomboy for her childhood excellence in sports generally associated with males. In grammar school, Patty quarterbacked a football team that included the future University of Oklahoma and National Football League Coach, Bud Wilkinson.

Golf, however, was part of her nature and nurturing. Her father, Herman Berg, was a golf fanatic who filmed players like Walter Hagen, Bobby Jones, and Gene Sarazen and then tried to improve his game by analyzing their swings. He passed on to his daughter his passion for the sport and encouraged her to study his home movies.

Patty Berg was still a seventeen-year-old school kid in 1935 when she lost in the finals to Glenna Collett Vare, then on her way to a sixth national championship. In 1937, Berg returned to the National Women's Amateur final only to be defeated by Estelle Lawson Page. She made herself 1938 women's amateur champion topping Page while still shy a few months of the

right to vote. Her feats on the links that year, which included the Curtis Cup, and wins in ten of the thirteen tournaments entered, brought election by the Associated Press as best female athlete of the year. Patty duplicated that honor in 1943 and 1955.

The red-headed Berg turned professional in 1940, in hopes of providing some income for her beleageured family. The tournament trail for pro women then amounted to three events with a total purse of 500 dollars. However, Wilson Sporting Goods Company, seeking to cash in on the female golfer market, signed her for endorsements and arranged a schedule of instruction clinics and exhibitions. At the Western Open for Women in 1941, she scored her first pro victory. A few months later, on the day after Pearl Harbor, she fractured her knee in three places in a Texas auto accident. Recovery and rehabilitation included a regimen ordinarily designed for boxers. She rode a bicycle, did bending exercises, hauled pulleys and weights, and punched a bag for ten minutes to restore her sense of timing.

She recuperated enough to participate in the 1943 Western Open and repeat her previous success. Berg then entered the U.S. Marine Corps unit for women. Commissioned a lieutenant, she, like other famous golfers, spent some of her military duty playing exhibitions to raise money for charity and on occasions received leave to appear in a tournament. After hostilities ended, Berg commenced where she left off, adding the National Open for Women in 1946 and challenging Babe Zaharias for the title of best woman golfer over the next decade. When she eventually retired from the competitive golf trail, she had won a total of eighty-three tournaments, seven Western Opens, and four championships George May arranged for women at Tam O'Shanter. For the lowest scoring average among women in 1953, '55, and '56, she received the female equivalent of the Vardon Trophy, the Vare Trophy.

While recognizing the financial benefits of Zaharias's membership in the LPGA, Berg chafed under the celebrity power of Zaharias, who was not shy of exploiting

(Left) *"At the final hole, with all the people lining the course and waiting to escort her home, she sliced her drive badly into a wicked place among trees. She could have used as many strokes as she pleased to finish and the sensible thing to do was to sacrifice a stroke and play back to the fairway. But The Babe took the position that this was no way to finish. She found a tiny opening and she took a long iron and went through it toward the distant green. It gave her a chance for a par-4. She missed it by an inch but she had finished in a champion's way."*—Al Laney, New York Herald Tribune, July 4, 1954. (COURTESY UPI/BETTMANN NEWSPHOTOS.)

her fame. In the final round of a 1951 tournament, playing with the Babe, Patty outshot her and passed her rival with only a few holes remaining. Rain started to fall and Zaharias tromped off to the clubhouse, announcing to the sponsors that the day's play should be canceled because of the downpour. They acceded even though the course was playable. A furious Berg feasted on sweet vengeance the following day when she whupped the Babe.

Other women had begun to scrap for the still-meager bucks of the tiny distaff pro circuit. A slightly built youngster from Atlanta, Louise Suggs, like Patty Berg, was steered into golf by her father and coached by him. She stepped into the amateur void left by Berg and Zaharias. Her ability to efficiently and swiftly mobilize her 112 pounds enabled Suggs to generate tremendous club head acceleration at the moment of impact, causing some to describe her as the "female Ben Hogan." As a nineteen year old in 1942, she collared her first major title, the North-South amateur championship. In succeeding years, Suggs held that honor twice more, as well as the Western Amateur on three occasions.

Suggs flashed her most impressive cre-

Dorothy Kielty (left) and Frank Stranahan clutched their trophies after their victories in the 1950 World's Championship at Tam O'Shanter, while Zaharias toted home a handful of silver and a large check as the top pro for her sex. (COURTESY CHICAGO SUN-TIMES.)

dentials at the 1946 Women's Western Open. First she vanquished the Babe, the defending champion in pursuit of her third successive title. The match attracted 2,000 sweating enthusiasts—an impressive number compared with the modest handful that witnessed the dramatic match of the Babe and Peggy Chandler some ten years before. The gallery witnessed a classic struggle between the slugger, Zaharias, and the boxer, Suggs. Babe belted huge drives and long irons while Louise countered with superb chipping and deadly putting, a hallmark of her game.

Babe was 1 up after fifteen holes but on the sixteenth, she missed a 4 footer while Louise knocked one of the same distance home to draw even. The seventeenth hole, a 115 yarder, saw a replay of the previous one. While Suggs nearly canned a 30 footer for a deuce, Zaharias blew another 4-foot stab, to fall one down. When Louise putted to within inches of the cup from 35 feet on eighteen, the match was over.

Victory over Babe created a final against the equally formidable Berg. It, too, was a see-saw struggle, with first one and then the other ahead during the thirty-six-hole match. At the thirty-third tee all seemed lost for Suggs as Berg stood a firm 2 up with only four to play. But Suggs then birdied the 482-yard par-5 thirty-third with an 18-foot putt. She pressed even harder on the thirty-fourth with a chip shot that trickled into the cup, then popped out to cost Suggs an eagle. Still, this bird put her even. When she parred the last holes while Berg slipped to a pair of bogeys, Louise had beaten the best two women on the scene. A gracious Berg declared: "Louise is a great golfer. She deserved to win. You'll hear a lot from her for a long time."

And indeed, the next decade saw Suggs, who won the Women's Amateur title in 1947 and turned pro in 1949, battling Berg and Zaharias, who rejoined the pro ranks in 1947. But before Berg or Zaharias entered the play-for-pay ranks, both of them traveled to England in 1947 for the British Ladies Golf Championship. The Scottish crowds adored the wise-cracking, unpretentious Babe. She entertained the gallery

Slender, young Patty Berg sits at right among a gathering of top women golfers. (COURTESY RAY DAVIS.)

with a running conversation and when someone asked how she was able to get such great distance on her drives, they delighted in her response:

"I just loosen my girdle, and let the ball have it." The torturous undergarment, however, was never part of her wardrobe; she had discarded it long ago.

What truly impressed the locals was the caliber of her game, which in the early rounds obliterated the British entries by lopsided scores. One writer remarked, "It seems cruel to send our girls out against a game like that."

One match lasted until the sixteenth hole. In the semi-final, the Scottish champion, Jean Donald, considered a long hitter, fell 7 and 5 as Babe added some brilliant putting touches. But the thirty-six holes for the championship brought out stiffer resistance. The foe, Jacqueline Gordon, a pupil of Henry Cotton, held her even over the first eighteen and had led by 2 through the thirteenth. The afternoon, however, was a massacre. Babe lost only one hole. The match ended on thirty-two as Babe won 5 up, to become the first American ever to win the British Ladies Amateur.

The conquering heroine returned to a welcome reminiscent of that accorded Bobby Jones in 1930. The celebration began as her train left Edinburgh for London, as hundreds of people crowded the plat-

form for choruses of "Auld Lang Syne." When the *Queen Mary* steamed near the New York harbor, a tugboat of newsmen and photographers pulled alongside. Also on hand was her sumo-size husband, George. For the benefit of the newsreels and stills, husband and wife donned tartan kilts and caps to dance for the cameras. At city hall in their hometown of Denver, she received a 250-pound key to the town and rode a rose-bedecked float in a parade before 50,000 people.

Although Babe had promised the Scottish fans she would return the following year to defend the title, she and George quickly realized it was time to cash in the amateur chips. His wrestling promotions let them afford the 15,000 dollars a year required for her to follow the amateur circuit, but an offer of 300,000 dollars for a series of short films on golf could not be overlooked.

Fred Corcoran became her agent and even that master of publicity was surprised by the instinctive skill of his new client. Corcoran remembered the press conference at Toots Shor's restaurant where she explained why she was turning pro:

The thing started to drag a little, so she opened it up for questions. A guy asked her what her plans were—where was she going to play? "Well," she said, "I'm going to enter the U.S. Open Championship—for

Patty Berg stands tied for third with Betsy Rawls among all-time tournament wins for women with fifty-five victories that include thirteen contests prior to the formation of the LPGA. (COURTESY BETTMANN/UPI NEWSPHOTOS.)

Berg campaigns at the Western Open in 1951. She won this event a record seven times. (COURTESY BETTMANN/UPI NEWSPHOTOS.)

Louise Suggs, "Miss Poker Face" from Georgia, holds the fifth slot on the all-time tournament list of the LPGA with fifty titles. (COURTESY UPI/BETTMANN NEWSPHOTOS.)

men." I didn't know she was going to say this. I don't think she did when she got up there. There was this stunned silence, mouths dropped and then the press—en masse—made a dash for the phones. At the time, there was no rule against women entering the men's Open, but the very next day the USGA put in a new rule forbidding it. However, Babe had gotten her headlines. She had upstaged them all.

Although by turning professional Babe was forced to renege on her pledge to defend the British Ladies Amateur Championship, Louise Suggs sailed to England in 1948, and made it two in a row for the Americans.

Over the years, Zaharias and Suggs competed against one another on and off the golf course. The somewhat reticent Suggs may well have resented the publicity that her frequent opponent received. She was, like Sarazen, offended by anyone who failed to maintain a dignified style on the links or adhere strictly to the rules. Decorum, she felt, was not high enough on the Babe's priorities.

While Zaharias prospered through her film deals and promotions by Corcoran, the women professionals as a group lacked recognition and decent purses. Babe and Fred Corcoran schemed to enlarge the tour for herself and colleagues. Corcoran explained:

We needed money, of course. L. B. Icely, the president of Wilson, thought he saw some kind of future in women's golf and he was willing to put up the money. There had been something called the Women's Professional Golf Association earlier. I called Hope Seignious, who was the head of it; she refused to sell us the charter. Well, okay, we thought, in England they call them "ladies" and in a way it sounded classier than "women." We decided to call our tour the "Ladies Professional Golf Association."

Thus, the word that would by the 1980s be regarded by feminists as one of opprobrium rather than "classier," was only the result of this unattainable charter.

There were eleven original members of the LPGA, formed in Wichita, Kansas, in

1950. Patty Berg served as the first president with the other members, Babe, Suggs, the Bauer sisters—Marlene and Alice—Sally Sessions, Betty Jameson, Bettye Danoff, Shirley Spork, Helen Dettweiler, and Marilynn Smith.

Corcoran was actually paid by Wilson and eventually MacGregor and Spalding also contributed towards his salary. While he booked the tournaments, the day-to-day management and details fell upon the working women of the new tour. They kept the accounts, wrote the checks and handled the correspondence. During some of the first years it was a hand-to-mouth business, with the hands occasionally coming up empty. The LPGA could not afford to hire officials; the USGA would only become involved later and so the players participating in a tournament sometimes found themselves obliged to make rulings on other competitors.

The first purses were small, averaging between 3,000 and 4,000 dollars, sums approximating those the men had fought for in the heart of the Depression. Nevertheless, the results of organizing were immediately visible. In 1948 and '49, Babe led the female money winners with totals of 3,400 and 4,650 dollars. In 1950 and '51, she topped out at 14,800 and 15,087 dollars. Betsy Rawls★ led with 14,505 dollars in 1952, and Louise Suggs banked 19,816 dollars the following year as the total purses climbed steadily, along with membership. Charter member Betty Jameson, in 1952, donated the trophy, named for Glenna Collett Vare, which honored the lowest scoring average.

The American women who successfully invaded Great Britain in the post–World War II year were only a part of the U.S. forces intent on dominating golf abroad. Sam Snead, in 1946, took the British Open in its first postwar appearance. Then Francis Ouimet captained a 1948 Walker Cup team that revenged the 1938 U.S. loss and one member, Willie Turnesa, added the British Amateur to the American laurels. Another of the Walker Cup squad, Frank Stranahan, followed with consecutive wins of the Amateur in '48 and '49.

But as other lands—particularly those of the now splintering British Empire—recovered from the vicissitudes of war, their golf stars began to strike back. In 1947, the first major threat arrived in the person of a jowly, mustachioed former South African bomber pilot, Arthur D'arcy "Bobby" Locke.★ Except for Gene Sarazen, American golf fashion now called for long trousers and short-sleeved, open-necked shirts. Locke, in his blousy plus 4, full-sleeve white shirt, and four-in-hand tie—no matter how high the temperature—stood out sartorially from the start.

During the several months he played the U.S. circuit in 1947, Locke piled up winnings of more than 27,000 dollars. He had quit school at seventeen in order to concentrate upon golf, winning both the amateur and open titles of his land. After he won the Transvaal Open as an amateur a friend said, "Congratulations, boy; you've got the publicity and Sid Brews [the pro low scorer] has got the money."

According to Locke, that remark prodded him into the professional ranks. "Golf is my pleasure. I love the game. But I made up my mind never to lose sight of the cash side of it."

As a twenty-one-year-old in 1939, he abandoned a post as clerk for a mining company and arrived in England as the choice to win the British Open. He failed miserably but regained his reputation with matches against 1938 Open winner, Reginald Whitcombe, and 1939 titleist, Richard Burton. His match-play victories in both instances were overwhelming, 6 up and 5 to go against Whitcombe and a 10 and 9 drubbing of Burton. He completed a triple of such engagements with a 4–3 beating of the British match-play champ, Dai Rees.

Sporting England at that time, in contrast to the expanding circuit traveled by Americans, featured challenge matches of this nature. Mining magnate and racehorse owner Len Oates backed Locke in two contests, the first of which was 500 pounds sterling winner-take-all and the second 250 pounds, handsome returns even compared with the going prizes in the States. Ultimately the gauntlet was flung at Henry Cotton. But even though a potential stake of 1,000 pounds was in the offing, Cotton insisted he would only meet the challenger if he won the British or U.S. Opens, and Locke accomplished neither.

Although a youngster, Locke, according to M. W., golf correspondent for a British newspaper, was:

(Above) *"I won fifty-five tournaments as a professional. I won ten of them in 1959 and won a little over 26,000 dollars. But I don't feel any resentment at the amount of money the girls are playing for now. That's not why I played, for the money. If it was a lot of money I was after, I probably would have done something else. I thoroughly enjoyed playing and got a lot of satisfaction out of it. I take pride in being a pioneer that helped make today's tour possible."—Betsy Rawls, quoted by Al Barkow,* Gettin' to the Dance Floor. (COURTESY UPI/ BETTMANN NEWSPHOTOS.)

(Below) *At Bloomfield Hills, Michigan, in 1956, three Hall of Famers and the best known sisters of the LPGA lined up on the practice tee. From left to right, they are: Louise Suggs, Alice Bauer, Betsy Rawls, Marlene Bauer, and Mickey Wright.* (COURTESY UPI/BETTMANN NEWSPHOTOS.)

(Right) *Bob Toski, a player the pros consult when their game is troubled, beamed alongside George May after his World Championship bonanaza of 50,000 dollars in 1954.* (COURTESY BETTMANN/UPI NEWSPHOTOS.)

(Below) *"The only thing that [Bobby] Locke did the least bit like any other professional in the world was win tournaments and even here he differed from the others in the way he won them. At a time when alligator shoes, canary-yellow slacks, and fuchsia sports shirts were practically the uniform of the day for the American professional, Locke dressed in grey flannel knickerbockers, white buckskin shoes and linen shirts complete with necktie. His swing was put together by exaggerating everything which the American pros had come to regard as anathema. . . . Locke hooked every shot in the bag, including his putts, and his method here had some purists among the pros kicking lockers in frustration." —Charles Price,* The World of Golf. (COURTESY UPI/BETTMANN NEWSPHOTOS.)

. . . one of the coolest, shrewdest and most unemotional players with whom I have ever come in contact. . . . I have never once seen him lose his temper or express annoyance . . . he is never flustered and never hurries.

Unlike a growing number of golfers, Locke did not believe in hitting dozens of balls to perfect a particular shot. He theorized that the process tired a golfer and tended to consolidate a fault rather than rectify it. His form of practice was to play as many rounds as possible, concentrating on the challenge of par. In that respect he agreed with the counsel not of Ben Hogan but of Bobby Jones. "Old Man Par is a severe enough taskmaster and the player who can keep in step with him has nothing to fear."

But unlike Jones and Cotton, who deliberately controlled the swiftness of their swings. Locke whipped his clubhead with express-train speed. One observer noted:

Every ball he hit headed to some distant target off to the right, and then made a sweeping turn like a boomerang and landed in the geometric center of every fairway. He even hooked his putts. Using a wristy stroke with a hickory shafted blade putter old enough to grow moss, he swept the face open on the backstroke, then flapped it closed coming through the ball. He holed everything he ever looked at.

Indeed, that uncanny ability to putt was the true source of Locke's success. Henry Longhurst observed:

One of Locke's canons of putting is "Thou shalt not be short," and it is a fact that in sixty-three holes of eager watching, I do not recall his once being short of the hole.

His greens work destroyed his opponents in the side matches of 1939. M. W. remarked:

When British professionals . . . learn how to putt, and can step up with confidence, as in the case of Locke, to the six-footers, they will have a chance of beating America in the Ryder Cup match.

World War II, of course, ended hopes

for the match with Cotton and the talk of the Ryder Cup. Locke spent more than five years flying 1,800 hours in single-, twin-, and four-engined aircraft, winding up in the Middle East and Italy as pilot of a B-24 Liberator bomber.

He resumed his golf career as if the long layoff was of no consequence. Although Lew Worsham beat out the perennial second, Sam Snead, in a playoff for the 1947 U.S. Open, Locke toted up the most earnings on the U.S. tour and he was Vardon winner for 1946, '50, and '54. When he finally hung up his tournament shoes, he could count four British Opens and earnings in excess of 600,000 dollars.

The dominant figure for the ten years that followed the end of World War II was, of course, Ben Hogan. Not only had he won four U.S. Opens (1948, '50, '51, and '53), the PGA twice (1946, '48), the Masters twice (1951, '53), and the British Open (1953), along with countless other tournaments, but the tale of his comeback from the near-fatal car wreck in February 1949 converted the "Wee Ice Mon," the unsmiling automaton, into something of a hero.

His resurgence after his accident was all the more remarkable since he faced ever stiffer competition. During WWII, some of the better golfers had been surprised by an army dentist who played them at least even in exhibitions. Cary Middlecoff, a six-foot two-inch, slender Tennessean, was well known in his home state where he had won four amateur championships from 1940–1943. Still an amateur, he took the 1945 North South Open, beating his closest rivals Denny Shute and Ben Hogan by 5 and 6. In 1947, he quit filling cavities and resigned a spot on the Walker Cup squad in order to make a living on the pro trail.

Middlecoff capitalized upon his height, taking back the club in a high arc and pausing momentarily before accelerating forward to strike, with a distinctive grunt, great soaring drives that split the fairways. A streaky putter, he rattled off long droppers in batches. If he had a fault it lay in his temperament. Not for him the slow purposeful strides of a Bobby Locke; Middlecoff was golf's man-in-motion, barely able

to stand still while foes stroked. He almost trotted after his ball. But then he switched to idle gear and vacillated over his choice of club and strategy, sorting out endless possibilities while he chain smoked cigarettes. When he succumbed to his inner rage, Vesuvian outbursts shattered the calm. One memorable moment at the 1953 Open he became so distraught he fired a ball onto the Pennsylvania Turnpike and stalked off the course.

Over the winter tour of 1949, he burnished his mettle with three victories and two seconds. While Ben Hogan could barely limp a few steps about his living room, Middlecoff and the rest of the gang assembled at the Medinah Club in Chicago. It seemed as if Middlecoff's nerves overwhelmed him on opening day when he bumbled home with a 75. But then he embarked on a binge of sub-par holes and scored 67 and 69 to take a 3-stroke lead over Clayton Heafner into the final round.

Once again, Middlecoff's touch deserted him and he shuffled through for a second 75 and a total of 286. Heafner evened the match on the fourteenth hole but then bogeyed sixteen and came in at 287. However, Sam Snead, still on the quest for an Open to go with all his other trophies, had started 6 behind, and with a par 36 for the front nine could catch Middlecoff with a do-able 33 for the remaining holes. Snead rose to the occasion, canning a flock of birdies and by the fourteenth hole needed only to meet par for a tie. On the par 3 seventeenth, he elected to putt from off the green. He knocked himself 8 feet from the cup and then missed the putt. Only a birdie on eighteen could save him now and the best he could achieve was a par. Middlecoff was the 1949 Open champ.

Seven years later at the Open over Oak Hill (the old stamping grounds of Walter Hagen in Rochester, N.Y.), with the 1955 Masters' green jacket in his closet, Middlecoff again could only fidget and wait for the others. He had recovered from an early pair of double-bogey 7s and moved ahead. The margin was slim, however, because on the final three holes the erstwhile tooth mechanic slumped with a pair of bogeys.

(Right, top) *Sam Snead and Ben Hogan palaver with the native son who would capture the 1954 British Open, Peter Thomson. Eleven years later, Thomson also beat off potent new invaders named Palmer and Nicklaus.* (COURTESY UPI/BETTMANN NEWSPHOTOS.)

(Right, bottom) *"Anyone who hasn't been nervous, or who hasn't choked somewhere down the line, is an idiot." —Cary Middlecoff,* Golf Digest, *July 1977.* (COURTESY UPI/BETTMANN NEWSPHOTOS.)

(Below) *No pain-wracked patient of erstwhile dentist Cary Middlecoff could outdo his agony and grimace over a blown shot.* (COURTESY UPI/BETTMANN NEWSPHOTOS.)

Three players could catch him. Ben Hogan, looking to revenge his 1955 loss in a playoff against the near-anonymous Jack Fleck, could tie with pars on the final two holes. He seemed nearly over the hump when he left himself a 3-footer on seventeen. But he missed and now only a bird would do. He drove far enough on eighteen but his wood shot left him a 30 footer and he settled for par and second place.

The next challenger, Julius Boros,★ was thirty-six years old but a relative newcomer to the pro ranks. He was a big man like Middlecoff, but a stark contrast in style. His easygoing swing mirrored his temperament. He seemed so calm it was tempting to think of him as a hacker out for a morning away from the office. On occasions, he trudged along the fairway, golf club slung over his shoulder, whistling a popular song. When it was his turn to putt, he was not like some who agonized over the geography like ancient navigators peering at the stars and their astrolabe. Instead Boros stepped up, quickly surveyed the terrain, and then smoothly put club to ball. The serenity was all the more remarkable for the traumas he had suffered. In 1952, only two years after he filed the last debits and credits of his accounting job and joined the tour, his wife died in childbirth. Still, the plucky Boros recorded a 4-stroke U.S. Open win at Dallas's Northwood Country Club. That same year the thick-set Boros collected an unheard of total of 50,000 dollars in prizes from George May's Tam O'Shanter World's Championship extravaganza.★ On the strength of these heroics, which helped make him the top earner for 1952, the PGA had named Boros golfer of the year.

At Oak Hill in 1956, Julius Boros needed only one birdie over the final four to tie. On fifteen, the ball teetered on the lip of the cup, but would not fall. On sixteen, it just skirted the rim. And on eighteen, the ball hesitated as it caught the right edge, and then decided to continue on an inch or so.

Seven years later in 1963, Boros, on the fiftieth anniversary of Francis Ouimet's upset of the British titans Vardon and Braid, and on the same site (The Country Club in Brookline, Massachusetts), ran away from the field for his second National Open title, short by a few months of tying Ted Ray, the 1920 victor, for oldest (forty-three) golfer to win that championship.

Middlecoff's last challenger at Oak Hill in 1956, Ted Kroll, needed a string of pars over the last four holes. But he bogeyed, double bogeyed, and bogeyed to collapse from contention. Middlecoff had his second national championship.

A year later, at Inverness, in Toledo, Cary defended his Open title. Hogan had entered but on the eve of the opening round, pleurisy, an inflammation of the lungs, made the simple act of lifting his arms above his chest excruciating. The USGA, in a rare effort to accommodate a player, volunteered to set back his starting time. But it was to no avail; Hogan withdrew.

Middlecoff faltered with a 146 for the first two rounds, 8 off the pace. He heated up on the morning of the final day, carding a 4-under 68. The leader, Dick Mayer, was in the clubhouse as Middlecoff, for once the pursuer, played out the string. To tie he would have to birdie two of the last four holes. He could only par 15 and on the 412-yard sixteenth, his pitch left him 20 feet from the cup. He sank it, leaving him in search of one more saved stroke. The seventeenth was just too long for such heroics; the only chance was eighteen. Cary launched one of his spectacular suborbit shots off the tee and then blasted an approach to within 9 feet of pay dirt. In his inimitable fashion he spent long minutes

---

*Impressive as Boros's take, the most memorable and rewarding blow of May's promotions came the next year. Chandler Harper had smacked his second shot on the 370-yard final hole to within 18 inches of the cup for a birdie for what everyone believed a winning score of 279 and the 25,000 dollars first money plus the series of exhibitions of 1,000 dollars a date. However, playing in a final threesome, was Lew Worsham who could tie Harper with his own birdie on that last hole. From 104 yards out, Worsham lofted a wedge shot that landed 25 feet from the pin, rolled over a slight ridge, and into the cup. The eagle deuce brought Worsham in at a winning 278. The purse and exhibitions fees made the shot worth a total of 62,000 dollars.

squinting, studying, calculating the line and force required. The hush of the crowd broke into sustained applause as the putt rolled to the right, then hooked left and fell for a tie.

The playoff was an anticlimax. The worst surfaced in Middlecoff's game as he lurched from bunker to green and stabbed at putts. Mayer carded a comfortable win with a 72 to the loser's 79. Middlecoff faded from the top ranks, flaring to the fore only briefly in 1959 as runner-up to Art Wall in the Masters. Soon time, the implacable enemy of the athlete, would steadily demand many new faces.

The old order changed most sadly with the illness and death of Babe Zaharias. The skinny girl who had wowed the fans at the Los Angeles Olympics in 1932 had filled out to 140 sinewy pounds. Between 1948 and 1955 she had won thirty-one professional tournaments, including three U.S. Women's Opens, the last of which was in 1954. A year before, however, doctors diagnosed her as suffering from cancer. It involved a colostomy and one of the attending physicians declared: "I don't know yet if surgery will cure her but I will say that she never again will play golf of championship caliber."

But a mere fourteen weeks after being wheeled into the operating room, Babe confounded the prediction by teeing off in May's All-American and over an abbreviated season finished sixth among the female money winners, earning the Ben Hogan Comeback of the Year award.

She resumed a full schedule for 1954, capping her five tournament victories with the Open at the Salem Country Club in Peabody, Massachusetts. But then the cancer reappeared and she died in 1956.

While the Zaharias-Suggs rivalry had been the first great confrontation of the newly formed LPGA, their achievements were challenged by a pair of young women. Betsy Rawls did not swing a club in earnest until age seventeen. A scant four years later in 1949, she won the Texas Amateur, then repeated in that event in 1950. That same year as an amateur she finished second behind Zaharias in the Women's Open.

She joined the LPGA tour a year later

and as a rookie captured the first of her four Open championships. Her second Open win came in 1953 over a burly Hawaiian, Jackie Pung. Jackie appeared to have revenged the defeat in 1957 at Winged Foot in Mamaroneck, New York, when she posted a 298 to Rawls's 299. However, officials discovered that Pung had signed a scorecard on which her sister competitor erroneously wrote down a 5 instead of the actual 6 Jackie took on the fourth hole. It did not matter that the 298 total was correct; the stiff-necked authorities disqualified Pung.

Rawls's game was dead-on as she drew closer to greens and she added the 1960 Open for a fourth championship, a feat equaled by only one other woman. Furthermore, Rawls notched two LPGAs and two Western Opens in her fifty-five first-place finishes. Long active in the affairs of the LPGA, she served as tournament director for six years following her retirement from the circuit in 1975.

The one woman who matched Rawls's four Open victories was a child of San Diego, Mickey Wright.★ A student of the game from her early adolescence, Mickey received her first lessons from the pro at the La Jolla Country Club and then developed her swing under the tutelage of Harry Pressler, the pro at the San Gabriel Country Club near Los Angeles. Every Saturday, for two years, her mother drove Mickey the 130 miles or so for sixty minutes of Pressler's guidance.

When Babe Zaharias scored her final U.S. Women's Open round, she paired with Wright, whose slender five-foot-nine build resembled that of the young Babe. Wright was only nineteen, and her fourth place that tournament beat out all other amateurs.

On the strength of that performance, Wright quit college to enlist in the pro ranks. She was not an instant success. She could hit farther than most of her rivals on the tour but she missed many fairways. Furthermore she was inept at the short game, the area where one makes up for mistakes and opens the doors to birdies. Her weakness within striking distance of the cup was discerned by the most expert of close-in play, Betsy Rawls:

Mickey had no touch at all on her chip shots, and she was absolutely the worst putter I have ever seen in professional golf. Her mental attitude was all wrong. She was preoccupied with playing flawlessly from tee to green. If she didn't hit fifteen of the eighteen greens in the regulation stroke, she was disgusted with herself. She had complete contempt for scrambling. It took Mickey two years to learn to respect the short game, and realize that even the top players have to be able to get down in two from off the green. Then her chipping and putting started to improve, and, of course, her scoring did, too.

Wright punched out her initial victory at the Jacksonville Open in 1956 and progressed steadily, winning three tournaments in 1957, five including the U.S. Women's Open in '58, four more and repeating in the Open in '59, six tournaments in '60, and then an overwhelming ten in 1961 as she added her third American championship.

Rawls, who went toe-to-toe with Zaharias and became Wright's closest pal on the tour, remarked:

Mickey was much better than Babe Zaharias. No comparison. Babe was stronger, maybe a better athlete—she was so well coordinated—but Mickey had a better golf swing, hit the ball better, could play rings around Babe.

Once queen of the hill, Wright remained on the throne. She led the LPGA in just about every area, tournaments taken, low average, and naturally most money. In 1965, somewhat burned out from an intensive ten years on the circuit, with a total of eighty-two career triumphs, all of the major titles and a female record for low eighteen-hole score (62), plagued by a sore wrist, she retired from competition at age thirty. This was almost as young as Bobby Jones who had similarly lost his competitive edge.

Just as Wright claimed the mantle of dominance in women's golf from the Babe, so to would a newcomer at the end of the 1950s usurp the men's crown abdicated by Ben Hogan.

(Opposite, top) Life *magazine and the PGA cosponsored a 1953 "Golf Day" promotion that invited challengers to pay a one dollar entry fee and match the net score for eighteen holes on their courses against Julius Boros, 1952 Open champ, playing the Oakmont layout, site of the coming Open. The receipts were to be split between the USO and the National Golf Fund, a nonprofit organization assisting worthy causes associated with the game.* (COURTESY RAY DAVIS.)

(Opposite, bottom) Boros and family relish the 50,000 dollar prize for his 1968 victory in the Western Classic.* (COURTESY UPI/ BETTMANN NEWSPHOTOS.)

(Above) "Thomson is a supremely good bunker player. Perhaps his finest exhibition of this art was when he won the Open at Lytham [1958] where they have innumerable bunkers, of which he encountered at least his share. I have always remembered his remark afterwards that he had 'never seen such a beautiful sand.' He sincerely regards 'splashing' the ball out of sand as the simplest shot in the whole game, if only because there is so much greater margin for error than with a similar shot off grass."—Henry Longhurst, The Best of Henry Longhurst. (COURTESY UPI/BETTMANN NEWSPHOTOS.)

With eighty-two wins, Mickey Wright places second on the women's all-time tournament victories list. "We had some great head-to-head matches. Nine times out of ten, she won."—Kathie Whitworth (No. 1 on the list with eighty-eight), Golf Magazine, June 1983. (COURTESY UPI/BETTMANN NEWSPHOTOS.)

17

The Army Mobilizes

The booster rocket that sent the men's tour into orbit was forged in the hamlet of Latrobe, Pennsylvania, hitherto known only as the 1896 site, perhaps, of the first professional football game in the United States. Now it's also known as the source of an irresistible force by the name of Arnold Palmer.

The golf gene permeated Arnold's body. His father, who had been on the construction crew that built the Latrobe Country Club, stayed on to become greenskeeper, then course superintendent and pro. Milfred "Deacon" Palmer fashioned a half-pint-sized set of clubs for his three-year-old son out of some wood-shafted sticks with rewrapped grips to accommodate the tiny fingers. Arnold credits such early familiarity with golf clubs with preventing him from having to overcome a baseball bat grip, a common failing of American boys who come to golf after learning to swing a bat. He modestly protests his early introduction to the sport did not make him "an instant champion. I was seven years old before I broke a hundred." (Of course, there are many who never get into the double figures.)

As a child, Arnold helped his father maintain the course.

Some people think I developed my strong arms by working in the steel mills around Latrobe. Not so. I got them when I was a little kid, seven or eight years old, working on the tractor for Pap. As I went chugging up and down those hills, it took everything I had—standing up and heaving the wheel with both arms—to "horse" that machine around.

Deacon Palmer taught his boy the rudiments of the stroke and advised him, "Always hit it hard." On his own, Arnold practiced for hours although his father, a stickler for club etiquette and rules, restricted his use of the course. One result was he often rehearsed from the rough, a habit he believes gave him the confidence to play out of what he laughingly calls his "natural environment."

Young Arnold continued to caddie, unblushingly offering his wisdom to the club members—his choice of club even at age eleven, was usually correct—and hustling his mother and her friends for a nickel or dime by offering to hit the tough shots over the creek on the fifth hole. But he had no notion of fame and celebrity through the game.

At the beginning golf was just another sport to me. I liked baseball and football and played whatever the gang was playing. Golf was just another version of cowboys and Indians.

He also distinguished himself at pool and cards but one trait emerged and remained. A high school classmate recalled: "He was a wild man—he'd press anything to the hilt on a gamble."

His all-or-nothing attitude hurt him in baseball: "I could really hit the ball—when I hit it at all." And while he was tall enough at five feet ten to play football, he weighed between 150 and 160 pounds, which is a prescription for significant bodily harm in the kind of football that permeates the Pennsylvania coal country.

Palmer accepted his father's advice to concentrate on what he could do well and that, of course, was golf. As a junior, on his high school team, or representing the Latrobe Country Club, he devastated the local amateur competition. A friend remembered: "Arnie had watches running up one arm and down the other and more luggage than you ever saw before."

A flash of the future Palmer illuminated a 1947 Pennsylvania high school tournament. The youthful Palmer had clouted one into the rough, a stiff 4-iron from the green. Distance was not the problem, however. The line of flight to paydirt, a piece of the green, ran through a narrow opening between two trees. The shot had to be low enough to pass beneath the branches yet strong enough to carry over a bunker guarding the front of the green.

Arnold reminisced:

No one knows how to hit a shot like that but I imagined what it looked like in flight, and my hands somehow had the feeling of what to do. I just knew that I was going to do it because I had to do it to win. It never occurred to me that I wouldn't pull it off.

And he did.

As a high school senior, Palmer met Buddy Worsham, Lew's brother, and they became best friends. Wake Forest University already had awarded a scholarship to Buddy on the strength of his golf, and he persuaded that institution to add Palmer to their roster. Golf, part of the American university scene since the dawn of the twentieth century when the best amateurs attended Ivy League schools, had now achieved a prestigious status in college athletics. Scholarships on the basis of golfing abilities educated the likes of Mike Souchak, Art Wall, Billy Maxwell, Dow Finsterwald, Ken Venturi, Gene Littler,★ and Don January.

For three years, Worsham and Palmer roomed together, partied together, and played together for Wake Forest. They turned the school into a golf powerhouse. Under their urging, Wake Forest even converted its old sand greens into grass ones, with the two stars and others on the golf team supplying the labor.

At this point in his career, Arnold relied almost exclusively on power, smiting 260- and 270-yard drives. He could putt decently but he ignored the less glamorous yet supremely important arts of chipping and bunker outs. On a whim he entered the

Azalea Open and against some excellent players finished fifth.

The fun halted when Buddy Worsham died in a car wreck while returning from a dance in Durham. Distraught, Palmer dropped out of Wake Forest and enlisted in the Coast Guard, then gearing up for duty in the Korean War. He spent much of his military time stationed in Cleveland where he managed to get in a considerable number of rounds. Among them was the 1953 U.S. Amateur in which he defeated Ken Venturi before losing in the fourth match. Gene Littler took the title.

Mustered out, Palmer returned to school for his degree. He accepted a job selling paint supplies in the Cleveland area, mixing in the role of golf companion to valued customers. But the urge to compete was too strong to be satisfied by casual play. Confidence was always one of his strong points. He remarked that even at that stage he never doubted that if given the opportunity he could beat Ben Hogan.

In 1954, Arnold Palmer entered the U.S. Amateur at the Country Club of Detroit against some experienced top flight talent. Among them was "the strong man," Frank Stranahan, a member of the Walker Cup squad, captained by Francis Ouimet, which vanquished the British in 1947 to start a string of 12 consecutive U.S. triumphs. Stranahan acquired the British amateur title the next two years, and at Detroit he ousted Harvie Ward, the winner of the 1951 British Amateur and U.S. Amateur champ in '54 and '55. When Stranahan met Palmer, who'd barely survived with a pair of 1-up matches, Arnold upset the Strong Man, 3-up, one to go.

Palmer then squeaked by Don Cherry, the crooner who abandoned night clubs for the tournament circuit, gaining a two and one lead after having trailed by a hole with just seven left. In the thirty-six-hole semi-finals, Arnold again confronted a much more experienced foe, Ed Meister, a thirty-eight-year-old publisher of fruit industry trade papers. Palmer hung on through the regulation rounds only because Meister blew putts of 10, 14, 5, and 16 feet over the final four, allowing Arnold to halve. The

(Opposite) Coast Guardsman Arnold Palmer obtained sufficient shore leave to pile up the silver plates. (COURTESY WILSON NEWS SERVICE.)

deadlock continued for two sudden-death holes. On the 510-yard thirty-ninth hole, Palmer overwhelmed Meister with sheer power, blasting an enormous monster of a drive that enabled him to reach the green with a 2-iron where he 2-putted for a bird and a win.

The other finalist was even older than Meister. Bob Sweeny, a forty-three-year-old banker, former Oxford scholar, and organizer of the Royal Air Force's American volunteers, the Eagle Squadron, had won the British Amateur seventeen years earlier. Sweeny struck like a dive bomber, scoring birdies on three of the first four holes to go 3-up. Even Sweeny thought it a bit much, Palmer remembered:

"Arnie," he said, as he threw an arm around me on our walk off the fourth green, "you *know* I can't keep this up."

Sweeny was a man of his word, losing three holes over the next six to even the match. But Palmer could not break away. Not until the thirty-second hole did he charge ahead. A birdie on thirty-three by the twenty-four year old supplied a big enough margin to win.

The victory convinced Palmer he could succeed as a touring pro. He quit selling paint and married a Coopersburg, Pennsylvania, girl, Winifred Walzer. He figured he would need 15,000 dollars to cover expenses. Several people offered to sponsor him, advancing 10,000 dollars to cover initial outlays. The investors did not demand repayment of the loan or even interest. But they wanted 50 percent of whatever he earned over a period of years. Palmer decided not to mortgage his future and luckily a sporting goods company offered him a few thousand dollars, in return for his endorsement of their products for three years. Palmer accepted the arrangement, which included a generous supply of balls, bags, and clubs, and he borrowed an additional sum from family and friends.

Thus began his ascent to golf's pinnacle. While not an instant threat to Hogan and company, he earned enough his first season to pay off the relatives and friends. The source of his early income was not the

PGA-certified tournaments, however. The rules barred any newcomer from receiving any tournament money for the first six months; not that Arnold had much of a claim, since his best were a handful of sixth and tenth places as well as a more distant seventeenth and even a fortieth. Instead, he picked up cash in the non-PGA pro-ams that frequently preceded major tournaments.

On the strength of his U.S. Amateur victory, the Masters invited him to Augusta and he finished a credible tenth, good for 696 dollars. (The Masters fell outside of the PGA tournament schedule, being operated entirely by its own authorities.) And when his six months in limbo ended, Palmer began to score. Most of his achievements were modest but there was a Canadian Open victory worth 2,400 dollars. At the close of 1955, he counted 8,226 dollars in PGA money. That stuck him well down on the earnings list, far below his college contemporaries Mike Souchak and Gene Littler, each of whom pocketed more than 29,000 dollars.

Three years later, Arnold's PGA take surpassed 45,000 dollars, and most importantly, he won his first major event. The site was Augusta National, whose green jacket trophies soon crowded Palmer's closet. Until the 1958 Masters, Palmer, while collecting a more than adequate number of dollars from the tour, had failed to score impressively in the major events, the ones that gave Nelson, Snead, and Hogan their stature.

A 68 in the third round of the Masters lifted Palmer to a tie with Snead, now a robust forty-six year old. For the final eighteen, Palmer paired up with Ken Venturi and when Snead faded, Arnold became the hare, Venturi the hound on his traces. The twosome teed off on the 155-yard twelfth, with the pin tucked away in a corner of the green protected in front by Rae's Creek and a rough adjoining the bunker behind.

Both players determined not to fall short. Venturi's ball glanced off the wall of rough and kicked back into the green. With two putts he had his par 3. Palmer's shot, however, struck the embankment low and dug its way into water-soaked turf. Because of heavy rains from the evening and morning, the tournament committee had decreed players could lift, clean, and drop without penalty any ball that buried itself in its own pitch-mark "through the green." Clearly any place other than the tee, green, water hazards, or traps, was covered by the language and Palmer was entitled to a lift. However, the official at the twelfth hole seemed not to have gotten the word. Unmoved by debate, he insisted Arnold play it as it lay. Palmer hacked at the ball, moving it a bare 2 feet. He then chipped poorly, and needed 2 putts for a 5. To the surprise of onlookers, Palmer returned to the point where his tee shot landed, dropped an "alternate" over his shoulder. He chipped dead on and sank the putt for what would be a 3. The question, however, was which score counted, 5 or 3?

The pair of contenders now confronted the 475-yard thirteenth with the sinister Rae's Creek lying in wait just below the green. Venturi, shorter than his companion off the tee, elected to lay up short of the stream with his second stroke. He planned to attack for the bird with his chip. Palmer, as usual, had boomed far down the course. Instead of opting for safety, he choked up slightly on his 3-wood and ripped into the ball. It screamed down the fairway, glided across the creek to land at the green's edge, and then coasted smoothly over the turf to a point 15 feet from the cup.

As he marched towards his ball, Palmer entered a walking discussion with one of Augusta's foremost authorities on the rules governing the contretemps on the twelfth. On the thirteenth green, however, Palmer shoved that business from his mind, concentrated on his putt and smacked it into the heart of the cup for an eagle. Two holes later, he received official notice that his card rightfully should bear a "3" for the twelfth. Coupled with his eagle, Palmer had an insurmountable lead.

The 1958 Masters established Palmer as a fellow of considerable, if reckless, skill. But the reign of Arnold truly began in 1960. It started with the Masters, where despite an opening round of 67, Palmer only led by a single stroke when the last day

dawned. He fell off the pace and after twelve holes trailed Venturi and Dow Finsterwald by a one. It was now birdie time, and the prime candidates were thirteen and fifteen, 475 and 520 yards in length, eminently accessible to a long hitter like Arnold Palmer.

Yet Palmer missed out on both. He overpowered on the thirteenth, banging his second shot across the green and into a trap. On the fifteenth his drive left him blocked by some trees and a deliberate hook with a 1-iron worked only partially.

Finsterwald had fallen out of contention as Palmer came to the seventeenth but Venturi was in the clubhouse with that one-stroke lead. Neither of the remaining two holes yielded easily to sub-par play and when he gave himself a 27 footer on seventeen the possibility there seemed remote. He lined up the shot, addressed the ball, then stepped away. He returned to the task, again readied the stroke, then walked off. The dreaded yips appeared to have struck. A third time he assumed his stance, and resolutely tapped the ball. It broke right, headed straight for the cup only to pause at the lip. But then it fell. He was even with Venturi.

In what was to be typical Palmer fashion, the birdie triggered streaky success. He followed a handsome drive on eighteen with a 6-iron that missed the pin by 2 feet before backspin spun it away, about 5 feet off. After he canned the putt, this Mas-

(Above) *Arnold curls in a tournament clinching putt at the 1960 U.S. Open.* (COURTESY JOHN G. ZIMMERMAN *SI.*)

(Below) *While Palmer won the Open at Cherry Hills in 1960, Tommy Bolt, the 1958 champion, demonstrated the into-the-pond club chuck. Notice the arm extension, the two-handed grip, the weight shift.* (COURTESY JOHN G. ZIMMERMAN, *SI.*)

ters was his, thanks to the birdie–birdie mini-charge in the final reel.

When Arnold went on to Cherry Hills in Denver for the National Open and delivered a sustained attack to card an incredible 30 for the front nine of the final day, what had been a rag-tag band of followers enlisted in Arnie's Army for the duration.

For the next five years, Palmer became the man to follow, the man to beat. Not since Walter Hagen had any golfer so caught the fancy of the fans. The hordes rooting for Arnold, often to the detriment of challengers, dwarfed the fandom of Sir Walter, playing in the primitive days of tournament golf and without the benefit of TV to capture his histrionics and derring-do.

Purists critiqued his stroke, describing it as "a lunge." "His swing is too fast, too violent, too lacking aesthetically," scoffed one authority. Others equally expert ignored the artistic failing. "If I ever needed an 8-foot putt and everything I owned depended on it," said Bobby Jones, "I would want Arnold Palmer to putt it for me."

The only major championship to escape Arnold was the PGA where three times he finished second. Still, he added two more Masters after 1960 as well as a pair of British Opens in '61 and '62. Cash values have always impressed American sports fans and Palmer added to his stature by piling up the bucks. He was the first golfer to pass the 100,000 dollar mark in annual earnings, the first to reach the 1 million dollars total mark reward. When he signed up for management under a Cleveland attorney, Mark McCormack, he also became the prototype of a new kind of financially powerful athlete. Indeed, because he breached the old fiscal frontiers, the annual trophy awarded to the tour's leading money winner was named for him in 1980.

The adoration of Arnold that burst into full-throated passion in 1960 coincides with another American love affair, that for the newly elected President John F. Kennedy. Perhaps no other individuals so embodied the buzzword of the day, "charisma." In both instances there was the feeling, expressed by JFK, that "the torch is passed" to another generation. The men Palmer

supplanted were not that many years his seniors but he stamped out the last embers of the pre-war firecrackers—Hogan, Snead, Middlecoff, and the like. Like the new man at the White House, Palmer exuded not only youth but also confidence and daring, commodities suddenly in demand after the cautious and "silent" 50s.

At the same time Arnold Palmer began to swashbuckle through the tournament thickets, several more representatives of the former British Empire followed the footsteps of Bobby Locke. It had taken some twenty years, but the prediction of Gene Sarazen that golfers from down under would come to challenge the very best began with the appearance of a curly-headed Australian, Peter Thomson.★

While Palmer was copping his U.S. Amateur and embarking on his professional career, Thomson mopped up abroad, winning three straight British Opens, 1954–1956, losing in '57 to Locke before adding a fourth Open at Royal Lytham, England. With his victory in the 1965 event, Thomson tied J. H. Taylor for five titles, a figure exceeded only by Harry Vardon's six.

Thomson revived arguments about the best way to practice. For many players, Ben Hogan's endless hours repeating particular shots were a revealed truth, in light of Hogan's accomplishments. Thomson took a tactical approach and explained his philosophy:

> . . . it's stupid to rely on the mechanical theory that what you did on the practice ground will repeat automatically on the course. The circumstances are entirely different. The view from the tee must affect you. Suddenly there are bunkers and out-of-bounds to think about. . . . My purpose in the practice round is to learn where the serious trouble is and to get the pace of the course, how the ball is bouncing.

Thomson, like others from abroad, fared better in British tournaments where the smaller ball and the low, running shots were less familiar to Americans. Although Thomson never captured an American major, he persistently scored well enough to make his appearances on the tour extremely profitable. And in the Canada Cup, an international test begun in 1953, Thomson and his fellow Aussie, Kel Nagle, prevailed twice.

The global bonhomie generated by the Canada Cup competition inspired Joe Dey and company at the USGA to create a world amateur championship. The Royal and Ancient enthusiastically agreed to the concept and thirty-two countries signed up. In honor of the White House resident, the competition was christened the Eisenhower Trophy. In the first incarnation, Australia again asserted its growing strength as four amateurs from down under tromped on the U.S. delegates in a playoff. Thereafter, the U.S. flexed its mettle, with such representatives as Deane Beman, Bob Gardner, William Hyndman III, Billy Joe Patton, and Jack Nicklaus.

Meanwhile, the success in the U.S. denied to invaders Henry Cotton, Bobby Locke, and Peter Thomson, could not be refused to the diminutive South African who first showed up in the late 1950s. Gary Player★

was only twenty when he wowed Britons with a stunning average of 67.5 strokes for five rounds to win, in a playoff, his first pro event in England. Subsequently, when he ventured to the U.S., Player became almost instantly recognizable on the courses, a small man totally dressed in black who whacked the ball a more than respectable distance.

Gary had realized early he would need to compensate for his lack of size if he were ever to compete against the longer hitting, bigger men. He declared: "Whoever thought of that silly expression, 'Drive for show and putt for dough,' did not understand modern golf."

He added megawatts of power through an intensive schedule of body building techniques. He ran daily, long before the infatuation with jogging. He strengthened his hands via fingertip pushups. He sweated through various exercises designed for arm and back development, and adopted various diets calculated to preserve and enhance his physique. First, he ate raisins

(Above) *Counting his one U.S. Amateur championship, Palmer captured eight major tournaments, but the PGA title escaped him entirely.* (COURTESY BETTMANN/UPI NEWSPHOTOS.)

(Above) *"He [Arnold Palmer] can take between 5,000 and 10,000 pounds for giving a golf clinic or turning up to play at a company outing, and in Palmer's case particularly, the millions rolled in from the use of his name in promoting products that had no direct connection with golf. All this in essence derived from the drama of the man's play; the fact that he swung a driver with such patent violence; that his recoveries from rough and woodland caused both turf and bushes to fly; and not least, that he was an aggressive putter—in watching most players, one is aware that putting is a matter of some delicacy, of coasting the ball up to the hole. Palmer almost gave it a bang, confident that if he went a few feet past, there would be no problem in getting the return putt in."—Michael Hobbs,* In Celebration of Golf. (COURTESY UPI/BETTMANN NEWSPHOTOS.)

for good health, then decided their sugar damaged his teeth. Bananas became the food of choice. He feasted on wheat germ, ordered his bacon burned for easier digestion, and stood on his head on the theory that the increased blood flow to the brain boosted mental alertness. In an ambience noted more for the pleasures of the nineteenth hole than reverie, he cited four books as profoundly influencing him: *The Bible, The Power of Positive Thinking, Imitation of Christ,* and *Yoga and Health.*

Player showed a natural affinity for the game. He took it up at fourteen and parred his first three holes. By age seventeen he had turned pro. When he began, a pronounced hook afflicted him due to his grip and a stance well away from the ball. He shifted his hands to reduce the hook but throughout his career his ball tended to start out towards his right before a midcourse correction towards the fairway center. In his practice habits, Player was the spiritual son of Hogan. No one ever hit more balls to perfect a particular shot. A South African pro remembered seeing the teenage Player working on his bunker problems at 6 A.M. and, when the pro passed by at noon, the youngster was still sand bound. Late in his career, however, he declared that practice tired a golfer.

In contrast to Peter Thomson's notion, Gary Player would create tactical laboratory situations. He would set up an obstacle of a tree branch and try to punch the ball beneath it ten straight times. If he hit the limb, the exercise would start all over. Before heading for Great Britain, Player deliberately seized opportunities to play in South African downpours, the better to acclimate himself to British weather conditions.

He insisted one must master all of the available weapons.

A golfer should never stop using a certain club because he believes he cannot use it well. It's best to practice your inability; chances are the swing errors that are causing the trouble with that club will creep into the rest of the game.

He had a reputation for leaving nothing to chance: checking the depth of the soil above the cup; examining the wear of grass on the basis of the frequency of putts from one side or the other; diagnosing the direction of the grain from dead blades of grass, caused by cutting that severed root systems.

A psychiatrist might mumble about an obsessive-compulsive personality, but Player's way cashed impressive dividends. With his first British Open title behind him in 1959, Player mounted his first truly successful campaign in the U.S. in 1961. He challenged Arnold Palmer early in April at the Masters. They were all even after thirty-six holes. But Palmer slipped in the third round while Player carded a 69 to give him a comfortable four-stroke lead for the finale.

Slowly, however, the lead eroded in the face of a Palmer charge and a Player falter. In particular, on thirteen, with Rae's Creek lying in wait, the South African tried for one of those whiz bang recoveries, a real life application of his experiments. He planned to punch a ball beneath the abundant pine growth blocking the green. But he duck hooked into the water and double bogied. Even the most focused of individuals might have been shaken, particularly as Player then added another bogey, which put Palmer 1 ahead. All Arnold needed over the final five were pars.

He rattled off four of them, then miscalculated slightly on the par 4 eighteenth. His 7-iron carried too far to the right and landed in a trap. He was still in position, however. Player had gotten down in 2 from that very same location moments before. Palmer sprang out of the trap, far too hard. When the ball finally halted it had crossed the green and rolled down an incline until it was 25 feet away from the cup. Now he needed to 2-putt just for a draw. He plotted the rub of the green perfectly but smacked it much too hard, leaving himself a 15-footer. When Arnold missed that shot to double bogey, Player had backed into his first Masters victory.

He demonstrated in the following months he was no fluke, as he outearned Palmer for the 1961 tour. Gary's next major victory in the U.S. was the 1962 PGA champion-

(Opposite, right) *The Palmer putt posture knocked his knees.* (COURTESY CLARK'S PHOTOGRAPHY.)

(Above) *"Player is gifted, of course, but I hardly think he is overburdened with natural ability. His immense success comes from hard work, and a capacity to concentrate on the job in hand given to few.... On the putting green, and with an iron club in his hand, he has an agreeable style, and is at all times well balanced, but strangely enough when it comes to wooden-club shots he hits out so hard that he loses his poise, and therefore from a distance it is hard to detect whether or not he is pleased with the shot. I cannot see that the extra yard or two he gains by this violence is worthwhile." —Leonard Crawley,* London Daily Telegraph, *October 18, 1965.*

Gary Player counts twenty-one USPGA tournament wins, nine majors, and altogether 130 victories around the world. (COURTESY UPI/ BETTMANN NEWSPHOTOS.)

(Right) *"I loved Westerns and the cowboys always looked good in black." —Gary Player.* (COURTESY UPI/BETTMANN NEWSPHOTOS.)

ship. He was the first foreigner to take that title. And in 1965 he became the first visitor since Ted Ray in 1920 to become U.S. Open champion.

The site was the Bellerive Country Club in St. Louis, one of the new tournament-level courses designed by Robert Trent Jones. Gary got out in front after thirty-six holes and with only three to play in the tournament, he held a margin of 3 over the Australian, Kel Nagle. But when he double bogied the par-3 sixteenth while Nagle chopped one off the standard for seventeen, it became a tie. The playoff was an anticlimax; Nagle missed fairways, twice driving balls into the spectators. The only surprise occurred at the presentation when Player donated his entire prize, giv-

ing 5,000 dollars to cancer research and 20,000 dollars to the USGA for the promotion of junior work.

In this same season, Player, along with countryman Harold Henning, brought South Africa first place in the Canada Cup. In fact, of all of the golfers in his era, Player won more major events around the world than anyone, adding to his three British Opens (1959, '68, and '74) the Piccadilly World Match Play Championship in England on five occasions, the Egyptian Match Play Championship, the Japan Air Lines Open, the Australian Open six times, that country's PGA twice, and the Brazilian Open twice.

The stamina from his intensive physical conditioning program paid off in 1978. An ancient forty-two year old, Player was not considered much of a threat to an excellent field at the Masters. When the final round began he lay a large 7 strokes off the pace, well behind the 1977 U.S. Open victor, Hubert Green, a streaking Rod Funseth, two years Player's senior, and a new titan, Stanford graduate Tom Watson.★

With the leaders scheduled to tee off later, hardly anyone watched Player start his last round. He steadily chopped strokes off par, going out in a distinguished 34 and then birdying six of the final nine for a fantastic 30. The mark he set allowed no margin for error to those who followed. Watson could have tied with a par on eighteen but when he hooked into the trees he was a goner. Funseth and Green needed birdies on eighteen to tie. Both missed the requisite putts, Funseth by a hair from 20 feet and Green by inches from less than a yard off. Player would be the oldest fellow to take the Masters until the 1986 triumph of forty-six-year-old Jack Nicklaus.

Further evidence of golf's global grip was the appearance of one of the best traveled and most durable pros since Ha-gen and Sarazen spread the gospel. Born into modest circumstances in Buenos Aires, Roberto De Vincenzo★ began somewhere beneath the bottom rung of the ladder, as a caddie's assistant.

De Vincenzo won Argentina's Open and its PGA in 1944 before testing the waters in the U.S. in 1947. He dueled Ben Hogan in his prime and twenty years later outshot Jack Nicklaus by two strokes to become British Open champ. In between, De Vincenzo locked up five more of his native land's Opens, the French Open thrice, the Belgian Open, the Dutch Open, the Mexican Open three times, the Spanish Open and the Brazilian Open on four occasions. De Vincenzo, a very popular pro on the tour, captured more than 200 tournaments around the world.

In the United States he had seventeen victories but he is probably best remembered for a mistake on the scorecard that cost him a playoff shot at the Masters. Starting the last eighteen of the 1968 Augusta fiesta, one stroke behind Bob Goalby, De Vincenzo banged home an eagle on the very first hole. He nearly birdied two and three as well with a chip and a wedge,

"Playing against him, you begin hoping he'll be on grass rather than in sand. From grass you expect him to pitch the ball close. From a bunker you're afraid he'll hole it out."—Jack Nicklaus, Golf Magazine, *1982.* (COURTESY UPI/BETTMANN NEWSPHOTOS.)

"[Roberto] De Vincenzo had a devotion approaching that of Ben Hogan to the art and the delights of striking a golf ball as well as is humanly possible. Hogan liked to get away to remote parts of the practice ground and seek perfection; de Vicenzo was more companionable but it was still his routine to hit balls for four hours and then go out for a round once he was satisfied. He paid equal attention to his putting, but here there was something of a desperation about the hours spent. He was looking for a stroke that would get the ball into the hole more frequently, that would not break down when the pressures of competition were at a height. He did not hope for perfection."
—Michael Hobbs, Great Opens.
(COURTESY UPI/BETTMANN NEWSPHOTOS.)

both of which sat the ball down within 2 feet of the cups. He went on to birdie eight, twelve, and thirteen. On the seventeenth hole, a par 4, De Vincenzo sank his third shot to cut off one more stroke, so it was thought. He decided to play eighteen safe, taking a bit off the drive to stay in the fairway. But his second shot with a 4-iron hooked through the crowd and bumped down a well-trod path 30 feet from the green. He used his putter and knocked it 5 feet from home. But when he flubbed the putt and took a bogey, the irritated De Vincenzo hardly looked as he signed the card. It was to be a fatal error for his companion, Tommy Aaron, had mistakenly given him a 4 for the seventeenth instead of his birdie 3. De Vincenzo signed off on a 66 instead of his actual 65. The false figure gave him a total of 278.

Meanwhile, Goalby had come to eighteen seemingly needing a par to beat De Vincenzo. When he pushed his 3-wood off the tee into the trees he could have been doomed. But the ball rebounded smack in the middle of the fairway. Goalby rifled a

2-iron onto the green and 2 putted for a triumphant 277. Had Aaron marked the Argentinian's card correctly, he too would have toted up a 277. Under the rules of the USGA, a player who signs his card with an error in his favor is disqualified. If the mistake, however, is against the player, the overage simply becomes official. De Vincenzo thus finished one behind. Later that spring, the Argentinian retired after posting the low card in the Houston Open.

Almost, but not quite, buried in the hoopla of Palmer and his overseas rivals, one of his collegiate contemporaries, Gene Littler, steadily stroked his way toward the head of the pack. After taking the National Amateur in 1953, he boldly challenged for the U.S. Open at Baltusrol the following year. He finished one strike down to Ed Furgol. (The winner himself was a story of pluck. A journeyman tour competitor, Furgol forged an effective swing despite a permanently bent left arm, the residue of a childhood accident.)

Over the years, Littler was doomed to come up a mite short in the majors, finishing in the top ten twenty times, but copping the prize only in the 1961 Open. On the other hand, Littler salted away a total of twenty-nine PGA-recognized titles.

Littler accepted his role as a part of the hero's entourage. On one occasion he remarked, "I drew a big gallery today. I was paired with Palmer."

Still, his contemporaries recognized his fine stroke. After watching Littler on the practice tee, Tommy Aaron said, "Doesn't take long for a Rolls-Royce to warm up, does it?"

Perhaps his most significant triumph came after surgery for cancer in the spring of 1972. By autumn, he was back on the tour and his comeback was honored with the Bob Jones and Ben Hogan awards in 1973.

The professional sport had begun to overwhelm the amateur version in the 1930s, and with the end of WWII the trend became the dominant mode. Few excellent players could resist the lure of larger and larger sums of cash. One who did was William Campbell,★ the pride of West Vir-

ginia. His degree in history and his collegiate golf at Princeton were temporarily delayed by service as an infantry captain. But once demobilized he returned both to his studies and to golf as an avocation.

Only Chick Evans, with his forty qualifications for the U.S. Amateur, competed in that event more than Campbell, who entered on thirty-seven occasions. In 1964, at age forty-one, he finally won, adding that trophy to fifteen West Virginia Amateur titles, and three of his home state opens. Campbell appeared in the Masters and U.S. Open many times, and served on Walker Cup squads on eight meetings with the foreign rivals, captaining the team in 1955.

Campbell, a businessman in West Vir-

ginia, also served for three years as head of the USGA. He accepted his honor as the third American nominated to be captain of the Royal and Ancient with a sense of mission, which he expressed in an interview with John M. Olman in *Golfiana*:

One of the things I spoke for [when asked his hopes for the coming year] was a reaffirmation of the manners that go with golf. Not that they're in jeopardy, but just to remind ourselves that it's a game of relationships and of dignity and self-respect. It's an honorable game, an honorable institution, if you will, so that people shouldn't need policemen to keep them straight. That goes with being a golfer.

"Perhaps the desire to improve is greater in golfers than in any other sportsmen, possibly because there are other opponents besides your fellow-competitor. There is the constant battle against par and the even greater struggle within yourself."—Gary Player, quoted in The Golfer's Bedside Book. (COURTESY UPI/BETTMANN NEWSPHOTOS.)

Dan Jenkins on
ARNOLD PALMER

Arnold Palmer may have meant more to golf than anyone in history, including Mary Queen of Scots, who did not invent the game, according to the Dutch, the French, and most Scotsmen.

Arnold Palmer, in fact, invented golf on television.

Arnold Palmer, in fact, invented increased prize money for touring professionals.

Arnold Palmer, in fact, took golf to the masses.

Arnold Palmer, in fact, invented sweating, the shirttail coming out, visor-tossing, "going for it," driving the ball through tree trunks, sinking unmakable putts, and all the while being nice to everybody. Arnold Palmer invented nice.

Arnold Palmer, in fact, invented agent-managers when he shook hands with Mark McCormack one day on the Augusta National veranda. And Mark McCormack invented money.

Arnold Palmer, in fact, had a lot to do with inventing Jack Nicklaus by losing to him at a time when the public demanded otherwise.

Arnold Palmer did all these things in the course of inventing Arnold Palmer, and it is difficult to imagine that anyone could have enjoyed being Arnold Palmer more than Arnold has.

For more than thirty years he has been Arnold Palmer, the biggest name in town when he came to town, and the biggest name on the golf course when he was on the golf course.

Being Arnold Palmer meant that Arnold never had to apologize for not winning, even after he stopped winning.

Name another athlete in any other sport who can claim this. You can't.

Arnold *was* and Arnold *is*.

It all came about in the late 1950s because the sport of golf needed a hero. The consistently winning days of Ben Hogan and Sam Snead were behind them. Who would fill the void?

That it would turn out to be someone named Arnold D. Palmer of Latrobe, Pennsylvania, was something nobody could have guessed, for at the time it was looking as if Ken Venturi and Gene Littler were the heir apparents.

Even when Arnold won the first of his four Masters tournaments in 1958, it was regarded as something of a fluke. Then as now, one major didn't make a star, and Arnold was still a guy in clashing colors with the cuffs of his slacks turned up, a guy who might make 6 or 8 birdies in a single round but would cancel them out with 6 or 8 bogeys, owning to his daring style of attacking a golf course.

Under the guidance of "Pap," his father and the Latrobe Country Club pro, the young Palmer led high school and college golf teams. (COURTESY RAY DAVIS.)

It wasn't until 1960 that he actually became Arnold Palmer, the Arnold of "Whoo-ha, go get 'em, Arnie!"

This was the spring that Arnold birdied the last two holes in the final round of the Masters to beat Venturi by a stroke, to capture his second Masters. It was also the year that he came from fourteen players and 7 strokes behind with a blazing 65 in the last round to win the U.S. Open championship at Cherry Hills in Denver.

Only three other men had won the Masters and the U.S. Open in the same year and Ben Hogan was two of them.

Arnold's victory in the Open probably did more for his reputation than anything else, and it certainly provided golfing lore with a gem.

Before the final eighteen on "Open Saturday" that June in Denver, Arnold had lunch with a couple of writer friends. One was Bob Drum of the *Pittsburgh Press*, the other happened to be myself, then a servant of the old *Fort Worth Press*.

(Right) *Winnie Palmer stuck with her husband's decision to turn pro and abandon a promising career as a golf-playing paint salesman.* (COURTESY PGA OF AMERICA.)

(Below) *"For Arnold Palmer, it's let it go or let it blow—all or nothing. This man just don't know when to play safe."—caddie Nathaniel Avery.* (COURTESY PGA OF AMERICA.)

(Right) *"The foundation of his [Arnold Palmer's] huge success as a golfer is the strength of his response to challenge and competition, and as a person the genuine, unaffected warmth of his response with whom he comes in contact. . . . Palmer's greatness as a competitor stems from his reaction to challenge in any form. The difficult recovery, the telling putt, the long dangerous carry, the desperate situation when all seems lost; any form of adversity is adrenalin to him. With a hitch of the pants and a grim smile he gets to work; his attitude is that of a man fighting and loving it—as indeed he does."—Pat Ward Thomas,* The Golfer's Bedside Book. (COURTESY FRANK CHRISTIAN STUDIOS.)

(Left) *"Palmer usually walks to the first tee unlike any other pro. He doesn't walk on to it, as much as climb into it, almost as though it were a prize ring."—Will Grimsley, AP.* (COURTESY PGA OF AMERICA.)

(Below) *"If I ever needed an 8-foot putt and everything I owned depended on it, I would want Arnold Palmer to putt it for me."—Bobby Jones, quoted by Stanley Paul*, Masters of Golf.

In this instance, the putt brings a victory at the Masters. (COURTESY FRANK CHRISTIAN STUDIOS.)

Palmer combined the rare qualities of an intense champion with an accessibility to the media that added to his popularity. (COURTESY PGA OF AMERICA.)

The first hole at Cherry Hills had been bugging Arnold all week. It was a downhill par 4 that seemed reachable from the tee if a man could hit a career drive and bounce the ball through the USGA's high grass that guarded the entrance to the putting surface.

"I'm gonna drive that first green this afternoon," Arnold said in the locker room.

"Good," Drum said. "Maybe you can finish twelfth."

Arnold said, "If I drive the first green and get an eagle or a birdie, I might shoot 65. That would be 280. Doesn't 280 always win the Open?"

"Yeah," I grinned. "When Hogan shoots it."

Arnold went out on the course and promptly drove the first green and two-putted for a birdie. He then birdied the next three holes.

Bob Drum and I wandered out on the clubhouse veranda and saw his name go up on the scoreboard. Four birdies in a row for Arnold D. Palmer, Latrobe, Pa.

"Jesus Christ!" said Drum, and we took off running to catch Arnold at the fifth hole.

We caught up with him on the sixth tee, after he had merely parred the fifth. Out of breath, we climbed under the gallery ropes as our press armbands permitted.

"Fancy seeing you here," Arnold smiled.

Whereupon he birdied the sixth, then the seventh.

On the senior circuit, he blasts out of a trap. Palmer added more than a million dollars in winnings in his first ten years on the abbreviated tour. (COURTESY JOHN COLEY.)

Arnold was now 6 under par through the first seven holes—and leading the Open! He had zoomed past fourteen players, two of which were Ben Hogan and a beefy young amateur named Jack Nicklaus.

He turned with a remarkable 30 on the front nine and played even par over the last nine to post his 65, his 280, and win that Open. Along the way, Drum or I would get him a Coke, and I would loan him a cigarette—he was smoking in those days.

Over a span of seven years, Arnold won the Masters four times, the British Open twice, and that one U.S. Open; seven majors, in other words. From 1958 through 1964, he *was* golf. And it was during this period that the tournament purses began to double, triple, and quadruple, heading toward the million-dollar level they reached in the 1980s.

One thing about Arnold, for all the big bucks that came his way, he knew who had gone before him. Back in the 1960s they held a do for Walter Hagen. Palmer spoke for the touring pros when he remarked, "If it were not for you, Walter, this dinner would be downstairs in the pro shop and not in the ballroom." And it is largely because of Arnold, with help from Mark McCormack, that there are pros, including Palmer, who own a chunk of the pro shop, the ballroom, the course, and the surrounding real estate.

Simultaneously, Arnold single-handedly resurrected the British Open by simply entering it, returning it to the major status it had once enjoyed in the days of Bobby Jones and Walter Hagen. Other American stars began following Palmer to England and Scotland.

Thus, Arnold must also be given credit for establishing what has come to be recognized as the modern professional Grand Slam, the Big Four, or what *would be* a Grand Slam if anyone could take all four in the same year.

So far, Arnold has come as close as anyone. Back in 1960, after winning the Masters and U.S. Open, he went to St. Andrews and lost by a single stroke to Kel Nagle in the British Open, thereby ending his chance at it.

Strangely, Arnold has almost been as good at losing as he was at winning. Part of his charm, one supposes.

One of his most memorable losses came at Augusta in 1961. He needed only a par at the seventy-second to win back-to-back Masters tournaments but implausibly hit into a bunker and made a double bogey 6 to give the title to Gary Player.

"I was in too big of a hurry to win it," was all he said about it later.

In the 1966 U.S. Open at the Olympic Club in San Francisco, Arnold blew the championship so badly and so incredulously, it is hard to recall that Billy Casper's name is in the record book.

Dominating the tournament and the headlines from start to finish, Arnold was a whopping 7 strokes ahead of the field with only nine to play, and later on 5 strokes ahead with only four to play, and yet he found a way to hook some tee shots and hack around in the rough and permit Casper to tie him, then beat him in the playoff.

And what did Arnold say of this?

He said, "I was thinking about Hogan's seventy-two-hole record and forgot there was another guy on the golf course."

As usual, the affable Palmer found time to chat with fans during a seniors tournament. (COURTESY JOHN COLEY.)

This was the third Open playoff Arnold had lost in five years. Nicklaus had beaten him at Oakmont in '62, Julius Boros had beaten him at The Country Club in Brookline, Massachusetts, in 1963, and now Casper at Olympic.

In those days, Arnold had a coffee table in his home at Latrobe inlayed with all the gold medals he had won in various tournaments. Visiting him one day, I noticed that the table included the three silver medals for being a runnerup in the U.S. Open.

"What are those silver medals doing in here?" I asked him.

"Well, they aren't bad looking," he said.

Reminders, I thought. Reminders of other majors he should have won.

For several years, Arnold wondered why some of us called him "Bubba."

It went back to a day in Augusta, Georgia, during a Masters in the early 1960s. As Arnold stood over a birdie putt on the fourth green, Drum and I overheard a Southern fan say to himself, "You make this one, Bubba, and you the leader of the tribe."

Arnold could always laugh. He has always laughed at the fact that nobody who knew him ever called him "Arnie." Arnie was the man in the headlines, the general of "Arnie's Army." Winnie, his wife, usually calls him "Arn," and his friends mostly know him as Arnold.

One afternoon he doubled over with laughter on the seventy-second tee when he was leading by 6 strokes and poised to win his fourth Masters.

That day, he was paired with Dave Marr, a good friend on the tour, a player who was about to finish second in the tournament and make a very handsome (and much needed) check.

As Arnold addressed his ball, he said to Dave, "Anything I can do to help you here?"

"Yeah," said Marr. "Make a twelve."

Though gray-haired today, Arnold Palmer is a trim, bronze, vigorous figure, as friendly and cooperative as ever, and surely one of the richest athletes who ever lived. His golf course design business flourishes, as does most any business endeavor he goes near, but the Arnold Palmer *I* know is still happiest when he's out on a golf course or on a practice range beating balls.

Nobody before or since ever mustered such a massive band of loyal rooters. It's partly because everyone recognizes that mysterious fury with which Arnold would rally himself, and partly because of the nobility with which he has carried himself when he lost.

"Arnie's Army" is a phrase coined long ago by a sportswriter named Johnny Hendrix in the *Augusta Chronicle*, and now that Arnold has passed sixty—a bald spot peeking through the gray, a senior on the tour packaged for seniors, walking a step slower up to still-one-more green—the Army now includes those who never saw him in his prime. But it salutes. The Army applauds not for the shot he'll hit or the score he'll shoot but for what he gave the game and them.

Of all the greats who have come before him and after him, there was never one in his prime who created so much suspense and drama when he addressed a shot. One way or another, you knew something was going to happen.

18

Claimants, Nobles, and Pretenders

The advent of Gary Player on the American scene coincided with the gathering momentum of the U.S. Civil Rights movement. As a citizen of South Africa, Player became an occasional target for demonstrators. He was neither an apostle nor apologist for apartheid, but the time had finally come for golf in the U.S. to let down its barriers.

According to Al Barkow, at the second U.S. Open in 1896, one participant was a caddie named John Shippen whose father was a West Indian black, and whose mother was a Shinnecock Indian. A second outsider among the white professionals was Oscar Bunn, a full-blooded Shinnecock. The Caucasian professionals threatened to quit the Open if Shippen played. (Organized baseball had drawn its color line a decade earlier.)

Theodore Havemeyer, the sugar king and first president of the USGA, issued his own ultimatum. Nothing in the USGA constitution defined eligibility in terms of race. Either the pros teed off, or Shippen and Bunn would be the only competitors. The rebels surrendered and the entire field played. Shippen, after sharing the first round lead, finished fifth behind Jim Foulis. Shippen entered two more Opens without incident but on both occasions placed low in the standings.

Over the years, people of color teed off in a handful of major events. But the PGA Constitution of 1916, in Article Three, Section One, dictated that only Caucasians could be members.

In the days before World War II, the question of nonwhites competing in tournaments, much less being admitted to membership in country clubs, was never raised. Even in those few instances where nonwhites might have been welcomed in a country club, the economic circumstances of non-Caucasians meant a dearth of candidates. The Michigan delegation to the PGA in 1943 reinforced the prohibition on nonwhites with a resolution to that effect.

Shut out by the established organizations, the nonwhites, just as in baseball, in 1928 created their own group, the United Golf Association, with twenty-six clubs as members. The first UGA National Open went to Pat Ball, who collected a 100-dollar first prize. Loosely formed regional groups such as the Eastern Golf Association also held tournaments.

No black pro could possibly survive on the take from the tiny tour, nicknamed the "peanut circuit." The only significant events that accepted them were the U.S. Open, Western Open, Los Angeles Open, and the Tam O'Shanter. But without either championship-course facilities or sustained high-level competition, and because economics as well as social barriers reduced the pool of nonwhite golfers to a mere drop, white supremacy in golf went unthreatened. Bill Spiller, among the best of them, survived as a redcap. Ted Rhodes earned his keep as the traveling pro for the best-known nonwhite golfer of the 1930s and '40s, heavyweight champion Joe Louis.* Sugar Ray

"The most famous black golfer between World War II and 1970 was cigar-chomping Charlie Sifford from Charlotte, North Carolina. Sifford hustled bets like the other pros from anyone foolish enough to play with him, and he was a fixture at UGA events. 'We didn't have no other way to play,' he observed. Black newspapers, which had begun sponsoring golf tournaments, lowered their contributions if Sifford were not entered."—Arthur Ashe, The Black Athlete. (COURTESY UPI/BETTMANN NEWSPHOTOS.)

---

*The fighter frequently entered the Tam O'Shanter. There was no shortage of white professionals willing to go a practice round or two with him. It was not his celebrity they admired as much as that Louis was golf's all-time, champion patsy, hustled for thousands upon thousands of dollars.

"All I had was a stupid head, a raggedy golf game, and determination to be a golfer; one of the best in the world, not a black golfer."—Charlie Sifford, quoted in The Black Athlete. (COURTESY UPI/ BETTMANN NEWSPHOTOS.)

had been regulars in professional football for half a dozen years, Bill Spiller (who had won the UGA title four times), Ted Rhodes and Madison Gunter, challenged, then sued the PGA and the Richmond (California) Golf Club for refusing their entries into a tournament. Spiller and Rhodes had both qualified with their previous week's finishes of twenty-fifth and eleventh in the Los Angeles Open. The PGA pledged to remove its "Caucasians only" restrictions in return for the golfers dropping the 315,000 dollar claim.

Over the following decades, a host of appeals to the courts, particularly on the heels of the 1954 *Brown* v. *Board of Education* decision, widened opportunities for nonwhite golfers. Municipalities that had sought to maintain segregation through building whites-only and blacks-only courses now yielded to legal pressure for integration.

In the mid-1950s, Charlie Sifford was the lone representative of black golfers, entering tournaments as an "approved player" rather than as a fully certified member of the PGA. In 1957, he won the first sanctioned event by a member of his race, the Long Beach (California) Open. Still, attitudes at tournaments in the South forced Sifford to detour for three months as the country clubs tried to avoid confrontation with local law by making "opens" into "invitationals."

There were signs of change in attitude at the PGA. Horton Smith, as president of the organization, paired himself in 1952 with Joe Louis at the San Diego Open. Gene Sarazen, Cary Middlecoff, and Bo Wininger, were among the professionals who spoke out on behalf of blacks seeking admission to the tour. But it was not until 1959 that the restrictive clause in the PGA constitution was formally removed. In the same year, Sifford fractured the Mason-Dixon line of resistance when he played in the Greensboro (North Carolina) Open. It was not a happy experience, said Sifford.

Robinson, often Louis's companion, hired his own instructor, Joe Roach. Singer Billy Eckstine employed a fellow named Charlie Sifford, who picked up a few more bucks selling clubs from the trunk of his car.

In 1948, a year after Jackie Robinson broke baseball's color line and when blacks

I had a good chance to get in the Masters if I finished good. And I was going good. Suddenly, I was intercepted by five white men who started following me around the course. They threw beer cans at me and called me "nigger" and other names. This went on for several holes, and the men were finally arrested, but after that I lost a lot of strokes and finished far down the list.

Sifford capped his career with the Los Angeles Open victory in 1969. Although his appearance on the tour was belated he managed to earn a total of 339,000 dollars on the circuit, and through the PGA Seniors' events of 1989, his take approached another 300,000 dollars.

The two most prominent male blacks after Sifford were Lee Elder and Calvin Peete. Elder benefited from the coaching of Lloyd Mangrum, who convinced Lee to abandon his cross-handed grip and obtained an assistant's job for him. Working the Peanut Circuit, he once won twenty-one of twenty-three events, but the prizes seldom amounted to more than 2,500 dollars. He supplemented his income hustling chumps, playing on one leg, from his knees, and in ninety-five-degree weather bundled in a zipped-up rainsuit. When he sank a long birdie putt on the fourth hole of a sudden death playoff in the 1974 Monsanto Open, Elder automatically qualified for the Masters, the first of his race to earn an automatic invite to that event. Cliff Roberts took pains to personally welcome Elder. During his thirty years as a PGA player and senior, Elder garnered well over 1 million dollars.

Peete was the first who had never caddied or played in the UGA. In fact, the best black golfer to date first laid club against ball at age twenty-three. An itinerant salesman to migrant farm workers, Peete seemed to suffer an insurmountable handicap apart from his age. As a child he broke his left arm. When the fracture failed to heal properly, Peete drew a permanent handicap: an inability to completely straighten the arm. The experts insisted the bent limb would prevent him from consistently hitting straight.

Joining the money chase so late and with family responsibilities, Peete hovered around the 20,000 dollars-a-year mark in earnings during the 1970s, barely enough to cover expenses. But in 1978, at thirty-five, he took his first tournament, the Greater Milwaukee Open, which Elder had won the year before. Peete's income soared to 122,481 dollars for the year. Like Elder he accepted a bid to a Ryder Cup team, and a decade after the initial win in Milwaukee, Peete drew a bead on the 2 million dollar mark in total PGA earnings.

Blacks continue to be an endangered species on the tour. During the 1970s, as many as a dozen Afro-Americans could be seen on the circuit. But in 1990, only Calvin Peete at forty-six, and Jim Thorpe, forty-two, were active. Peete has taken steps to remedy the lack of candidates. Through his Calvin Peete Minority Foundation, he hopes to raise money from corporations and pro-am events that will develop golf programs aimed at minority kids.

Unlike in baseball, the struggle for equality did not radically change the complexion of the scene. Economics and more subtle discrimination limited the golf experience of nonwhites.

Lee Elder chipped a huge chunk off the "whites only" wall at the Augusta National Course in 1975 as the first black to play in the Masters. (COURTESY UPI/BETTMANN NEWSPHOTOS.)

Elder relishes his first PGA victory, the Monsanto Open in 1975, which brought him a berth in the Masters. (COURTESY UPI/BETTMANN NEWS-PHOTOS.)

The issue boiled over onto front pages and the nightly news shows just before the 1990 PGA at Shoal Creek Golf Club in Birmingham, Alabama. Local civil rights groups threatened to picket the all-white club. Sponsors withdrew rather than risk a boycott or criticism. After considerable talk, the Club agreed to admit one or two people of color. To avoid conflicts in the future, both the PGA and the PGA Tour announced that the membership policies of clubs holding certified tournaments would be a factor. The aim was to pressure the private clubs to open their doors not only to people of color but also to women who were denied admittance.

The 1960s, '70s, and '80s were tempestuous times all across the United States, and the major team sports of baseball and football suffered through strikes and lockouts along with expensive, drawn-out battles in the courts of law. Professional golf, with every competitor in effect an independent contractor, was not beset by conflicts between capital and labor. However, there were ongoing differences between the touring pros and the other members of the PGA.

By 1979, Elder, here winning the 1976 Houston Open, was mainstream enough to play for the U.S. Ryder Cup team. (COURTESY UPI/ BETTMANN NEWSPHOTOS.)

One argument centered around the division of the TV spoils. A mini crisis arose in 1968 as leading tour players, including Jack Nicklaus, announced they would form the American Professional Golfers to operate their own circuit. The potential rupture was avoided with the establishment of the autonomous Tournament Players Division as part of the PGA. Joe Dey was installed as its commissioner.

After Dey, Deane Beman was chosen commissioner. During his stewardship, the tour faced the problem of an overabundance of fortune seekers on the circuit. Qualifying rounds were not enough to satisfy both the veterans and the newcomers. Previously, the top sixty winners and those who had made the cut the preceding week received an exemption to a PGA event. The solution, invoked in 1983, created an "all-exempt tour," with places reserved for the top 125 money winners from the previous year.

The size of the purses over more than forty weeks of tournament play, the ever swelling galleries, and the respectable (if less than spectacular) Nielsens for the TV coverage all have contributed to the elevation of the best of the pros into international celebrities. Back in 1940, Fred Corcoran, inspired by the monument to baseball at Cooperstown, New York, promoted a Golf Hall of Fame under the auspices of the PGA. In April 1941, PGA President Tom Walsh announced the first fourteen to be honored. The list included Bobby Jones, Francis Ouimet, Walter Hagen, and Gene Sarazen, but the bombs that fell on Pearl Harbor eight months later brought a twelve-year hiatus before more names were added. But since there was no visible Hall of Fame, the institution was more a back room than museum and nominations ended in 1982.

In 1974, an independent group opened a World Golf Hall of Fame in Pinehurst. The inductees included Jones, Sarazen, Hagen, and Ouimet from the PGA's 1940 list, plus Patty Berg, Ben Hogan, Byron Nelson, Jack Nicklaus, Babe Zaharias, Arnold Palmer, Gary Player, Sam Snead, and Harry Vardon. Subsequently, a real estate development firm bought out the original creators and in 1984, the PGA acquired the institution, which includes a museum of golf artifacts, such as ancient clubs, featheries, gutties, Walter Hagen's putter, a 23-ounce sand wedge with a concave face (the kind used by Bobby Jones), trophies, the earliest golf carts, and jackets for the Ryder Cup teams and for winning the Masters. Many of the oldest items came from collection of Laurie Auchterlonie, who had been curator of the World Golf Hall of Fame and Honorary Professional of the Royal and Ancient Golf Club at Saint Andrews.*

The museum also displays photographs and illustrations devoted to the history of the game and the illustrious enshrined there. Unlike the USGA's museum, the PGA expects to constantly add items for exhibition. In addition, the PGA World Golf Hall of Fame operates a research library with rare books that date back to the 16th century and which is valued at 2 million dollars. It has been enriched by the 5,000 volumes from the collection of golf antiquarian and bibliophile Otto Probst and contributions from noted historians like Herb Graffis, C. B. Clapcott, and Judge Earl Tilley. Not the least of the Hall's memorabilia are the personal files of the current curator, Ray Davis. Now seventy-eight, Davis first developed an interest in Scottish clubs when he was only ten years old. At a tender age, he prowled the libraries to locate antique dealers in New York who might have historical information on the sport. He has amassed his own unique photographic library, which adds to the pictures and illustrations possessed by the Hall of Fame.

According to Hall of Fame Director Peter R. Stillwell, the aim is to bring new exhibits to the institution constantly. "We never want anyone to say, 'I've been to the Hall of Fame. I don't need to go again.'" Toward that end, the storage rooms bulge with items, hundreds of antique clubs, more than 12,000 logoed balls, 500 tees in carrot, goblet, funnel, and trumpet shapes, and over 350 pieces of artwork. Stillwell declares, "We want the golf world to give as much thought to Pinehurst as baseball does to Cooperstown, as football does to Canton, as basketball does to Springfield. Since the PGA came into the picture, there's been a 360-degree change in attitude. People in golf understand now that the Hall of Fame is solid and headed toward bigger and better things."

One unique aspect of the Hall is a plan for a "hands-on" exhibit. Explains Stillwell, "A majority of the people who come to the Hall of Fame actually play the sport—they're not just spectators. We want to give them opportunities to participate, to have their swings analyzed, and to interact with teaching videos and other devices to

---

* The USGA maintains a museum at its headquarters, Golf House, in Far Hills, New Jersey. On display are the trophies for the major tournaments under its aegis, artwork, photographs, and artifacts covering the history of the sport. The R and A opened a new museum at St. Andrews in 1990.

(Left) *"For six years [Calvin] Peete was just another middle-of-the-road pack pro, one of the Tour's purest swingers and worst putters. Then, late last season as 1982 wound to a close, Peete suddenly turned one of those mystical corners in sport; he won four tournaments in four months and jumped to the top in every category; money ($318,470—fourth), victories (tied for first), and stroke average (70.33—second). Suddenly, Peete went from a heart-warming human-interest story to one of the half-dozen best golfers in the world."* —Tom Boswell, Strokes of Genius. (COURTESY UPI/BETTMANN NEWSPHOTOS.)

(Below) *By winning the Tournament Players Championship in 1985, Peete gained exempt status for ten years. A year earlier, he copped the Vardon Trophy for low average.* (COURTESY UPI/BETTMANN NEWSPHOTOS.)

help them improve their games. They will learn not only the history and background of golf but also something about the latest teaching techniques and equipment."

By 1990, sixty individuals had been named to the Hall. Nominees for the modern era are selected by a committee solely on the basis of achievement of the past twenty years. To be eligible, a player must have ten years of major competition and win 75 percent of the votes cast by members of the Golf Writers Association of America. Those whose careers ended before the modern era are chosen by a special committee appointed by the Golf Writers Association of America.*

Just as the pantheon at Pinehurst continued to grow, on the tournament trail there was a steady parade of new faces. In 1959, Billy Casper★ exploited his expertise with the high irons, particularly the seven, and a marvelous touch on the greens to succeed Tommy Bolt at Winged Foot, Mamaroneck, New York, as U.S. Open champion.

The tempestuous Bolt flashed thunder and lightning to the delight of the media but to the detriment of his game. On one occasion he supposedly faced a 325-yard shot and, when his caddie handed him a 3-iron, Bolt snarled that he wanted a 3-wood. The bag toter nervously explained to him that the iron was the only club left in the bag; Bolt had broken or hurled away all the

---

*The Ladies Professional Golf Association formed its own Hall of Fame. Nomination for modern players there turns on a formula of tournaments won and money earned.

others, with the exception of the putter and Tommy had broken its handle earlier.

Bolt was not the main U.S. Open contender in 1959. Instead, Ben Hogan, at forty-seven, and after having been runner-up in 1955 and '56, appeared grimly determined to stuff the whippersnappers in their place. Spotting Casper twenty years, Hogan trailed Casper by only a stroke after thirty-six holes, and by just 3 after fifty-four. But in the final round, age caught up with Hogan as he sagged to a 76 and tenth place. Meanwhile, Casper turned in a 74, hardly sensational but enough to eke out a 1-stroke victory over a fast-closing Bob Rosburg.

Casper owed his victory at Winged Foot to his art with a mallet-headed putter he'd never used before then. He 1-putted thirty-one greens—partially, of course, a result of adroit shots from the fairway—and only 3-putted once.

When he scored his Open win, Casper weighed in at a portly 212 pounds. Over the next few seasons, Casper struggled to maintain that same high level of play. Convinced nutrition affected his stroke, Casper slimmed down with a diet said to include swordfish, avocado pears, and buffalo meat. He gobbled large slices of the financial pie, ranking among the ten top money-winners for all but one of the fifteen years between 1956 and 1971. His consistency with all clubs, except for a tendency to smite the long irons so low his ball occasionally bolted across the green, granted him the Vardon Trophy for low-average five times over a nine-year stretch.

His steadiness and lack of emotion on the links hid his achievements from all but the cognoscenti. However, in the 1966 Open at the Olympic Country Club in San Francisco, he was pitted against the people's choice, Palmer, and his performance became very noticeable. Olympic, at 6,719 yards, was shorter than many championship layouts, but the moisture-laden ocean air dampened drives and long irons. A seeming 420-yard par 4 played more like a 440 yarder.

After two rounds, Palmer and Casper, tied at 137, had left the others in the dust. The USGA paired them on the third round, which saw Billy lose control of his driver, spray balls to the edge of trouble, and spend the afternoon scrambling. Palmer displayed brilliance much of the time and only an occasional lapse prevented a rout. The day ended with Palmer holding a comfortable three stroke advantage, thanks to his 70 and Casper's 73.

On Sunday, Palmer and Casper resumed their duel, Arnold blazed away in the front nine; his 32 lengthened his lead to a seemingly insurmountable 7. The only question was whether Palmer could smash the record of 276 Ben Hogan had scored in the 1948 Open. There seemed no way for Casper to save himself. And in fact, it was Palmer who rescued Casper. He bogeyed ten and thirteen. giving back a pair. Still, he held a margin of 5 with five to play.

After both parred fourteen, Palmer, still in hot pursuit of Hogan, charged on the 150-yard fifteenth. Said he:

I chose the bold shot, to go for the cup. Unfortunately, the ball hit an inch wrong, an inch or so the other way to the left, and it would have licked in to the left and held near the cup, in good birdie distance. But it went an inch or so the wrong way and trickled down into the trap on the right side. I blasted up onto the green and two-putted.

Meanwhile, his adversary had resorted to his faithful 7-iron and the ball plopped safely on the green. When he canned the long putt, he had a birdie and the lead had shrunk to 3 strokes, with three holes to play.

At that moment, Palmer says he finally took his eye off the hole and regarded the doughnut.

. . . it dawned on me that Billy Casper had a chance to win this tournament. But, to me, it didn't look like a very good chance. The sixteenth was a long, par-5—604 yards. . . . It was not an easy birdie hole. Neither was the seventeenth. The eighteenth was a possible birdie. So I didn't see him making up three shots in those three holes. . . .

As I stood on the sixteenth tee, I knew that I could play it safe and shut Billy off completely. I could take out a 1-iron and bump and nudge the ball down the fairway, keeping it under control—while sacrificing distance—and accepting that it would take three shots to get to the green. If I played it safe all the way, I'd be in a good position to two-putt and get my par. Then I thought of how I'd look to myself: "There goes Arnold Palmer, playing it safe with a one-iron when he's got a three-stroke lead with three holes to play. . . ."

I couldn't do it. I have to be aggressive. I have to play the hole as I *feel* it, not as somebody else plays it. So I decided to go for broke; to use my driver.

Few wielded a more deadly putter than Casper. Winning the 1959 Open at Winged Foot, he stroked a total of 114 times on the green, 30 less than par for the seventy-two holes. In 1966 at Olympic, Casper putted 117 times, 27 below par, and finished the regulation four rounds tied with Palmer. In the head-to-head match that followed, he walloped Arnold, 69–73. (COURTESY UPI/BETTMANN NEWSPHOTOS.)

(Opposite, top) *Peete sprays sand in the U.S. Open of 1986.* (COURTESY UPI/BETTMANN.)

(Opposite, bottom) *The PGA World Golf Hall of Fame in the woods of Pinehurst backs up Donald Ross's famous Number Two Course.* (COURTESY PGA WGHF.)

Charles Coody surprised the cognoscenti and the titans of the game with an upset win in the 1971 Masters. He followed up with first prize in the then-unofficial Tournament of Champions. (COURTESY UPI/BETTMANN NEWSPHOTOS.)

Broke is what he got. He pulled his drive into a stand of trees amid the rough. Again he chose valor instead of discretion, aiming for the green with a 3-iron. The rough overpowered him and he moved the ball only 75 yards, remaining mired in the tall grass.

From his vantage point Casper was pleasantly wondrous. "I was surprised when I saw Arnold take such a shallow club for his second shot, but nothing Arnold does really surprises me. When he is playing well, he feels he can do anything."

Palmer surrendered to caution, temporarily, poling a safe 9-iron onto the fairway. But then he let fly a 3-wood that put him in the bunker to lie 4 while Casper sat on the green with a 3, and then canned the birdie putt. Palmer could have lost 3 strokes getting from the trap to the cup but he managed to get down in 2, losing only a pair. A stroke separated the pair.

Palmer appeared to have collapsed entirely on the seventeenth when his second shot left him in the rough while Casper lay on the fringe of the green. But here Arnold lived by his sword, lofting a wedge to within 2 yards of the pin for an eminently makeable par. He missed by an inch; Casper did not and they were all square. On eighteen only another disaster-defying 9-iron lifted Palmer out of a matted, tangled rough to the green. When Casper missed his 14-foot birdie putt by inches, the two men met in a playoff and a third day of head-to-head combat. Finally, Casper walloped Palmer 69 to 73 as Arnold again led by 2

after nine and then after the turn home floundered to a 40.

Casper added the 1970 Masters to his laurels, again via the playoff route. He could also point pridefully to a record membership on eight Ryder Cup teams. By the time he joined the Senior Tour in 1981 he could count fifty-one titles. As a Senior, he carted a generous amount of avoirdupois, writ larger with bright colored shirts and blossoming, canary yellow plus 4s.

Regardless of how much he damaged the scales, Casper was a consistent performer. There were others, however, who rocketed across the tournament circuit for a brief period. Then, like some whistler off the tee, having soared down the fairway, they suddenly hooked far out of bounds, hardly to be heard from again. For example, in the 1955 Open, a drained Ben Hogan grimly gimped through a U.S. Open playoff against an unknown using Ben Hogan–model clubs. Jack Fleck beat out the four-time champion who double bogeyed the final hole. As a reward, Fleck was toasted by President Eisenhower, in town for a United Nations bash, but never again would he approach the front rank of the pros. Charles Coody was the 1971 Masters winner over Johnny Miller and Jack Nicklaus but he also disappeared into the shadows, reappearing only as a Seniors' threat.

On the other hand, Ken Venturi, a contemporary of Palmer, always seemed poised for a grand splash in the elite pool. His father managed a San Francisco municipal course and, despite a maiden round of 172 at age twelve, Venturi soon improved. As an amateur, Venturi spearheaded U.S. teams in the 1952 Americas Cup Match and the 1953 Walker Cup. Still an amateur, he sprinted to a 4-stroke lead in the 1956 Masters with only eighteen holes to play. A dismal 80 enabled Jack Burke, Jr., to eke out a one-stroke victory. He turned pro, rattled off a number of tournament wins, and placed high on the earnings lists. At the Masters in 1960, Venturi again became the man to beat, and Palmer did it with his birdie-birdie finish.

In succeeding years, Venturi's name slipped farther and farther down on the leader board, so much so that he was forced to qualify for the 1964 National Open at Congressional. He hung in, finishing the morning of the last day at 208, 2 down to leader Tommy Jacobs. The torrid temperatures dehydrated him and sapped his energy to near exhaustion, forcing him to bed down for fifty minutes before the afternoon play. He revived and in a semidaze carded a 70 for the final eighteen to earn a major victory at last.

Others strutted in triumph for brief moments upon the links. One of the saddest tales is that of Tony Lema. In contrast to many of the newer stars, Lema did not come from the college and country club ranks but was a former U.S. Marine and bottle washer in a San Francisco cannery. Well over six feet but weighing little more than 180, he learned his strokes from Lucius Bateman, a black driving-range pro working in Oakland, California. Lema, incidentally, was not the only white kid to profit from Bateman's instruction. Brothers John and Dick Lotz, and Don Whitt all hit the pro tour with a game and an attitude inspired by Bateman.

Lema filed his pro papers in 1955 and two years later joined the circuit. He scraped along for five years, never earning more than 12,000 dollars a year when the minimum in expenses added up to 10,000 dollars. Occasionally, he boiled over in frustration. Once, after hitting his ball into a ditch, he pitched his club after it, then heaved his bag of sticks. He paid more than his share of fines for unseemly behavior. Suddenly, in 1963, he showed up

fourth on the money list with 67,112 dollars, which enabled him to marry an airline stewardess he'd met on his travels. At the Orange County Open in California, he made an off-hand remark to beer-swilling newsmen—"Fellows, if I win this tournament, we'll all have champagne." The promise fulfilled, they hyped him as "Champagne Tony."

The sobriquet not withstanding, Lema would have vanished had he not suddenly become all-conquering in 1964. After winning the Crosby, his game lay becalmed. At the Oklahoma City Open, Arnold Palmer heard him grouse about his putting. Palmer offered an old putter of his. The club seemed bewitched. Lema knocked off the Thunderbird tournament and the Buick Open. He faltered in the U.S. Open, finishing twentieth, but then squeaked by Palmer in a playoff for the Cleveland Open. A sure sign of his prominence: He signed up for personal management by Fred Corcoran.

Lema flew off to Britain and his easy, cheerful manner endeared him to the Scots who packed St. Andrews for the British Open. Lema squeezed in a single practice round over the tricky layout, hardly enough to become familiar with the conditions of climate and the smaller ball. Yet, after eighteen holes, he held a 9-stroke margin over Jack Nicklaus. Nicklaus struck back: His 66 and 68 on the two final rounds is the best ever in the event, but Lema scored a 68 and 70 to preserve his victory. Naturally, the champagne was on him. Unhappily, Lema and his wife, making a quick getaway from a tournament in 1966, died in a plane crash.

(Below) *Ken Venturi staggered through the heat for his greatest win, the 1964 U.S. Open, but within a year his career declined because of circulatory problems in his hands.* (COURTESY UPI/BETTMANN NEWSPHOTOS.)

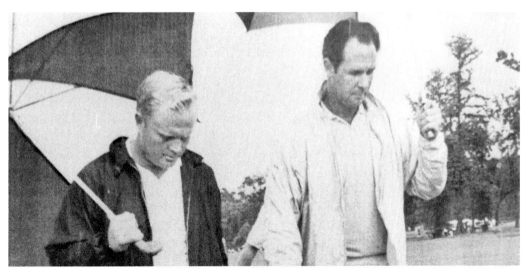

(Left) *For a few brief years, Tony Lema (right), the driving range graduate, jousted with Jack Nicklaus on equal terms. "Anthony David Lema, the new Open champion [British, 1964], is really rather a splendid fellow, absolutely in the Hagen tradition of not wanting to be a millionaire, but possessed of a strong determination to live like one. Gay, debonair, handsome, and at the age of thirty, something of a reformed character, he now has the world before him." —Henry Longhurst,* The Best of Henry Longhurst. (COURTESY UPI/ BETTMANN NEWSPHOTOS.)

19

Jack the Giant and the Would-Be Killers

When Arnold Palmer charged at Cherry Hills for the 1960 U.S. Open during the final Saturday double round, he started in fifteenth place. The leader, Mike Souchak, led the nearest horses—Julius Boros, Dow Finsterwald, and Jerry Barber—by two. Suddenly, as the golfers made the last round, a new challenger surfaced—the twenty-year-old son of a Columbus, Ohio, pharmacist: Jack Nicklaus.

When his son Jack was ten years old, Charles Nicklaus underwent three operations on an ankle. For physical rehabilitation, doctors advised walking, and what better way to put in five or six miles than over the rolling fairways? But the elder Nicklaus needed to rest his aching leg frequently, and few adults enjoyed the delays between holes. So he began taking Jack with him. The game quickly fascinated the boy, and the time-outs taken by his dad allowed him to practice on the course.

The family belonged to the Scioto Country Club, and a fine teaching pro, Jack Grout, inculcated a firm grasp of fundamentals in his young pupil. At twelve, he broke 80, and a year later shot a sub-70 round. By age thirteen, the youth was Ohio State Junior champion, and as an adolescent he quickly advanced to the front ranks of his contemporaries. His father encouraged him with a home indoor practice range.

As a thirteen-year-old himself, the elder Nicklaus had obtained a ticket to the National Open played at Scioto in 1926. He tagged along after Bob Jones and those memories poured into the ears of Young Jack, who chose Jones as his golf idol. Nicklaus qualified for the U.S. Amateur in 1955 as a fifteen-year-old. Since the date was both the silver anniversary of the Grand Slam and his victory at the Amateur over the Merion course, Jones spoke at a dinner celebrating the event.

During the tournament, the boy reached the green of a par 4, hilly, 460-yard hole with two huge woods. No other player had reached the green in 2. Having heard of the feat, Jones invited Nicklaus to chat. Accompanied by his father, the awestruck boy listened to his hero. Much of the talk concerned Scioto almost thirty years before but, at the conclusion, Jones announced: "Young man, I've heard that you're a very fine golfer. I'm coming out and watch you play a few holes tomorrow."

When Nicklaus noticed Jones as he reached the eleventh tee, he choked. He bogeyed the hole and worse followed on twelve. "I was even more brilliant—I took a double bogey; a drive pushed into the trees on the right, a choppy recovery, an underclubbed approach and three more to get down from the apron."

He dropped the next hole to his opponent also, going from 1 up at eleven to 2 down. Jones departed, sensitive that his presence might have affected Nicklaus, who eventually lost the match on the final hole.

Impressed nevertheless, Jones contacted Nicklaus's father, who passed along a message to his son.

I think I was a fairly good young golfer, but I never became what I would call a really good golfer until I had been competing for quite a number of seasons. You see, when I first started to play in the big tournaments, whenever anything went wrong, I'd run home to Steward Maiden, our pro at East Lake. Finally, I matured to

Crew-cut Jackie Nicklaus abandoned football for golf. (COURTESY UPI/BETTMANN NEWSPHOTOS.)

the point where I understood my game well enough to make my own corrections during the course of a tournament, and *that's* when I'd say I became a *good* golfer.

It was advice that the youth carefully absorbed. From that moment on, he says, he became determined to learn all there was to know about his swing in order to

diagnose his game and make adjustments as needed.

The double round on the final Saturday of the U.S. Open at Cherry Hills in 1960 was another painful learning experience. In the morning, the twenty-year-old was paired with Hogan. The pressure of the tournament plus the presence of so formidable a personality could easily have unnerved the young amateur. However, Hogan was extremely courteous, complimenting Jack on several shots without overdoing it. And the somewhat odd couple had to be pleased since their 69s moved them to 3 behind the leader, Mike Souchak.

By the thirteenth hole, the talk of the galleries and broadcasters was all Nicklaus. He held a 1-stroke lead over Boros, Palmer, and Fleck. Facing the 385-yard, par 4 with a creek some 70 yards before the green, Nicklaus blasted a 3-wood to the precise site targeted, a flat section of fairway from which he lofted a 9-iron only 12 feet from the cup.

Then I became just a shade excited. If I got that putt, it would place me 2 strokes in front, and a 2-stroke lead might stand up regardless of what anyone else managed to do. I hit a pretty fair putt that just slid by the cup and went about 18 inches past. And then I saw something that bothered me: directly on my line there was a small indentation, the remains of a ball mark which someone hadn't repaired properly. I remember well my thoughts at that moment. "I'm playing good golf and I'm twenty years old, though I know I shouldn't be."

Nicklaus's awe of his circumstances—and his ignorance of the rules—prevented him from repairing the ball mark. When he putted, the tiny depression in the green caught his ball and shifted it to the left where it rimmed the cup before spinning out. Instead of a birdie 3, he saddled himself with a bogey 5.

The miss at thirteen pushed Nicklaus back into a tie with the others. He bogeyed fourteen to fall behind. Given an opening, Palmer charged through and the final tallies showed a 280 for Arnold, 282 for Jack, good only for second place but still the record low for an amateur in the U.S. Open.

Nicklaus already had one U.S. Amateur championship under his belt from 1959 and, after a second victory in that event in 1961, he chose the life of a tournament pro. During his first months on the circuit, sixteen tournaments passed without a victory. But only a year after he joined the

tour, he tied Palmer in regulation play for the U.S. Open before whipping him in a playoff. From then on, for close to twenty years, longer than anyone in the history of the sport, Nicklaus bore the crown.

Nicklaus entered golf from a solid middle-income family with easy access to the country club and lessons. Lee Trevino★ traveled a markedly different route. As a seven-year-old living with his gravedigger grandfather, a 9-iron from the seventh fairway of the Dallas Athletic Club course, Lee discovered golf. Or rather, he discovered that he could pocket silver, by selling balls he found in the deep rough. By age eight, he had graduated to the post of caddie, where he taught himself how to play.

Trevino floated through the golf world as a teenager, caddying, then after quitting high school at fifteen, taking a job at a driving range. The owner, Hardy Greenwood, was impressed with the youth's ability and inspired Trevino to think of a career as a professional.

Trevino enlisted in the marines during the late 1950s. A rambunctious adolescent, Trevino thought he could easily conquer a rotund army sergeant in a military tournament over a Japanese course. This sergeant was Orville Moody, who some ten years later, having left the army after fourteen years of service, became U.S. Open champ in 1969. He walloped Trevino by 19 strokes.

After his honorable discharge, Trevino returned to Dallas to raise hell and play golf. Hardy Greenwood urged a more serious attitude, and Trevino obtained membership in the North Texas chapter of the PGA. But for the most part he gambled and hustled a living on the course. He even invented what he called the "Dr Pepper" club by wrapping a family-size bottle of the soft drink with adhesive tape. He used it to outshoot suckers over a par-3 layout.

Sponsored by Greenwood, and stimulated by a second marriage, Trevino attended the PGA Business School for two weeks, earning some of the credits a club pro needed for the tour's Class A card. After an initial success taking the Texas Open, Trevino, Mexican by ancestry but

In the great tradition, Arnold Palmer slips the Masters' green jacket over the shoulders of new champion Nicklaus. (COURTESY FRANK CHRISTIAN STUDIOS.)

with no knowledge of Spanish, rattled around Central America, jouncing over rutted, unpaved roads and coping with bats flitting through hotel rooms, in pursuit of the Panama Open title. Fifth place earned him 716 dollars and sixteen cents. he returned home dead broke but more aware of what his game needed.

Fate intervened in the person of a long-suffering cotton farmer in El Paso. Having heard of Trevino's talents, he recruited him for a match against a wealthy rival. The deal offered expenses and a share of the winnings. Trevino scored a 66 and 67, pocketed 300 dollars, and received an offer to serve as pro at Horizon Hills, a local club. On the job, Trevino worked on his stroke. Trevino observed how Ben Hogan cut the ball slightly to substitute a mild left-to-right trajectory for the more violent right-to-left that frequently submerged Trevino in the sticker bushes or the rough. While he taught himself the art of the fade, he gave lessons, shagged range balls, and cleaned members' shoes.

He exhibited his new form in the 1966 National Open, using an unmatched set of clubs made up from seven separate brands. No one paid him much heed: He wound up 10 strokes behind Casper and Palmer and the 600 dollars he earned just about paid his way. The following year, he figured he'd skip the Open. However, his wife, Claudia, had enough faith in him to remit the twenty-dollar entry fee for the 1967 U.S. Open at Baltusrol, and Lee borrowed his expense money.

Husbanding his resources, Trevino stayed in a cheap motel and kept himself in beer through his skills as a raconteur. Had he not 3-putted twice on his final round, he could have finished third. Instead, he had to be content with fifth but the 6,000 dollar check enabled him to buy a share in the ownership of Horizon Hills with a pair of brothers who also agreed to sponsor him on the tour.

On the road he scored well enough to earn more than 27,000 dollars and rookie of the year. Still, he was more noticeable

A magnificent out from a Muirfield bunker aided Nicklaus in 1966, his first successful quest for a British Open. (COURTESY UPI/BETTMANN NEWS-PHOTOS.)

A rare gathering united the only four men ever to win all four of the professional majors: Gene Sarazen, Ben Hogan, Gary Player, and Jack Nicklaus. (COURTESY RAY DAVIS.)

for his singularities than as a threat to Palmer or Nicklaus. With the TV eye now intensely focused on major tournaments and big money offered by clothing makers to the pros, Trevino's appearance as he teed off for the 1968 Open at Oak Hill seemed as inappropriate as his homemade swing. At five foot seven, 180 pounds, he advanced the wrong shape for a fashion statement. And his faded red or green shirt, baggy black pants, black shoes, and black baseball-style cap growled driving range rather than country club. To complete his bizarre appearance, Trevino occasionally masked his face with large scuba goggles, a trick he acquired in El Paso where some golfers wore them to keep windblown sand out of their eyes.

Nor were experts impressed by the stroke. One British commentator later described Trevino's technique as the "agricultural method," suited to a scythe rather than a golf club. Instead of the magnificent soaring parabolas of a Cary Middlecoff, Trevino swatted low liners; the only golfer of any note who had struck the ball with comparable lack of altitude was the abbreviated back swinger, Doug Sanders. But while the purists moaned, Lee Trevino's ball stayed on the fairway and his putts rolled true.

And at Rochester in 1968, Trevino performed as no other Open entry had ever done, with a 69, 68, 69, and 69 for four rounds in the 60s. The victor's prize amounted to 30,000 dollars, but his new fame piled up far more in rewards. Instead of the mixed bag previously toted by his caddies, Trevino now represented Faultless Golf Equipment with a deal that amounted to 350,000 dollars over four years. He also signed up with a clothing company, agreed to speak for Dodge cars (which added two automobiles and 40,000 dollars to his coffers), and even did a pair of Bayer Aspirin commercials worth 50,000 dollars.

The new Open champ quickly challenged the very best before again teetering on the edge of oblivion. He mixed some respectable finishes with missed cuts and blown opportunities, like the Open taken by Vincenzo after Trevino badly misplayed a pair of irons. He had followed up the triumph at Oak Hill with the Hawaiian Open and the low score in the World Cup competition, banked a total of 400,000 dol-

"There ain't nothin' relaxed about me on a golf course. I'm very tightly wound. All that jabbering is a pressure valve. I couldn't do without it. The competitor inside you knows what has to be done. If the game doesn't eat you up inside, you can't possibly be a great player. I still get mad, but not nearly like I once did. In the last ten years [1981] that's probably the biggest improvement in my game."—Lee Trevino, *quoted in* Strokes of Genius *by Tom Boswell.* (COURTESY UPI/ BETTMANN NEWS-PHOTOS.)

In spite of this missed putt, Trevino at Muirfield shut down the favorite Jack Nicklaus, and posted his second consecutive British Open. (COURTESY UPI/BETTMANN NEWSPHOTOS.)

lars in tournament monies in just two-and-one-half years, and earned the Vardon Trophy for 1970. His agent, Bucky Woy, handed the press a nickname: "Super Mex." But even as the high tide swept over him, Trevino struggled to keep himself afloat. His marriage started to fall apart; he broke up with his backers and Woy; and he began to party to such excess that he missed starting times. His game suffered. He received a salutary jolt one day in a locker room, when Jack Nicklaus remarked, "I hope you go right on clowning, and never learn how good you are, because if you do, the rest of us might just have to pack up and go home."

In 1971, Trevino reformed—somewhat. He curbed his carousing sufficiently to win three tournaments before the U.S. Open. That Open, during a shootout with Nicklaus after both carded 280s, Lee turned in a 68 while Jack could only manage a 71. Just as Nicklaus predicted, when Trevino paid attention to business, even Jack could be sent packing.

Trevino followed that success with a sudden–death birdie putt for the Canadian Open, outlasting Art Wall, the U.S. Open champ of 1959.

Immediately following the Canadian coup, Trevino rushed to the airport for a flight to England for that country's Open at Birkdale. As a former member of a Ryder Cup team, Trevino knew the course. More importantly, his flat, punchy stroke and low-flying shots were well suited to both the course and the British ball. But unlike everyone else (except Gary Player, another tardy arrival), Trevino had neither an opportunity to practice at Birkdale nor to restore himself after the rigors of a battery of tournaments and the long trip.

For a time, though, it seemed as if Super Mex was indefatigable. He scored well enough in the first two rounds to be paired with Tony Jacklin, the local hero. Jacklin, in 1969, became the first Briton to capture its Open since Max Faulkner in 1951, and Jacklin fueled home pride further after he added the U.S. Open title for 1970. Consequently, a large gallery followed these leaders. The subterranean fires of British resentment soon enveloped the spectators.

Over the years, the dominance of the Americans had rankled the citizens of the faded Empire. In fact, in 1964, a management efficiency expert, Ernest Butten, bought an ad in British golf publications, to wit:

£3,000 per annum plus bonus is offered to leading golfer (professional or amateur),

"By the time I was five I was out in the fields, too. I thought hard work was just how life was. I was twenty-one years old before I knew Manuel Labor wasn't a Mexican." —Lee Trevino, They Call Me Super Mex (COURTESY CHUCK KIRMAN.)

" . . . Trevino was imprisoned in some far-off corner of the green. Trevino glowered as he stalked the ball. He studied it from all angles and, the ritual complete, hunched himself over the ball and eased it into life. . . . It took an eternity to cover the distance on that green—down little valleys, up and over some hills, skirting the sides of others until it settled on the true course close to the hole that Trevino had perceived. The ball vanished into the hole and there effectively Nicklaus lost the Open and Trevino was champion for the second time."—*Michael McDonnell*, Great Moments in Sport. (COURTESY UPI/BETTMANN NEWSPHOTOS.)

"*This guy is beautiful. He not only won but also saved the National Open. It was threatening to become strictly Dullsville until Lee Trevino stayed hot, stayed talkative, remained what he is—Lee Buck Trevino out of Dallas, El Paso, and of Mexican parentage.*" —*Francis Stann*, The Washington Post. (COURTESY UPI/BETTMANN NEWS-PHOTOS.)

"In his prime, most things about Lee Trevino were underrated, though nothing more than his serious side. His temper was underrated. He wasn't usually, or even typically the Merry Mexican. His depth was underrated. He has always been a thoughtful man."—Tom Callahan, Golf Digest, December 1989. (COURTESY UPI/BETTMANN NEWSPHOTOS.)

or other suitable candidate with wide knowledge of golf and experience of managing and training international sportsmen, who could select and successfully train a team of four to six tournament players. The appointment is full time and the objective is to win the British and American Open championships.

The ad resulted in a program managed by Max Faulkner but it came to naught. Still, the sentiment gripped many golf fans and the press in Great Britain. Lamentations about the weaknesses of the Britons representing the nation were a newspaper staple as Ryder Cup, Walker Cup, and Curtis Cup squads from the States drubbed them regularly, moving Henry Longhurst to say that "it is now manifestly impossible for Britain ever again to beat the Americans, professional or amateur, at normal golf. . . ."

The crowds at Royal Birkdale, as Jacklin and Trevino started their round in 1971, discarded any British reserve to openly root for the native son. They booed when Super Mex struck a telling blow and cheered his errant shots. The boorish behavior by those whose cause he represented probably upset Jacklin more than Trevino.

When the day ended, Trevino, on the strength of 5 birdies over the final seven holes, held a 1-stroke advantage over Jacklin and a total outsider, Lu Liang Huan of Taiwan. In the final round, Trevino quickly sprinted to a commanding 5-stroke lead with a 31 for the first nine. But, suddenly, the engine started to misfire. Jacklin had run into trouble, but the Taiwanese (who grinned widely and doffed his hat following the drop of each birdie putt), hung in there, only three back.

Still, as only two holes remained, Trevino hardly expected that the short-hitting Lu could gain that much ground. But on the seventeenth, out from the tee, toward the left, lay hills of sand that threatened hookers and short hitters. Trevino smacked a drive calculated to fly straight toward the dunes before the usual drift to the right and the hospitable down of the fairway. To his horror, his ball hewed to the straight and narrow and plonked smack in the sand.

Trevino mushed up the incline to his ball. He swung a wedge; sand exploded from the point of impact but the ball plowed only a few yards farther through the sand bank. Again he clubbed away and the ball soared clear. Unfortunately, it flew over the fairway before diving into the rough on the other side. Opportunity beckoned Lu: If he could reach the green with his 2nd shot, his finesse with the putter could knot the match. But the tiny Lu could not muster quite enough power, and he left himself just short. Trevino, however, remained at risk as his fourth stroke died well shy of the green. The match now lay on Lu's club. Even though off the green, a chip close to the cup would ensure a par. Unsmiling, Lu huddled over the ball, eyed the pin placement, and then gently attacked. It lofted onto the green, bounced, and rolled—farther away than desired but still a makeable putt.

Trevino then chipped up, but failed to add pressure, coming to rest a good distance from paydirt. He putted poorly and the final count added up to 7 strokes, a triple bogey. Now Lu bent over for the putt that could tie. He tapped the ball—a miss. Trevino clung to a 1-stroke lead. Reprieved, Trevino birdied the eighteenth and became British Open champion. In four weeks, he had bagged three major titles.

It was a soul-satisfying victory: He had actually been the leader by 2 strokes a year before at St. Andrews, but after firing a shot at the wrong target, he had compounded his problems with a series of 3 putts and had been blown away by Nicklaus and Doug Sanders. Furthermore, in the face of the less than hospitable reception he received, Trevino donated 4,800 dollars of the purse to a local orphanage. Charity dotted his career: In 1968, while he was still building his fortunes, he contributed 10,000 dollars of the prize for the Hawaiian Open to the family of a pro pal from the Islands, Ted Makalena, who drowned while surfing.

Trevino repeated in the British Open of 1972 with another cliff-hanger. The match came down to Jacklin vs. Super Mex. Even as they played the par-5 seventeenth at Muirfield, Jacklin lay less than 5 feet from the cup with his try for a birdie. Trevino, on the other hand, after his fourth shot with a wedge, lay in a patch of rough, 20 feet from the cup. Said Trevino:

> . . . I was so damned mad with myself when I went over to play my fifth that I didn't take any time at all with it. I just grabbed my nine iron from the bag and hit the ball. The film shows I didn't even have my feet planted when I chipped it. The ball just happened to go into the cup.

Jacklin, who had been looking at a putt that would have given him a one stroke advantage, was shocked enough to miss and now trail by one. When Trevino parred the final hole, he had won his second British Open.

Trevino filled out his trophy case with the PGA title in 1974. But a year later, at the Butler National Golf Club in Chicago where the Western Open was being played, a thunderstorm halted play. Near the thirteenth green, Trevino and Jerry Heard opted to rest beside the lake until the storm subsided. Trevino later recounted:

> There was a thunderous crack like cannonfire and suddenly I was lifted a foot and a half off the ground. There was a loud, steady ringing in my ears like a tuning fork, my hands were flailing and I couldn't breathe. I was stretched out like a vibrator.

His companion, Heard, suffered only minor injuries; the fiery blast burned off his pubic hair. But Trevino blacked out and, when physicians examined him, they discovered four burn spots on his left shoulder. The lightning had ricocheted off the lake, glanced off the metal shafts of the clubs in the bag propping him up, and then struck his back. Upon his discharge from the hospital, he could barely walk, and the electrical shock affected the fluid that normally lubricates the vertabrae. Lifting a heavy flower pot, the bones ground together, popping a disk. For two years he suffered agonizing pains until surgery repaired the damage. Eight months after his operation, Trevino claimed his second Canadian Open. And in 1984, at the venera-

ble age of forty-five, he secured his second PGA title.

When Ken Venturi, on the verge of heat prostration, staggered through the final two rounds for his 1964 U.S. Open championship, he was paired with a twenty-one-year-old pro who'd joined the tour only a year before. In fact, it was Ray Floyd★ who sought out Venturi's wife to warn her of the seriousness of her husband's condition. Some twenty-two years would pass before Floyd himself would command first place in the U.S. Open, making him, at forty-three, the most senior fellow after Ted Ray ever to hold that title.

Britain's Tony Jacklin followed up his 1969 British Open championship with a stunning victory in the 1970 U.S. version. (COURTESY RAY DAVIS.)

"Raymond [Floyd] has done it all. If he were playing Sunday in Miami and there was a party that night in Dallas, he'd charter a plane."—Lanny Wadkins, Golf Digest, *September 1982. And indeed he had done almost all, for among his 21 tournament victories are the Masters (1976), the USPGA twice (1969, 1982), and the U.S. Open (1986).* (COURTESY UPI/BETTMANN NEWSPHOTOS.)

At the Colgate Hall of Fame Classic in 1979, Miller sinks a bird. (COURTESY BETTMANN/UPI NEWSPHOTOS.)

An army brat, Floyd had taken to the game early enough. "Erratic" was the favorite adjective to precede his name, particularly when he initially ventured forth on the tour. He never even made the cut in his first ten efforts, but on the eleventh won the St. Petersburg Open to become one of the youngest victors in a PGA-approved tournament.

Power rather than pinpoint accuracy marked his long game, but on the greens he showed a truly canny ability. Floyd was noted for the painstaking care with which he lined up the putter's face and set his feet. But while the process seemed tedious, you couldn't argue with results.

After St. Pete, however, he lapsed deep into the also-entered ranks for the next half-dozen years. Some ascribed this to his appetite for the night life of the tour. In 1969, Floyd reasserted himself with a string of three tournaments, including his first major, the PGA. Six somewhat leaner years followed, although they were still good for big bucks. Then, in the 1976 Masters, Floyd astounded the experts and the public by tying the tournament record of 271 set by Nicklaus in 1965. Ben Crenshaw finished second, 8 strokes behind the winner.

Floyd achieved his magnificent score with the help of a seldom-used club, a 5-wood. He wielded it for approach shots on the par-5 holes where others employed long irons. The wood launched balls in a high arc from which they descended to a soft, sedate stroll over the greens. In contrast, the lower-trajectory irons had a tendency to send balls skittering across the hard-packed, close-cropped Augusta greens. Following Floyd's win, hackers across the land besieged their local sporting goods stores for 5-woods in hopes of emulating Floyd's feat.

In 1982, Floyd added his second PGA championship, and at the 1986 U.S. Open at Shinnecock Hills, gave notice that youth would not always be served. The advantage during the first rounds had passed among a group of new faces—Bob Tway, Lanny Wadkins, Chip Beck, Mark McCumber, Greg Norman (the Great White Shark Australian to be celebrated for blowing tournaments with injudicious strategy), and Payne Stewart, who wore knickerbockers with a color scheme that resembled a barber pole or punk rocker.

On the final nine, Floyd lay two back of Stewart as he teed off at the thirteenth. So far, Floyd had stuck to the philosophy that the bogey lies in wait for those who seek to force birdies. But he chose this moment to gamble. The green was some 150 yards from the tee but the pin lay on an isthmus between a pair of monstrous bunkers. Using a 6-iron, he smacked a lofty drive that bit the green and halted 4 feet from the pin. Stewart, paired with Floyd sought to avoid losing a stroke but came on too strong. He rolled over the back of the green. Nevertheless, using his putter, he stroked an almost-perfect recovery. The ball rolled true, only to lip the cup, then trickle another 5 feet. Stewart, who, like Greg Norman, acquired an undeserved reputation as a choker, missed coming back and scored a bogey 4. Floyd coolly knocked his putt home and it was all even.

Floyd now dumped caution and pressed his case, attacking the remaining holes with a fury that allowed him to turn the final nine in 32, winding up with a total of 279 for a margin of 2 over Chip Beck and Lanny Wadkins, who briefly threatened on the strength of 66 for their final cards.

Ray Floyd and Ted Ray held honors as the most-aged U.S. Open winners only until 1990. The course at the Medinah Country Club in Chicago, expected to severely test skills, instead saw Old Man Par sacked and burned by a furious barrage of low scores as rain-soaked greens held balls and encouraged boldness. On the final afternoon, anyone of a dozen men, including Jack Nicklaus, Nick Faldo, and Curtis Strange, lay in easy reach of the lead. Unnoticed by the star gazers was Hale Irwin, a creaky forty-five, on hand only because of a special exemption, but a winner in seventeen PGA events, including the Opens of 1974 and 1979.

On the seventy-second hole, Irwin canned

a 60-footer to tie Mike Donald, more than twenty years his junior. At a time when blandness tends to dominate, Irwin treated fans to an exuberant victory lap around the green. In a rare eighteen-hole playoff the following day, Irwin and Donald again matched strokes until the ancient birdied a sudden-death ninety-first hole. Apart from being the oldest winner, Irwin achieved another special class as the only three-time Open champion (Willie Anderson, Bob Jones, Ben Hogan, and Jack Nicklaus all won four times).

The most obvious usurper of the Nicklaus crown was a lanky, six foot three, blond dropout from Brigham Young University, Johnny Miller. In 1969 he had joined the tour and, as play for the U.S. Open at Oakmont in Pittsburgh began in 1973, he counted a modest pair of victories. Miller had blown prime opportunities to take a Masters in 1971 and the Bob Hope Desert Classic a few months before the Open. The course seemed its usual intractable self on the first day with only four sub-par rounds—Gary Player at 67, Ray Floyd, Lee Trevino, and Jim Colbert with 70s. Jack Nicklaus managed to card a par 71 on the strength of a gigantic drive on the 322-yard seventeenth hole, the ball rolling to within

"[Johnny] Miller's 63 is the lowest round ever shot in our national championship. It is also the lowest final round ever shot by the winner of any major championship, eclipsing Palmer's final 65 in the 1960 Open, at Cherry Hills, near Denver, and Nicklaus's matching 65 in the 1967 Open at Baltusrol. It was an astounding effort in that Miller was on each green in the regulation stroke and that his card—shades of Jones at Sunningdale in 1926—contained not a single 5."—Herbert Warren Wind, Following Through. (COURTESY UPI/BETTMANN NEWSPHOTOS.)

12 feet of the cup. He sank his putt for a bird. Miller, who had a reputation as a tournament rabbit, marked by opening rounds in the 60s before slumping to an also-entered, posted a respectable 71.

Overnight, human error drastically changed the complexion of play. It had been a wet spring, but Oakmont by the first day was dry enough for the usual testing fast greens. But after the opening day, greenskeepers mistakenly left the sprinkler system on all night. The soaked greens were defenseless and the pros attacked without mercy, aiming dead on the flagsticks, and happily watching balls hit the turf and stick. And if one faced a downhill 5-footer, he could dismiss the danger of a miss that left one even farther off. Old Man Par withered under the assault; twenty-seven shooters bettered or equaled 71 and a club pro set a course record of 65.

Miller carded an excellent 69, but his total of 140 left him 3 back of Player, who trimmed 1 off par with a 70. Player obviously was still rusty, having joined the tour only three weeks earlier after major surgery at the start of the year. A squad of top names—Palmer, Nicklaus, Trevino, and Boros among others—nipped at his heels as fourteen men were within 6 strokes.

Then weather teed off on the vulnerable course. Heavy rains almost halted play on Saturday, the third day. The greens remained easy meat; the only restraint upon the par busters were the soggy fairways, which prevented any roll. When all had repaired to their various nineteenth holes,

four men held the lead. They included forty-three-year-old Arnold Palmer, raising the Army's hopes for one more major win; even more elderly Julius Boros, ten years Arnold's senior; Jerry Heard; and John Schlee, distinguished at the time not only for his Open rounds but for his astrological explanations: "My horoscope is just outstanding. Mars is in conjunction with my natal moon."

Meanwhile, Miller, true to his accepted form, ballooned to a 76, setting him 6 back of the leaders. On the final round, his position sent him off a full hour before the low scorers. While the galleries flocked around the likes of Palmer, Nicklaus, Trevino, and the other probable winners, Miller snipped stroke after stroke off par with long and short irons to birdie range of the cup, and an explosion from a trap to within inches. He ended his day at the office with a card dappled by birdies for an 8 under, brilliant 63 that stood as the best eighteen in an Open until tied by Nicklaus and Weiskopf in 1980. For a good sixty minutes, Johnny Miller sweated out the efforts by those still on the course. But no one managed to catch him; Schlee took second, leading Herb Wind to remark that "the old zodiac had given it a damn good try."

Miller showed he was no fluke when he won eight tournaments in 1975, and then beat out Nicklaus and Seve Ballesteros for the 1976 British Open. But the following year, the true heir to the Palmer and Nicklaus eras took the field.

Thomas Boswell on

JACK NICKLAUS

All in all, it's probably good that Jack Nicklaus never completely lost his love handles, always had a squeaky voice, couldn't tell a joke, was color blind, couldn't resist raiding the refrigerator for ice cream, and had a lousy sand game. (Yes, and he backslid a thousand times on the damn cigarettes, too.)

Otherwise, in the future when his career and his legend are discussed, few would be able to believe that such a person—almost embarrassingly close to being an ideal competitor and sportsman—could actually have existed. In fact, as he ages, it might be helpful if Nicklaus would do something wrong—get a parking ticket or make a bad business deal—just so his psychobiographers won't have to throw up their hands in despair.

Few careers in any walk of life have started so spectacularly, then continued steadily upward, almost without interruption for so long. Success, which has ruined many, only refueled Nicklaus. Each piece of good fortune seemed to be reinvested at compound interest. Neither twenty major golf championships, spread over twenty-seven years from 1959 to 1986, nor a personal empire worth hundreds of millions of dollars, seemed to disorient this son of a midwestern drug store pharmacist. He took himself seriously, but not as seriously as his responsibilities to his talent, his sport, his family, even his public image.

Yet, just as soon as you started to think you had his diligent dutiful character pinned down and encircled, word would seep back to the PGA tour that Nicklaus The Practical Joker had struck again, usually in some new installment of his lifelong battle with his friend John McCormack, a tournament director.

Once, after blowing a tournament that McCormack had run, the eternally stoic, always utterly self-controlled Nicklaus walked calmly into McCormack's office and destroyed everything in the room, right down to the picture frames.

After the sounds of smashing and crashing had stopped, Nicklaus walked out, composed and smiling, leaving McCormack and the rest of the golf world to wonder—and never find out—whether his true feelings had been rage or amusement.

Even Nicklaus recognized the problem of living such a relentlessly mythological life. (Let's see, is that five Masters and six PGAs that I've won or six Masters and five PGAs?) Once, while playing in the 1975 Doral Open, he sank a 76-yard wedge shot for an eagle at the tenth. Then, two holes later, he holed a 77-yard shot for another eagle to take the lead. No TV cameras were on him. His gallery, on a remote part of the course, was only a hundred people. For once, he was

(Above) *"As an amateur I was essentially a one-dimensional golfer; a left-to-right player. I was also mostly a one-style golfer; hit it hard, find it, and hit it hard again .... the amount of raw strength I had at my disposal tended to make me somewhat cavalier about the sort of problems that less-powerful players usually rely upon finesse to overcome. Frequently, I could simply whale the ball over obstacles that others would prefer to finesse their way around with artfully flighted shots."* —*Stanley Paul,* On and Off the Fairway. (COURTESY RAY DAVIS.)

(Opposite) *Jack Nicklaus sounds his last major hurrah as he birdies the seventeenth hole at Augusta to wrap up the 1986 Masters at age forty-six.* (COURTESY UPI/BETTMANN NEWSPHOTOS.)

almost unobserved. When the second eagle disappeared, Nicklaus dropped his club and began spinning around in circles like a little boy who makes himself dizzy until he falls down. He finally stopped before he flopped.

After his round, after he had won again, he was asked why he had gotten such an attack of silliness. "When I made the second one, it just all felt so crazy," Jack said. "I was almost beginning to believe some of the stuff you guys write about me."

For such a down-to-earth man (sometimes even a slightly boring man), to become so genuinely heroic almost seems like a joke on the rest of us. Everybody talks about maturing—getting better, not older. More than any athlete of his era, Nicklaus did it.

In the 1960s, as he surpassed Arnold Palmer, and established himself as a Goliath of golf, Nicklaus was a sports hero but nothing more. Call him Fat Jack. Then, the young, tubby, and titanically powerful Nicklaus may have been the most awesome golfer who ever lived. Bobby Jones watched Nicklaus as his towering 300-yard drives air-mailed the farthest fairway traps and as his iron shots from the rough snapped back with mystical backspin. Jones's pronouncement: "Jack Nicklaus plays a game with which I am not familiar."

In the 1970s, as he lost weight and (to his shock) turned from a frumpy fashion frog into a coverboy, Nicklaus established himself as the greatest and most dignified of all golf champions. Slowly, he became a true national hero: The Golden Bear. He not only carried his sport, to most people he actually *was* his sport.

Finally, in the 1980s, when he recreated himself once more as an aging, flawed, and beloved everyman—winning the Masters in the age of forty-six with his adult son as a caddie—he became a world hero: The Olden Bear.

Perhaps someday we will learn that Nicklaus was, in some respect, not entirely what he appeared to be. In an age when athletes often seem to be made entirely of clay, Nicklaus remained almost too good to be true for decades at a time. Not "too good" in the goody-two-shoes sense. (Ask McCormack about the morning he woke up to discover that "somebody" had ordered that his entire front lawn be buried under several tons of horse shit.) But "too good" in the sense of too decent, too organized, too creative, too lucky, too smart in business, too good a father to his five hell-raising children, too solid a husband, too wise in his self-analysis, too gracious in defeat, too cheerfully and generously joyful in victory.

How'd this guy get so squared away, so sane, so productive? How come his children didn't hate him? How come the small-print news items always said, "Third-round leader Jack Nicklaus flew home last night in his private jet to watch a Little League game, attend a school play, and grill a few steaks in the backyard. He will return in time for Sunday's final round." How could this guy, by age thirty, be on vacation more than half the year so he could raise his family, yet

In his thirties, the once-porky Nicklaus slimmed down and, according to him, swtiched from an "explosive" style to "greatly improved shot-making versatility." (COURTESY RAY DAVIS.)

still crush everybody's bones? Chi Chi Rodriguez called him "a legend in his spare time."

Where's the divorce, the scandal? How come, for thirty years and still counting, Jack always looked at Barbara as though she were the real reason for it all. And she looked at him like she was fairly proud, but like she might also have to grab him by the ear and straighten him out at any moment. Once, in the late '70s, I stepped into a hotel elevator and caught the old married Nicklauses doing a little necking between floors.

Why weren't his foes, men that he inevitably diminished, insanely jealous of him? How many victories did he take from Arnold Palmer, Lee Trevino, Tom Watson, Seve Ballesteros, and Greg Norman? Yet many of his adversaries became his true friends, all were his admirers, and some, like Norman, practically worshipped him and sought his advice, which he always gave. Perhaps only Watson, the Stanford psychology major, kept a prickly distance and successfully resisted Nicklaus's subtle seduction. Almost all Watson's greatest victories, in particular the 1982 U.S Open, the 1977 and '81 Masters, and the 1977 British Open, were snatched directly from Nicklaus in confrontations, which, while formally respectful, had a certain amount of tangy spin and edged byplay. Once, the pair even went jaw to jaw in the scorers' tent behind the seventy-second green at the Masters because Watson thought that Nicklaus, playing ahead, had been waving derisively at him (Take that, kid) as he pulled the ball from the cup after a birdie.

Sometimes, he failed to "whale the ball over obstacles," and the results could be costly. (COURTESY PGA OF AMERICA.)

How could Nicklaus set out to build a fabulous golf course and a great tournament in his home town—The Memorial in Columbus, Ohio—and have it work, right off the bat? Okay, having amassed a fortune estimated at several hundred million dollars doesn't hurt. The proud bear, son of a pharmacist, would have used dollar bills to fertilize Muirfield if that's what it took. But it's also true that Nicklaus the course designer and tournament director was as much an instant success as Nicklaus the teenage superstar.

Perhaps part of the reason is that Nicklaus was, and remains, a man who is inspired by failure, or even the thought of failure. Defeat always prodded his bearish nature into slow, inexorable, productive action. For example, in the spring of 1980, Nicklaus, then forty, had been in a two-year slump. "Is Nicklaus Washed Up?" was the standing headline. "I'm sick of playing lousy," said Nicklaus, publicly. "I've just been going through the motions for two years. First, it irritates you, then it really bothers you, until finally you get so damn blasted mad at yourself that you decide to do something about it. I've decided to do something. And I will. Or I'll quit."

Privately, he was even more blunt. At about this time, I casually mentioned to Nicklaus how nice it was that Lee Trevino had made a strong comeback the previous two years. "Yes," said Nicklaus, suddenly grabbing me by both shoulders, "it's almost as nice as this year when Nicklaus made his great comeback."

That year, Nicklaus won the U.S. Open and the PGA. No player (until Nick Faldo in 1990) had won two major tournaments in the same season.

Typically, Nicklaus loved periods of struggle even better than those periods when his game was ticking smoothly. "These are interesting times," he said during one of his slumps. "The game is most fun when you are experimenting. One day you're great, the next day scatterload. But you're learning. No, that's not right. I probably have forgotten more about golf than I will ever learn. What you do is remember some of the things you thought you'd never forget."

Because he never feared failure or experimentation, Nicklaus seemed especially suited to golf, the game of perpetual humiliation and embarrassment. Nicklaus approached his whole game, perhaps his whole life, the same way he lined up a putt—slowly, confidently, and from every angle. When the ball went in the hole, he would give a pleasant perfunctory smile—mostly to please his gallery since he'd expected to make it anyway. When he missed, his look of fierce, sometimes forbidding concentration deepened as he analyzed the problem. What had he forgotten? The grain of the grass, the evaporation of the dew? This was a man who once explained casually that he had chosen an odd-shaped putter because it combined "the largest possible moment of inertia and the smallest dispersion factor."

"When you lip out several putts in a row, you should never think that means that you're putting well and that 'your shares' are about to start falling," Nicklaus once said in the mid-1970s when he was at the peak of his powers. "The difference between 'in' and 'almost' is all in here. If you think the game is just a

Gary Player, as defending champion, assists the winner of the 1975 Masters into the traditional green blazer. It was the fifth such jacket awarded Nicklaus and, with the victory in 1986, he set a record that seems destined to stand forever. (COURTESY BILL KNIGHT.)

matter of getting it close and letting the law of averages do your work for you, you'll find a different way to miss every time. Your frame of reference must be exactly the width of the cup, not the general vicinity. When you're putting well, the only question is what part of the hole it's going to fall in, not if it's going in."

Whether Nicklaus, or Jones in his heyday, was the greatest golfer of the twentieth century is a question that they will probably have to decide at match play over the next few eons in the Elysian Fields. Perhaps Nicklaus will be allowed a millennium to practice with hickory shafts, while Jones will be given a few thousand years to decide whether graphite, beryllium, or square grooves suit his taste.

It will not require eternity, however, to decide which man had the greatest golf career of the twentieth century. On that score, Jones, the amateur who retired at thirty with no worlds to conquer, abdicated the crown. At a comparable age, Nicklaus also ruled his sport. But he kept competing at or near the mountaintop until he was past forty-five, accomplishing more great feats at later ages than any player.

Only Jones was as dominant in his youth as the 215-pound Fat Jack, who won his first U.S. Amateur at nineteen, his first U.S. Open at twenty-one, and then quickly added his first Masters and PGA at twenty-two. (In the first thirty-four major championships of his pro career, Nicklaus had seven victories, eighteen trips to the top three, and twenty majors in the top seven.)

No one, however, was ever as consistently exceptional in his thirties as the trimmed-down and glamorous Golden Bear. He took a physique and a game that others thought was the best of all time and radically remodeled it in the interests of consistency and longevity. And he actually got a little better. In what we might call the middle third of his career, starting with his 1970 win at the British Open, Nicklaus had eight wins and twenty finishes in the top three in the span of thirty-three majors. He also finished fourth four times and was in the top ten in the majors thirty-one times in those thirty-three events. Feel free to do a double take. That streak is beyond comparison and almost beyond belief. In that period, Nicklaus also won the TPC and the Tournament of Champions—perhaps the next most prestigious events—three times each.

Finally, only Ben Hogan, after his car wreck, was as inspirational at the end of his career as Nicklaus, who was, by then, a ridiculously beloved Olden Bear.

Most golf fans assume that Nicklaus's greatest accomplishment, in his own eyes, was his record in the majors. In his first twenty-five years as a pro, from 1961 through 1986, Nicklaus played in exactly 100 majors. He had eighteen wins, eighteen runner-ups, nine third places, and sixty-six visits to the top ten. Yet, ask Nicklaus if his play in golf's biggest events is in fact his defining accomplishment, and he balks. He knows that what he's done in the majors is bound, hand and foot, with something vaguer, yet of broader importance.

"Basically, the majors are the only comparisons over time . . . played on the same courses for generations. All the best players are always there. But I'm just

At forty-one, Nicklaus faced off against an equally graying competitor, Lee Trevino. (COURTESY RAY DAVIS.)

as proud of the whole way I've managed my career, the longevity of it. . . . You only have so much juice. You try to keep what you've got left so you can use it when it means the most."

Nicklaus has illustrated as vividly as any public figure in our national life how to manage talent over time, how to organize a balanced and productive life, how to continually revitalize our enthusiasm for our work. To many, Nicklaus is a symbol of successful labor. But he is also a marvelous symbol of creative laziness. By age twenty-five, he was already cutting back his tournament appearances. By thirty, he played barely twenty times a year.

However, when he worked, he concentrated utterly. No player ever changed his game more radically than Nicklaus after his weight loss, then again after his thirty-fifth birthday when he (essentially) tinkered with every aspect of his swing to create a more aesthetically pleasing whole. No player ever attacked the short game after his fortieth birthday and improved so immeasurably, partly because he had been so bad for so long. And nobody ever tore apart his putting, and even came out with a new, goofy-looking kind of putter, after age forty-five to then win the Masters with it.

As Nicklaus recedes from golf's center stage, his victories in athletic old age now seem to hold us most tightly. Why? Because they prove that (as we suspected and very much prefer to believe) he was a special person, not just a special athlete. By craft and canniness, he discovered a succession of temporary stays against age and self-doubt—almost against mortality itself. And, repeatedly, he prevailed. With dignity. With easy good grace. With many of the qualities that seem to lose their substance unless some special person can live them out, embody them on his own terms.

"If you don't mind, I'm just going to stand here and enjoy this," said Nicklaus at the massive press conference after his shocking "Jack Is Back" victory in the

An uncharacteristically unshaven Nicklaus discoursed on his design for a course in Orlando, Florida. "Power in golf has become totally out of proportion. This is a game of precision, not strength.... Where is the challenge in just beating at the ball? Any idiot can do that. Length is only one factor, and if everyone is to enjoy golf, the course must be within his capabilities. Golf should make you think, and use your eyes, your intelligence, and your imagination. Then, if you hit your best shots, you should be rewarded. To me, variety and precision are more important than power and length." —Jack Nicklaus, *quoted in* The World of Golf *by Peter Dobereiner.*

1980 U.S. Open at Baltusrol. When he finally spoke, he said, "I have to start with self-doubt. I kept wondering all week when my wheels would come off like they have for the last year and a half. But they never came off. When I needed a crucial putt, or needed to call on myself for a good shot, I did it. And those are the things I have expected from myself for twenty years.

"I've wondered if I should still be playing this silly game. . . . You see guys who have been winners who get to the point where they ought to get out of their game. They are the last to know. They make themselves seem pathetic. It hurts to think that that is you. . . .

"Once a time is past, it's past. I'll never be 215 pounds, hit it so far, or have my hair so short again as I did when I was here in 1967 and won the Open at Baltusrol. You can never return. I've lost the '60s and '70s. We all have. I'm not the same. I have to look to the future. I have to see what skills I have now. I have to find out what is in store for Jack Nicklaus in the '80s. I can't look backwards, because that man doesn't exist anymore."

Nicklaus tests himself in opposition not to any one man, but to everyone in his game simultaneously. He measures himself by only one standard: The attempt to be the best golfer who ever lived and the best who ever will live.

Throughout his career, Nicklaus has confronted his own limits and flaws with less desire to blink or turn away than any golfer, perhaps any athlete, of his time. Only reality interested him, not self-delusion. When thwarted by bad luck, injury, poor performance, or better foes, he suffered, accepted his situation, regrouped, and then relentlessly returned.

His greatest return (unless, of course, he wins the British Open on the Old Course at the age of seventy-five) came at the 1986 Masters in what, by something approaching consensus, was the Golf Event of the Century.

The moment when Nicklaus walked up the final fairway at Augusta National became the frontispiece in a whole generation's book of sports memories. The place of respect that the Louis-Schmeling fight, for example, may have held for our grandfathers is held for millions of today's generation by that image of Nicklaus. In the last half-century, perhaps only the U.S.–U.S.S.R. Olympic hockey game of 1980 has had a comparable transcendant power over the general non-sporting public.

An exemplary man, a full and rounded adult, was doing an almost impossible athletic deed, and doing it with amazing cheerful grace—ignoring every odd, lovin' every minute of it, waving his putter to the crowd like a scepter. Nicklaus later freely admitted everyone could see he had tears in his eyes "four or five times" as he played, so moved was he by the standing ovations that swept him along through every hole of a tumultuous, cascadingly dramatic final nine.

Despite all that emotion, despite the depths of his famous concentration on every swing, Nicklaus also walked between shots at times with a bemused, almost disbelieving expression on his face, as though he were sharing an inside joke with the world, but not with his competitors, who could only see his closing scores being posted. Starting at the ninth: Birdie, birdie, birdie, bogey, birdie, par, eagle, birdie, birdie, and finally one more par as his last long birdie putt stopped in front of the hole—1 inch from a 29 on the homeward nine.

Of all his victories, all his glory days, this was the most accessible. After all, Nicklaus had spent nearly two years reading stories about how he should stop embarrassing himself and retire. All around him, eyes were being turned away. He arrived at the Masters, for the first time in his career, almost an object of pity.

After leaving the representation of Mark McCormack, Nicklaus created his own off-course empire, Golden Bear Enterprises.

Nicklaus actually stuck a "Jack Should Quit" story to his refrigerator door during Masters week.

"I kept saying to myself, 'Done. Washed up. Finished.' I was trying to make myself mad, but it didn't really work too well because I thought it might be true."

As he walked the closing holes, Nicklaus was talking to himself some more, but the words were very different. The crowds had him crying, something that had happened to him at the 1978 British Open and 1980 U.S. Open—two of his previous premature valedictories. "We have to play golf. This isn't over," he kept telling himself. "What I really don't understand is how I could keep making putts in the state I was in. I was so excited I shouldn't have been able to pull it back at all, much less pull it back like I wanted to. But I did. One perfect stroke after another. When I don't get nervous, I don't make anything. Maybe I've been doing it backwards."

Bobby Jones was certainly golf's best player writer, but Nicklaus may have been its best extemporaneous player talker. He wasn't funny or colorful or charismatic. Instead, he seemed to have a rarer gift: simple, unadorned insight. He knew exactly what was on his mind and, whenever politic, he said exactly that. He spoke almost without spin, with no double meaning or hidden agenda. His words were a pane of glass that revealed an analytical, well-lit, and fairly guileless mind. Of course, maybe it's only decent for a fellow to be candid and sporting when he can spot the world one-a-side by the age of twenty-one.

Jack Nicklaus never gave better press conferences than describing how he agonized while watching Greg Norman's final 15-foot par-putt at the seventy-second hole, which would have forced a playoff. Nicklaus had never before rooted against a foe.

"I was sitting watching TV as Norman kept making birdies. So when he came to the last putt, I said, 'Maybe I'll stand up.' I like to win golf tournaments with my clubs, not on other people's mistakes. But when you're coming to the finish . . . I'm in the December of my career . . . Well, somebody did something to me at Pebble Beach as I remember," said Nicklaus, recalling Tom Watson's seventy-first-hole chip-in at the 1982 U.S. Open.

Perhaps the 1986 Masters crystalized three aspects of Nicklaus's character, which, independent of his enormous talent, will be remembered and revered as long as golf is played.

First, Nicklaus was appreciated as a man who loved his family as much as (and probably more than) his fame. "To have your own son with you to share an experience like that is so great for him, so great for me. I have great admiration for him. He's done a wonderful job of handling the burden of my name," said Nicklaus of son Jack, Jr., twenty-four. ". . . If it wasn't for my kids, I probably wouldn't be playing now. You've got to have a reason for doing things. Last time I won [at the 1984 Memorial], Jackie caddied for me."

Second, his late-career success deomonstrated Nicklaus's ability to accept the fact that golf is an unmasterable game. That knowledge was his key to being a

(Above) *In 1984, the University of St. Andrews awarded the winner of three British Opens, two of them on the St. Andrews course, an honorary degree.* (COURTESY UPI/BETTMANN NEWSPHOTOS.)

(Opposite) *For all his traveling, Nicklaus remained devoted to his wife, Barb, and their brood.* (COURTESY PGA OF AMERICA.)

master. Instead of searching for the perfect method, or clinging to what had worked in the past, Nicklaus constantly reworked and remodeled his game, enjoying the very same process of perpetual loss and rediscovery that panicked and infuriated other players. In the two weeks before the 1986 Masters, Nicklaus had made key changes in his full swing and his chipping method, as well as using a new putter.

Finally, Nicklaus's old-age triumphs exhibited to everyone the unmistakably clean core of his competitiveness. A regal sense of joy in combat, which is the heart of great sportsmanship, was evident throughout those victories. Nicklaus was having fun, expressing his best gifts, actually enjoying the same kinds of pressure that crush so many people in so many walks of life. And he was doing it long after he should have been washed up.

By the end, with many of his golfing gifts gone but his character intact, Nicklaus's play seemed to speak for itself: "This is life. Look how hard it is. Look how great it is."

"Nicklaus accepts victory simply as the natural outcome of the event. His manner shows less of joy and relief than that of other men, and conversely failure never disturbs his remarkable equilibrium and self-assurance. Obviously, he hates losing; there never was a worthwhile champion who did not, but the only effect is to harden his determination; there is no self deception in the philosophy of Nicklaus."—Pat Ward Thomas, The Golfer's Bedside Book. (COURTESY PGA OF AMERICA.)

20

King Tom, Queen Nancy

Despite the individual successes of foreigners on the U.S. circuit, Americans continued to batter Britain regularly in team competition. A few exceptions were the 1957 Ryder Cup in England and several Walker Cups. In 1965, the amateur Britons on U.S. turf managed an 11–11 tie and at St. Andrews in 1971 the locals triumphed 12–10, with two matches halved.

With golf a mass-participant sport in the States, the British, drawing from a much smaller population pool were at a distinct disadvantage. Adding golfers from Ireland to the 1973 Ryder Cup roster helped a bit but Tony Jacklin, Bernard Gallagher, Christy O'Connor, Peter Oosterhiuis, and company were no match for Jack Nicklaus, Lee Trevino, Billy Casper, Gene Littler, Tom Weiskopf, and Ray Floyd (who would eventually earn the dubious distinction of most matches lost).

Starting in 1979, the U.S. faced a more equal opponent as the enemy became an all European team. In succeeding years that meant competing against not only Tony Jacklin and Nick Faldo (British Open victor in 1987, and Master's champion of 1989 after both Greg Norman and Payne Stewart slumped in the last round), but also Spain's Seve Ballesteros (1979 British Open champion, at twenty-three the youngest to win the Masters in 1980, a repeater at Augusta in 1983), his countryman Antonio Garrido, and West Germany's Bernhard Langer. In 1985, the year Langer joined the ranks, the Europeans, led by Manuel Pinero and Ballesteros, defeated the Americans for the first time in twenty-eight years. Two years later, in Dublin, Ohio, at the Muirfield Village Golf Club designed by Jack Nicklaus, the visitors, again boosted by Ballesteros's play, whipped the U.S. Ryders.

Since most U.S. tournaments are medal play, American golfers tend to lack experience in match play, the format for Ryder, Walker, and Curtis Cup competition. Ben Crenshaw has suggested that the course design in the States, with its heavy emphasis upon water hazards, encourages playing through the air, in contrast to the European mode, which includes flight and roll over the ground. Because more of the foreigners now make the American scene, they are familiar with both forms of attack. That also holds for the ball size as well. Because of their frequent presence on the U.S. circuit, the visitors are better able to adapt to the different weights than the Americans.

Nothing better demonstrated the growing equality of international play than the scramble of winners for major tournaments once considered the home boys' preserve. Ballesteros won the British Open in 1984 but Scot Sandy Lyle took it the following year only to be succeeded by Australian Greg Norman in '86. Briton Nick Faldo captured his land's Open the next year with Seve repeating in 1988 before American Mark Calcavecchia in '89.

The Masters went to Briton Lyle in '88 and then Faldo toted off sudden-death victories for '89 and '90. In the first of these, a flubbed short putt by Scott Hoch enabled him to squeak through. In the second, Raymond Floyd, already the oldest ever to win the U.S. Open, at age forty-seven headed for a similar honor at Augusta as he savored a 3-stroke lead with only six holes to play. But the thirty-two-year-old Faldo rattled off birdies on thirteen, fifteen, and sixteen, while Floyd struggled to par for the final half dozen. On the initial playoff hole, Faldo staved off defeat getting down in 2 after he bunkered his 2nd shot. He survived only because Raymond missed a 15-foot birdie putt for the green jacket. When Floyd then

(Top, left) *"It's tempting to say that Seve is the greatest foreign player since Harry Vardon, but that would only make Gary Player grumpy."—Dan Jenkins,* Golf Digest, *February 1990.* (COURTESY UPI/ BETTMANN NEWSPHOTOS.)

(Top, right) *At the 1988 British Open which he eventually won, Ballesteros delights with a chip that edges the cup. This was his second of these championships, the first dating to 1984. The Ballesteros trophy collection includes a green jacket for the 1983 Masters.* (COURTESY UPI/BETTMANN NEWSPHOTOS.)

splashed down on the second hole, the six-foot three-inch, very deliberate, even slower-playing Faldo became only the second to successfully defend a Master's title (Nicklaus did it first). Faldo became the headline name with his easy victory in the 1990 British Open.

On the other hand, both the PGA championship and the U.S. Open have repelled foreigners with Americans in exclusive control of the former since 1972, although admittedly the birthplace of the 1990 PGA champion, Wayne Grady, is Australian. However, he lives in Florida. The Opens have been won in both '88 and '89 by Curtis Strange and in '90 by Irwin.

As the pro tour attracted more and more of the better players among U.S. women, the country's Curtis Cup entry weakened. In 1986, a British team defeated the Americans on their home turf for the first time. There was no challenge to the U.S. professional women. They more or less had the course to themselves as other nations failed to develop a female pro tradition parallel to the male one. The women's circuit then was barely a toddler; the purses a fraction

of the men's. And Mickey Wright seemed intent on winning everything in sight. Kathy Whitworth remembered: "We had some great head-to-head matches. Nine times out of ten she won."

Whitworth, Texas-bred and New Mexico–raised, maintained her amateur status just long enough to cop her home state's championships in 1958–1959 before turning pro at age twenty. Not until 1963 did Whitworth capture her first victory but that helped her finish second to Wright in the run-for-the-money. Within a couple of years, Whitworth's toughest rival had quit the tour and she reigned supreme. She notched three LPGA titles (1967, '71, and '75), posted the low-scoring average for six seasons to earn the sextet of Vare Trophies. As she stroked toward her fourth decade of professional golf, she counted eighty-eight official LPGA victories, a total that not only surpasses Mickey Wright, winner of eighty-two, but also Sam Snead, the U.S. men's leader with eighty-four. In the beginning, for all her success, the rewards were barely enough to pay the freight. Not until 1972 did her annual take pass 50,000 dollars.

(Above) *The 1957 British Ryder Cup squad beat the visiting Americans at Lindrick 7½–4½ for the first U.S. defeat since 1933.* (COURTESY BRITISH PGA.)

(Left) *The victorious Ryder Cup team of 1987 included not only players such as Nick Faldo and Ian Woosnam from the British Isles, but also Continental Europeans like Seve Ballesteros, Bernhard Langer, and Jose Maria Olazabal.* (COURTESY FRANK CHRISTIAN STUDIOS.)

(Right) *Nick Faldo (front row, extreme right) led another European Ryder team in 1989 at the Belfry Golf Club, Coldfield, England. The U.S. reps tied the home boys 14–14.* (COURTESY BRITISH PGA.)

(Left) *Bill Campbell, U.S. Amateur champ for 1964, became the third American named Captain of the Royal and Ancient Golf Club of St. Andrews in 1987.* (COURTESY RAY DAVIS.)

(Right) *Tony Jacklin proudly hailed the Union Jack after the Ryder Cup triumph of 1985.* (COURTESY UPI/ BETTMANN NEWSPHOTOS.)

(Opposite, top left) *"I believe that no other woman has ever played a long, exacting course quite as magnificently as Miss [Mickey] Wright did that last day at Baltusrol [1961]. In fact, I can think of only one comparable exhibition of beautifully sustained golf over thirty-six holes in a national championship—Ben Hogan's last two rounds at Oakland Hills in the 1951 Open."—Herbert Warren Wind,* Following Through. (COURTESY UPI/BETTMANN NEWSPHOTOS.)

(Opposite, top right) *Happy Carner waves after one of her forty-two victories in an LPGA championship event.* (COURTESY UPI/BETTMANN NEWSPHOTOS.)

(Opposite, bottom left) *"The hardest thing in golf is controlling your emotions," says the affable Mrs. [JoAnne] Carner, who can belt the ball 250 yards with her "mannish swing." "You're facing a dead still object, something you can only address with your golf club after a long wait between shots. Your hands are tied in knots, your mind begins to wander and you've got to find a release from tension."—United Press International, December 1974.* (COURTESY UPI/BETTMANN NEWSPHOTOS.)

(Opposite, bottom right) *On her way to eighty-eight tournament victories, Kathy Whitworth chalked up seven Vare trophies as best scorer, two more than her closest rivals, Mickey Wright and JoAnne Carner.* (COURTESY UPI/BETTMANN NEWSPHOTOS.)

But as the women's game drew more generous sponsors, the dollars increased almost geometrically, making her, by 1981, the first millionaire in career earnings.

She credited the game for more than her financial security. "I'd probably be the fat lady in a circus right now if it hadn't been for golf. It kept me on the course and out of the refrigerator," she said.

Whitworth's biggest rival after Wright quit the tour was JoAnne Gunderson Carner. Unlike either Wright or Whitworth, Carner remained an amateur for twelve years, during which she captured every major amateur event at one time or another, including five U.S. Women's Amateur championships (1957, '60, '62, '66, and '68). She held a slot on four consecutive Curtis Cup teams from 1958 to 1964. In 1969 she won the Burdine's Invitational, making her the last amateur to ever win an LPGA-certified event.

Her husband suggested she turn pro to avoid boredom, and at the age of thirty, Carner challenged Whitworth and the other top players on the tour. An affable, unpretentious woman, Carner basked in the favor of the galleries. Before marriage, she was known as "Great Gundy" and on the tour Sandra Palmer nicknamed her "Big Momma," because "the ground shakes when she hits it."

Whatever they called Carner, she quickly demonstrated her talent. She was rookie of the year in 1970 and eleventh in earn-

ings with one tournament win. Over the succeeding years Carner received the Vare Trophy five times and captured the U.S. Women's Opens of 1971 and '76. In 1982 her five tournament victories earned her more than 300,000 dollars, helping push her over the 2 million mark four years later, even though she saw limited duty because of back aches. She was, however, not the first of her sex to reach that mark; Pat Bradley preceded her that same year.

The successor to the Whitworth-Carner joint occupancy atop the LPGA heap was, like Whitworth, a New Mexican. But Nancy Lopez,★ daughter of Domingo Lopez, owner of a small auto body shop, learned her golf at her father's knee rather than from a country club pro. Learning from her father (at his best a 4-handicap) and what he and she could pick up from instructional books and magazine pieces, Nancy developed something less than a classically structured swing. But it was stunningly effective. Domingo and his wife quickly recognized the precocity of his youngest child with a golf club. Despite the family's modest circumstances, they set aside 100 dollars a month for Nancy's golfing needs.

Her ethnic background barred her from the local country club in Roswell and she played on a flat, dry muny course. At age twelve, the husky kid startled the local golf fans and, like Babe Zaharias, miffed the snooty as she won the state amateur

championship. By age fifteen she owned the event, with three victories there to go with titles as U.S. Junior champion and the Western Junior's best. The University of Tulsa, responding some say to the pressure for equal treatment of women, offered an athletic scholarship.

Lopez spent two years on the campus before dropping out to become a professional golfer. To finance her, her father obtained a 50,000-dollar loan from a bank. It proved unnecessary; she won almost instantly. Herb Graffis, writing for *Golf Digest*, was among those who sang her praises early on: "She just goes to prove that golf is not a hard game to learn. Her old man could fix a fender in the morning and teach her how to play golf in the afternoon."

During her early days on the circuit she weighed in at a nearly 160 pounds, but when she slimmed down it did not reduce her distance any more than it had for Jack Nicklaus.

By 1989, she had bagged every major championship open to women, most of them several times over, with a single exception. Just as Arnold Palmer could never capture a PGA Championship, and Sam Snead and Tom Watson the U.S. Open, Lopez has never been able to win the USGA's Open, although she won the LPGA crown thrice. She and Pat Bradley stand at the top of the money list, both over the 2 million dollar mark.

The question of who in women's golf was fairest of them all temporarily was settled with the advent of Nancy Lopez. Nor was there any doubt about the identity of the royal descendent in the line of Palmer and Nicklaus. Tom Watson, like Palmer and Nicklaus before him, picked up the game as a lad from his father and also traveled the college route—in Watson's case to Stanford University. While Palmer and Nicklaus matriculated with athletic scholarships, the Watson family paid Tom's

academic way. In his four years at Stanford, he acquired a degree in psychology.

Perhaps that training lies behind his success. Byron Nelson, the man who fine-tuned Watson and was king of the tour almost forty years before, said:

Tom listens better than anyone I've taught. You don't have to go over things twice. We work one point at a time, because I'm afraid he'll want to absorb too much. He has a very active mind. Our goal remains constant: to develop a simple repeatable swing, one where Tom will never have to think of the parts. His major flaw has been a tendency to come over the top, when he should be staying down and under the ball.

Arnold Palmer watched Watson chip into the cup on the seventeenth hole at Pebble Beach for his 1982 Open title and remarked: "Watson is doing to Nicklaus what Nicklaus was doing to me twenty years ago. I know exactly what Nicklaus was thinking when Watson's chip went in."

Because of his Missouri background, his reddish blond hair, and freckles, some characterized Watson as Huck Finn with a wedge. But he was never tempted to shirk hard work or to take the sport lightly. Instead he was among the most dedicated, even when Mother Nature frowned.

I love rotten weather. The founders of the game accepted nature for what it gave, or what it took away. Wind and rain are great challenges. They separate real golfers. Let the seas pound against the shore, let the rains pour.

When asked about his great rival Nicklaus, Watson deadpanned: "I never thought his short game was very good. Of course, he hit so many damn greens, it didn't make any difference."

Dick Taylor on
NANCY LOPEZ

Unlike the majority of golfers on our big-time circuits, Nancy Lopez was not born with a silver spoon (or driver, for that matter) in her mouth. She is the adopted daughter of an auto body repair shop owner who recognized her talent, nurtured it through financial sacrifice, and encouraged it through love. Hollywood may portray successful career women as tough dames who stepped on a few faces on the way up, but this success story would baffle screen writers.

It has taken the better part of half her career for contemporaries, some fans, and some writers, to understand that Nancy Lopez is a true lady, thoughtful and unspoiled by her meteoric rise and instant riches. "Instant" may be unfair—she paid her dues. But she has it all now, and she did it the hard way, by dint of hard work, not ruthlessly climbing over the bodies of those in her way

The tournament circuit may stretch out forty weeks. It's a suitcase and restaurant life both in the air and on the road, with home an occasional pit stop. In between tournaments, there's an endless string of demands for interviews, business meetings, personal appearances for private and public causes, and, of course, practice sessions to keep the source of all of the above—winning golf—alive. It all leaves little time for a loving relationship with a husband, even less for raising kids.

But Nancy Lopez, Mrs. Ray Knight, mother of two, confounds the pundits. Of all women athletes of today, she seems to have it all. She has more than forty notches on her tournament belt, including three LPGA championships. She has been named player of the year three times, and has earned the Glenna Collett Vare award for low-score average, an indicator in which she places great stock for determining who is best. In 1989, she charged past the 2 million dollar mark in winnings; only her contemporary Pat Bradley has put away more. In 1987, Lopez, by dint of tournament wins, automatically entered the LPGA Hall of Fame and, on the strength of her overall achievements, electors named her to the PGA World Golf Hall of Fame in 1989. Like fellow legends Sam Snead, Arnold Palmer, and Tom Watson, she lacks one major—the USGA Women's Open, in her case. But, Nancy could store away her clubs tomorrow and still be part of the pantheon that includes "The Babe," Suggsy, Patty, Mickey, "Whit," and Gundy. Close by her side, along for the ride, is her husband Ray Knight, the former major league baseball star who was the most valuable player for the New York Mets in the 1986 World Series, now a baseball announcer. And for much of the year, while Ray serves as baggage handler, manager, and cheerleader, the two little girls toddle and chirp about their mother in her digs at tournaments.

313

An exuberant Nancy Lopez bird-ies the ninth hole en route to win-ning the 1985 LPGA Open by 8 strokes. (COURTESY UPI/BETTMAN NEWS-PHOTOS.)

The one to beat in any tournament, just thirty-four-years-old with many peak years left—Nicklaus was forty-six when he won a Masters in 1986—surrounded by her family, Lopez graces her domain with a championship personality. She really is that nice—warm, with a lilting half-laugh, half giggle, a woman who wants to be remembered first as an unselfish person and then as the best golfer ever. In the world of high-level professional sports, where the words "me," "I," and "mine" dominate, Nancy is an anomaly.

In 1969, as editor of *Golf World Magazine*, I saw a report from our New Mexico correspondent that identified the winner of the state's women's amateur cham-pion as a twelve-year-old. That triggered a phone call to ensure it wasn't a typo, that the winner was actually twenty-one. Nosir, the age was correct and, further-more, she had been playing in the event since she was ten. Further investigation revealed the prodigy was not the daughter of a club pro—a female Arnold Palmer—but, instead, the daughter of Santiago "Domingo" Lopez, who owned and operated an auto-body repair shop in Roswell, New Mexico.

Santiago Lopez and his wife, Maria, relaxed over rounds of golf at the local municipal course. Nancy tagged along, and to keep her quiet was handed a cut-down iron to play tag-along.

"At age eight, I was still teeing the ball up in the fairway because I couldn't get it off the ground. During this period, my mother had a gall bladder operation and I used her Patty Berg clubs while she recovered. When mom got well, the clubs became mine and she walked with us for exercise. Dad was a really good player (a 4 handicapper).

"We really couldn't afford to pay for three of us playing and that's why she gave up the game. I had announced I wanted to learn to play, and well. At age ten, dad got me a set of men's Wilson 1200 clubs. He taught me a proper grip, made me understand hitting toward a target, and just let me have my lead. The forward press I have—arching my wrists and taking the club back at the same time—is something I have always done and never tried to change."

"When I played badly I would cry, and daddy would say, 'You can't see the ball if you cry.' And that made a lot of sense at that age. I was so competitive I wanted to play really well, and when I didn't I would get mad. Daddy would say, 'If you get mad you will shoot 50; if you don't it could be 49. Now which do you want?' And that made sense, too. And it still does."

Her father was also smart enough not to be confused by the hokum of sport's most entrenched shibboleth. "I remember being upset once and telling my Dad I wasn't following through right, and he replied, 'Nancy, it doesn't make any difference to a ball what you do after you hit it.' "

As a youngster she showed a single-minded devotion to her dream of playing well. "All I did as a kid was practice and play. I gave up boyfriends and I know I gave up part of growing up, where you can be carefree. My parents had sacrificed too much for me to put away the clubs and just play around." Indeed, her parents, despite their modest income, set aside 100 dollars a month to cover her golf expenses.

"I was comfortable at the muny course, although I knew the daughter of the pro at the country club. But I never have felt particularly welcome or comfortable there. I also played a lot at the New Mexico Military Institute course."

She measured her progress on a hole at the city course. "It was a par 3 over a tree and at first I had to hit a drive, usually hitting it into the tree. What a triumph when I finally got over it using a 4-iron."

On the heels of the victory that first brought her to my attention, Nancy won two more successive state titles, stepped up in class to the national level, and was an immediate sensation. In a whirlwind junior career, she twice won the USGA Girls' title, the Western Junior thrice. Golf writers and golf watchers took notice of the sweet-faced, pudgy Mexican American.

On the surface the kid may have seemed unfazed, but it took the firm stand of her father at her initial Western to instill self-control. "It was different away from home, even though I had only qualified for the first flight, I threw up every morning. I had to take a waste basket with me in the car. Once I hit the ball I was okay, but I feared I would throw up on the ball. Daddy told me, 'You will eventually get over these nerves, so I think you had better start now or quit playing.' I loved golf. Loved to practice and play and he startled me.

"I was scared out of it! I knew he would make me quit if I didn't stop it. The first time, as a little girl, I slammed a club in the ground he told me he'd hit me with it the next time I did that! I know he meant it. But the Western was another lesson. I've never, ever been nervous since."

"The strongest part of Nancy's game is that she plays by feel. All her senses come into play. That's when golf is an art. She has a sense of self ..." —Carol Mann, quoted by Dudley Doust, Sunday Times, *July 2, 1978.* (COURTESY USGA.)

"... Lopez burst on the scene with five wins in a row and as much charisma as anyone since Babe Didrikson Zaharias."—Jaime Diaz, Sports Illustrated, *1987.* (COURTESY USGA.)

Over the hurdle of pre-tournament jitters, Nancy continued her march to national prominence with a third USGA junior and made a dazzling TV (second) debut in the 1975 USGA Women's Open at the Atlantic City Country Club. "My head was in the clouds," recalls Lopez. "I was surrounded by my idols. And when I was paired with JoAnne Carner the last day I was in heaven. She was my main idol. That time I did get nervous. I had been working on taming a slice and there she was doing the same thing, this great player. At the short seventeenth, she hit it far to the right, into a backyard. I remember her getting a 4 out of the hole and, then and there, I knew that you just kept hanging in and even the great ones make mistakes." To manage that 4, incidentally, Carner bunkered her third shot, then holed out.

Still uncertain of her career future, Lopez accepted a golf scholarship at the University of Tulsa, seeking a degree in engineering, "because I was so good at math." Calculus, trigonometry, and a big time college golf schedule did not mix well. "Next year," recalls Nancy, "it was business administration, which was my final year. One more and I would have majored in basket weaving. I tried to dedicate myself to my studies. I won't do anything unless I can do it well, and I wasn't giving myself a chance. I was not a good student."

While in school she continued to march to a single drummer. "During the early days a lot of people wanted to help me. I just had to decide I was not going to listen to any of them; it was in one ear and out the other. When I was at Tulsa, Buddy Phillips was the pro there and he gave me tips to make a good player better. But daddy has been my only teacher."

As a collegian, she won the NCAA women's title, and her Tulsa team topped all competitors. She also served on the U.S. Curtis Cup squad.

Late in 1977, as her father urged her, Nancy Lopez turned professional, teeing off on the tour a few months later. She had her qualms. "I was scared. I couldn't help notice the pros out there didn't look particularly happy. And I was afraid of being alone out there. I worried because I love to play, but I also wanted to have a family, and not just play golf. Week after week of golf, moving from place to place, would make it impossible to establish any kind of relationship. I had to ask myself if that was going to happen to me. Was I just going to play golf all my life?"

Her 1977 debut was as incandescent as Nicklaus's in 1962 as she earned both rookie and player of the year honors. Altogether she captured nine events, five in succession (with a one-week rest during the span). The victories were not over easy fields either. The titles included the LPGA, the European, and Far East Opens, and her 71.76 scoring over the season copped the Vare trophy.

"I satisfied my curiosity when I got on the tour. All of a sudden I was 'there' and I couldn't believe it. I thought, 'boy, this is really easy!' It seemed weird to me. My first check was for 800 dollars. That was like a million to me. I just could not bear to cash it. I carried it around for months just so I could look at it. But

By 1980, Lopez had added the name of her husband Tim Melton to hers, and marital problems contributed to a loss of concentration and the winning touch. (COURTESY UPI/BETTMANN NEWSPHOTOS.)

then my accountant at IMG [International Management Group] told me she needed money in my account to pay my bills." The fact that IMG signed up Lopez before she even played a pro round suggested how highly regarded she was.

That first circuit should have been a sheer delight, a whirlwind year of great expectations greatly achieved. Outwardly, she remained the poised kid from next door. Her face shone on slick magazine covers; *Sports Illustrated* gave her an in-depth feature, the ultimate in U.S. sports print exposure. But she played the season heartsick, for her beloved mother, Maria, had died. To this day tears well up as she speaks of her mother, who sacrificed so much to give her daughter her chance. "My mother never knew what I had accomplished."

The following year, Nancy came out firing to repeat as winner of all year-end honors. She added eight more tournament titles, including a second European championship over the demanding Sunningdale layout near London. Fame also brought home the downside of instant celebrity. She was on a natural high when she arrived for the Colgate–Dinah Shore tournament at Rancho Mirage in Palm Springs. As the new sensation, the vivacious Lopez radiated talent, smiled easily, and gave her fans the time of day (or night) if they asked.

At Dinah's do, the preferential treatment got out of hand. For the first time, the defending champion, Canadian star Sandra Post, was not on the cover of the tournament program. For the first time the defender did not play in the pro-am with Dinah. In both instances, Nancy supplanted Post who was rightfully offended, as her friends constantly reminded her of the mighty slight.

Years later, Nancy says, "I would certainly have felt that way, too. She earned those honors. It was out of my control, just as were most of the nice things people were doing for me. I remember one place where I spotted a reserved parking space for me. No other contestant had one. I didn't even have a car that week; instead I used the courtesy car transportation."

Colgate CEO David Foster thought it would be fun to throw a 15 handicapper in fast company, so I played in the pro-am as one of Post's partners. Somewhere along the line, "Posty" asked how she should handle the situation. I asked if she really felt put out by it all. She replied she didn't and I suggested she go with how she felt. Subsequently, Sandra responded to all complaints about the situation with a turn of the cheek. She graciously explained that Nancy deserved such treatment as she was the new, gate-pulling star on the LPGA circuit.

When Nancy was introduced at the tee ahead of us, Post exhibited even more charm by joining in the applause. And the experience seemed to motivate her, for she repeated as champion.

Lopez's opponents quickly recognized her awesome talent. "They've got the wrong person playing Wonder Woman on television," joked Judy Rankin. And a few years later, JoAnne Carner remarked, "We're all trying to steal Nancy's birth-control pills, but so far we've been unsuccessful."

For her part, she continued to suffer celebrity shock. "I found out people were crazy; they will pay money just to see your face. I now understand something of the corporate business scene and I went from 500 dollars for an outing to five figures for an appearance, and it still shocks me. This was all so new to me and was also so much fun. I felt I had the world by the tail and everyone was there to do anything they could for me. I love to play and to win and I was getting all this money, just for doing that.

"I began hearing and feeling the animosity growing among some of the players, and that was a shame. I think I'm a nice person and wouldn't hurt anyone."

The coolness of some of her sister players on the tour and the death of her mother left her lonely. And she had resolved not to let the game interfere with her quest for a relationship and a family, to have it all quickly. The result was the brief, unhappy marriage to TV sportscaster Tim Melton early in the wonder years following her entrance into pro golf.

The breakup with Melton and the divorce depressed Nancy. And while she kept her troubles to herself, it is a fact that from 1980 to 1984, although she won a dozen titles, the luster of Lopez faded. Even her natural stroke deteriorated. "Suddenly, I couldn't hit the ball where I wanted to, and I'd been able to do that since I was twelve. There were times when every day I'd go back to the hotel crying."

Life began to perk up with the marriage to Knight, and then she played a shortened schedule for 1983–1984 as golf went on the back-burner for the birth of daughter Ashley. In 1985 the new mother boldly reasserted her supremacy in the controversial LPGA championship at Kings Island, Ohio. In the opening round, Nancy had scorched the course, arriving at the sixteenth hole with 6 birdies and an eagle. Her threesome had been delayed by a series of rulings, none of which involved Lopez, by tournament officials. Concerned about the slowness of the competition, someone held a stopwatch on Nancy as she pondered which club to use off the tee for the windswept 180-yard hole. She had a reputation for deliberate play that caused some detractors to call her "Slopez." When her club finally met the ball, the clock said she had used 83 seconds, 23 more than permissible. After she tapped in a short putt for a par, an official announced a 2-stroke penalty.

Lopez protested, to no avail. With tears running down her face—"I was crying like a baby"—she cracked a fine drive, approached to within 10 feet, and canned the putt for another bird. Her score for the day was 65, *including* the 2-stroke assessment.

Some players might have crumbled, even though the 65 did give her a 3-stroke lead. J. J. "Dee" Darden, a retired lieutenant colonel and fighter pilot for the U.S. Air Force, her steady caddie, said, "It got her mad. People don't realize how tough she is. There's no 'give up' in her. She's the damndest woman I ever saw. You watch her eyes. She's like a bulldog with a bone."

Lopez described herself as "super motivated, mad, disillusioned, and frustrated." She fired a 71 in the second round to increase her lead but slipped to a par 72 on the third day, which left her tied with Alice Miller. With the kind of resolve that enabled her to overcome social and economic handicaps and to pull herself up from the wreckage of a marriage, Lopez recorded another 65 in the final round to win by an 8-stroke margin. The penalty, however, cost her the tournament-scoring record by 1.

She was back on top. Whatever troubles had afflicted her game, they had proved minor. Says Darden, "She is a quick study. She can iron out problems quickly. She is not a ball-beater, but a tuner. I help her alignment on course, as she tends to move to the right, and give her exact yardage. Her greatest talent is hitting the ball flush more times than anyone in golf. Her hitting plane at the bottom of her swing is very long before coming out of the swing in the follow-through. After watching her I wonder why our great men pros don't work on that. You never see Nancy in bunkers or pitching on from far off the green."

She agrees with Darden's analysis for corrections. "I won't tire myself hitting golf balls; you can groove bad habits. If the 5-iron was a problem, then I hit twenty practice shots with it until it's right again."

Nancy Lopez watches her shot as she tees off at the 2nd hole during the U.S. Women's Open at the Salem Country Club, 1984. (COURTESY UPI/BETTMANN NEWSPHOTOS.)

Lopez surveys a putt. (COURTESY USGA.)

In the middle 1980s, Knight was still a major leaguer himself. The family, enlarged by a second daughter, Erin Shea, jockeyed appearances and travel arrangements to maximize their time together. As much as Knight now agonizes over her golf battles, she seized every opportunity to see him on the diamond. "I used to arrange my playing schedule so I could watch him as often as possible. And in that World Series [1986] I cried during the last game. I knew how much that ring would mean to him. I have my Hall of Fame jewelry. I also knew what a rotten winter it would be if he lost!"

When Ray finally laid down his bat, he briefly supplanted Dee Darden, but his superheated intensity on the course restored the former aviator to the post. "I fired Ray," she smiles. He retorts, "She couldn't fire me. She never paid me, so I quit."

The family travels with an Irish nanny and Ray deals with the fourteen pieces of luggage, including the cumbersome golf gear, at the airports. Nancy is in charge of business at the counter. But he is not a "tour husband," walking every round, hanging over each green. Instead, Knight spends his time either with the kids or out on a course himself. "He's absolutely gone on the game," she laughs. "He's given up on the idea of beating me, finally. But he's working to lower his handicap from the high single figures."

Knight does show up for the kill—the finales. And she believes his presence during a tournament helps. "I want him with me, I feel so much strength coming from him. He's quiet on the golf course. Only at night will he quiz me, and that's the word for it, wondering why I played certain shots. He is very, very analytical."

Her experiences over the years have toughened Lopez as a competitor. In the 1989 LPGA, she blundered on the tenth green of the last round, to fall 2 behind. "Those are the kind of putts I hate to miss," she said later. "On the other hand, it was very good because it really made me mad." In fact, she was sore enough to birdie five of the last eight holes and score her third LPGA title.

But for all of the fire with club in hand, she remains accessible to the galleries. She seems never to have met a fan she didn't like. "I'm certainly no better than they are. I may play better golf than they do, but does that make me a better person than them? I don't think so. Daddy took me to a pro tour event when I was a kid and I saw an example of really bad manners and I felt embarrassed for the player who thought he could act that way toward fans. In my fantasy of playing before a gallery, I vowed then I'd always have time for them."

It is the nature of life that even in those rare instances where someone really seems to have it all, the terms are more like a short lease than something permanent. Recently, her father's health made the point. "I almost lost Dad in 1989. He had cancer of the colon and successful surgery but had a relapse of some sort. He was put in intensive care. One doctor told us time was short, and then the surgeon came in and told us the opposite. We were furious over such treatment. We had really panicked over the first diagnosis. But Ray had a great way of looking at it. Dad is seventy-four now and the doctors expect at least five

She shared with her third-sacker spouse the glory of his MVP trophy after the 1986 World Series. (COURTESY UPI/BETTMANN NEWSPHOTOS.)

more years of quality living. Ray said, 'Give me a contract that I'll live to seventy-nine and I'll sign right now.'

"We have a beautiful marriage. We are both very happy. He does set high goals for me each season and I answer, 'Give me a break!' There are times on tour when I wonder what I'm doing out there when I could be at home doing what I'd rather do—enjoy a home I love, sleep in a bed I seldom see, and do all those wonderful things most housewives and mothers take for granted and some even consider boring, a chore, but not me. But Ray knows I'm not ready to retire, not as long as I can play to my standards. If you are judged the greatest, is it based on tournaments won? Longevity as a top player? I don't know the answer but I will know when it is time to go home."

Dave Anderson on

TOM WATSON

Beyond the slender white Turnberry lighthouse and across the sun-splashed water, Ailsa Craig resembled the bald dome of a deep-sea monster. Until the final round of the 1977 British Open, this roundish rock symbolized the Scottish resort. But ever since, when people think of Turnberry, they think of the duel between the world's best golfer at the time and the world's best golfer ever.

Out on the 209-yard fifteenth hole, known as *ca canny* (take care) on the scorecard, Tom Watson's 4-iron missed the green. His ball stopped on a hardpan upslope about 10 feet from the green, about 60 feet from the flagstick. When Jack Nicklaus's tee shot stopped about 12 feet below the cup, it appeared that the Golden Bear might increase his 1-stroke lead to 2 strokes, maybe 3. Moments later, using a "Texas wedge," a putter from off the green, Watson rapped his ball. Rapped it too hard, most people thought.

Sensing that the speed of Watson's ball would take it perhaps 10 feet past the cup, Nicklaus leaned over to place his ball next to his mark.

Instead, like a field mouse scurrying home, Watson's ball dove into the hole. Birdie! Stunned and shaken, Nicklaus missed his birdie putt. When he tapped in for his par, they were tied at 11 under par after sixty-nine holes of what is considered the most memorable medal-play duel in golf history. For nearly four rounds they had matched each other's score: 2-under-par 68s in the opening round, even-par 70s in the second, 5-under-par 65s in the third, and, after fifteen holes of the final round, each was 4 under.

To appreciate how those two golfers dominated the 1977 British Open, consider that nobody else would finish within 10 shots of the champion.

Now, on the sixteenth tee, twenty-seven-year-old Tom Watson understood, and appreciated the moment. With his reddish brown hair fluttering in the breeze above his firm jaw, he glanced at the golfer that he and just about everybody else considered to be the best in history.

"This," said Watson, smiling, "is what it's all about, isn't it?"

Jack Nicklaus grinned. He, too, understood and appreciated the moment. For the Golden Bear, husky and blond and intimidating by his very presence, this was what it had been all about and what it would be all about for a quarter of a century: Winning a major championship on the final holes in the crucible of competition.

But in this 1977 British Open, as in the 1977 Masters, as in the 1981 Masters, and the 1982 United States Open, this was what Tom Watson will be remembered as

being all about: Defeating Jack Nicklaus on the final holes of a major championship, *mano a mano.*

That sunny Saturday afternoon at Turnberry, their duel turned on the seventeenth hole, a par 5 of 515 yards. After a drive and a 3-iron, Watson had a 12-foot eagle putt. Nicklaus pushed his approach, a 4-iron that drifted into the brownish rough some 50 feet up a slope from the green, then chipped to within 4 feet. Watson missed his eagle and tapped in for a birdie, but Nicklaus's birdie putt slid to the right. Watson had gained the stroke that would make the difference. But not easily. Nicklaus holed a 32-foot putt for a birdie at the eighteenth forcing

Watson to make a 3-footer for the birdie that assured his second of five British Open titles.

"I gave you my best shot," Nicklaus would say graciously before the old silver trophy was presented to Watson. "But it just wasn't good enough. You were better."

Over the last two days while paired with each other, Jack Nicklaus shot 65–66, 9 under par, but Tom Watson shot 65–65. Their duel at Turnberry was framed forever in heather and gorse. In the process, Tom Watson's reputation was forged forever in steel. For all the accolades that Nicklaus deserves, Watson was creating his credentials for the bronze engraving that accompanied his 1988 induction into the PGA World Golf Hall of Fame in Pinehurst, North Carolina.

In time, Watson emerged during 1989 as the PGA Tour's leading career money-winner with more than 5 million dollars, finally overtaking Nicklaus. (Subsequently, Tom Kite passed them both, as others will.)

Money, however, has never impressed Tom Watson as much as the silver trophies for his eight major titles: five British Opens, two Masters, and one United States Open. He also cherishes his six PGA Player of the Year plaques and his three Vardon Trophies, awarded each year for the lowest stroke average on the PGA Tour.

"I'm not a specific-goal oriented person," he once said, "but the Vardon Trophy is important. That's a standard. Money changes. But basically over the years we've played the same courses so the stroke average means something. And if you win the Vardon Trophy, you're going to win some money along the way."

Watson won the Vardon Trophy in 1977, 1978, and 1979. He was the PGA Player of the Year in 1977, 1978, 1979, 1980, 1982, and 1984, an eight-year span in which he reigned as the world's best golfer.

But the trophies that most appealed to Watson, as they do to all golfers with a sense of history, are the shining silver symbols of the four major tournaments: the Masters, the U.S. Open, the British Open, and the Professional Golfers Championship.

"No matter how much money you get for winning a major, you cash the check, you spend the money," he has said. "But your name is on the trophy forever."

And for Watson, his one U.S. Open trophy is as meaningful as all his others because, for him, that trophy had been so elusive for so long.

In golf, as in all sports, the burden of excellence for the best competitors is that they're expected to win the best championships. If they don't, their skill is suspect. So is their nerve. So is their place in history. And in golf, the U.S. Open is considered by many people to be the best championship. The most difficult to win. The most prestigious.

"If you don't win the Open," Gene Sarazen, who won it twice, often said, "there's a gap in your record."

Even during Watson's reign as the world's best golfer, he was aware of that gap. As he prepared for the 1982 U.S. Open at Pebble Beach, he had won three British Opens, two Masters, and nearly 3 million dollars. He was known as a bold putter who never worried about missing because he knew he'd make the 4-footer coming back. He usually did. But in the U.S. Open, he had been frustrated. He had been the leader after three rounds in 1974 at Winged Foot, but shot 79 the last day for fifth place. He had been in contention on the final holes in 1975 at Medinah but finished with a 77 that dropped him into a tie for ninth. And at Inverness in 1979, he had missed the thirty-six-hole cut. All of which increased his burden of knowing that he had to win the Open.

"To be a complete golfer," Watson often said, "you have to win the Open, you just have to."

And when he had to make a miraculous shot to win the 1982 Open at Pebble Beach, he not only made it, he called it.

Walking to where his 2-iron tee shot had snuggled into the high grass about 16 feet to the left of the pin on the 209-yard seventeenth hole, Watson knew the Open had dissolved into another duel with Nicklaus, who was waiting in the scorer's tent after having shot 69 for 284, 4 under par. Now, as Watson peered at his lie and at the downslope of the green, he needed a par 3 to remain at 4 under par for the tournament going to the eighteenth tee.

"Get it close," his caddie Bruce Edwards said.

"I'm not going to get it close," Watson said, about to lob the ball from the high grass with his sand wedge. "I'm going to make it."

Incredibly, he did make it.

In the scorer's tent Nicklaus, having seen on a television monitor that Watson was in the high grass, had hoped to take the lead for what would be his record fifth U.S. Open title. But as Watson celebrated his birdie, Nicklaus heard the roar that erupted from the gallery at the seventeenth hole.

"It's happened to me before, but I didn't think it would happen again," Nicklaus would say later, alluding to Lee Trevino's chip-in at the seventeenth hole at Muirfield that won the 1972 British Open by a stroke. "When you think you've won, it's disappointing."

To win, Watson still needed a par at the 548-yard eighteenth hole threatened on the left by the seawall and Carmel Bay's rocky beach. Wisely, he played it cautiously with a 3-wood off the tee, a 7-iron, a 9-iron onto the green and a 25-foot lag putt that dropped into the cup. With that birdie, he took a 2-under-par 70 for 282 to the scorers tent where Nicklaus was waiting.

"You little son of a bitch," Nicklaus said, smiling. "You're really something. I'm proud of you. I'm pleased for you."

Watson had made a shot heard 'round the golf world, a shot that had won the U.S. Open and closed the gap in his record, a shot that he called "the best shot of my life," a shot that "had more meaning to me than any other shot of my career," a shot that will be remembered as long as golf is played.

At Turnberry in the 1977 British Open, the championship settled into a duel betwen Jack Nicklaus and Watson. Both men battered the old record of 277 for a British Open, with Watson besting his rival by a single stroke at 268. "What underlies the confidence that Watson exhibited throughout his extended duel with Nicklaus? For one thing, his triumph in the Masters undoubtedly convinced him that he had reached the point where he could stand up to a giant like Nicklaus. For another, he is able to get himself up very high when he faces Nicklaus .... He also knows that he is a sound driver and a sound putter, and, though he doesn't make this kind of pronouncement, he believes he hits the ball as well as anyone ... when a golfer like Watson feels that he is swinging just the way he wants to, it affirms his feeling of confidence and imbues him with an extraordinary resilience." —Herbert Warren Wind, The New Yorker, *August, 1977.* (COURTESY UPI/ BETTMANN NEWSPHOTOS.)

"But it's also a shot that I practiced," he said. "At the Open where they let the grass grow high around the greens, you need that shot."

Even so, Bill Rogers, the 1981 British Open champion who was paired with Watson in that final round, suggested that if Watson were to go out and chip 100 balls from the high grass off the seventeenth green, he would not hole one ball. And when Rogers's prediction was relayed to Nicklaus, the Golden Bear nodded.

"Try about 1,000 balls," he said.

When Watson was informed that Nicklaus doubted he could duplicate that shot with 1,000 balls, the champion smiled.

"Let's go out and do it," Watson joked, laughing. "I might make a little more money."

But making money has never meant as much to him as, quite simply, winning tournaments. Maybe that's why he has won more than forty tournaments world-wide, including the 1984 Australian Open and the 1980 Dunlop Phoenix tournament in Japan. His obsession with winning, as opposed to merely making money, was apparent in his early years as a touring pro. When he earned more than 70,000 dollars without having won a tournament in 1973, his second year on the PGA Tour, his wife, Linda, tried to console him.

At Royal Birkdale in 1983, Watson tees off in what became a successful quest for his fifth British Open. Only Harry Vardon surpassed him in victories in this event. (COURTESY UPI/BETTMANN NEWS-PHOTOS.)

"If you made 70,000 dollars every year," she said, "we could live very nicely."

"Don't ever say that again," he said. "I've got to win tournaments."

Several months later he won the 1974 Western Open. In 1975 he won the Byron Nelson Classic and his first British Open. In 1982 he accomplished what Jack Nicklaus never did and what only Bobby Jones, Gene Sarazen, Ben Hogan, and

Lee Trevino had done: win the U.S. Open and the British Open in the same year. At the time he had won as many major championships as Sarazen, Sam Snead, and Harry Vardon. With his 1983 British Open, he matched Arnold Palmer's total of eight majors. He was already a golfer of history and he relished it.

"Just winning money isn't enough," he often said. "In this game, you are measured by your major titles."

But his struggle had not been easy. In golf, it never is. The game is too difficult to be easy for anyone.

"I learned how to win by losing and not liking it," he once said. "Losing at the Hawaiian Open in 1973, at the World Open at Pinehurst in 1973, at the U.S. Open at Medinah in 1975. You have to learn from losing. You can't dwell on it, but you can't forget it. You hate to lose and you don't want it to happen again."

In that Hawaiian Open he had a 4-stroke lead going into the final round.

"I couldn't handle the lead, I couldn't sleep that Saturday night," Watson recalled. "Now when I'm nervous, I sleep too long. But in Hawaii that last day, I had no feel."

In that 1973 World Open, he shot a 62 in the fifth round of what was an eight-round event over two weekends.

"But then I shot 76, 76, 77," he said, rattling off the scores that had been burned into his memory. "Miller Barber won, Ben Crenshaw finished second, Leonard Thompson finished third. I finished fourth by 6 shots. I won 17,400 dollars, but it bothered me. I lost and it bothered me."

(Left) *At the 1985 PGA over the Cherry Hills, Colorado, course, Watson explodes from a bunker. The PGA championship is the one major he never captured.* (COURTESY UPI/ BETTMANN NEWSPHOTOS.)

(Right) *Watson splashed down at Rae's Creek in the 1987 Masters, an event that added two green blazers to his wardrobe.* (COURTESY UPI/ BETTMANN NEWSPHOTOS.)

At the 1974 U.S. Open at Winged Foot, he took a 1-stroke lead into the final round but soared to a 79.

"That didn't bother me," he said, "I didn't deserve to win the Open there. One day I hit only eight or nine greens and had a good score, but I wasn't playing well. When you're not playing well, you can't expect to win. But what happened in 1975 in the Open at Medinah did bother me. I shot 67 the first round, 68 the second round. I should've won that Open, but I kissed it away."

He finished with 78–77.

"And I didn't like it."

Three weeks later, Watson won his first major, the 1975 British Open at Carnoustie, Scotland, in an eighteen-hole playoff with Jack Newton, an Australian who would later lose an arm in an airplane accident. But even then Watson's gift for the spectacular was on display. His 25-foot putt on the final green put him into the playoff. The next day, his 71 won by a stroke.

"Losing at Medinah had a lot to do with me winning at Carnoustie," he has said. "I hated performing at Medinah the way I did. Basically, I just wasn't going to let myself lose again."

Thomas Sturges Watson learned how to be a winner while growing up in Kansas City, Missouri, where his father, Ray, was an insurance executive and the Kansas City Country Club golf champion. Born on September 4, 1949, Tom was the second of Ray and Sallie Watson's three sons; Ridge is a California vineyard executive, John an interior designer. At Pembroke Country Day, a small private school, Tom was a football quarterback and a basketball guard. His coaches there nicknamed him "Huckleberry Dillinger" for his freckle-faced appearance and cold-blooded intensity.

"But in team sports, there's always somebody to help you win," he has said. "In golf, you have to learn to win by yourself. That's why golf is the greatest game. You win by yourself and for yourself. You hear that winning breeds winning. But no, winners are bred from losing. They learn that they don't like it."

For all the pressure of winning that Tom Watson has had to endure in golf tournaments all over the world, perhaps none compared, relatively, with the tee shot he was asked to hit one day when he was seven years old.

On a family vacation through the Rocky Mountains that summer, the Watsons stopped in a small Colorado town with a municipal golf course. But when Ray Watson and his small son arrived at the course with their golf bags, the man behind the counter in the pro shop shook his head.

"The kid can't play," the man said. "He's too young."

Ray Watson explained that young Tom had been playing at the Kansas City CC for more than a year, that he was not a beginner.

"Sorry, he's too young," the man said.

"I'll make a deal with you," Ray Watson said. "I noticed that on the first hole there, there's a ditch about 40 yards out. If my son hits his tee shot over that ditch, will you let him play?"

"Fair enough," the man said.

Moments later, young Tom pulled his sawed-off 3-wood out of his bag, teed up a ball, and knocked it high over the ditch, about 100 yards down the fairway.

"The kid can play," the man said.

That's coping with pressure. That's competing. That's displaying a dislike for not winning. Whatever you want to call it, Tom Watson cultivated that spirit so evident that day in the mountains of Colorado, that spirit in his genes. One of his great-grandfathers, Isaac Newton Watson, cleaned up Kansas City politics by busting the Boss Pendergast political machine. Another great-grandfather, Dr. Simeon Bishop Bell, who arrived in Kansas in a covered wagon, created a real-estate empire that provided land and money for the University of Kansas medical school. But young Tom not only cultivated that spirit, he thrived on it.

Even in the years before young Tom was a teenager, he was playing two-dollar nassau matches on Saturday afternoons with his father, Stan Thirsk, the Kansas City CC pro, and Bob Willits, the 1947 Missouri Amateur champion.

At age thirteen, young Tom shot a 67 and at fourteen he won the men's Kansas City match-play tournament. At fifteen he appeared in an eighteen-hole charity exhibition match with Arnold Palmer, then at the height of his charismatic career. When they arrived at the first tee, the galleries lined both sides of the fairway. Not that young that Tom was intimidated. With that long full swing that would become so familiar to golf aficionadoes all over the world, he crashed a 270-yard drive.

"Who is this kid?" Palmer asked?

"Most professionals can fiddle their way around in respectable figures when they lose their edge. The only way Watson knows to play the game is to go for the flag. . . . Golf courses are arranged so that such shots, unless executed perfectly, are punished most severely. When Watson is off his stick his scores zoom up to the 78–79 levels, but when he is sniffing close on the scent of that elusive quarry, his golf is sublime."—Peter Dobereiner, The Observer, *July 1980.*

At a Crosby Pro-Am, Watson played from the rough, retaining his rep as a man who finds trouble frequently. (COURTESY UPI/BETTMANN NEWSPHOTOS.)

As the Missouri high-school champion, this kid also played an exhibition with Jack Nicklaus, a preview of duels to come. But young Tom often was reminded by his father not to merely hit the ball far, but to "shape his shots" as he practiced on the Kansas City CC range.

"Bring it in from left to right," his father might say. "Now hit a slight draw. Now a high one. Now knock one down."

That spirit of creativity also inspired young Tom to practice all-but-impossible shots around the greens out on the course by himself in the late afternoons. All those hours would be reflected and rewarded in the 1982 U.S. Open at Pebble Beach, with that holed shot from the high grass alongside the seventeenth green, where he also had rehearsed the theatrics of the Open.

As a psychology major at Stanford University in Palo Alto, California, he had often played Pebble Beach in those years before it hosted its first United States Open in 1972, those years before it emerged as a crowded corporate golf shrine.

"I'd drive down to tee it up at 7 o'clock when I'd have the course all to myself," he has said. "Honestly, I did fantasize about coming down the stretch head to head with Jack Nicklaus in the U.S. Open. When I'd get to the last couple of holes, I'd say, 'You've got to play them 1 under par to win the Open.' Of course I'd always play 'em 2 over and I'd tell myself, 'You've got a long way to go, kid.' "

As it turned out, he didn't have that far to go. On his journey, he would be accompanied by his wife, the former Linda Rubin, the sister of Chuck Rubin, an attorney who has been his longtime agent and advisor. Tom and Linda met as teenagers when their schools jointly staged *The Pirates of Penzance.* Linda was in the chorus, and Tom was the stage manager.

But when Tom announced that he intended to try the PGA Tour instead of getting a real job, Linda didn't know if she wanted to be married to a touring pro. Staying in a different motel every week. Eating in restaurants. Driving from one tournament to another. Wondering when the next paycheck would arrive. And more than anything else, not really having a home.

"I was family-oriented," Linda once said. "My father was in commercial real estate, he worked 9 to 5 every day. I was accustomed to a certain atmosphere. I wasn't sure about living on the run. I wasn't sure it was right for our marriage, or for me. But if I'd known how great the tour was going to be, I'd have married Tom in college."

Living on the tour was one thing. Winning on the tour was quite another. But even Watson's final-round 79 in the U.S. Open at Winged Foot turned out to be a blessing. In his disappointment, he sat on a wooden bench in the men's locker room. Soon he was no longer alone. He looked up to see Byron Nelson and hear words of encouragement from one of history's legendary golfers.

"Everybody who has ever played this game has had a round like that once in a while," Nelson said. "You're too good a golfer to let it get you down. If you ever want to come to Dallas and let me help you with your game, just call me."

Several weeks later the five-foot-nine-inch, one-hundred-and-sixty-pound Wat-

son took his first of many trips to Nelson's cattle ranch. Nelson's influence embellished the game that Stan Thirsk, the Kansas City CC pro, had nurtured. Nelson also tutored Watson's mental approach to winning. On the windy, threatening morning of the final round of the 1975 British Open at Carnoustie, Nelson spoke to Watson, who was 3 strokes off the lead.

"No matter what happens out there," Nelson said, "don't let the weather or some bad shots discourage you. Everybody else will be making bogies. Just play the best you can."

Watson 3-putted three consecutive greens, but kept battling the elements. His par 72 for 279 was equalled only by Jack Newton, creating an eighteen-hole playoff the next day that boiled down to the final hole. After a weak drive, Newton pulled a 2-iron into a greenside bunker and finished with a bogey. Watson rolled a 2-iron onto the green and two-putted for a 1-under-par 71 to Newton's 72.

At age twenty-five, Watson had won his first major. Two years later, in the 1977 Masters, he would win his first of four duels with Jack Nicklaus in a major. But that Masters is also remembered for their momentary misunderstanding.

From the thirteenth fairway, Watson saw Nicklaus, in the twosome ahead, tap in a birdie putt and wave to the gallery. But as Watson waited for Nicklaus to leave the green, he took that wave to mean that the Golden Bear was challenging him to match that birdie. And the more Watson thought about it, the more he seethed.

"I thought, Nicklaus, how can you do that?" Watson would say later. "And then I talked to him about it when we finished."

Nicklaus explained to Watson that he had just been waving at the gallery, not waving at him as a challenge. But in his annoyance at the time, Watson answered the challenge with a birdie there. And after Nicklaus birdied the fifteenth hole, Watson answered with his own birdie to remain tied with Nicklaus with three holes to go. On the seventeenth Watson sank a breaking downhill 20-foot birdie putt. Moments later Nicklaus bogied the eighteenth for the eventual 2-stroke difference.

"Not only winning the Masters," Watson said later in the interview area, "but winning it by beating Jack head-to-head over the last three holes gives me great satisfaction. Great, great satisfaction."

But while Watson waited at the door for Nicklaus to finish answering questions in the interview area, another tableau developed. The day before, Ben Crenshaw had mentioned that while the younger touring pros still respected the then thirty-seven-year-old Nicklaus as "the best," their attitude, according to Crenshaw, was "if they have their day, they're going to win." Nicklaus was asked if Crenshaw's quote had contributed to his final-round 66, but before Nicklaus could respond, Watson interrupted.

"I'll answer that," Watson said, standing near the door. "I'm always afraid of that man."

"No, he's not," Nicklaus said, smiling. "He's not afraid of anyone. That's why he won."

During the 1979 Memorial tournament Watson wasn't even afraid of bone-chilling windy weather, the bane of most golfers. In a raw rain and a 30-m.p.h. wind, the 45-degree weather felt more like the wind-chill factor of 13 degrees. But he shot 69, with 3 birdies and no bogeys. The average score for that Friday's second round was 78.75, which made Watson's 69 amount to 10 under par that day. Some people argue that, considering the conditions, Watson's 69 was the best round of golf ever played. And when some touring pros complained about having to play in that day's weather, Chi Chi Rodriguez put their griping in perspective.

"Hey, guys, tell me something," Chi Chi said. "How come the best player in the world is leading the tournament?"

With a grin, "the best player in the world" at that time joked about how he was accustomed to "playing in this kind of weather, it's good Kansas City weather." Unlike most touring pros who reside in Florida, Texas, or California in order to

On the final round of the 1982 U.S. Open at Pebble Beach, Tom Watson chips from the rough, 8 feet from the 17th green. The ball lifts 2 feet off the ground, then rolls across 20 feet of green to hit the pin and drop in. The sensational birdie enabled Watson to beat out Nicklaus for the title. (COURTESY SPORTS ILLUSTRATED.)

practice in warm weather when they're home, Watson has not only remained in the Kansas City area but contributed to the community.

His annual golf exhibition there has raised more than 3 million dollars for Children's Mercy Hospital. He also presides at a Junior Golf Clinic and Clubs for Kids program.

But while other golfers practice among palm trees, he's out at the Kansas City CC in cold weather. When snow covers the course, he'll go to the swimming-pool house, open the 4-foot wide glass door and hit orange balls through the opening into the drifts on the nearby practice fairway.

"I hit about 100 balls into the snow one day," he once recalled, "and only lost four balls."

But after having won his fifth British Open in 1983 at Royal Birkdale, and after having been the PGA Tour's leading money winner for the fifth time the next year, Watson suddenly lost his magic. Maybe it was all those winters he didn't practice among palm trees. Maybe it was his devotion to staying in his red-brick French provincial Mission Hills, Kansas, home with Linda and their two children, Meg and Michael. Maybe it was just that his competitive flame burned out.

Whatever it was, even though he was in contention every so often, his face reflected a certain sadness that wasn't there before.

"The second time around, it's harder to do it than the first time, no question about it," he said during the 1989 British Open. "When I get a little too frustrated, it affects me quicker than it did before. The frustration level before, I just passed it off. I said, 'I'll do it.' But now sometimes I feel, 'Well, today is not the day.' In the past, any day was a day I could play well, and that's something I'd like to try to get back instead of having it happen by the luck of the draw, so to speak. Have that feeling that you can do it anytime you want to. I hope this is the beginning of maybe the second career for Tom Watson."

But if not, Tom Watson's first career would still be glorious enough. For any golfer.

21

Old Man Par and Colonel Bogey Ascendent

Tom Watson's success and that of Jack Nicklaus, who comes from a similar economic background, contradicts the adage that an athlete must be hungry to win. "The money changes," remarked Watson, "but the achievement the Vardon [award] represents doesn't."

The money, however, changed enough so that Watson overall topped Nicklaus as he surpassed the 5 million dollar mark in tournament earnings, although he won fewer than half as many events. For that matter, Curtis Strange in 1985 and '87, and Greg Norman in 1986, both banked more than Watson in his most lucrative year, 530,808 dollars and 33 cents in 1980. Strange had approached the 1 million dollar mark with his 925,941 dollars in 1987. The record for both the highest annual take and career winnings, however, passed to a nonhousehold name, the bespectacled Tom Kite. With a mere thirteen tournament titles in his eighteen seasons on the tour, Kite fattened his wallet with a 450,000 dollar first prize for the richest of all tournaments, the Nabisco Championship at Hilton Head Island, South Carolina. That made him the big money man for 1989, which in turn added a bonus of 175,000 dollars. Kite, who won three events that year, pocketed a total of 1,395,278 dollars, which made him a 5,600,691-dollar man for his career, roughly half a million better than Nicklaus, and 340,000 dollars ahead of Watson. Kite became the game's first 6-million-dollar man in 1990, following his victory in the St. Jude Classic.

The rewards beyond purses are even greater. *Golf Digest* reports twenty-three individuals earn better than 1 million dollars through endorsements. Atop the list is Arnold Palmer, raking in an estimated 9 million annually for the use of his name. Greg Norman is worth 8 million, Nicklaus 7 million. The names include several players from Japan, indicating the enormous interest in golf there.

As golf headed into the 1990s, the media discovered another boom in the sport. In 1964, the National Golf Foundation reported the number of golfers stood at 8 million, and the regulation-size courses numbered 7,000. Those figures were the bottom of the graph in what has been a steep ascent upward to more than 15 million in 1980, and nearly 25 million on the links in 1990 with 13,000 full-length playpens to service them. Projections indicate a total of 40 million divot diggers by the turn of the century. Indeed, research from the National Golf Foundation warns that, since 1970, facilities have increased by only 24 percent compared to a 94 percent rise in the number of golfers.*

Economists now calculate golf is a 20-billion-dollar industry. Balls alone are a 462-million-dollar market. In 1925, balls were a 30-million-dollar item. One sign of golf's investment potential is International Golf Inc., a company that retrieves balls

Bernhard Langer, Germany's top pro and the 1985 Masters winner, plays a difficult lie during a Benson and Hedges Tournament in England. (COURTESY KEN LEWIS, SPORTS PHOTO-GRAPHICS.)

---

*The inability to supply enough courses to meet the player demand in the U.S. is minor compared with the problem in Japan. There, an estimated 12 million golfers seek to tee off on only 1,600 courses, a ratio of 7,500 players for every eighteen-hole layout. In the U.S., the statistics indicate fewer than 2,000 per links. Unfortunately, the facilities are not evenly spread over the country. Public courses often have long waiting times and even some of the more exclusive clubs, forced by economics to recruit a bigger membership, suffer near linkslock as players turn out in force.

Nick Faldo, a home-grown product prepares to putt out for his 1987 British Open title at Muirfield. "Early in the decade he was El Foldo *to the British press, a talented player who had not fulfilled his promise. This may or may not have been the reason he chose to go into hibernation and completely rebuild his game. Grip, stance, arc, everything. What emerged was a straight-hitting stylist. He won the British Open in 1987 and the Masters in 1989 and lost a playoff to Curtis Strange in the 1988 U.S. Open."—Dan Jenkins,* Golf Digest, *February 1990. Faldo repeated in the 1990 Masters, and took the British Open that year as well.* (COURTESY REUTERS/BETTMANN NEWS-PHOTOS.)

from water hazards at 600 courses all over the world, paying half a million for the right to send its scuba divers in search of fatal hooks and slices. Clothes and shoes total 2 billion dollars a year. During the 1920s the figure was 50 million dollars. Real estate connected with golf courses turns over 4 billion dollars a year, and golf travel (including hotel rooms), adds up to 7.8 billion, according to the National Institute of Business Management. Partly responsible for the flourishing trade is the PGA's huge annual Merchandise Show, which Bob Harlow had inaugurated in a desperate effort to publicize the organization during the Depression. Space for the show now sells out months in advance.

Golf paraphernalia has become one of the mysterious assets known as collectibles. An estimated 3,000 individuals around the world prowl auctions and read special publications. A 1910 rake iron received a bid of 80,000 dollars through Christie's outlet in Glasgow, four times as much as the previous record price paid for an eighteenth century iron in 1986. A featherie from W & J Gourlay, manufactured around 1840, brought a bid of 5,500 dollars.

TV and corporate sponsorship of the Tour is worth half a billion. As a consequence, close to twenty events on the regular circuit offer purses of 1 million dollars or more. Well over 100 tournament regulars have become millionaires. A major reason for the increasing challenge to U.S. hegemony has been the incentives offered around the world. European sponsors boosted their tournament prizes from 5.8 million dollars in 1984 to 22.5 million dollars by 1989. Even U.S. companies like American Express have begun to shower dollars on the competitions there. British TV networks cover twenty-four tournaments for an audience of fourteen countries. The Japanese have also stimulated their pros with rewards totalling 19.1 million dollars, spread over forty-one tournaments.

Incidentally, the Japanese seem to have overcome the limitations on distance due to restrictions on balls. The country's best player, Masashi "Jumbo" Ozaki, one of a brotherly threesome—with Naomichi (Joe) and Tateo (Jet) Ozaki—designed a driver with a metal head and graphite shaft. Known as the "J's Professional Weapon" (in honor of the Ozaki trio), it was eagerly adopted by Jack Nicklaus, Ray Floyd, and Greg Norman. "I not only hit it longer, I hit it straighter," insists Norman. Among the first nonpros to swing a "J" were a pair of Washington weekend duffers—George Bush and Dan Quayle.

The PGA Tour has added a new kind of operation, the Tournament Players Club. There are a dozen of these owned, managed, or licensed by the PGA Tour in the United States, and there are others in construction or projected for Japan. They feature so-called "stadium golf" in which a majority of the holes are designed to enhance the spectators' views without sacrificing the strategic concepts.

Mindful of its obligation to encourage younger pros, the PGA Tour has also created its Ben Hogan Tour with purses of 100,000 dollars, where novices can sharpen

(Left) *Greg Norman, the "Great White Shark" from Australia was the 1989 Vardon Trophy victor, the first foreigner to win since Bruce Crampton in 1973. His finest hours came during his victorious rounds in the 1986 British Open at Turnberry. Either snake-bit or strategically flawed, Norman has lost playoffs in the U.S. Open (1984), the Masters (1987), and the British Open (1989). He also is known as the player to lose majors on miracle shots—Bob Tway sank a trap shot on the final hole of the 1986 PGA and Larry Mize pitched into the cup on the second hole of the playoff in the Masters. Some sweet satisfaction followed in the 1990 Doral Ryder Open. Greg came from 7 down on the final round with a 10-under-par 62, then canned a chip from the apron to win a four-way playoff with an eagle.* (COURTESY UPI/BETTMANN NEWSPHOTOS.)

(Right) *Tom Watson played a familiar scene with the emblem of the British Open championship at Troon in 1982 as he captured his fourth title. A year later his fifth win tied him with James Braid and Peter Thomson for second place to Harry Vardon who notched six British Opens.* (COURTESY UPI/ BETTMANN NEWSPHOTOS.)

their competitive teeth and prove themselves worthy of joining the regular tour.

The PGA of America itself has grown enormously. It now counts about fifteen thousand members and some five thousand apprentices. The PGA not only conducts the business of the World Golf Hall of Fame, but is responsible for other major honors—its own "Player of the Year," the Vardon Trophy, and Professional of the Year for the club pro who's done the most for the sport. While supervising fourteen major tournaments, including the oldest event for pros, the PGA championship, the U.S. Ryder Cup matches, the PGA Seniors Championship, and several events such as National Golf Day (which raises funds for charities), the PGA involves itself in broadening the game's base. The organization has taken the lead in promoting junior golf, from whose ranks will undoubtedly come the Hogans, Palmers, Nicklauses, and Watsons of the future, as well as the armies of amateurs, late afternoon and weekend swingers who will know how to play and to appreciate the skills of those earning a living on the tour. Its aim was expressed by PGA president Pat Rielly:

"Making your golf game better; making golf a better game."

Some of the golf popularity undoubtedly stems from the Senior Tour, which the PGA Tour division began to operate in 1980. The first year there were only two events under the PGA aegis, and the prize money a mere 250,000 dollars. As the better-known names became older, they did not fade away but joined the senior tour. Don January became the first of the breed to earn a million dollars in Senior Tour money. Corporate sponsors Mazda, Vantage, Pepsi Cola, GTE, General Foods, and others, agreed to sponsor tournaments.

The Senior Tour was a heart transplant for those whose bodies could no longer accommodate their ambitions. For Gary Player, "This Senior Tour is a bloody joy." Australian Bruce Crampton quit the regular circuit for nine years. Then the two-time Vardon Trophy winner discovered the afterlife: "I never thought I'd wish for my fiftieth birthday to come. But I was counting the days, chomping at the bit. I feel like I've been reborn. I'm having a ball."

For Billy Casper it also enabled him to show another face.

(Top, left) *Even as little more than an adolescent, Nancy Lopez dominated her contemporaries.* (COURTESY USGA.)

(Top, right) *At age fifteen, Nancy outshot all rivals for the U.S. Juniors title.* (COURTESY USGA.)

It's a second chance for some of us to change our personalities . . . I used to be known as a grouch and a grump. Look at me now. Wearing knickers and [argyle] plus fours and silly hats . . . "But we're out here playing golf with people we've known all our lives. We get to meet some really great fans who appreciate us. We're not faced with a cut. At the end of the week, you're going to get a nice check.

By 1989 the growing list of notable eligibles could skirmish in forty-one events worth more than 14 million dollars, and elder statesmen like Lee Trevino and Jack Nicklaus joined in 1990 and a middle-aged Tom Watson could look forward to a life after fifty. (Nicklaus refused to concede to the passage of time, declaring he saw no glory in playing against people whom he had beaten so often when they were at the top of their games.)

Indeed, the durability of golf is a major component in its unflagging grip on the public. It is a game in which the individual may struggle and achieve, without defeating another human being. Old Man Par does not suddenly slip in a split-fingered fastball, nor does he destroy one with a top-spin lob, or befuddle one with a knight's gambit. Instead, the golfer's demon presents itself in the form of courses, produced by nature and man, that challenge the individual to take his or her best shot. From day to day, from lie to lie, the duel differs. A game that can last a lifetime, it utters a metaphor for human endeavor. As in life, one may temporarily get the upper hand, but then on the next round, on a different (or even the same) course, surrender to the Colonel Bogey.

Golf in the English-speaking lands offers one more imprecise but nevertheless useful insight into the nature of the prevalent culture. It is certainly one of the most democratic activities. Height and weight seem immaterial. Some of the best players have been slight of build. And what was once a pursuit open only to the moneyed of stratified Great Britain has evolved into a game of the people. It is pursued *en masse*, particularly in the U.S., by men, women, and children, from all segments of society.

"The Country Gentleman" eighty years ago sneered at the American approach— the fierce desire to win rather than the "lighthearted and cheery matches and foursomes which form the main part of golf as it is played in the United Kingdom." It is true that golf (along with other sports in the States) has been pursued with a zeal and an industry usually associated with commercial enterprises. And, as in business, golf in America has also been the subject of concentrated science, research, and technology. Few individuals casually take up the game; hours of lessons or days of practice precede or accompany actual combat on the links. The cottage industry of a few instructional articles and

a handful of books has grown into a library of how-to literature, along with an outpouring of videotapes demanding a substantial investment of cash and study time. (Some might argue that in light of the parlous state of basic U.S. industries competing with Japan and Germany, the business side of the country might draw inspiration from the ways of the golfers.)

To be sure, business and careers are frequently part of a round. Indeed, commerce often carries golfers to the course as companies and organizations arrange conventions at resorts or clubs, with golf as a major feature. But contrary to the grumps of "The Country Gentleman," the desire to win has never squashed the "lighthearted or cheery." Anyone who has ever teed off in a foursome at the country club or the local muny, or has seen the pros up close, knows that golf in America also incorporates fun, be it the needle deftly applied to the overbearing, the self-deprecating jab, the gossip about the high and the familiar, or the gamey locker room anecdote. All are touches common to the entire scene.

Curtis Strange fires the ball towards the massive Royal and Ancient Golf Clubhouse on his way to an Old Course record 10-under-par 62 during the Dunhill Cup play of 1987. (COURTESY UPI/BETTMANN NEWSPHOTOS.)

On his way to the first of his con-
secutive U.S. Open wins, Curtis
Strange blasts out of a trap at The
Country Club, Brookline, Massa-
chusetts, in 1988. (COURTESY UPI/
BETTMANN NEWSPHOTOS.)

Ben Crenshaw with fourteen tour
titles delights the media and the
gallery with his willingness to talk
the game.

A round of golf is a social affair. This quality dominates not only the conversation that flourishes between strokes, but also the recollections bandied about in the tranquility of the post-match atmosphere. The locker room has its own special character. Something about people when they congregate without their clothes on spurs revelations, exchanges of confidences. Today's nineteenth hole may be light years away in decor from the apple tree gang's jug and tub of ice, but it frees the mind, loosens the tongue, and binds us with the warmth of camaraderie. Golf as pursued in the democratic societies brings people together in a way unseen in authoritarian lands.

That mixture of high seriousness and low humor, the pursuit of material gain and the pleasure of physical achievement, and the fine glow polished by competition, are essences of the game. Beyond these lie another great attraction, the solitary struggle, the metaphor for the individual nature of the human. Sam Snead, who continued to harass Old Man Par even as he approached his seventieth birthday, re-

marked: "Golf is the only sport where a man [of] sixty can play with the best. That's why golf is such a great game. And no one has ever licked it."

For the professional who once regularly brought the enemy to his knees, decline can be frustrating. An aging Walter Hagan could not accept defeat. "I can't stand the thought of shooting another 80." On the other hand, a hacker can cheerfully devote a lifetime to the duel. Wrote John Updike:

What other sport holds out hope of improvement to a man or woman over fifty? . . . For a duffer . . . the room for improvement is so vast that three lifetimes could be spent roaming the fairways carving away at it, convinced that perfection lies just over the next rise.

That dream of perfection over the next rise is not exclusively reserved for the duffer. It is the same stuff that fuels the young in pursuit of fame and glory, from whose ranks will come the newest entrants at the Pinehurst shrine, the PGA World Golf Hall of Fame.

(Top, left) *Tom Kite never won a major, lies back in the ruck for total tournament victories but a career of finishing in the money made him top buck earner through 1990 with more than 6 million dollars for his nineteen years on the tour. "It's a distorted statistic. I'd be foolish to say this makes me better than Jack Nicklaus."—Tom Kite,* Golf Digest, *February 1990.* (COURTESY UPI/BETTMANN NEWSPHOTOS.)

(Top, right) *On his way to the Nabisco Championship at Hilton Head, SC, Kite lifts off from a bunker. The victory brought the biggest check of the Tour, 450,000 dollars.* (COURTESY WIDE WORLD.)

The major symbols of achievement: The British Open (top left), the PGA Rodman Wanamaker Trophy (top center), the United States Open (top right), and the Masters (forefront). (COURTESY PGA WGHF.)

S O U R C E   N O T E S

(1) "The third of April . . ." From Willie Ogg in *The Professional Golfer of America*, May, 1940.

(1) "On the 5th . . ." From Willie Ogg.

(5) "After dinner the mysteries . . ." From James K. Robertson, *St. Andrews*, Fife, Citizen Office, 1967.

(10) "on account of his . . ." *Golfiana*, Spring/Summer 1989.

(10) "It appeals to the . . ." *Golfiana*, Spring/Summer 1989.

(10) ". . . the 'Royal and Ancient' . . ." *Chambers's Edinburgh Journal*, October 8, 1842.

(13) "I had been out . . ." From Henry Leach, *Great Golfers in the Making*, U.S. Golf Association facsimilie of 1907 edition.

(16) "Eh, they potties—. . ." From Horace G. Hutchinson, *50 Years of Golf*, U.S. Golf Association facsimilie of 1919 edition.

(22) "One bright Sunday morning . . ." From H. G. Martin, *Fifty Years of American Golf*, Dodd, Mead, 1936.

(26) ". . . as the short rightfield . . ." From Herbert Warren Wind, *The Story of American Golf*, Alfred A. Knopf, 1975.

(26) "I do not think . . ." From Herbert Warren Wind, 1975.

(27) "[It] furnishes great . . ." From Henry Howland, *Scribner's Magazine*, May 1895.

(29) "Gentlemen, this beats rifle . . ." From Al Barkow, *Golf's Golden Grind*, Harcourt Brace Jovanovich, 1974.

(30) "I like to play golf . . ." From Allan Nevins, *Study in Power, John D. Rockefeller*, Scribner's, 1953.

(30) "Hold your head down . . ." From Allan Nevins.

(30) "If you suppose I . . ." From Allan Nevins.

(33) "The object of a . . ." From Herbert Warren Wind, 1975.

(37) "a guttie on the . . ." From John Stuart Martin, *The Curious History of the Golf Ball*, Horizon Press, 1968.

(38) ". . . managed to turn . . ." From Henry Cotton, *A History of Golf*, J. B. Lippincott, 1975.

(38) "At Earlsferry and Elie . . ." From Henry Leach, 1907.

(40) ". . . though the kindliest of men . . ." From Bernard Darwin, in *The American Golfer*, January 1934.

(40) "They were short holes . . ." From Henry Leach, 1907.

(41) "He smiles as he . . ." From Al Barkow, 1974.

(41) ". . . with a flower . . ." From Horace Hutchinson, 1919.

(42) ". . . he would mark . . ." From Charles Price, *The World of Golf*, Random House, 1962.

(42) "At that period . . ." From Al Barkow, 1974.

(43) "Mr. John Ball . . ." From *The Professional Golfer of America*, May, 1939.

(44) "standard . . . would destroy . . ." From *New York Times*, November 16, 1902.

(57) "The first thing that . . ." From Henry Leach, 1907.

(58) "A reasonable number . . ." From Charles Price, 1962.

(60) "Some day I hope . . ." From Henry Leach, 1907.

(60) "Travis could write . . ." From Herbert Warren Wind, 1975.

(61) "I never hit a . . ." From Charles Price, 1962.

(65) "Drop it anyway . . ." From Herbert Warren Wind, 1975.

(65) "I guess the Old . . ." From Herbert Warren Wind, 1975.

(72) "The first golf course . . ." From *St. Nicholas Magazine*, March, 1914.

(76) "I realized I was . . ." From *Golfiana*, Spring, 1988.

(76) "You're hitting the ball . . ." From Charles Price, 1962.

(77) "We finally found . . ." *New York Herald Tribune*, 1938, date unknown.

(78) "For the first time . . ." From Francis Ouimet, *A Game of Golf*, Houghton Mifflin, 1932.

(78) "Thank you, Mother . . ." From *Boston Traveler*, September 21, 1913.

(78) "It is customary . . ." From *Boston Traveler*, September 21, 1913.

(78) "Naturally, it is always . . ." From Herbert Warren Wind, 1975.

(83) "Hagen returned to . . ." From Ron Fimrite, *Sports Illustrated*, June 19, 1989.

(83) ". . . if Evans could putt . . ." From Herbert Warren Wind, 1975.

(84) " 'Listen, Mike' said Hagen . . ." From John Lardner, *True*, 1959.

(87) "Do you know what . . ." From the *Professional Golfer of America*, December, 1930.

(88) "Who is going to . . ." From Robert E. Harlow, *Esquire*, May 1945.

(88) "Overseas entries have added . . ." From *The Professional Golfer of America*, June 1928.

(89) "Golf has never had . . ." From John Lardner, *True*.

(89) ". . . he released the professional . . ." From Henry Cotton, 1975.

(92) ". . . not because we doubt . . ." From Tom Scott and Geoffrey Cousins, *The Golf Immortals*, Hart Publishing, 1969.

(95) "I have not played . . ." From Robert T. Jones, Jr., *The American Golfer*, 1930.

(95) "Miss Leitch brought power . . ." From Tom Scott and Geoffrey Cousins, 1939.

(102) "Chief Justice Taft was . . ." From Bob Addie, *Washington Post*, December, 1971.

(104) ". . . encourages idleness, shiftlessness . . ." From Herbert Warren Wind, 1975.

(105) ". . . if he could draw . . ." From *The Professional Golfer of America*, March 1931.

(106) "He handed his club . . ." O. B. Keeler (edited by Grantland Rice), *The Bobby Jones Story*, Tupper & Love, 1933.

(106) "From a national . . ." From *Golf Illustrated*, August 20, 1920.

(111) "You come into the shop . . ." From Clarence Budington Keeland, *The American Golfer*, 1935.

(114) "I started out with . . ." From Robert T. Jones, Jr., *Down the Fairway*, Minton Balch, 1937.

(115) "The sports writers loved . . ." From O. B. Keeler, 1933.

(116) "Jones, beaten year after . . ." From O. B. Keeler, 1933.

(141) "I heard somebody say . . ." From Al Barkow, *Gettin to the Dance Floor*, Atheneum, 1986.

(141) "I don't think I . . ." From Herbert Warren Wind, *Following Through*, Ticknor & Fields, 1985.

(142) "I use to pal . . ." From Al Barkow, 1986.

(142) "I was absolutely flat . . ." From Al Barkow, 1986.

(143) "I can make the green . . ." From Gene Sarazen, *Coronet*, August, 1945.

(145) ". . . the men who build . . ." From *The Professional Golfer of America*, June, 1924.

(153) "I believe that . . ." From *The Professional Golfer of America*, February, 1931.

(157) "Chinese burial customs . . ." From Associated Press, March, 1936.

(158) "Somehow I felt . . ." From Sam Snead (with Al Stump), *The Education of a Golfer*, Simon and Schuster, 1962.

(160) "Is that your idea . . ." From Associated Press, April 8, 1942.

(177) "It was a wee . . ." From O. B. Keeler, *Atlanta Journal*, June, 1937.

(178) "I shot 118 . . ." From Al Barkow, 1986.

(180) "We've got to hide . . ." From Dan Jenkins, *The Dogged Victims of Inexorable Fate*, Little, Brown, and Co., 1970.

(186) "After a light lunch . . ." From Henry Cotton, 1975.

(197) "We knew everybody . . ." From Dan Jenkins, 1970.

(200) "The average American soldier . . ." From Associated Press, April 25, 1944.

(208) "The bunkers were put . . ." From Gene Gregston, *Hogan, the Man Who Played for Glory*, Prentice Hall, 1978.

(233) "Granny was always loud . . ." From William Oscar Johnson and Nancy P. Williamson, *Whatta Gal*, Little, Brown and Co., 1975.

(235) "We don't need any . . ." From William Oscar Johnson and Nancy P. Williamson, 1975.

(239) "The thing started to . . ." From Fred Corcoran, *Unplayable Lies*, Duell, Sloan and Pearce, 1965.

(240) "We needed money . . ." From Fred Corcoran, 1965.

(241) "Congratulations, boy . . ." From Frank Moran, *Weekly Scotsman*, April 30, 1953.

(242) "Every ball he hit . . ." From M. W. (undated newspaper clipping).

(247) "Mickey had no touch . . ." From Herbert Warren Wind, 1985.

(247) "Mickey was much better . . ." From Al Barkow, 1986.

(249) "Some people think I . . ." From Arnold Palmer (with William Barry Furlong), *Go for Broke*, Simon and Schuster, 1973.

(250) "No one knows how . . ." From Arnold Palmer (with William Barry Furlong), 1973.

(252) " 'Arnie,' he said . . ." From Arnold Palmer (with William Barry Furlong), 1973.

(254) ". . . it's stupid to rely . . ." From Peter Dobereiner, *The World of Golf*, Atheneum, 1981.

(257) "A golfer should never . . ." From Michael Hobbs, *In Celebration of Golf*, Charles Scribner's Sons, 1983.

(260) "I drew a big . . ." From Bob Chieger and Pat Sullivan, *Inside Golf*, Atheneum, 1985.

(260) "Doesn't take a . . ." From Bob Chieger and Pat Sullivan, 1985.

(272) "I had a good . . ." From Arthur Ashe, *A Hard Road*, Warner Books, 1988.

(279) "I chose the bold . . ." From Arnold Palmer (with William Barry Furlong), 1973.

(280) "I was surprised . . ." From Arnold Palmer (with William Barry Furlong), 1973.

(282) "Young man, I've heard . . ." From Jack Nicklaus (with Herbert Warren Wind), *My Life in Golf*, Simon and Schuster, 1969.

(282) "I think I was . . ." From Jack Nicklaus (with Herbert Warren Wind), 1969.

(284) "Then I became . . ." From Jack Nicklaus (with Herbert Warren Wind), 1969.

(288) "I hope you go . . ." From Lee Trevino and Sam Blair, *Supermex*, Random House, 1982.

(288) "£3000, per annum . . ." From Henry Longhurst, *Never on Weekdays*, Cassell, 1968.

(291) "There was a thunderous . . ." From Lee Trevino and Sam Blair, 1982.

(312) "Tom listens better . . ." From Michael Bartlett, *Sport*, June 1980.

(312) "I love rotten weather . . ." From Bob Chieger and Pat Sullivan, 1985.

(338) "It's a second . . ." From Thomas Boswell, *Strokes of Genius*, Doubleday & Co., 1987.

(341) "What other sport . . ." John Updike (From Bob Chieger and Pat Sullivan), 1985.

B I B L I O G R A P H Y

Barkow, Al. *Golf's Golden Grind.* New York: Harcourt Brace Jovanovich, 1974.

Barkow, Al. *Gettin' to the Dance Floor.* New York: Atheneum, 1986.

Bartlett, Michael, ed. *The Golf Book.* New York: Arbor House, 1980.

Boswell, Thomas. *Strokes of Genius.* Garden City, NY: Doubleday, 1987.

Chieger, Bob and Pat Sullivan. *Inside Golf.* New York: Atheneum, 1985.

Corcoran, Fred (with Bud Harvy). *Unplayable Lies.* New York: Duell, Sloan & Pearce, 1965.

Cotton, Henry. *A History of Golf.* Philadelphia: J. B. Lippincott Co., 1975.

Cromie, Robert. *Par for the Course.* New York: Macmillan, 1964.

Demaret, Jimmy. *My Partner, Ben Hogan.* New York: McGraw-Hill, 1954.

Dobereiner, Peter. *The World of Golf.* New York: Atheneum, 1981.

Evans, Webster. *The Encyclopedia of Golf.* New York: St. Martins Press, 1971.

Gallico, Paul. *The Golden People.* Garden City, NY: Doubleday, 1965.

Golf Magazine. America's Golf Book. New York: Charles Scribner's Sons, 1970.

Graffis, Herb. *The PGA.* New York: Thomas Y. Crowell, 1975.

Gregson, Gene. *Hogan: The Man Who Played for Glory.* Englewood Cliffs, NJ: Prentice Hall, 1978.

Grimsley, Will. *Golf, Its History, People and Events.* Englewood Cliffs, NJ: Prentice Hall, 1966.

Hobbs, Michael. *Great Opens.* New York: A.S. Barnes, 1977.

Hobbs, Michael, ed. *In Celebration of Golf.* New York: Charles Scribner's Sons, 1983.

Hope, Bob. *Confessions of a Hooker.* Garden City, NY: Doubleday, 1985.

Hutchinson, Horace G. *Fifty Years of Golf.* Far Hills, NJ: United States Golf Association, 1985.

Jenkins, Dan. *The Dogged Victims of Inexorable Fate.* Boston: Little, Brown, 1970.

Jenkins, Dan. *You Call It Sports But I Say It's a Jungle Out There.* New York: Simon and Schuster, 1989.

Johnson, William Oscar and Nancy P. Williamson. *Whatta-Gal.* Boston: Little, Brown, 1975.

Jones, Robert Tyre. *Golf Is My Game.* Garden City, NY: Doubleday, 1960.

Leach, Henry, ed. *Great Golfers in the Making.* Far Hills, NJ: United States Golf Association, 1988.

Longhurst, Henry. Edited by Mark Wilson with Ken Bowden. *The Best of Henry Longhurst,* Norwalk, CN: Golf Digest, 1978.

Longhurst, Henry. *Never on Weekdays.* London: Cassell, 1968.

Lopez, Nancy (with Peter Schwed). *The Education of a Woman Golfer.* New York: Simon and Schuster, 1979.

McCormack, Mark. *The Wonderful World of Professional Golf.* New York: Atheneum, 1973.

McDonnell, Michael. *Great Moments in Sport.* Toronto: Pagurian Press, 1974.

Martin, Harold. *50 Years of American Golf.* New York: Dodd, Mead & Co., 1936.

Martin, John Stuart. *The Curious History of the Golf Ball.* New York: Horizon Press, 1965.

Nicklaus, Jack (with Herbert Warren Wind). *The Greatest Game of All.* New York: Simon and Schuster, 1969.

Palmer, Arnold (with William Barry Furlong). *Go for Broke.* New York: Simon and Schuster, 1973.

Peper, George. *The First 100 Years.* New York: Harry Abrams, 1988.

Price, Charles. *Golfer-at-Large*. New York: Atheneum, 1982.

Price, Charles. *The World of Golf*. New York: Random House, 1962.

Price, Charles, ed. *The American Golfer*. New York: Random House, 1964.

Rice, Grantland (from the writings of O. B. Keeler). *The Bobby Jones Story*. Atlanta, GA: Tupper & Love, 1933.

Robertson, James K. *St. Andrews*. Fife, Scotland: Citizen Office, 1967.

Sarazen, Gene (with Herbert Warren Wind). *Thirty Years of Golf*. Englewood Cliffs, NJ: Prentice Hall, 1950.

Scott, Tom and Geoffrey Cousins. *The Golf Immortals*. New York: Hart, 1969.

Shapiro, Mel, Warren Dohn, and Leonard Bergur. *Golf, A Turn-of-the-Century Treasury*. Secaucus, NJ: Castle, 1986.

Snead, Sam (with Al Stump). *The Education of a Golfer*. New York: Simon and Schuster, 1962.

Sommers, Robert. *The U.S. Open*. New York: Atheneum, 1987.

Steel, Donald, ed. *The Golfer's Bedside Book*. London: B. T. Batsford, 1965.

Taylor, Dawson, *The Masters*. Chicago: Contemporary Books, 1986.

Trevino, Lee (with Sam Blair). *They Call Me Super Mex*. New York: Random House, 1982.

Wind, Herbert Warren. *The Story of American Golf*. New York: Farrar, Straus, 1948.

Wind, Herbert Warren. *Following Through*. New York: Ticknor & Fields, 1985.

I N D E X

KEY TO IDENTIFICATION OF CLUBS

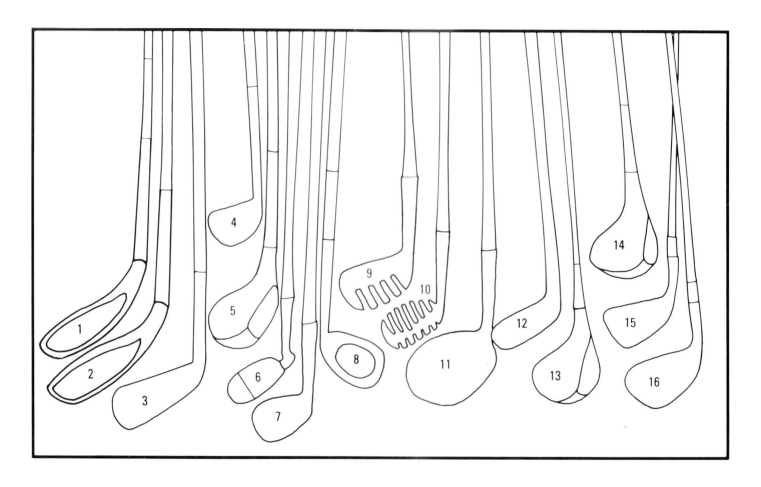

1. Play Club, 1770.

2. Short Spoon, 1865.

3. Sand Iron (with concave face), 1860.

4. Rut Iron, 1850.

5. Dreadnought Driver, 1900.

6. Urquhart Adjustable Iron, 1900.

7. Fairlie Patent Offset Iron, 1890.

8. Water Iron, 1900.

9. Rake Niblick, 1990.

10. Brown Toothed Water Mashie, 1900.

11. Mammoth Niblick, 1905.

12. Ted Ray Model Putter, 1920.

13. Bert Dargie (spoon made of dogwood), 1915.

14. Chieftain Driver (ivory backweight and pins), 1925.

15. Michael Jordan 6 Iron, 1989.

16. Tom Watson Sand Wedge, 1988.